The Corporate Finance Reader

The Corporate Finance Reader

Edited by

Robert W. Kolb

**School of Business Administration
University of Miami**

KOLB *Kolb Publishing Company*   *Miami, Florida*

A list of sources appears on pages 215–216 at the end of this text.

Printed in the United States of America.

Library of Congress Catalog Card Number   91–90007

ISBN: 1–878975–04–8

ЖK
KOLB
Kolb Publishing Company
7175 S.W. 47th Street, Suite 210   Miami, Florida 33155
(305) 663-0550   FAX (305) 663-6579

Preface

In many respects, the 1980s was the decade of finance. Those years witnessed an unprecedented wave of merger activity, the flourishing of the junk bond market, and a seemingly endless rush of innovative financial products. The end of the decade saw a financial marketplace ready for a lull. However, it seems that no lull is in sight. The financial restructuring of many firms that occurred in the 1980s caused an upheaval that will take another decade to resolve. The 1990s may well be a decade of assimilation as managers seek to fully comprehend the new financial structures created so rapidly in the 1980s.

The Corporate Finance Reader presents a range of articles to illuminate this brave new world of finance. The articles are all quite timely. Every article originally appeared in 1989 or later, with fully half being published in 1990. Consistent with their timeliness, the articles in *The Corporate Finance Reader* focus on the key current issues in finance today: radical changes in corporate debt and capital structure, the merger-driven metamorphosis in corporate form, and the new relationship between the firm and the investor that emerges from a new financing mix and new trends in the market for corporate control.

The text is intended to serve as a course supplement for a corporate finance survey at either the undergraduate or MBA level. The text does not attempt to cover every area of corporate finance. Instead, the articles in *The Corporate Finance Reader* attempt to compensate for a necessary weakness of most finance textbooks: Corporate finance survey texts must encompass the entire domain of finance, without undue emphasis on certain features merely because of timeliness. By contrast, the readings in this book deal with the topics that are timely and most clearly before the mind of business executives and the informed public. This focus helps students to understand the dynamic and contemporary nature of the subject matter of finance. The readings are organized into five sections:

I. The Contemporary Setting of Corporate Finance

This section considers recent trends in corporate financing and the movement toward a global financial system. It also considers the changing attitude toward debt and analyzes anew the inflation issue.

II. Corporate Debt

Section II focuses on the new financing mix adopted by may corporations. Articles in this section focus on the level and suitability of new levels of corporate debt.

III. Capital Structure

The great increase in corporate debt during the 1980s caused changes in corporate capital structure. Not surprisingly, the question of capital structure remains a hot issue in finance, particularly because Merton Miller won his Nobel prize for his work on this topic.

IV. Changes of Corporate Form

Judged by media attention, the merger boom was one of the most important finance issues in the 1980s. This section considers leveraged buyouts, hostile takeovers, and corporate bankruptcies.

V. Corporate Financial Management and the Investor

The sweeping changes in corporate organizational form and corporate leverage have helped to redefine the relationship between the firm and the firm's investors. This section considers this new relationship, from cash payments to shareholders to the underpricing of new stock issues.

A special word of thanks goes to the authors represented in the pages that follow. Without their creativity and labor, this book could never have appeared. We also want to thank the publications where these articles originally appeared for allowing the articles to be collected in *The Corporate Finance Reader*. While it is customary to praise others for making a book possible, such praise has a special meaning for this book. The original work by the authors represented in this text really did make this book possible.

Robert W. Kolb
University of Miami

Contents

V. Corporate Financial Management and the Investor 179

Section I
The Contemporary Setting of Corporate Finance

Section I sets the contemporary scene for financial management. As we noted in the preface, the big contemporary issues in financial management focus on the merger boom, the globalization of financial markets, the greater reliance on debt financing, and the changing relationship between firms and their investors. The articles of this section touch on these broad issues.

"Recent Developments in Corporate Finance," by Leland E. Crabbe, Margaret H. Pickering, and Stephen D. Prowse, provides a broad background of all of these issues. The article relies on graphs to show the dramatic increase in merger activity and the sharp drop-off in equity financing. In addition, the article highlights the increase in the amount of debt that firms must service relative to their operating cash flows. Crabbe, Pickering, and Prowse also show how the increase in debt financing is tied to merger activity. Not surprisingly, the authors are able to show how the movement toward more debt financing leads to an overall deterioration in firm's credit ratings. Finally, the authors provide a brief survey of bond issuances in foreign markets.

In "Globalization in the Financial Services Industry," Christine Pavel and John N. McElravey survey the current status of globalization in financial services. They also examine how future movements toward globalization are likely to proceed. They find that globalization has already been achieved to a large extent for wholesale banking markets, and they foresee an increasing pace to globalization, particularly in Europe. For the firm interested in raising capital, the movement toward globalization implies that the financial manager must consider foreign, as well as domestic, financing sources. As Pavel and McElravey show, the market value of stocks traded in Japan now exceeds that of the U.S. Also, foreign bonds have become increasingly important in recent years, emphasizing the increasingly global character of capital markets.

In his article, "The Changing American Attitude Toward Debt, and Its Consequences," Frank E. Morris focuses on the debt of the U.S. government. Stemming from the continuing budget deficits, the large increase in Treasury debt has helped transform the United States from the largest net creditor nation in the world to the largest debtor nation. Thus, the movement toward increasing levels of debt has characterized both the public and private sectors. Morris draws some potentially grim implications of this public debt for firms and society at large. Morris fears that high governmental debt can lead to increases in interest rates, which would increase the cost of capital for corporations. Similarly, a higher cost of capital will reduce the level of investment that firms undertake. Therefore, continuing budget deficits have a fairly direct impact on the firm's capital budgeting decision. Based on the arguments advanced by Morris, the federal debt presents a problem of substantial magnitude that will affect firms directly in the years ahead.

High federal debt and high interest rates are likely to stimulate inflation, a persistent increase in the general level of prices. The important point in this definition is the focus on the general level of prices, not the price change of a single commodity such as beef or gasoline. Over time, prices generally seem to drift higher, giving an inflationary tendency. Michelle R. Garfinkel asks, "What Is an 'Acceptable' Rate of Inflation?—A Review of the Issues." Like almost every issue in economics, inflation involves costs and benefits. Surging prices hurt some economic agents and benefit others. As Garfinkel points out, zero inflation might be the most desirable target, but the costs to the economy necessary to achieve zero inflation may be undesirably high. During the latter half of the 1980s, inflation was relatively modest. However, some signs in the economy point toward higher inflation, making Garfinkel's study of this issue particularly timely.

Article 1

Recent Developments in Corporate Finance

This article was prepared by Leland E. Crabbe, Margaret H. Pickering, and Stephen D. Prowse of the Board's Division of Research and Statistics. Brian H. Levey provided research assistance.

Recent years have seen dramatic changes in the financial structure of U.S. nonfinancial corporations, in corporate securities markets, and in corporate financing techniques. Many of these changes have been associated with the wave of mergers, acquisitions, and other corporate restructurings during the last half of the 1980s. In particular, the outstanding debt of the nonfinancial corporate sector soared as corporations borrowed heavily to finance retirements of equity resulting from restructuring activity. Furthermore, a substantial portion of this step-up in borrowing involved low-grade debt. At the same time, investors became more receptive to these bonds, responding to the promise of attractive yields and recognizing the opportunities for diversification of their portfolios. This shift not only provided funds for mergers and restructurings, but also enabled more firms that were less well-known to tap public debt markets.

With the repayment of the debt from many mergers hinging on subsequent sales of assets, acquirers turned to new sources of temporary financing from commercial and investment banks and made innovative use of bonds with deferred interest payments and variable coupon rates. Because bondholders were dissatisfied with losses occasioned by downgradings in the wake of unanticipated restructurings, many corporations included protection against this special risk in their new bond issues to reduce borrowing costs.

With the rise in debt, many measures of corporate financial condition deteriorated: Interest expenses claimed a significantly higher share of corporate cash flow; downgradings of debt accelerated; and bond default rates, while still relatively low, began to climb. In contrast, debt–equity ratios based on market values increased very little, as higher stock prices offset much of the growth in corporate indebtedness. Nonetheless, the nonfinancial corporate sector appears, on balance, to be more exposed to potential financial problems than it was in 1984. In this environment, banks and other investors have become more cautious in extending credit to finance highly leveraged mergers and acquisitions, a shift that has contributed to an increase in the use of equity financing and to a slowing in merger activity.

While the changes associated with the restructurings captured the public's attention, significant developments were occurring elsewhere during the last half of the decade. The differences between debt and equity as sources of funds to finance corporate activity narrowed significantly with the expansion in the use of financial instruments having features of both. Interest rate swaps and other methods for hedging interest rate risk also blurred the traditional distinction between short-term and long-term debt. Nonfinancial corporations relied more heavily on bonds, commercial paper, and loans from foreign banks for new funding and less on credit extended by domestic banks. For investment-grade nonfinancial corporations, medium-term notes became a growing source of funds. Issuance of privately placed debt was robust over the last half of the 1980s, despite growth in the public junk bond market, which many believed might supplant the private market. Moreover, in a recent ruling the Securities and Exchange Commission removed restrictions on secondary trading of private placements by larger institutional investors. The ruling likely will spur continued growth in the private market fed by increases in the participation by foreign issuers and, perhaps, by domestic issuers drawn from the public market.

RESTRUCTURINGS AND CORPORATE FINANCIAL DEVELOPMENTS

Merger and acquisition activity, which was instrumental in shaping corporate financial patterns, was strong throughout the decade (chart 1). The number of transactions rose moderately through 1983 and then accelerated between 1984 and 1986. Although the number fell over the remainder of the decade, it remained high by past standards. More important, the dollar value of the transactions continued to climb rapidly until 1989, easing only briefly in 1987, after the October stock market break. Acquisitions of U.S. firms by foreign companies since 1987 have added significantly to the volume of merger activity. Divestitures rose at a strong pace throughout the 1980s, accounting in the last five years for nearly one-third of the dollar value of all mergers and acquisitions.

Many explanations have been offered for the dramatic expansion of mergers and acquisitions. One is the search for the fullest potential of the firm's assets through a transfer of corporate control to new management teams. Another focuses on the tax benefits of higher leverage, the capture of tax-loss carryovers, and an increase in the asset basis used for depreciation allowances and other purposes (although the Tax Reform Act of 1986 and subsequent legislation essentially eliminated the last two incentives). A third explanation views the restructurings as vehicles for transferring wealth from bondholders, workers, and other corporate stakeholders to shareholders. A fourth ascribes the merger boom to highly sophisticated investors who doubted that the equity values of many firms fully reflected the appreciation in their assets during the inflation of the 1970s and early 1980s. These investors were aided by legal advisers and financial intermediaries who increased investors' awareness of the potential gains and developed financial instruments to facilitate the transactions. A final explanation points to a less restrictive antitrust enforcement policy that permitted most of the proposed mergers and acquisitions to go unchallenged. Although it is early to draw firm conclusions, preliminary research has suggested that several of these factors played a role in the restructuring boom.

Corporate Balance Sheets and Profitability

Whatever their cause, corporate restructurings have resulted in an unprecedented retirement of outstanding equity shares, which far outstripped the moderate level of new equity issuance (chart 2). Overall, retirements of nonfinancial corporate stock have exceeded new issues by about $600 billion since 1983, in sharp contrast to the rest of the postwar period, when retirements of shares exceeded new issues in only a handful of years, and then by very small amounts. Even the stock market break in 1987 had little effect on retirements because a pickup in stock repurchases by many corporations largely offset the brief pause in merger activity.

Unlike the mergers of the 1960s, which were financed largely by an exchange of securities,

1. Mergers and acquisitions

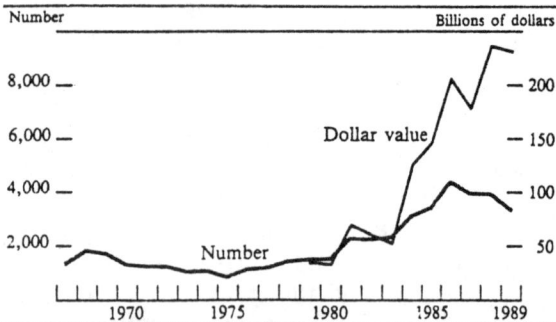

The data reflect transactions of $1 million or more of all corporations, including financial firms. Partial acquisitions and divestitures are included. The dollar value is not available before 1979.
SOURCE. *Mergers & Acquisitions*, various issues.

2. Net equity financing of nonfinancial corporations

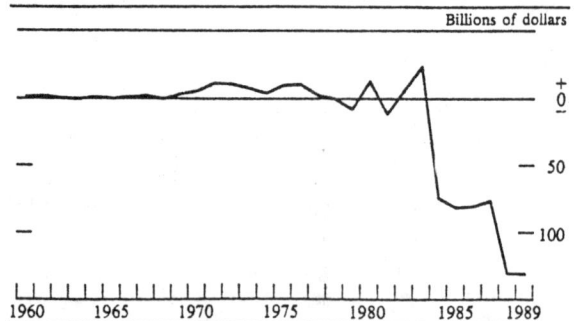

Annual data. Net equity financing is gross equity issuance less retirements. Gross issues include public offerings and private placements for cash, stock issued for stock dividends, dividend reinvestment programs, and employee participation programs, and stock issues arising from the exercise of warrants and conversion privileges. Retirements include equity retired through leveraged buyouts, other mergers and acquisitions, and share repurchases.

acquisitions in the 1980s relied heavily on borrowed funds to pay cash to selling shareholders. Leveraged buyouts (LBOs), the most highly leveraged acquisitions, mushroomed from less than $5 billion in 1983 to more than $60 billion in 1989, the year that included the $25 billion RJR–Nabisco transaction. LBOs served to transfer assets from publicly held corporations to closely held partnerships and private corporations. Some were structured with as little as 10 percent equity, provided largely by buyout pools that takeover specialists assembled. To finance the remainder, the new firm effectively pledged the assets of the acquired company as collateral for new debt obligations. The LBO firms then sought to lower the debt burden through improved cash flow and sales of some operations. Many of these divestitures were themselves structured as LBOs.

In addition to financing LBOs and other mergers and acquisitions, debt commonly was used to finance defensive measures such as leveraged recapitalizations undertaken to discourage unsolicited or "hostile" takeovers. As a result of all these restructuring activities, the indebtedness of nonfinancial corporations grew rapidly, as illustrated by the sharp increase in the ratio of the market value of debt to the gross domestic product of nonfinancial corporations (chart 3).

The rapid buildup of debt in the nonfinancial corporate sector was accompanied by rising net interest payments that absorbed a growing share of corporate gross product (chart 4). The interest share expanded even though interest rates were lower, on balance, during the last half of the

3. Ratio of corporate credit market debt to corporate gross domestic product of nonfinancial corporations

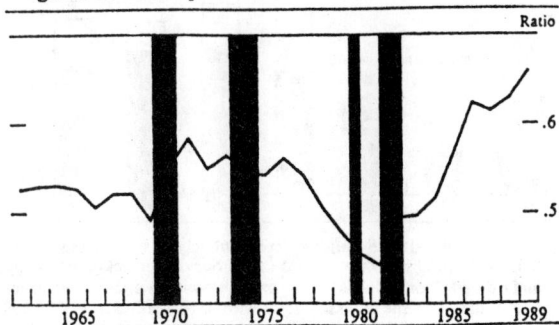

Annual data. The data on debt are based on market value. Shaded areas indicate business recessions.

4. Domestic profits, net interest payments, and capital income of nonfinancial corporations

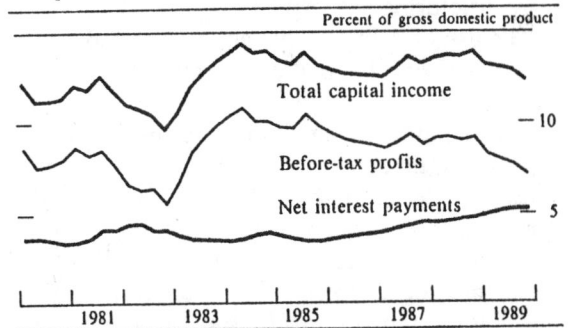

Quarterly data. Total capital income is before-tax profits plus net interest payments.

1980s, and that expansion was one factor acting to depress corporate profitability. Before-tax profits slipped from roughly 9 percent of corporate output in 1987 to about 7¾ percent in 1989. Over the same period, net interest payments rose from about 4¼ percent to more than 5 percent of corporate gross product, accounting for more than half of the drop in the profits share.

Cyclical developments also played a part in the shrinkage of the share of before-tax profits. The slowing of gains in output and productivity toward the end of the decade, along with faster gains in compensation, squeezed corporate profits, especially in 1989. Moreover, in the face of foreign competition, businesses were forced to exercise restraint in passing rising production costs through to prices, further damping corporate profits originating from domestic operations.

The Tax Reform Act of 1986 had important effects on after-tax profitability. The average corporate tax rate on nonfinancial corporations—the ratio of federal, state, and local tax accruals to economic profits—rose from 31 percent in 1985 to 44 percent in 1989. Although the act reduced the maximum marginal rate of corporate taxation and permitted more accelerated depreciation for tax purposes, the elimination of the investment tax credit and of the preferential taxation of long-term capital gains more than offset these benefits. The increase in the corporate tax rate has meant that, over the past five years, before-tax profits have shown more strength, on balance, than after-tax profits. Combined with the loss of some nondebt tax shields, the increase in the effective corporate tax rate also may have strengthened the incentive to use debt finance, even for firms not directly involved in restructuring activity.

The use of debt to retire equity boosted corporate borrowing beyond that required to finance capital outlays. The financing gap, the difference between capital expenditures and internal funds, represents the extent to which corporations must draw on external sources of funds—credit market borrowing, new equity issuance, or asset liquidations—to finance capital expenditures. Although credit market borrowing exceeded corporations' needs for external funds for most of the postwar period, changes in total borrowing generally reflected changes in the financing gap. However, this pattern changed dramatically after 1983 (chart 5). The financing gap showed little trend between 1982 and 1989, while borrowing increased sharply, reflecting the surge in merger activity.

Merger Financing and the Junk Bond Market

Although the merger and buyout activity of the past decade contributed significantly to the radical transformation of the junk bond market, part of the early growth of that market was related to developments in private placements. Before the 1980s, few new speculative-grade bonds (bonds rated below Baa3 by Moody's Investors Service or below BBB– by Standard and Poor's Corporation) were publicly offered because most investors shied away from their higher risk of default. Higher-risk borrowers, typically small and medium-sized companies, tended instead to rely on loans from commercial banks and on private placements, primarily with life insurance companies. When policy loans began to absorb the investible assets of life insurance companies in the late 1970s and early 1980s, these institutions turned from the private placement market toward more liquid investments. Consequently, many of these higher-risk companies were forced to seek new sources of credit. In response, securities firms, led by Drexel Burnham Lambert, began actively promoting public offerings of high-yield bonds in the early 1980s. At the same time, institutional investors in the public market became convinced that the bonds' higher yields more than compensated for their greater risks, especially when the bonds were held in a diversified portfolio. The economic expansion also provided a favorable environment by seeming to mitigate risk.

These developments interacted with the growth of financing needs arising from mergers and restructurings to spur a dramatic increase in the issuance of junk bonds. Between 1983 and 1989, nonfinancial corporations issued $160 billion of junk bonds to the public; that sum accounted for more than 35 percent of public bond offerings by the sector. About two-thirds of the high-yield bonds offered during this period were associated with restructurings—leveraged buyouts, other mergers and acquisitions, divestitures, stock repurchases, leveraged recapitalizations, or other restructuring activities (chart 6). In most cases, junk bonds provided permanent

6. New public issues of low-rated bonds by nonfinancial corporations

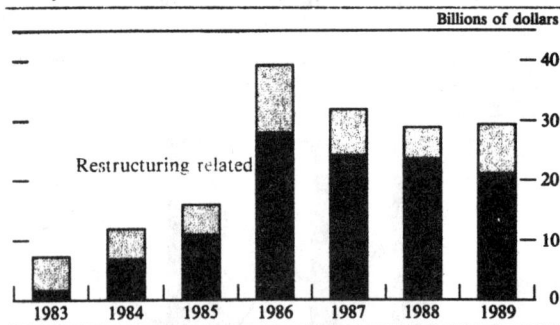

Low-rated bonds are bonds offered publicly in the United States rated below Baa3 by Moody's Investors Service or below BBB– by Standard and Poor's Corporation, or with no known rating. Restructuring issues are those associated with leveraged buyouts, other mergers and acquisitions, divestitures, stock repurchases, leveraged recapitalizations, and other restructuring activities.

5. Total credit market borrowing and financing gap of nonfinancial corporations

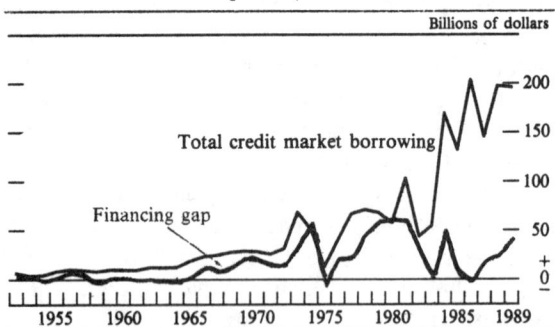

Annual data. The financing gap is defined as capital expenditures less internal funds.

financing for cash buyouts, which replaced part or all of the funds supplied initially by commercial or investment banks.

As the high-yield market matured, new instruments that offered issuers greater leeway in managing the timing of their interest payments were introduced. These instruments grew out of the need to minimize interest payments until cash flow improved or until debt loads could be reduced with the proceeds from sales of assets. The deferred-cash-payment bond and the reset note were commonly used for these purposes.

Deferred-Cash-Payment Bonds. Several types of bonds enable borrowers to postpone the cash payment of interest. Payment-in-kind (PIK) bonds give the issuer the option of issuing more debt in lieu of a cash coupon payment over the first years of the bond's life. These bonds typically have a stated maturity of about ten years, and a payment-in-kind period of about five years. After this period, the issuer must make the coupon payment in cash. Original-issue-discount (OID) bonds also delay cash interest payments. These bonds, which are issued at a large discount from par, include zero coupon bonds and bonds with coupon rates set well below market yields at the time of issuance. After an initial period, the coupon rate is raised. Because securities with deferred cash payment typically have a subordinated standing in the issuer's capital structure and shorter call protection than conventional debt, their yields to maturity tend to be at least 200 basis points above those on conventional debt. Moreover, the returns on deferred-cash-payment bonds usually are more volatile than those on straight debt, reflecting their junior standing and longer duration.

During the years 1987–89, PIK and OID bonds accounted for more than 15 percent of new funds raised in the junk bond market (table 1). Until recently, issuers of PIK bonds were allowed to deduct coupon payments on the additional debt as an interest expense, even though no cash outlay was made. Similarly, issuers of OID bonds were allowed to deduct the accrued interest as an expense. As a result of legislation passed in 1989, however, no interest deductions are allowed on that portion of the accrued interest that is 6 percentage points above the yield on

1. OID and PIK bonds as percentages of gross issuance of junk bonds, 1985–89

Year	Type of bond		
	Zero coupon	Deferred coupon	Payment in kind
1985	4.57	. . .	. . .
1986	.94	3.06	2.30
1987	.96	7.16	4.39
1988	1.29	14.66	4.49
1989	2.00	9.22	4.08

comparable Treasury securities; and the interest expense corresponding to the yield that is between 5 and 6 percentage points above comparable Treasury securities can be deducted only at maturity. The legislation has greatly reduced the attractiveness of issuing debt with delayed cash payments.

Reset Notes. Reset notes have characteristics of both floating- and fixed-rate debt. The coupon rate is fixed for an initial period, usually one to three years, after which it is reset to make the bond trade at a predetermined, or reset, price, usually 100 to 102 percent of par value. The coupon rate would be raised if the market price were less than the reset price and lowered if the market price were greater than the reset price.

The reset feature appeals particularly to firms that anticipate improvements in their credit quality before the reset date, for they will be able to benefit from lower borrowing costs. The appeal may be especially great to companies that have experienced a downgrading in credit rating as a result of a buyout but expect debt paydowns from asset sales to lead to an upgrade.

From the investor's viewpoint, the reset feature offers some protection against a deterioration in an issuer's credit quality. This protection is, however, limited to modest declines in credit quality because if the issuer faces severe financial distress, there may be no affordable coupon rate that makes the note trade at its reset price. Moreover, even if its financial condition is not deteriorating, the company may have to raise the coupon rate if the reset date falls in a period of heightened concerns about credit quality. To lessen the risk that reset notes will exacerbate financial stress, many issuers place caps on the coupon rate. More than two-thirds of the notes yet to be reset have caps, generally ranging from

100 to 400 basis points above the original coupon rate. Since this type of security first appeared in the U.S. public market in 1985, more than fifty reset notes, with an aggregate face value of about $13½ billion, have been issued in the junk bond market. The dollar volume accounts for about 7½ percent of public issuance of junk bonds during this period. By year-end 1989, about a dozen of these publicly issued reset notes had been either called or reset. In addition to issuance in the public market, at least $2¾ billion was placed privately between 1987 and 1989.

Corporate Credit Quality

The increase in the use of debt finance has been associated with a deterioration in many indicators of corporate financial health. Interest payments in the aggregate have claimed an increasing proportion of the cash flow of nonfinancial corporations since 1983 (chart 7). Furthermore, the number of firms whose interest expense exceeded cash flow rose significantly between 1983 and 1988, despite favorable economic conditions and falling interest rates. In these circumstances, concerns have arisen about the ability of highly leveraged firms to service their debt, especially in light of the slowing of the economy in 1989.

The secular erosion in corporate credit quality accelerated in the last half of the 1980s, an erosion evidenced by the increase in downgradings of corporate bonds relative to upgradings. The growth in new issues by lower-rated firms, which are more prone to downgradings, has meant that more frequent changes in credit ratings are likely. Nonetheless, the general deterio-

ration in creditworthiness is noteworthy because it occurred while the economy was expanding.

As a result of these changes in ratings, the median rating that Standard and Poor's assigned to industrial bonds dropped from an investment-grade A in the early 1980s to a below-investment-grade BB at the close of the decade (chart 8). One-third of the estimated $600 billion of rated nonfinancial corporate bonds outstanding at the end of 1989 was rated as noninvestment grade. In the early 1980s, before the recent wave of restructurings, these low-grade bonds accounted for less than one-tenth of the total outstanding.

Some of the growth in below-investment-grade debt stemmed from the downgrading of outstanding debt to speculative grade because of events related to restructuring. More important, that growth was boosted by new debt issues of these downgraded companies. Furthermore, in the late 1980s, many new issues carried ratings at the lower end of the credit spectrum—B and Caa on Moody's scale. In the past these ratings generally appeared only when corporations on the edge of default were downgraded. The relative importance of the other component of speculative issuers, those companies downgraded to noninvestment grade because of a long-term decline in business fundamentals, has changed little over the past ten years.

Default rates on corporate bonds of below-investment grade, while still low, have risen, from 1.4 percent of outstanding bonds in 1987 to 4 percent in 1989 (table 2). Moreover, many market analysts expect much higher default rates over the next few years, both because the overall

7. Ratio of gross interest payments to cash flow of nonfinancial corporations

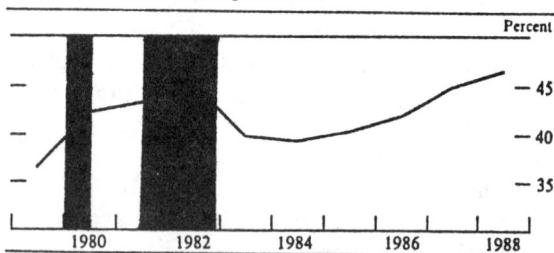

Annual data. Cash flow includes after-tax economic profits, depreciation, and gross interest expense less dividends. Shaded areas indicate business recessions.

8. Distribution of bonds by rating, 1983 and 1989

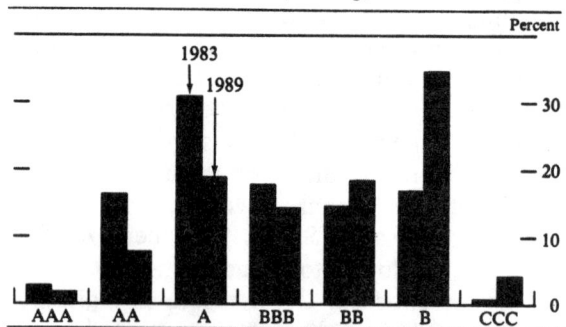

The distribution is based on ratings of outstanding industrial issues by Standard and Poor's Corporation. The median rating was A in 1983 and BB in 1989.

2. Outstanding amount and default rate of low-rated corporate bonds, 1980–89

Year	Outstanding amount (par value, billions of dollars)[1]	Default rate (percent)
1980	15.13	1.48
1981	17.36	.16
1982	18.54	3.11
1983	28.23	1.07
1984	41.70	.82
1985	59.08	1.68
1986	92.98	3.39
1987	136.95	1.35[2]
1988	159.22	2.48
1989	201.00	4.03

1. Par value of straight debt. Financial issues are included.
2. Excludes Texaco default of $1.8 billion; with Texaco, the rate was 5.5 percent.
SOURCE. Edward Altman, New York University.

quality of the noninvestment-grade bonds has declined and because defaults tend to rise as bonds age. Indeed, several recent studies have found cumulative default rates for particular cohorts of bonds to be as high as 30 percent over the first ten years after issue.

Other measures of the condition of corporate balance sheets suggest that stockholders have not been overly concerned with the growing indebtedness of corporations. In particular, the ratio of debt to equity, both measured at market values, has increased only slightly since 1982, as rising equity prices have largely countered the rise in corporate indebtedness (chart 9). Nevertheless, the deterioration in other indicators of corporate financial condition, especially the ratio of interest expense to cash flow, indicates that the financial health of the business sector may be vulnerable to a significant slowing in economic activity.

9. Ratio of debt to equity of nonfinancial corporations

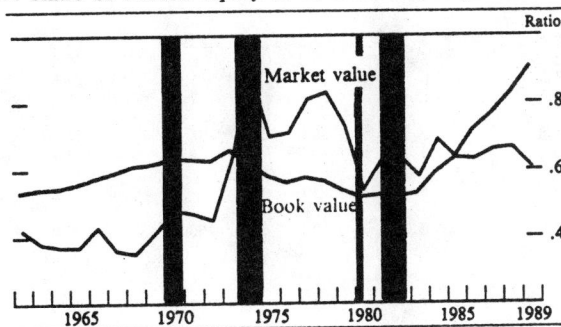

Annual data. Shaded areas indicate business recessions.

Event Risk

About one-fourth of the reductions of ratings in the past five years were related to restructurings. The downgradings were concentrated in the industrial sector, where leverage-increasing events occasioned downgradings for about 40 percent of outstanding bonds. According to Moody's Investors Service, these downgradings inflicted losses of nearly $14 billion on bondholders between 1984 and 1988.

As a result, investors in industrial bonds became increasingly sensitive to event risk—the risk that an unforeseen, major change in a firm's capital structure will lead to a large decline in the market value of the firm's outstanding bonds. To compensate investors for event risk, yields on investment-grade industrial bonds rose relative to yields on high-grade utility bonds. After the RJR–Nabisco buyout proposal in late 1988 dispelled the notion that bonds of very large industrial corporations were free of event risk, investors stepped up their demands for stronger bond covenants for protection against that risk, and several issuers have found it worthwhile to comply. The terms of the covenants have varied from issue to issue, but they have had common features. For example, most covenants written since late 1988 have specified that bondholders may sell their bonds back to the issuer at par if two events occur: a major change in the issuing firm's capital structure and a downgrading of the bond by the major rating agencies from investment grade to speculative grade. In 1989, nearly half of the new offerings of long-term bonds by investment-grade industrial firms included event-risk covenants. Estimates suggest that industrial firms have saved about ¼ percentage point on borrowing costs by including this protection.

RECENT DEVELOPMENTS IN MERGER AND RESTRUCTURING ACTIVITY

Early in 1989, the hectic pace of debt-financed restructuring began to subside. The amount of stock-for-stock exchanges in merger transactions rebounded in 1989 from the extremely low levels of 1987 and 1988. This rebound largely reflected the increase in emphasis last year on friendly strategic corporate acquisitions in which the new, combined company issued new common shares to stockholders of the two original companies. Then, late in the year, the deepening difficulties in the market for below-investment-grade bonds further encouraged combination offers of cash and securities, particularly preferred stock, to shareholders of the acquired company.

The acquisition market was jolted last fall when a few companies involved in highly leveraged transactions failed to perform up to expectations, defaulted on bond issues, and sought bankruptcy protection. Others, seeking to prevent default, have reached agreement with bondholders to reschedule debt or are attempting to do so. These "distressed" exchanges typically replace existing debt with securities carrying a longer maturity, lower interest rate, some substitution of equity, or a combination of these features; and they must be approved by a predetermined share of bondholders specified in the original bond's covenant. Whereas such exchanges are still few, these unravelings of acquisitions and the general vulnerability of highly leveraged firms to adverse economic developments have heightened concerns in the financial markets; and thus they have made investors much more cautious in extending funds to highly leveraged borrowers.

Uneasiness about rising bond defaults contributed to chaotic conditions in the market for speculative-grade bonds early this year as prices of restructuring-related issues dropped precipitously. The withdrawal of the savings and loan associations from the junk bond market and outflows from high-yield mutual funds further curtailed demand for these issues. The liquidation of Drexel Burnham Lambert early this year was another negative factor for the market to absorb, even though Drexel's participation had already dwindled.

New merger proposals dropped off noticeably during the first part of 1990 as a consequence of the virtual unavailability of funds for new financing in the low-grade bond market; the more cautious attitude of commercial banks, both domestic and foreign; and the weakening in the market for asset sales. Nevertheless, although restructuring activity is considerably less than it was in 1988 and 1989, it remains substantial. Despite the disarray in the junk bond market and investor caution, well-structured acquisition proposals, especially those aimed at enhancing a firm's competitiveness within its own lines of business, have been well received by investors.

IMPLICATIONS OF FINANCIAL INNOVATIONS

The past several years have seen many shifts in the relative importance of various debt instruments in financing business activity (table 3). One of the most significant changes has been the increase in the importance of bonds and notes, which were responsible for roughly 58 percent of estimated total credit market debt raised in 1989, compared with 46 percent in 1983. Another has

3. Distribution of funds raised in credit markets by nonfinancial corporations, by type of instrument, 1983–89

Percent

Type of instrument	1983	1984	1985	1986	1987	1988	1989
Bank loans							
U.S. banks	32.1	28.8	22.6	24.4	3.2	15.7	14.2
Foreign banks	4.9	7.7	1.1	5.5	1.3	5.3	6.8
Commercial paper	-1.5	12.8	11.0	-4.6	1.6	5.6	10.6
Finance company loans	14.1	9.7	9.6	5.5	11.6	7.6	5.4
Bonds and notes[1]	46.5	39.3	72.8	54.7	68.0	58.3	57.7
Mortgages	-8.0	-.8	-13.5	13.9	10.7	8.3	3.1
Bankers acceptances and							
U.S. government loans	11.9	2.5	-3.6	.6	3.6	-.8	2.2
Total	100.0	100.0	100.0	100.0	100.0	100.0	100.0
MEMO							
Total funds raised in credit							
markets (billions of dollars)	54.8	169.6	132.4	203.8	145.5	207.5	196.0

1. Includes bonds and notes issued abroad by U.S. corporations and tax-exempt bonds issued for the benefit of nonfinancial corporations.

been the steady decline in loans from domestic banks over the same period, from 32 percent of total credit market debt to 14 percent. Loans from foreign banks, on the other hand, increased, to just under 7 percent of total credit market debt raised in 1989; and the issuance of commercial paper continued its rapid expansion, interrupted only by a pause in 1986. The strong growth has been fueled by heavy inflows to money market mutual funds, which are the largest buyers of commercial paper.

The implications of these changes for the maturity structure of the corporate sector's debt are not so clear as they would have been in the past. For one thing, many of the financial developments and innovations in the past decade have eroded the traditional distinctions between short- and long-term debt, as well as those between debt and equity. Furthermore, a recent regulatory change by the Securities and Exchange Commission (which is discussed in some detail below), has blurred the traditional distinction between private and public markets for securities.

Short-Term and Long-Term Debt

Before the 1980s, it was reasonable in aggregate analysis to characterize commercial paper and bank loans as short-term debt and corporate bonds and mortgages as long-term debt. Such characterizations often were used to gauge corporate exposure to interest rate and liquidity risk, under the assumption that interest rates on short-term debt were variable whereas those on long-term debt were fixed.

Financial developments and innovations in the past decade have made this classification of debt less useful. One such development is the $1.3 trillion swap market. In an interest rate swap, an issuer of fixed-rate debt, for example, agrees with a counterparty—typically a swaps dealer—to make floating-rate payments in exchange for fixed-rate payments. Because the fixed-rate issue often has an intermediate or long-term maturity, the exchange effectively allows the fixed-rate issuer to convert its debt into an obligation with an essential feature of short-term debt. By the same token, a floating-rate issuer can convert its interest obligations to a fixed rate through a swap, thereby lengthening the duration of its

debt. In a similar sense, currency swaps have blurred the distinction between debt denominated in dollars and in foreign currencies. In a currency swap, an issuer of, say, dollar-denominated bonds agrees with a dealer to make principal and interest payments in, say, French francs, and in return the dealer provides the issuer with dollar payments for the principal and interest on the issuer's bonds. The swap protects against foreign exchange risk.

Related transactions, such as caps, floors, and collars, can be used to alter the characteristics of floating- and fixed-rate debt. A cap places a maximum on the interest rate paid by a floating-rate issuer: The seller of the cap agrees to provide funds to the holder of the cap to cover the interest payments that exceed a specified rate. Similarly, a floor places a minimum on the interest rate a floating-rate issuer is required to pay. And a collar combines a cap and a floor to confine the interest rate to a given range. The tighter the range associated with the collar, the closer the floating-rate obligation comes to fixed-rate debt. By similar reasoning, an issuer of a fixed-rate security can use caps, floors, and collars to introduce elements of short-term debt into its obligation.

The introduction of extendible notes, which give the issuer the option of extending the maturity of an issue, also has eroded the differences between intermediate- and long-term securities. Some extendible issues permit the issuer to extend the maturity for one, two, or three years and permit the exercise of this option for up to seven years. On other notes, the feature is more rigid, specifying a date on which the option may be exercised to extend the maturity to a specified number of years. Frequently, the option to extend has been included in offerings of reset notes, with the coupon reset if the issuer exercises the option.

Medium-Term Notes

In the corporate bond market, the classification of bond issuance as long-term financing also has become less meaningful as the market for medium-term notes has grown. Medium-term notes are continuously offered corporate bonds that generally are sold by agents on a "best efforts" basis; they have maturities that usually range from one to five years (utility issues, however, routinely have thirty-year maturities). The market for medium-term notes, which expanded rapidly after the Securities and Exchange Commission began permitting so-called shelf registration of security offerings in 1982, was dominated at first by the finance subsidiaries of automobile companies, but by 1989 more than 200 U.S. corporations had raised funds in the market; the gross issuance in that year was $35 billion (table 4). Offerings of medium-term notes by nonfinancial firms are likely to rise further as more of these issuers establish new programs and as others draw down on established programs. Continued growth of issuance by nonfinancial corporations also appears likely to produce a lengthening in maturities.

At first, many borrowers used medium-term notes to raise relatively small amounts of funds quickly, since the market afforded a flexible means to match the maturities of intermediate-term assets. Primary issues averaged about $5 million. As the market has matured, medium-term notes have become more competitive with traditional corporate underwritings, and trades have approached $50 million to $100 million. Most issuers have investment-grade ratings: Of the $72 billion in medium-term notes outstanding at the end of 1989, only $1¼ billion had ratings below investment grade, and most of those notes were issued originally as investment-grade debt. Some recent programs by nonfinancial issuers have included covenants that protect against event risk.

Although the market for medium-term notes was structured as an extension of the commercial paper market, its recent growth may be attributable to a shift from traditional markets for inter-

10. New issues of securities
by nonfinancial corporations

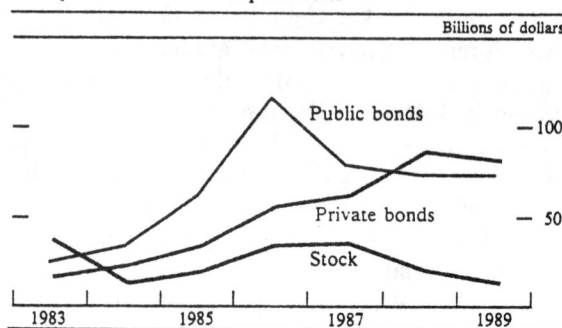

Billions of dollars

mediate-term financing, particularly the Eurobond market. (Eurobonds are bonds issued outside of the home market.) Favorable interest rates and the removal of the withholding tax on interest paid on bonds to foreign investors fostered borrowing by U.S. corporations in the Eurobond market in the mid-1980s (table 5). Since 1986, as the rate advantage in the Euromarket has diminished, U.S. corporate borrowing in that market has fallen off. Although several U.S. corporations have established global programs for issuing medium-term notes, issuance abroad has not grown so fast as domestic issuance. On the demand side, a high degree of sensitivity of foreign investors to the threat of event risk damped demand in the Euromarket for U.S. corporate issues, particularly issues of nonfinancial corporations.

Debt and Equity

The difference between debt and equity as sources of corporate financing has narrowed significantly. One factor has been the expansion of the market for speculative-grade bonds. Because low-grade bonds typically have a junior standing

4. Gross issuance of medium-term notes by U.S. firms, 1983–89

Billions of dollars

Type of issuer	1983	1984	1985	1986	1987	1988	1989	Total, 1983–89
Auto finance companies	4.8	6.8	6.8	8.9	11.0	7.7	11.1	57.0
Bank holding companies	.1	.9	2.0	2.6	2.5	4.3	3.7	16.0
Business and personal finance companies	.4	1.3	2.0	2.0	3.0	4.3	7.1	20.0
Other financial companies	.2	.9	1.5	3.6	4.8	6.8	6.5	24.3
Nonfinancial companies	*	.4	1.3	3.0	3.2	8.1	6.5	22.5
Total	5.5	10.2	13.6	20.0	24.3	31.3	34.9	139.8

*Less than $50 million.

in the issuing firm's capital structure and, more important, because their high returns are particularly vulnerable to a drop in earnings, these bonds have risk and return characteristics similar to those of both common stock and debt. In addition, many new offerings of speculative-grade bonds have been convertible into equity or have included equity-like features, such as warrants. There also has been an expansion in the issuance of a kind of preferred stock that gives the issuer the option to exchange it for debt. Most of this exchangeable preferred stock has been placed directly with shareholders as part of leveraged restructurings. Many of the issuing firms have exercised the exchange option.

Innovations in the use of variable-rate preferred stock likewise have served to narrow the difference between debt and equity. Because corporations are allowed to deduct 70 percent of the dividend income they receive from unaffiliated corporations, fully taxed corporate investors, given all else, favor preferred stock over debt investments. Variable-rate preferred stock combines this tax advantage with a floating dividend rate that makes the stock a substitute for commercial paper. The dividend rate is commonly adjusted several times a year either by a remarketing agent or through a Dutch auction, in which bids are ranked from lowest to highest and the highest bid that clears the issue will be the price paid for the bids by all winning bidders regardless of their initial bid. The rate is often capped at 110 percent of the AA-rated commercial paper rate. The caps lend variable-rate preferred stock an equity feature, inasmuch as buyers of these securities bear the risk of a price decline should the cap become effective.

Private Placements

The private market, in which corporate securities are placed directly with institutional investors, has grown steadily since the early 1980s, and in 1988 and 1989, the volume of privately placed bonds exceeded that of publicly offered bonds (chart 10). While the extraordinary expansion in the public market for non-investment-grade debt is partly an outgrowth of the private placement market, the public market has not supplanted the private one. Life insurance companies and pen-

5. Gross bond issuance by U.S. firms in foreign markets, 1983-89[1]

Billions of dollars

Year	All corporations	Nonfinancial corporations	Financial corporations
1983	8.3	4.1	4.2
1984	22.6	10.1	12.5
1985	37.8	14.9	22.9
1986	42.8	18.0	24.8
1987	24.3	11.3	13.0
1988	23.2	8.8	14.3
1989	22.8	5.7	17.0
Total, 1983-89	181.8	72.9	108.7

1. Details may not sum to totals because of rounding
Annual data.

sion funds have found in the private market an attractive outlet for their growing pool of investible funds. The wave of corporate restructurings spurred this growth, as many firms involved in restructuring tapped the private market for part of their financing.

The lines between public and private markets have faded because major lending institutions and corporations participate in both markets. The difference between private and public offerings is expected to narrow even further now that the Securities and Exchange Commission has adopted Rule 144A. The rule exempts U.S. and foreign corporations from registration requirements for bonds and stock sold to institutional investors with investment assets of $100 million or more (and, in the case of banks and thrift institutions, net worth of at least $25 million). Perhaps more important, the rule permits the resale of these private securities to qualified institutions at any time. Before the new rule was promulgated, private securities generally could not be resold for two years, although some carried registration rights that permitted their subsequent unrestricted resale in the public market. The National Association of Securities Dealers' screen-based trading system, called Portal, is designed to increase liquidity in the marketplace for primary and secondary market sales of 144A securities. The additional liquidity in the private market is likely to attract new buyers and issuers, both domestic and foreign. It also may draw in mutual funds, pension funds, and other lenders who have faced restrictions or limitations on their holdings of nonregistered securities.

Article 2

Globalization in the financial services industry

The pace has been most rapid at the wholesale, bank-to-bank and bank-to-multinational level; at the retail customer level, globalization will soon quicken, particularly in Europe.

Christine Pavel and John N. McElravey

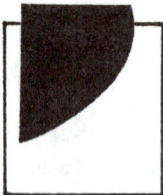

Globalization can be defined as the act or state of becoming worldwide in scope or application. Apart from this geographical application, globalization can also be defined as becoming universal. For the financial services industry, this second meaning implies both a harmonization of rules and a reduction of barriers that will allow for the free flow of capital and permit all firms to compete in all markets.

This article looks at how global the financial services industry already is, and will likely become, by examining the nature and trends of globalization in the industry. It will also draw lessons from global nonfinancial industries and from recent geographic expansion of banking firms within the United States.

Financial globalization is being driven by advances in data processing and telecommunications, liberalization of restrictions on cross-border capital flows, deregulation of domestic capital markets, and greater competition among these markets for a share of the world's trading volume. It is growing rapidly, but primarily at the intermediary, rather than the customer, level. Its effects are felt at the customer level mainly because prices and interest rates are influenced by worldwide economic and financial conditions, rather than because direct customer access to suppliers has increased. However, globalization at the customer level will soon become apparent, at least in Europe after 1992, when European Community banking firms will be allowed to cross national borders.

Trends in other industries and lessons from interstate banking in the United States suggest that as financial globalization progresses, financial services will become more integrated, more competitive, and more concentrated. Also, firms that survive will become more efficient, and consumers of financial services will benefit considerably. Reciprocity is likely to be an important factor for those countries not already part of a regional compact, as it has been for interstate banking to proceed in the United States.

International commercial banking

The international banking market consists of the foreign sector of domestic banking markets and the unregulated offshore markets. It has undergone important structural changes over the last decade.

Like domestic banking, international banking involves lending and deposit taking. The primary distinction between the two types of banking lies in their customer bases. Since 1982, international lending and deposit taking have both been growing at roughly 15 percent annually. At year-end 1988, foreign loans and foreign liabilities at the world's banks each totalled more than $5 trillion. The extent, nature, and growth of international banking, however, are not the same in all countries.

When she wrote this article, Christine Pavel was an economist at the Federal Reserve Bank of Chicago. She is now an assistant vice president at Citicorp North America Inc. John N. McElravey is an associate economist at the Federal Reserve Bank of Chicago.

Figures 1 and 2 show the ten countries whose banks have the largest shares of foreign banking assets and liabilities. Combined, these ten countries account for nearly three-quarters of all foreign assets and liabilities. Nearly half of all foreign banking assets and liabilities are held by banks in the United Kingdom, Japan, the United States, and Switzerland, up from 47 percent in 1982. This increase is almost entirely due to the meteoric rise in foreign lending by Japanese banks.

Perhaps the most notable event in international banking has been the rapid growth of Japanese banks. This extraordinary growth can be traced to deregulation in Japan, as well as to its banks' high market capitalization, the country's high savings rate, and its large current account surplus. Japanese foreign exchange controls and restrictions on capital outflows were removed in 1980. This allowed the banks' industrial customers to go directly to the capital markets for financing. The loss of some of their best customers, along with deposit rate deregulation and stiffer competition from other types of institutions, reduced profits.[1] To improve their profitability and to service Japanese nonfinancial firms that had expanded overseas, Japanese banks moved into new markets abroad. While a large part of the business of Japanese banks abroad is with

Japanese firms, Japanese banks have been very successful lending to foreign industrial firms because of a competitive advantage conferred by a more favorable regulatory environment. Japan's capital requirements have been relatively easy, allowing banks to hold assets at 25 to 30 times book capital.[2] Japan's share of all foreign assets and liabilities rose from 4 percent in 1982 to more than 14 percent in 1988, surpassing the U.S. and second only to the U.K.

While many banks have significant international operations, only a few are truly international in scope. More than one-half of the total banking assets and liabilities in Switzerland, nearly one-half of total banking assets and liabilities in the United Kingdom, and over one-quarter of total banking assets and liabilities in France are foreign. In contrast, less than 25 percent of the balance sheets of German, Japanese, and U.S. banks consist of foreign assets and liabilities.

The United Kingdom and Switzerland have long been international financial centers. For more than 100 years Swiss bankers have been raising loans for foreigners. The largest Swiss banks, in fact, try to maintain a 50–50 split between their foreign and domestic assets for strategic and marketing reasons.[3] Deregulation, or the lack of regulation in some cases,

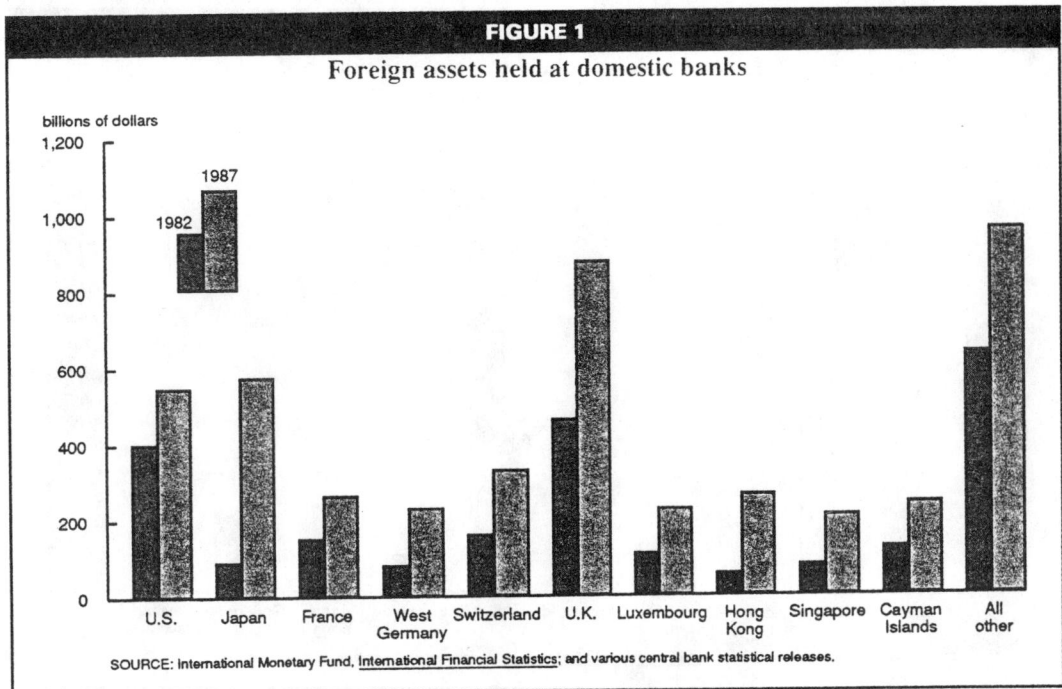

FIGURE 1

Foreign assets held at domestic banks

billions of dollars

SOURCE: International Monetary Fund, _International Financial Statistics_; and various central bank statistical releases.

and the restructuring of the British financial system have made London a powerful international financial center. More than half of all banking institutions in the U.K. are foreign-owned, and 59 percent of all assets of banks in the U.K. are denominated in foreign currency.[4]

At the aggregate level, the proportion of bank assets that are claims on foreigners is roughly equivalent to the proportion of liabilities that are claims of foreigners. This is not true of individual countries. Some countries' banks lend more to foreigners than they borrow from them. Foreign assets of German banks are almost twice the size of foreign liabilities, and Swiss banks hold about 34 percent more foreign assets than liabilities. For banks in these countries, the combination of international orientation and their country's high domestic saving rates makes them strong net lenders. Banks in the United States, Japan, and France, however, have more foreign liabilities than foreign assets, although in each case the difference is less than 5 percent.

U.S. banks have not always been net foreign borrowers. In 1982, foreign deposits at U.S. banks accounted for less than 13 percent of total liabilities, while foreign assets accounted for over 20 percent of total assets. Foreign deposits at U.S. banks have more than doubled over the 1982–87 period, growing far

more rapidly than domestic deposits. Foreign assets increased only 37 percent over that time and more slowly than domestic assets. This is due largely to the reduction in LDC lending and to the writing down of LDC loans by U.S. banks.

Foreign deposit growth also outpaced domestic deposit growth at Japanese banks. In 1982, foreign deposits accounted for 9 percent of total liabilities, and by 1987, they accounted for 18 percent. Similarly Japanese banks booked foreign assets about twice as fast as domestic assets over the 1982–87 period.

Offshore banking centers

A considerable portion of international banking activity occurs in unregulated offshore banking centers commonly known as the Euromarkets.[5] The Euromarkets, unlike the domestic markets, are virtually free of regulation. Euromarkets consist of Eurocurrency deposits, Eurobonds, and Euro-commercial paper. Eurocurrency deposits are bank deposits denominated in a foreign currency, and account for 86 percent of banks' foreign-owned deposits.

The development of Eurocurrency deposits marked the inauguration of the Euromarket in the mid-1950s. Eurocurrency deposits grew at a moderate rate until the mid-1960s when they began to grow more rapidly.[6] At that

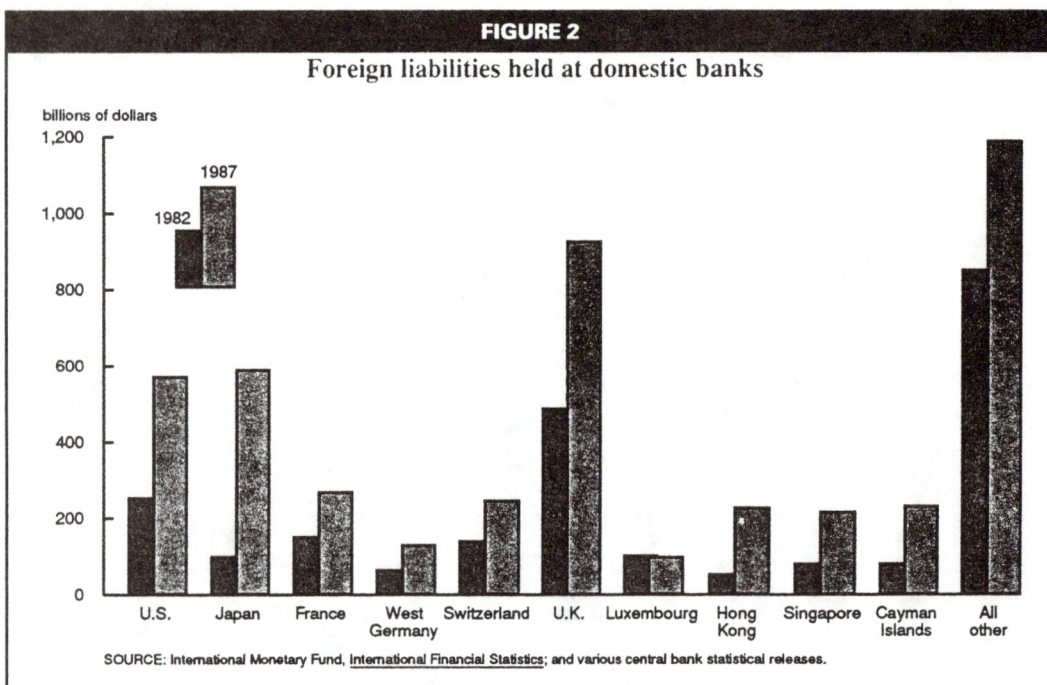

FIGURE 2

Foreign liabilities held at domestic banks

billions of dollars

SOURCE: International Monetary Fund, International Financial Statistics; and various central bank statistical releases.

time, the U.S. government imposed severe controls on the movement of capital, which "deflected a substantial amount of borrowing demand to the young Eurodollar market."[7] These U.S. capital controls were dismantled in 1974, but the oil crisis of the 1970s helped to fuel the continued growth of the Eurocurrency market. The U.S. oil embargo made oil-exporting countries fearful of placing their funds in domestic branches of U.S. banks. In the late 1970s and early 1980s, high interest rates bolstered the growth of Eurocurrency deposits, which are free of interest-rate ceilings and not subject to reserve requirements or deposit insurance premiums. From 1975 to 1980, Eurocurrency deposits grew over threefold.

Since 1980, Eurocurrency deposits have continued to grow quite rapidly, reaching a gross value of $4.5 trillion outstanding in 1987 and a net value of nearly $2.6 trillion (net of interbank claims). Eurodollar deposits, however, have not grown as rapidly. During the early 1980s, Eurodollars represented over 80 percent of all Eurocurrency deposits outstanding, but by 1987, they represented only 66 percent (see Figure 3). The declining importance of Eurodollar deposits can be explained, at least partially, by the decline in the cost of holding noninterest-bearing reserves against domestic deposits in the United States.[8]

Many Eurocenters have developed throughout the world. They have developed where local governments allow them to thrive, i.e., where regulation is favorable to offshore

markets. Consequently, some countries with relatively small domestic financial markets, such as the Bahamas, have become important Eurocenters. Similarly, some countries with major domestic financial markets have no or very small offshore markets. In the United States, for example, the offshore market was prohibited until 1981 when International Banking Facilities (IBFs) were authorized.

Japan did not permit an offshore market to develop until late in 1986. Until then the "Asian dollar" market consisted primarily of the Eurocenters of Singapore, Bahrain, and Hong Kong. Now Japan's offshore market is about $400 billion in size, over twice as large as the U.S. offshore market, but still smaller than that in the United Kingdom.[9]

The interbank market

The international lending activities of most banks, aside from the money centers, are concentrated heavily in the area of providing a variety of credit facilities to banks in other countries. Consequently, a large proportion of banks' foreign assets and liabilities are claims on or claims of foreign banks. Eighty percent of all foreign assets are claims on other banks.[10] This ratio varies somewhat by country; however, since 1982, it has been increasing for all the major industrialized countries.

Similarly, nearly 80 percent of all banks' foreign liabilities are claims of other banks.[11] In Japan, 99 percent of all foreign liabilities at banks are deposits of foreign banks. Swiss banks are the exception, where only 28 percent of foreign liabilities are claims of banks.

The Swiss have a long history of providing banking services directly to foreign corporate and individual customers, which explains their relatively low proportion of interbank claims. A favorable legal and regulatory climate aided the development of a system that caters to foreigners, especially those wishing to shelter income from taxes. Confidentiality is recognized as a right of the bank customer, and stiff penalties can be imposed on bank officials who violate that right. In effect, no information about a client can be given to any third party.[12]

Since a very large portion of foreign deposits are Eurocurrency deposits, it is no surprise that about half of all Eurocurrency deposits are interbank claims. Eurocurrency

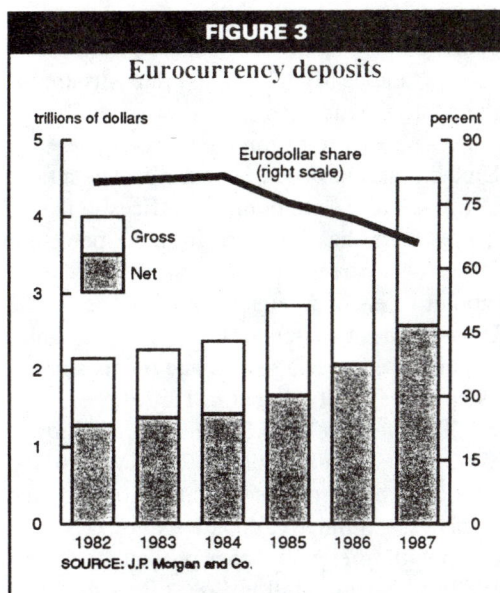

FIGURE 3

Eurocurrency deposits

trillions of dollars / percent

Eurodollar share (right scale)

Gross
Net

1982 1983 1984 1985 1986 1987

SOURCE: J.P. Morgan and Co.

deposits are frequently re-lent to other, often smaller, banks in the interbank market.[13]

The Japanese have become very large borrowers in the interbank market in response to domestic restrictions on prices and volumes of certain activities. Japanese banks operating overseas have been funding their activities by borrowing domestically (from nonresidents) in one market (e.g., the U.K.), and lending the funds through the interbank market to affiliates in other countries (e.g., the U.S.).[14]

Foreign exchange trading

Foreign exchange (forex) trading is another important international banking activity. Informal estimates place daily foreign exchange trading at $400 billion.[15] Like the loan markets, forex markets are primarily interbank markets. The primary players involved in the United States are the large money center and regional commercial banks, Edge Act corporations, and U.S. branches and agencies of foreign banks. Forex trading also involves some large nonbank financial firms, primarily large investment banks and foreign exchange brokers. However, according to the Federal Reserve Bank of New York's *U.S. Foreign Exchange Market Survey* for April 1989, 82 percent of the forex trading volume of banks was with other banks. Foreign exchange trading in New York grew at about 40 percent annually since 1986 to reach more than $130 billion by April 1989. In contrast, foreign trade (imports plus exports) has been growing at only about 6 percent annually since 1982 (3 percent on an inflation-adjusted basis).

The German mark is the most actively traded currency, followed by the Japanese yen, British pound, Swiss franc, and Canadian dollar. Since 1986, however, the German mark has lost some ground to the Japanese yen and the Swiss franc.[16]

The explosion of forex trading can, at least partly, be explained by the high rate of growth in cross-border financial transactions. Capital and foreign exchange controls were reduced or eliminated in a number of countries during the 1980s.

An international banking presence

There are several ways that commercial banks engage in international banking activities—through representative offices, agencies, foreign branches, and foreign subsidiary banks and affiliates. In addition, in the United States, commercial banks may operate International Banking Facilities (IBFs) and Edge Act corporations, which unlike the other means, do not involve a physical presence abroad. The primary difference among these types of foreign offices centers on how customer needs are met (often because of regulation). For example, agencies of foreign banks are essentially branches that cannot accept deposits from the general public, while branches, as well as subsidiary banks, can offer a full range of banking services.

U.S. branches and agencies of foreign banks devote well over half of their assets to loans, about the same proportion as the domestic offices of U.S. commercial banks. U.S. commercial banks, however, hold a much larger proportion of their assets in securities and a much smaller proportion in customer's liability on acceptances.[17] This latter situation reflects the international trade financings of U.S. foreign offices.

U.S. offices of foreign banks compete with domestic banks primarily in commercial lending and, to a lesser extent, in real estate lending.[18] However, a significant portion of the commercial loans held at U.S. offices of foreign banks were purchased from U.S. banks, rather than originated by the foreign offices themselves.[19]

Both U.S. offices of foreign banks and domestic offices of U.S. commercial banks primarily fund their operations with deposits of individuals, partnerships and corporations (IPC).[20] Offices of foreign banks currently gather 23 percent of these deposits from foreigners, and nearly all of these deposits are of the nontransaction type.

The presence of foreign banks in the United States has been increasing. The ratio of foreign offices to domestic offices in the United States has increased from 2.8 percent in 1981 to 4.4 percent in 1987. Similarly, the ratio of assets of foreign banking offices in the United States to assets of U.S. domestic banks has increased over 5 percentage points since 1981 to nearly 21 percent in 1987.[21]

The presence of U.S. banks abroad, however, has been falling since 1985. At that time, U.S. banks operated nearly 1,000 foreign branches.[22] Similarly, the number of U.S. banks with foreign branches peaked at 163 in 1982 and began to fall in 1986. By 1988, the number of banks with foreign branches had fallen to 147. On an inflation-adjusted basis, total assets of foreign branches of U.S. banks fell 12 percent since 1983 to $506 billion in 1988. The number of IBFs and Edge Act Corporations has also been waning. Edge Acts numbered 146 in 1984 and were down to 112 by 1988.[23] This retrenchment reflects the lessening attractiveness of foreign operations as losses on LDC loans have mounted.

Implications of Europe after 1992

The presence of foreign banking firms in European domestic markets will likely increase over the next few years as the 12 European Community states become, at least economically, a "United States of Europe." The EC plans to issue a single license that will allow banks to expand their networks throughout the Community, governed by their home country's regulations.[24]

Since banking powers will be determined by the rules of the home country, banks from countries with more liberal banking laws operating in countries with more restrictive banking laws will have an advantage over their domestic competitors. Consequently, the most efficient form of banking will prevail. Countries with more fragmented banking systems will need to liberalize for their banks to compete with banks from countries with universal banking.

While reciprocity will not be important for nations within the EC, it will be an issue for banks from countries outside the EC, especially those from Japan and the U.S. As financial services companies in Europe begin to operate with fewer restrictions, there will be competitive pressure on the U.S. and Japan to remove the barriers between commercial and investment banking. To be most efficient, firms operating in various markets want similar powers in each market. The EC, as previously noted, solved this problem with a Community banking license. Thus, the EC's efforts at regulatory harmonization may hasten the demise of Glass-Steagall in the U.S. and Article 65 in Japan.[25]

The implications for European banking will be similar to the experience in the United States following the introduction of interstate banking in the early to mid-1980s. Since that time, the U.S. commercial banking industry has been consolidating on nationwide, re-

gional, and statewide bases through mergers and acquisitions. Acquiring firms tend to be large, profitable organizations with expertise in operating geographically dispersed networks, while targets tend to be smaller, although still relatively large firms, in attractive banking markets. Large, poorly-capitalized firms will also find themselves to be potential takeover targets.

What these lessons imply for Europe in 1992 is that the largest and strongest organizations with the managerial talent to operate a geographically dispersed organization will become Europe-wide firms, while smaller firms will have a more regional focus and others will survive as niche players. In addition, just as different state laws have slowed the process of nationwide banking in the United States, language and cultural barriers will slow the process in Europe as well. The overall result of a more globally integrated financial sector in Europe, and elsewhere, will be that the organizations that survive will be more efficient, and customers will be better served. Also, it is very likely that the 1992 experience will improve European banks' ability to compete outside of Europe.

Size is not, and will not be, a sufficient ingredient for survival. In general, firms in protected industries, such as airlines, tend to be inefficient. Large banking organizations based in states with restrictive branching and multibank holding company laws tended to be less efficient than their peers in states that allow branches and, therefore, more competition. In addition, commercial banking organizations that operated in unit banking states had little expertise in operating a decentralized organization, and tended to focus primarily on large commercial customers. Consequently, these banking firms have not acquired banks far from home.

The process of consolidation has already begun within European countries and within Europe as firms prepare for a single European banking market. Unlike the Unites States' experience of outright mergers and acquisitions, however, the European experience centers on forming "partnerships." Partnerships have been formed Europe-wide, even though the most recent directive on commercial banking permits branching, because of the difficulties in managing an organization that spans several cultures and languages. Apparently, financial services firms want to get their feet wet first, rather than plunge into European banking and risk drowning before 1992 arrives. But also, until regulations among countries become more uniform, partnerships and joint ventures allow financial firms to arbitrage regulations.

The formation of partnerships and joint ventures is not only a European phenomenon. Indeed, U.S. firms have entered into such agreements with European and Japanese companies. For example, Wells Fargo and Nikko Securities have formed a joint venture to operate a global investment management firm, and Merrill Lynch and Société Générale are discussing a partnership to develop a French asset-backed securities market.

The experience of nonfinancial firms suggests that this arrangement can be a good way to establish an international presence. For example, in 1984, Toyota and General Motors entered into a joint manufacturing venture in California. Through this venture, the Japanese were able to acquaint themselves with American workers and suppliers before opening their own plants in the U.S. Since then, Toyota has opened two more manufacturing plants on its own in North America, and there is speculation in the auto industry that they will buy GM's share of the joint venture once the agreement ends in 1996.[26]

Another case of international expansion through joint ventures can be found in the petroleum industry. Oil companies from some oil-producing countries have been quite active in recent years buying stakes in refining and marketing operations in the United States and Europe. These acquisitions give producers an outlet for their crude in important retail markets, and refiners get a reliable source. Saudi Arabia purchased a 50 percent stake in Texaco's eastern and Gulf Coast refining and marketing operations in November 1988. The state-owned oil companies from Kuwait and Venezuela have joint ventures with European oil companies as well.[27] If joint ventures between financial services firms are as successful as nonfinancial ones have been, then global financial integration will benefit.

International securities markets

International securities include securities that are issued outside the issuer's home coun-

try. Some of these securities trade on foreign exchanges. Issuance and trading of international securities have grown considerably since 1986, as has the amount of such securities outstanding.

Greater demand for international financing is stimulating important changes in financial markets, especially in Europe. Regulations and procedures designed to shield domestic markets from foreign competition are gradually being dismantled. London's position as an international market was strengthened by the lack of sophistication of many other European markets. Greater demand for equity financing in Europe has been encouraged by private companies, and by governments privatizing large public-sector corporations. These measures to deregulate and, therefore, improve the efficiency, regulatory organizations, and settlement procedures are a response to competition from other markets, and the explosion of securities trading in the 1980s.[28]

It is estimated that the world bond markets at the end of 1988 consisted of about $9.8 trillion of publicly issued bonds outstanding, a nearly $2 trillion increase since 1986.[29] At year-end 1988, two-thirds of all bonds outstanding were obligations of central governments, their agencies, and state and local governments. This figure varies considerably across countries. Over two-thirds of bonds denominated in the U.S. dollar and the Japanese yen are government obligations, but less than one-third of bonds denominated in the German mark are government obligations, and only 10 percent of bonds denominated in the Swiss franc represent government debt.[30]

The international bond market includes foreign bonds, Eurobonds, and Euro-commercial paper. Foreign bonds are bonds issued in a foreign country and denominated in that country's currency. Eurobonds are long-term bonds issued and sold outside the country of the currency in which they are denominated. Similarly, Euro-commercial paper is a short-term debt instrument that is issued and sold outside the country of the currency in which it is denominated.

The Japanese are the biggest issuers of Eurobonds because it is easier and cheaper than issuing corporate bonds in Japan. Japanese companies issued 21 percent of all Eurobonds in 1988.[31] Ministry of Finance (MOF) regulations and the underwriting oligopoly of the four largest Japanese securities firms keep the issuance cost in the domestic bond market higher than in the Euromarket. The ministry would like to bring this bond market activity back to Japan, so it has been slowly liberalizing the rules for issuing yen bonds and samurai bonds (yen bonds issued by foreigners in Japan). So far, the impact of these changes has been small.[32]

International bonds accounted for almost 10 percent of bonds outstanding at the end of 1988 and over three-quarters are denominated in the U.S. dollar, Japanese yen, German mark and U.K. sterling (see Figure 4). These countries represent four of the largest economies and financial markets in the world.

The importance of international bond markets has increased considerably for many countries. As Table 1 shows, international bonds account for nearly half of all bonds denominated in the Swiss franc and over one-third of all bonds denominated in the Australian dollar. International bonds account for over 21 percent of bonds denominated in the British pound, up dramatically from less than 1 percent in 1980. The rise in importance of international bonds for these currencies can, at least in part, be explained by the budget surpluses in the countries in which these currencies are denominated and, therefore, the slower growth in the debt obligations of these countries' governments.

The value of world equity markets, at $9.6 trillion in 1988, is about equal to the value of world bond markets. Three countries—the United States, Japan, and the United Kingdom—account for three quarters of the total capitalization on world equity markets, and they account for nearly half of the 15,000 equity issues listed on the world's stock exchanges (see Figure 5).

American, Japanese, and British equity markets are the largest and most active. American and British markets are very open to foreign investors, but significant barriers to foreign competitors still exist in Japan.

Stocks have, historically, played a relatively minor role in corporate financing in many European countries. Various regulatory and traditional barriers to entry made these bourses financial backwaters. The stock exchanges in Switzerland, West Germany, France, and Italy have only recently taken steps to modernize in order to compete against exchanges in the U.S. and the U.K. It was estimated that about 20 percent of daily trad-

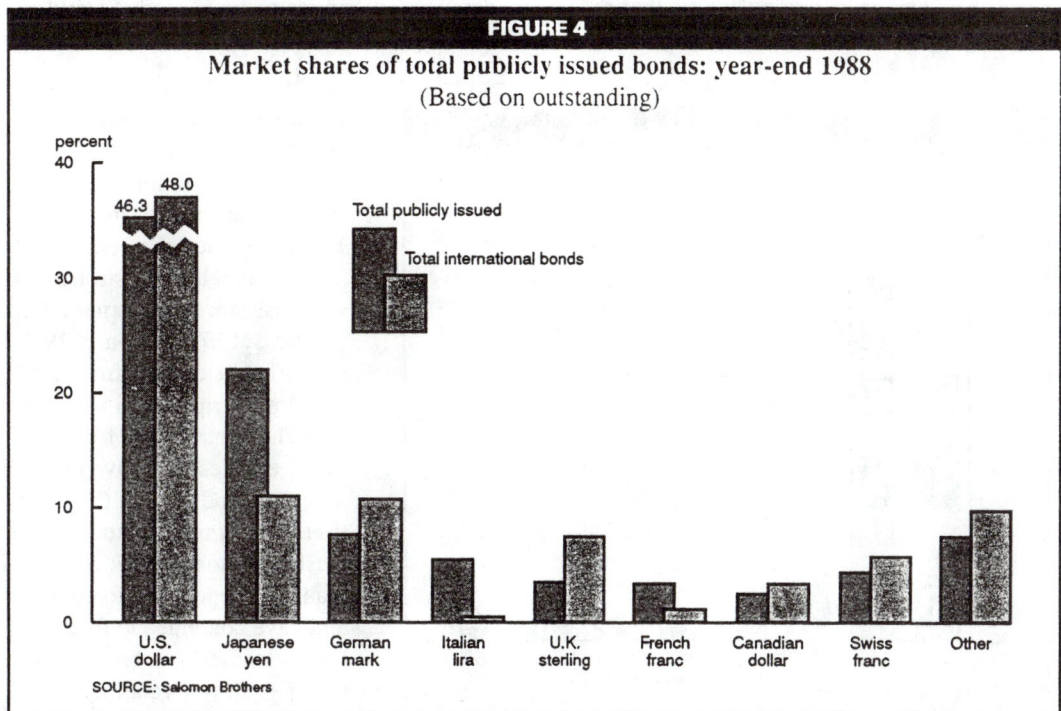

FIGURE 4

Market shares of total publicly issued bonds: year-end 1988
(Based on outstanding)

percent

Total publicly issued

Total international bonds

U.S. dollar Japanese yen German mark Italian lira U.K. sterling French franc Canadian dollar Swiss franc Other

SOURCE: Salomon Brothers

TABLE 1

International shares of the world's major bond markets
(Percent based on outstanding)

	1980	1985	1988
U.S. dollar	4.4	8.8	10.5
Japanese yen	1.6	3.2	5.0
German mark	12.6	11.2	14.2
U.K. sterling	0.9	9.4	21.3
Canadian dollar	3.1	5.5	13.7
Swiss franc	27.3	42.3	49.2
Australian dollar	n.a.	9.5	36.2

SOURCE: Salomon Brothers

ing in French equities was done in London in 1988.[33] French regulators hope that their improvements will lure some of that trading back to Paris.

West German equity markets, until recently, provided a good illustration of the kinds of barriers that keep stock exchanges small, inefficient, and illiquid. Access to the stock exchange was effectively controlled by the largest banks, which have a monopoly on brokerage. Under this arrangement, small firms were kept from issuing equity, thus remaining captive loan clients. Large German firms have traditionally relied more heavily on bank credit and bonds than on equity to finance growth. The integration of banking and commerce in Germany has contributed to this reliance. German banks, "through their equity holdings, exert significant ownership control over industrial firms."[34]

The fragmented structure of the West German system, which consists of eight independent exchanges each with its own interests, also helped check development. Over the last several years, though, rivalries between the exchanges have been somewhat buried, and they have been working to improve their integration and cooperation. One way is through computer links between exchanges to facilitate trading. A transaction that cannot be executed immediately at one of the smaller exchanges can be forwarded to Frankfurt to be completed. Overall, German liberalization efforts have been moderately successful, adding about 90 new companies to the stock exchange between 1984 and 1988.[35]

Active institutional investors, such as pension funds, which have a major position in the U.S. markets, have no tradition in the German equity market. Billions of marks in pension funds are on the balance sheets of German companies, treated as long-term loans from employees.[36] Freeing these funds in a deregulated and restructured market could have a profound effect on Germany's domestic equity markets.

FIGURE 5

World equity markets
(Market capitalization—1988)

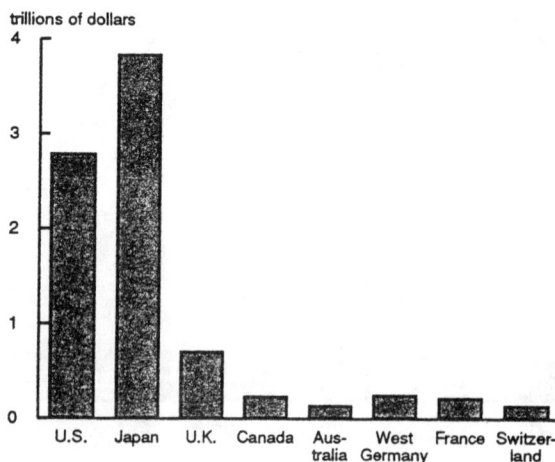

trillions of dollars

SOURCE: Salomon Brothers

Issuance of international securities

The issuance of international securities was mixed in 1988. Issuance of international bonds was relatively strong, while issuance of international equities, at $7.7 billion in 1988, was off considerably from 1987, but almost triple 1985 issuance.[37]

The contraction of international equities was driven by investors, and reflects their caution. Following the stock market crash in October 1987, portfolio managers reportedly focussed, and have continued to focus, on low-risk assets and on domestic issues.[38] Lower volatility of share prices on the world's major exchanges, however, would likely aid a rebound in the appetite for and in the issuance of international equities.

Some important structural changes took place in international financial markets between 1985 and 1987. A sharp increase in issuance for the U.K. translated into substantially greater market share of international equity issuance, from 3.7 percent in 1985 to 33.0 percent in 1987. This increased share of international activity reflects the deregulation and restructuring of the London markets that occurred in the fall of 1986, improving their place as an international marketplace for securities. Even with the retrenchment in 1988, London maintained its leading role, with twice the issuance of second-place U.S.[39]

Over this same three-year period, Switzerland's international equity issuance translated into a substantially smaller market share, falling from 40.7 percent to 6.0 percent. This sharp decline in market share, from undisputed leader to fourth, reveals Switzerland's failure to keep pace with deregulation in other countries. For years, a cartel system dominated by its three big banks has set prices and practices in the stock markets. It is only recently that competition from markets abroad has forced the cartel to liberalize its system.[40]

In contrast to the international equities markets, issuance of international bonds was very strong in 1988, following a sharp contraction in 1987 entirely due to a 25.5 percent decline in Eurobond issuance.[41] Eurobonds account for about 80 percent of international bond issues, and nearly two-thirds of all international issues are denominated in three currencies—the U.S. dollar, Swiss franc, and the Deutschemark. Nearly 60 percent of international bonds are issued by borrowers in Japan, the United Kingdom, the United States, France, Canada, and Germany.

The long-time importance of the United States and the U.S. dollar in the international bond market has been dwindling. In 1985, 54 percent of all Eurobonds were denominated in U.S. dollars, but by 1988 only 42 percent were in U.S. dollars.

Similarly, U.S. borrowers issued 24 percent of all international bonds in 1985, but issued only 8 percent in 1988. The impetus behind this decline lies in part with the investors who prefer low-risk securities and are

leery of U.S. bonds because of the perceived increase in "event risk" associated with restructurings and leveraged buyouts. Also, no doubt, developments such as the adoption of Rule 415 by the Securities and Exchange Commission (shelf registration) have encouraged U.S. firms to issue domestic securities by making it less costly to do so.

Trading in international securities

The United States is a major center of international securities trading. Foreign transactions in U.S. markets exceed U.S. transactions in foreign markets by a ratio of almost 7 to 1. This is a result of several factors. The United States has the largest and most developed securities markets in the world. U.S. equity markets are virtually free of controls on foreign involvement. SEC regulations on disclosure dissipate much uncertainty concerning the issuers of publicly listed securities in the United States while less, or inadequate, regulation in other countries makes investments more risky in those foreign markets. The market for U.S. Treasury securities has also been very attractive to foreign investors. In fact, large purchases of these securities by the Japanese have helped finance the U.S. government budget deficit.

Both foreign transactions in U.S. markets and U.S. transactions in foreign markets have been increasing at a very rapid pace. Foreign transactions in U.S. equity securities in U.S. markets plus such transactions in foreign equities in U.S. markets grew at almost 50 percent annually to exceed $670 billion in 1987.[42] Foreign transactions in U.S. stocks on U.S. equity markets have been increasing faster than domestic transactions; in 1988, foreign transactions accounted for 13 percent of the value of transactions on U.S. markets, up from 10 percent in 1986 (see Table 2).

Foreign transactions have increased in securities markets abroad as well; however, they have not, in general, kept pace with domestic trading. Consequently, foreign transactions as a percentage of all transactions has declined over the 1986-88 period for Japan, Canada, Germany, and the United Kingdom. Nevertheless, transactions by U.S. residents in foreign equity markets were estimated at about $188 billion in 1987, nearly 12 times as much as in 1982.[43]

TABLE 2

Foreign transactions in domestic equity markets: Share of domestic trading
(Percent of total volume)

	1985	1988
Japan	8.7	6.5
Canada	29.5	21.6
Germany	29.9	8.7
U.S.	9.7	13.1
U.K.	37.3	20.8
France	38.0	43.5
Switzerland	4.6	6.3

SOURCE: Salomon Brothers

Foreign transactions in U.S. bonds and foreign bonds in U.S. markets in 1988 increased to more than 13 times their 1982 level (see Figure 6). This trading boom was fueled mainly by growth in transactions for U.S. Treasury bonds, which accounted for about 84 percent of total foreign bond transactions in 1988, up from 63 percent in 1982. These transactions in U.S. Treasury bonds accounted for almost three-quarters of all foreign securities transactions in U.S. markets in 1988.

Bond transactions in other countries by nonresidents also increased dramatically. In Germany, for example, the value of such transactions increased by 300 percent over the 1985-88 period and now account for over half of the value of all transactions in German bond markets.[44] Foreign bond transactions by U.S. residents reached an estimated $380 billion in 1987, six times greater than the 1982 figure.

Derivative products

Globalization has affected derivative financial products in two ways. First, it has spurred the creation and rapid growth of internationally-related financial products, such as Eurodollar futures and options and foreign currency futures and options as well as futures and options on domestic securities that trade globally, such as U.S. Treasury securities. Trading hours on some U.S. futures and options exchanges have been expanded to support cross-border trading of underlying assets, such as Treasury securities. Second, globalization has lead to the establishment of futures and options exchanges worldwide. Once the exclusive domain of U.S. markets, especially in Chicago, financial derivative products are now traded in significant volumes throughout Europe and Asia.

The number of futures contracts on Eurodollar CDs and on foreign currencies as well as the number of open positions has increased rapidly (see Figure 7). The number of futures contracts on Eurodollar CDs traded worldwide increased almost 70 percent annually since 1983 to reach over 25 million in 1988. This compares with a 20 to 25 percent annual growth rate for Eurodollars.[45] Similarly, nearly 40 million futures and options contracts on various foreign currencies were traded worldwide in 1988, up from 14 million in 1983. This growth rate is roughly equivalent to that of forex trading.

The rapid increase in the volume of trading of internationally-linked futures and options contracts has largely benefited U.S. exchanges, which are the largest and sometimes the only exchanges where such products are traded. Nevertheless, the share of exchange traded futures and options volume commanded by the U.S. exchanges has dropped from 98 percent in 1983 to about 80 percent in 1988.

FIGURE 6

Foreign transactions in U.S. bond markets

trillions of dollars

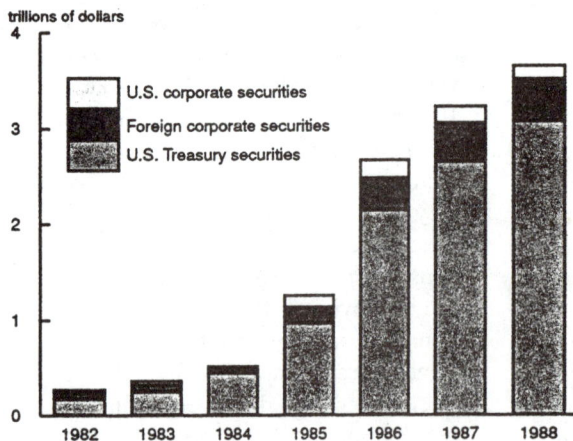

- U.S. corporate securities
- Foreign corporate securities
- U.S. Treasury securities

SOURCE: Board of Governors of the Federal Reserve System and U.S. Department of the Treasury

FIGURE 7

Contracts traded: Eurodollar CD futures and selected foreign curriencies

millions of contracts

Total foreign exchange
- Other
- Japanese yen
- Swiss franc
- German mark

Euro-dollar CD

SOURCE: Intermarkets

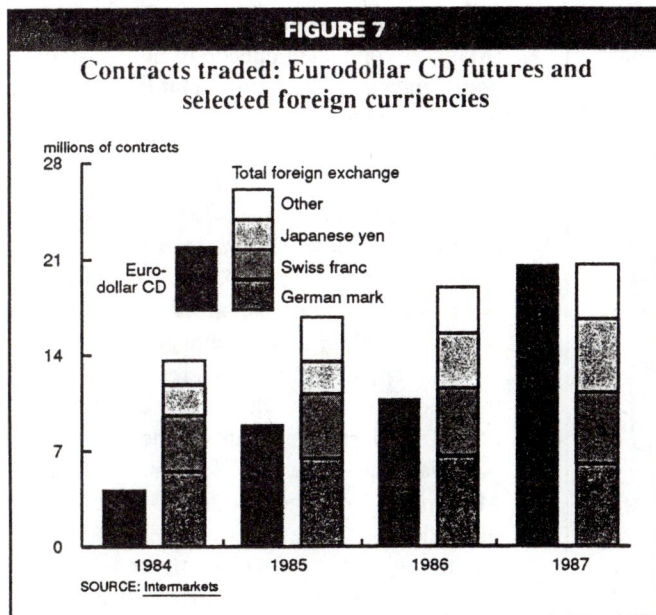

petition from London for business that the Germans felt should be in Frankfurt. LIFFE began trading futures on West German government bonds in September 1988, and, as of year-end 1989, it was the second most active contract on the exchange, trading about 20,000 contracts daily. It has been estimated that anywhere from 30 to 70 percent of this London-based trading is accounted for by the German business community.[50]

When an exchange is established, its product line usually includes a domestic government bond contract, a stock index futures contract, and, sometimes, a domestic/foreign currency futures or option contract.

These 18 percentage points were primarily lost to European and Japanese exchanges.

In the past four years, 20 new exchanges have been established, bringing the total to 72.[46] Many of these new exchanges are in Europe. In addition, foreign membership at many exchanges is considerable. For example, over two-thirds of LIFFE's (London International Financial Futures Exchange) membership is based outside of the United Kingdom.[47]

Two notable additions to futures and options trading are Switzerland and West Germany. The Swiss Options and Financial Futures Exchange (SOFFEX) was established in March 1988, and is the world's first fully-automated, computer-based exchange.[48] SOFFEX trades index options on the Swiss Market Index, which consists of 24 stocks traded on the three main stock exchanges in Geneva, Zurich, and Basle. Critics of the system contend that there is a lack of liquidity on the underlying stocks, thus limiting its effectiveness. Swiss banks control brokerage and can match trades internally with their own clients. This leaves a small amount for open trading on the exchange.[49]

The Germans will begin trading futures and options in 1990. The exchange will trade bond and stock-index futures, and options on 14 high-turnover German stocks. Trading will be executed entirely by computer, as on its Swiss counterpart. The main reason the government approved the new exchange was com-

Therefore, the number of contracts listed on foreign exchanges that compete with contracts on U.S. exchanges is small relative to the number of contracts traded throughout the world.

The U.S. exchanges' most formidable competitors are LIFFE and SIMEX (Singapore International Monetary Exchange). LIFFE competes with U.S. exchanges for trading volume in U.S. Treasury bond futures and options and in Eurodollar futures and options. SIMEX also competes for trading volume in Eurodollar futures as well as in Deutschemark and Japanese yen futures. But the SIMEX contracts are also complements to U.S. contracts in that a contract opened on the U.S. (Singapore) exchange can be closed on the Singapore (U.S.) exchange.

As shown in Figure 8, LIFFE commands less than 3 percent of trading volume in T-bond futures and options and Eurodollar options. Similarly, less than 3 percent of all Deutschemark futures trading occurs on SIMEX. LIFFE and SIMEX, however, are much more significant competitors for Eurodollar futures volume. SIMEX accounts for 7.5 percent of trading volume and LIFFE accounts for 6.5 percent.

Furthermore, in only three years, SIMEX managed to capture over 50 percent of the annual trading volume in the yen futures contract. The relatively greater success of SIMEX with the yen contract reflects the importance

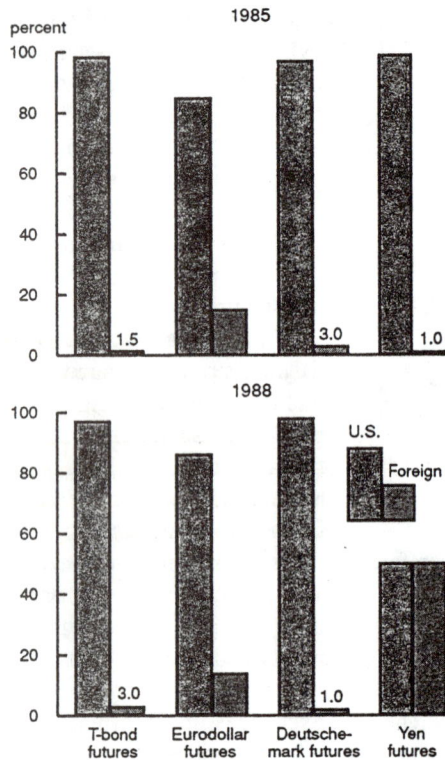

FIGURE 8

World competition for futures contracts
(Market share of world volume)

1985

1988

SOURCE: Intermarkets

of trading in the same time zone as one side of a foreign exchange transaction. In June 1989, a yen/dollar futures contract was launched in Tokyo, along with a Eurodollar contract. The experience of SIMEX suggests that the yen contract will attract market share away from SIMEX rather than from the CME because Singapore and Tokyo are in the same time zone. The above experiences suggest that once deutschemark futures begin trading on the German exchange, some proportion now traded in London will move to Germany.

24-hour trading

True 24-hour trading exists in only a few markets, and is most valuable for assets whose investors span several time zones. Major currencies are traded around the clock in at least seven major money centers. Precious metals, especially gold bullion, and oil, which trade in New York, London and Singapore, are traded 24 hours a day. U.S. Treasury bonds are traded around the clock as well, but overseas markets are thin. Twenty percent of the busi-

ness at the French futures exchange in Paris (Matif) is conducted outside of normal trading hours, indicating how important the extended hours can be.[51]

To a lesser extent, stocks of about 200 major multinational firms are traded in foreign markets as well as in their domestic markets, but foreign trading volume does not compare with that in domestic markets. One reason is that most information about a firm is revealed while domestic markets are open.

In preparation for the increase in round-the-clock trading and due to perceived competition from foreign exchanges, the National Association of Securities Dealers, the Chicago Mercantile Exchange, and the Chicago Board of Trade have made plans to extend their normal trading hours through computerized systems. The New York Stock Exchange is considering trading stocks electronically outside of normal trading hours, and the Cincinnati Stock Exchange and the CBOE are planning 24-hour electronic trading systems. The trading hours for foreign currency options on the Philadelphia Stock Exchange begin at 7:45 a.m. (Eastern Standard Time) to encompass more of the London business day.

International investment banking

As financial markets become more globally integrated, foreign investment banks are attempting to play larger roles in domestic markets. Overall, they are meeting with mixed results.

Foreign investment banks in the United States

Foreign-based investment banks have made some inroads into U.S. domestic capital markets. For the first time, two foreign firms ranked among the top ten advisers for U.S. mergers and acquisitions in the first quarter of 1989. Kleinwort Benson and S.G. Warburg, ranked sixth and seventh, respectively, according to the value of deals.[52] They placed ahead of Merrill Lynch and Kidder Peabody. No Japanese firms ranked among the top M&A advisers, although Fuji Bank of Japan has an ownership interest in Kleinwort Benson.

The Japanese are making a concerted effort to penetrate the U.S. investment banking market, but they have met with little success. The Big Four—Nomura Securities, Daiwa Securities, Nikko Securities, and Yamaichi

Securities Company—expanded in the United States in the mid-1980s, but have scaled back personnel due to unprofitable U.S. operations. Two of the Big Four—Nomura and Yamachi—have been trying to model their U.S. operations as identifiable Wall Street companies, and not just subsidiaries of Tokyo firms, by their appointment of Americans to head their U.S. operations. Nomura's strengths have been its primary dealership in U.S. government securities and U.S. stock trading unit, primarily for Japanese purchase. Nomura's weaknesses, however, are its lack of financial product development and its trading skills.

The Japanese have been more successful in U.S. derivative markets. In April 1988, Nikko Securities became the first Japanese securities firm to acquire a clearing membership at the Chicago Board of Trade (CBOT). Since then, fifteen others have joined the CBOT. The Chicago Mercantile Exchange (CME) has seventeen Japanese companies as members. Nikko, Daiwa, and Yamaichi are members of both the CBOT and CME. Recently, Nomura announced a cooperative agreement with Refco, one of the world's largest futures merchants. Consummation of the deal will assist Nomura in learning futures trading.

U.S. investment banks' activities abroad

Merger and acquisition activity has been slowing in the United States, prompting Wall Street firms to look to foreign markets. According to a 1988 survey, U.S. firms accounted for slightly more than half of all cross-border merger and acquisition activity. The most active U.S. investment banks were Shearson Lehman Hutton (57 deals), Goldman Sachs (46), and First Boston (34).[53]

U.S. investment banks represented about 12 percent of all mergers and acquisitions for European clients in 1988. The most active U.S. firms in this category were Security Pacific Group (37 deals), Shearson Lehman Hutton (26), and Goldman Sachs (22). Security Pacific has acquired two foreign investment banks, one Canadian and one British.[54]

U.S. firms expect to find some business in Asia as well. The newly formed investment bank, Wasserstein Perella, for example, recently dispatched merger and acquisition teams to Japan to set up the Tokyo joint venture, Nomura Wasserstein Perella.

In the area of securities underwriting, U.S. firms are quite strong. Seven of the top ten underwriters of debt and equity securities worldwide are U.S. firms; however, only three U.S. firms rank among the top underwriters of non-U.S. securities. Merrill Lynch was the top underwriter of all debt and equity offerings worldwide during the first half of 1989.[55]

The strength of U.S. firms abroad lies primarily in Europe. Foreign securities firms in Tokyo have found it difficult to establish themselves. Thirty-six of the 51 Tokyo branches of foreign securities houses lost a total of $164 million for the six months ending March 1989.[56] As a result of these losses, many foreign firms have cut back their Tokyo operations, concentrating on a particular product or service. Twenty-two out of the 115 Tokyo stock exchange members are foreign firms. Another 29 foreign securities houses have opened branch offices in Tokyo. Nevertheless, the Big Four dominate the Tokyo exchange, accounting for almost 50 percent of daily business. The foreign firms account for only 4.5 percent of this daily business.[57]

Three American investment banks, Salomon Brothers, Merrill Lynch, and First Boston, have been able to develop profitable operations in the Tokyo market. All three American firms attribute their success in part to a well-trained staff, and to hiring Japanese college graduates to fill positions. Salomon posted a $53.6 million pretax profit as of March 31, 1989. It also made a $300 million capital infusion, which has helped to make Salomon a challenger to the Big Four in bond trading.[58]

The U.S. government has been pressuring for greater access for U.S. firms to Japanese capital markets since 1984. For instance, Japanese government securities are predominantly sold through closed syndicates, in which foreign firms account for only about 8 percent of the total. Change has been slower than foreign investment banks and governments would like, but some progress has been made. The Japanese sold 40 percent of its 10-year bonds at an open auction in April 1989.[59]

Conclusion

Financial markets and financial services are becoming more globally integrated. As businesses expand into new markets around the world, there is greater demand for financing to follow them. All major areas of international finance have grown far more rapidly than foreign trade in recent years. Trading of securities in U.S. markets by nonresidents, trading volume of foreign currency futures and options, and foreign exchange trading have been growing at 40 percent or more a year. This rapid growth of international financial transactions reflects the growth in cross-border capital flows.

The major markets for domestic as well as international financial services are the United States, Japan, and the United Kingdom, although it is beginning to make more sense to talk about the dominant markets as the United States, Japan, and Europe. The reduction of regulatory barriers and harmonization of rules among countries have allowed more firms to compete in more markets around the world. These markets are also competing against each other for a share of the world's trading volume.

Today, a very large part of financial globalization involves financial intermediaries dealing with other, foreign, financial interme-diaries. Consequently, prices in one market are affected by conditions in other markets, but, with a few exceptions, of which commercial lending is the most notable, customers do not have direct access to more suppliers. Again, this could change as Europe moves toward economic and financial unification.

Lessons from industries such as automobiles and petroleum, as well as lessons from geographic expansion in the United States, indicate that the financial services industry will become more consolidated, with firms from a handful of countries garnering substantial market share. International joint ventures will be common and often precursors to outright acquisitions. For smaller firms to survive as global competitors, they will have to find and service a market niche.

As the financial services industry and financial markets become more globally integrated, the most efficient and best organized firms will prevail. Also, countries with the most efficient—but not necessarily the least—regulation will become the world's major international financial centers.

FOOTNOTES

[1]"Japanese Finance," Survey, *The Economist*, December 10, 1988, pp. 3 and 10.

[2]Ibid.

[3]Thomas H. Hanley, et. al., "The Swiss Banks: Universal Banks Poised to Prosper as Global Deregulation Unfolds," *Salomon Brothers Stock Research*, June 1986.

[4]See David T. Llewellyn, *Competition, Diversification, and Structural Change in the British Financial System*, 1989, unpublished xerox, p. 1.

[5]Christopher M. Korth, "International Financial Markets," in William H. Baughn and Donald R. Mandich, eds., *The International Banking Handbook*, Dow Jones-Irwin, 1983, pp. 9-13.

[6]During the Cold War, the U.S. dollar was the only universally accepted currency, and the Russians wanted to maintain their international reserves in dollars, but not at American banks for fear that the U.S government might freeze the funds. Therefore, the Russians found some British, French and German banks that would accept deposits in dollars. See Korth, p. 11.

[7]Christopher M. Korth, "The Eurocurrency Markets," in Baughn and Mandich, p. 26.

[8]Herbert L. Baer and Christine A. Pavel, "Does regulation drive innovation?," *Economic Perspectives*. Vol. 12, No. 2, March/April 1988, pp. 3-15, Federal Reserve Bank of Chicago.

[9]"Japanese banking booms offshore," *The Economist*, November 26, 1988, p. 87.

[10]*International Financial Statistics*, International Monetary Fund, various years.

[11]Ibid.

[12]This does not apply in criminal cases, bankruptcy, or debt collection. The disclosure of secret information to foreign authorities is not allowed, unless provided for in an international treaty. In such a case, which is an exception, the foreign authorities could obtain only the information available to Swiss authorities under similar circumstances. See Peat, Marwick, Mitchell & Co., *Banking in Switzerland*, 1979, pp. 35-6.

[13]Eurobanks have specific rates at which they are prepared either to borrow or lend Eurofunds. In London, this rate is known as LIBOR (the London Interbank Offer Rate). LIBOR dominates the Eurocurrency market.

[14]Henry S. Terrell, Robert S. Dohner, and Barbara R. Lowrey, "The Activities of Japanese Banks in the United

Kingdom and in the United States, 1980-88," *Federal Reserve Bulletin*, February 1990, p. 43.

[15]Michael R. Sesit and Craig Torres, "What if They Traded All Day and Nobody Came?," *Wall Street Journal*, June 14, 1989, p. C1.

[16]*U.S. Foreign Exchange Market Survey*, Federal Reserve Bank of New York, April 1989, pp. 5-7.

[17]"Report of Assets and Liabilities of U.S. Branches and Agencies of Foreign Banks," Table 4.30, *Federal Reserve Bulletin*, June 1989, Board of Governors of the Federal Reserve System; and *Annual Statistical Digest*, Board of Governors of the Federal Reserve System, Table 68.

[18]Ibid.

[19]*Senior Loan Officer Opinion Survey on Bank Lending Practices for August 1989*, Board of Governors of the Federal Reserve System.

[20]See footnote 17.

[21]*Annual Report*, Board of Governors of the Federal Reserve System, Banking Supervision and Regulation Section, various years; authors' calculations from Report of Condition and Income tapes, Board of Governors of the Federal Reserve System, various years.

[22]Ibid.

[23]Ibid.

[24]"European banking: Cheque list," *The Economist*, June 24, 1989, pp. 74-5.

[25]The Glass-Steagall Act is the law that separates commercial banking from investment banking in the U.S. Article 65 is its Japanese equivalent.

[26]James B. Treece, with John Hoerr, "Shaking Up Detroit," *Business Week*, August 14, 1989, pp. 74-80.

[27]*Standard and Poor's Oil Industry Survey*, August 3, 1989, p. 26.

[28]"European Stock Exchanges," *A supplement to Euromoney*, August 1987, pp. 2-5.

[29]Rosario Benvides, "How Big is the World Bond Market?—1989 Update" *International Bond Markets*, Salomon Brothers, June 24, 1989.

[30]Ibid.

[31]"Look east. young Eurobond," *The Economist*, September 16, 1989, pp. 83-4; "Japanese paper fills the void," *A supplement to Euromoney*, March 1989, p. 2.

[32]See *The Economist*, Sept. 16, 1989, pp. 83-4.

[33]"La grande boum," *The Economist*, October 1, 1988, pp. 83-4.

[34]Christine M. Cumming and Lawrence M. Sweet, "Financial Structure of the G-7 Countries: How Does the United States Compare?," Federal Reserve Bank of New York, *Quarterly Review*, Winter 1987/88, pp. 15-16.

[35]"Sweeping away Frankfurt's old-fashioned habits," *The Economist*, January 28, 1989, pp. 73-4.

[36]Ibid.

[37]*Financial Market Trends*, OECD, February 1989, pp.85-6.

[38]Ibid.

[39]Ibid.

[40]"A smooth run for Switzerland's big banks," *The Economist*, June 17, 1989, pp. 87-8.

[41]*World Financial Markets*, J.P. Morgan & Co., November 29, 1988.

[42]"Foreign Transactions in Securities," Table 3.24, *Federal Reserve Bulletin*, June 1989, Board of Governors of the Federal Reserve System.

[43]Ibid.

[44]Various central bank statistical releases.

[45]The underlying instrument is worth $1 million.

[46]"US exchanges fight for market share," *A supplement to Euromoney*, July 1989, p. 9.

[47]Elizabeth R. Thagard, "London's Jump," *Intermarkets*, May 1989, p. 22.

[48]See *A supplement to Euromoney*, August 1987, p. 28.

[49]Ginger Szala, "Financial walls tumble for German investors," *Futures*, January 1990, p. 44.

[50]Ibid., p. 42.

[51]See Thagard, p. 23.

[52]Ted Weissberg, "Wall Street Seeks Global Merger Market: IDD's First-quarter M&A Rankings," *Investment Dealers Digest*, May 8, 1989, pp. 17-21.

[53]"The World Champions of M&A," *Euromoney*, February 1989, pp. 96-102.

[54]Ibid.

[55]Philip Maher, "Merrill Lynch Holds on to Top International Spot," *Investment Dealers Digest*, July 10, 1989, pp. 23-25.

[56]"Japan proving tough for foreign brokerage," *Chicago Tribune*, September 11, 1989, section 4, pp. 1-2

[57]Ibid.

[58]Ibid.

[59]Ibid.

Article 3

The Changing American Attitude toward Debt, and Its Consequences

Frank E. Morris

Peter F. Drucker Professor of Management Science, Wallace E. Carroll School of Management, Boston College, and former President of the Federal Reserve Bank of Boston. This article is based on his remarks at his installation, February 12, 1990.

The Congress and the President have been struggling with the federal government budget deficit for six years, thus far with little result. The fundamental reason for their failure is the fact that the American people no longer view the deficit as a significant problem. This represents a radical change in the attitude of Americans from thirty years ago, when even small deficits were viewed with great concern. People are not much concerned about our long string of trade deficits, either. Those working in industries affected by foreign competition are, of course, worried about their jobs; others may feel uneasy about Mitsubishi buying Rockefeller Center; but people in general are not clamoring for the steps needed to eliminate the trade deficit. Moreover, there is no perception of the linkage between the federal budget deficit and the trade deficit.

This article will describe the factors that have produced this change in American values and assess the consequences, both past and future. Although society's values most often refer to social issues, they also help to shape the macroeconomic options open to a democratic government.

Early Influences

Dean Acheson chose as the title for his autobiography *Present at the Creation.* He was referring, of course, to the creation of the Marshall Plan, NATO and other aspects of U.S. foreign policy in the years following World War II. I was present at the creation of the changed American attitude toward national debts.

It began in the Kennedy Administration in the early 1960s. The President had run on a platform of getting the American economy going again. His principal economic advisers, Walter Heller, Chairman of the Council of Economic Advisers, and Douglas Dillon, Secretary of the Treasury, argued that the way to achieve that objective was through a major tax cut, which would stimulate economic growth and, in the process, increase Treasury revenues sufficiently that the tax cut would not result in any substantial increase in the federal deficit.

This was a radical idea in those days and President Kennedy was quite conservative in fiscal matters. It took a long time for his advisers to persuade the President that it made economic sense to cut taxes even though the government was already running a deficit. It took much longer to persuade the Congress. One of the key features of the Kennedy tax program was the investment tax credit. I remember being stunned to learn that the leading business organizations had testified against the investment tax credit. In part it was due to a preference for accelerated depreciation, but in part it reflected an uneasiness with the general idea of cutting taxes when the government budget was in deficit.

The popular view of the day was the view of President Eisenhower—that the federal budget was akin to a family budget and if the government ran deficits, trouble was certain to ensue. Walter Heller complained that what he called the "Puritan Ethic," an unreasoning fear of deficits, was keeping the government from following sound economic policies. And so a big educational effort was undertaken to deal with the "Puritan Ethic."

My small role was to talk to the banking groups that regularly visited the Treasury. We argued that there certainly were times when an increase in the

---

The popular view of the day was that if the government ran deficits, trouble was certain to ensue.

---

deficit would be inappropriate. If the economy were operating close to capacity, an increase in the deficit could be inflationary, and would raise interest rates and squeeze out private investment. But in the conditions of 1962 and 1963, when the economy was operating well below capacity, a tax cut would raise total output and increase private investment, without enlarging the deficit significantly.

In the event, the Kennedy tax cut was a triumph.

In the first three years that the tax cut was in effect, 1964–66, the growth rate of real GNP averaged 5.6 percent, federal government revenues rose by 23 percent, and the fiscal 1966 deficit was slightly less than in fiscal 1963.

This was the first of five factors that changed American attitudes toward the federal debt, and perhaps the most important, because if the Kennedy tax cut had been viewed as a failure, subsequent U.S. fiscal history would have been very different and the "Puritan Ethic" might be alive and well today.

Theoretical Justifications

The second factor changing attitudes was the emergence of the doctrine that large deficits were needed to control federal government spending. A principal advocate of this position was Milton Friedman. He argued that deficits were not important; what was important was the percentage of the GNP absorbed by federal government spending. Government deficits would not be inflationary if the Federal Reserve refused to monetize the debt, and the presence of large deficits would constrain spending. What Friedman did not emphasize was that this combination of a loose fiscal policy and a tight monetary policy would, in an economy operating close to capacity, drive up interest rates, squeeze out private investment, and make American industry less competitive in world markets.

The large deficits have had the effect that Friedman anticipated. Because of the rise in military spending, total federal government spending as a percent of the GNP was higher in the last year of the Reagan administration than it was in Carter's last year. However, excluding the military, entitlement programs, and interest costs, the remainder of the budget declined as a percentage of the GNP. More important, the deficits have restrained the Congress from initiating new social programs. President Bush has been talking about establishing a new space program, improving the educational system, initiating a war on drugs, and aiding the Eastern European countries. Because of the deficit, however, only nominal amounts of money are being allocated to these programs. The United States is not in a financial position to undertake new initiatives or address new challenges. Because of the restraint on spending, conservatives who traditionally have opposed government deficits are now comfortable in defending a policy of continuing deficits.

The *Wall Street Journal* has been a constant advocate of this position on its editorial pages. The following is from an editorial of January 31, 1990:

> Spending measures the government's real command over resources; it's a secondary matter whether it's financed by taxes, by borrowing or by even higher taxes with a budget surplus. While we'd like something a lot more surgical, an item veto for example, the deficit has been the only spending restraint we've had. The inexorable climb of outlays as a percent of GNP was checked by holding the line on taxes even at the expense of a budget deficit. Revenues are already climbing back toward their postwar high. On that ground alone it's time to cut them again, letting the people who earned the money decide how to consume, save and invest.

Other Contributing Factors

The third factor affecting attitudes has been the massive net inflow of foreign savings, totaling about $800 billion during the past seven years, which has mitigated the effect of the deficits on interest rates and private investment. Without this $800 billion in foreign savings, interest rates in the United States would have been much higher and the man in the street would be much less complacent about the deficits than he is today.

The fourth factor changing attitudes toward debt is the apparent success of the Reagan economic policies. I say "apparent" because we lack historical perspective, but without question a good feeling is widespread in the country. The unemployment rate is low. The inflation rate and interest rates are high by historical standards, but they are so much lower than they were in the early years of the decade that they seem quite satisfactory. For example, students today cannot relate to the fact that the mortgage rate on a house built in 1970 is 5½ percent—they think anything below 10 percent is pretty good. The very fact that the economy is in the eighth year of economic expansion with no recession in sight has caused people to discount concerns about the deficits.

The fifth and a very important factor changing attitudes toward debt, is the fact that the United States has not had a major depression in fifty years. This has made people much less cautious in financial matters. The clearest examples are in corporate finance, with many major companies taking on levels of debt that would not permit them to survive a serious depression. Some are even having trouble

dealing with a slower growth rate. The top managers of American companies in the 1950s and 1960s were people who had come to maturity during the Great Depression. The willingness of today's managers to leverage their companies must seem to them to be reckless behavior, and the willingness, until recently, of investors to buy the bonds of such highly leveraged corporations must seem to them to be naive. The fact that nobody under the age of sixty has any memory of the Great Depression has contributed substantially to the new attitudes about debt.

The massive net inflow of foreign savings has mitigated the effect of the deficits on interest rates and private investment.

The Consequences

Having discussed the reasons for the changed American attitude toward debt, I would like to turn to the consequences of that change. Economic theory tells us that if the government runs large deficits when the economy is running close to capacity, the result will be high interest rates, the squeezing out of private investment, and a slower rate of growth in productivity and real income. All of these consequences are clearly apparent in the 1980s, mitigated only by the large inflows of foreign capital.

Since World War II the U.S. economy has had two economic expansions that lasted more than seven years. It may be instructive to compare the first seven years of the present expansion (1983–89) with the first seven years of the earlier expansion (1961–67).

During the 1961–67 period the federal government budget deficits averaged 0.8 percent of the GNP versus 4.5 percent in the 1983–89 period, almost six times as large. At the same time, the gross private savings rate dropped from 17.2 percent during the 1961–67 period to 15.8 percent during 1983–89, which means that the burden of the deficits on our capital markets in the 1980s was even greater than the ratios of the deficits to the GNP would suggest. During the 1961–67 period, U.S. government long-term bond yields averaged 4.25 percent and the bank prime lending rate averaged 4.8 percent. These interest rates seem almost impossibly low today, but they are not very low relative to the rates that have prevailed in recent years in Japan and Germany, our major competitors.

Given the high cost of capital, it is not surprising that the investment performance of the United States in the 1980s was the poorest of any decade since

---

One of the most worrisome aspects of the large international deficit is that the United States has lost sovereignty over its financial markets.

World War II and that the rate of growth of productivity and real income was also the poorest. Net fixed domestic investment as a percentage of GNP during the 1983–89 period was only 72 percent of the 1961–67 level, and net fixed nonresidential domestic investment as a percentage of the GNP was only 58 percent of the 1961–67 level. We shall note later that the rate of growth of output per person in the nonfarm business sector during 1983–89 was 56 percent of the 1961–67 level. These domestic investment figures tell only part of the story. During the 1961–67 period the United States invested more abroad than foreigners invested in the United States, in an amount averaging 0.8 percent of the GNP. Net foreign investment during 1983–89 averaged a *negative* 2.7 percent of the GNP.

Since 1983 the level of investment in the United States has clearly been subpar despite the fact that in the past seven years the economy has enjoyed net imports of foreign savings totaling more than $800 billion. If this inflow had been associated with an exceptionally high level of investment in state-of-the-art plant and equipment, this country's future prospects would be greatly enhanced, but the facts clearly indicate that this inflow was consumed rather than invested.

While a national budget deficit is clearly not like a family's budget deficit, an international deficit is very similar. A family can consume beyond its in-

come as long as its credit remains good. The same is true of a nation in international transactions. The credit of the United States has been amazingly strong during the past seven years. This has led one prominent economist to argue that the United States can sustain current account deficits indefinitely at around the $100 billion level. I am skeptical of this proposition. My experience suggests that the fact that something has gone on for several years is no basis for assuming that it can go on forever.

When I was a graduate student in the 1950s, a common theme was that the world was going to have a perpetual shortage of dollars. When I arrived in the Treasury in 1961, I found that the dollar shortage was over. Foreign central banks had more dollars than they wanted to hold. The span of time between perpetual dollar shortage and dollar glut was very short.

One of the most worrisome aspects of the large international deficit is that the United States has lost sovereignty over its financial markets. The year 1987 was a case in point. In the spring of 1987 the inflow of private foreign capital suddenly dried up. Private foreign investors were unwilling to finance our deficit at prevailing interest rates and exchange rates. The dollar dropped and the deficit was financed entirely by an inflow of foreign central bank funds, as these banks sought to dampen the rate of decline of the dollar. While private foreign investors had been absorbing 30 percent or more of our new bond issues, central banks do not buy bonds; they invest short-term. As a consequence long-term bond yields rose by 150 basis points and this, in turn, triggered the great stock market collapse of 1987.

Prospects

The United States is currently vulnerable to another financial shock stemming from any change in the attitudes of private foreign investors. The major interest rate advantage that the United States offered in earlier years has largely been eliminated for German investors and is very much smaller for Japanese investors. The dollar has fallen by 18 percent against the deutsche mark since September, although it has thus far been steady against the yen. There could well be ahead of us another period in which the demand for U.S. assets by private foreign investors dries up. Again the United States would experience a sharp decline in the dollar and a rise in long-term interest rates. Despite an easing in Federal Reserve policy, long-term government bond yields have increased 75 basis points since December 20. At least in part, this rise in long-term yields reflects a recognition by the market that U.S. assets may be less attractive to foreign investors than they have been in the past. This is a matter of concern, since the economy in 1990 may be less capable of absorbing financial shocks than it was in 1987.

In 1981 the United States had net investment income of $34 billion, meaning that income on U.S. foreign investment exceeded income on foreign investment in the United States by that amount. This was a substantial American asset, the product of decades of heavy investment abroad. It permitted the country to run a trade deficit that in 1989 dollars would amount to $700 for every American family, and still balance its international accounts. In seven years this asset was dissipated; net investment income turned negative in 1989. At some point in the future, the United States will have to run a trade surplus in order to cover the interest payments due on the debt that we incurred so that we could consume more than we produced in the 1980s.

It should not be surprising that the poor investment performance of the 1980s has been associated with a poor productivity performance, the poorest of any major industrial country. Productivity growth during this expansion has been only 56 percent of the level of 1961–67, roughly the same proportion as the relative rates of growth of fixed nonresidential investment. Real compensation per hour in the nonfarm business sector rose by 20 percent during the expansion in the 1960s but only by 5 percent during this expansion.

With such an abysmal record of real income growth, why do Americans feel good about the 1980s? I think there are four reasons. First, the almost negligible real income growth dates back to 1973, the year of the first oil price shock. During the previous twenty-six years, 1947–73, real compensation per hour doubled. During the following sixteen years it rose by only 5 percent. Americans no longer expect a rapid rise in real income, as they did in the 1960s. Second, the decline of the inflation rate and interest rates from the high double-digit levels of the early 1980s is viewed, quite properly, as a success of economic policy. But there is no perception that the current levels of the inflation rate and interest rates are very high by historical standards. Young people find the cost of housing to be very high, and it is much higher in real terms than it was for my generation; but they do not understand that it is the higher

mortgage rates rather than the higher purchase price of housing that is the source of the problem. Third, the labor force participation rate for women has risen by almost 30 percent since 1973. The United States has many more two-earner families, and this has helped to mask the fact that real income per person has made little progress. Fourth, the poor U.S. economic performance was also masked by the large trade deficits that permitted us to consume more than we as a nation produced.

A prolonged reluctance of private foreign capital to finance our trade deficit would produce a declining dollar and sharply higher long-term interest rates.

Americans are a much less compassionate people than we were in the 1960s. We are now much less willing to sacrifice for the benefit of the disadvantaged, at home or abroad. The reason, I believe, is that with real incomes rising at 3 percent a year during the 1960s, Americans felt affluent. Today after sixteen years of little growth in real incomes the sense of affluence has gone and along with it some of our compassion for others.

In the American democracy, with all of its checks and balances and diffused power, we are often not able to act except in a crisis environment. While the economic policies of the 1980s have carried with them considerable costs, the costs are long-term in their impact, not the stuff to generate crises. The most likely disturbance to capture the attention of the American people would be a prolonged reluctance of private foreign capital to finance our trade deficit, which would produce a declining dollar and sharply higher long-term interest rates. We had a taste of this in 1987. More may come.

In the early 1960s economists of all persuasions agreed with President Kennedy's theme of the need to get the economy going again. In a congressional hearing in 1964, Keynesians argued that fiscal policies were too restrictive in the 1950s and monetarists complained that the Federal Reserve had not permitted the money supply to grow fast enough. They agreed on the need for more expansionary policies to enable the economy to reach its full potential. I shared this conventional wisdom.

President Eisenhower and William McChesney Martin, Jr., who presided over fiscal and monetary policies during most of the 1950s, were indeed conservative men. However, if we look at the economic statistics of the 1950s in the perspective of history, we might wonder why economists of that era were so unanimously dissatisfied with the results. During the 1950s we had an average rate of growth of real GNP of 4.1 percent, the unemployment rate averaged 4.5 percent, the increase in the Consumer Price Index averaged 2.3 percent per year. Not too shabby, but the dramatic numbers were those for productivity and real incomes. During the decade of the 1950s, output per hour rose by almost 30 percent, an average of 2.6 percent per annum, and real compensation per hour rose by almost 37 percent, averaging 3.2 percent per annum. We are unlikely to achieve that kind of economic performance in the 1990s.

In retrospect, I have reluctantly come to the conclusion that the country would be a lot better off today if we in the Kennedy Administration had failed to destroy the "Puritan Ethic" in the early 1960s.

Article 4

Michelle R. Garfinkel

Michelle R. Garfinkel is an economist at the Federal Reserve Bank of St. Louis. Thomas A. Pollmann provided research assistance.

What Is an "Acceptable" Rate of Inflation?—A Review of the Issues

"Our strategy continues to be centered on moving toward, and ultimately reaching, stable prices, that is, price levels sufficiently stable so that expectations of change do not become major factors in key economic decisions."

Alan Greenspan, *Testimony to House Committee on Banking, Finance, and Urban Affairs,* January 24, 1989

RECENT fears of increased future inflationary pressures, heightened by high rates of capacity utilization, have generated a large body of commentary concerning what level of inflation would be desirable or at least acceptable.[1] While there appears to be a general consensus that a rise in the rate of inflation is not desirable, whether or not many would agree with Mr. Greenspan's statement above is not clear. Indeed, his statement makes a stronger suggestion that even the current rate of inflation is not acceptable.[2]

This article points out three central issues for determining what constitutes an "acceptable" rate of inflation. The first issue concerns the costs of inflation. The second issue is whether, despite these costs, inflation's benefits are suffi-

ciently large to justify some positive rate of inflation. The final issue concerns the costs of reducing inflation. Even if there were convincing reasons for ultimately eliminating inflation, some analysts would argue that a positive inflation could be acceptable in the short-run; the optimal time path along which a long-run goal of zero inflation is achieved depends on the temporary costs of adjustment to reach that goal eventually.

WHAT ARE THE COSTS OF INFLATION?

Examining the effects of inflation sheds light on why price stabilization is a primary objective of monetary policy. This section focuses on

---

[1]See, for example, Clark (1989) and Stein (1989).

[2]Mr. Greenspan expressed this view more clearly in his testimony to Congress in February 1989: ". . . let me stress that the current rate of inflation, let alone an increase, is not acceptable, and our policies are designed to

reduce inflation in coming years." [Greenspan (1989), p. 274.] Elsewhere, he has been quoted as suggesting that the ultimate objective of the Fed is to eradicate inflation [Murray (1989)].

Table 1

Some Effects of Inflation

Anticipated Inflation	Unanticipated Inflation
1. Inflation tax on money balances: transfers resources from money holders to government and reduces money demand.	1. Reduction in real value of gross return from holding nominal debt: transfers resources from net monetary creditors to net monetary debtors.
2. Inflation-induced increase in marginal income taxes: transfers resources from taxpayers to the government and reduces labor supply.	2. Reduction in real wages if wages are fixed in nominal terms: transfers resources from labor to employers.
3. Taxation of nominal interest income: transfers resources from savers to the government and reduced savings.	**Inflation Uncertainty**
4. Interaction with tax incentives: reduces cost of borrowing and increases debt finance.	1. Increase in reluctance to enter into nominal wage contracts and increase in cost of nominal wage contract negotiations: increases indexation of nominal contracts and reduces real economic growth.
5. Costs of price adjustments: produces excessive relative price variability and a misallocation of resources.	2. Increase in risk premia of longer maturity nominal bonds: causes a movement from longer to shorter term maturities and increases the real cost of capital.
	3. Increase in incentive to hedge against unanticipated inflation: transaction costs incurred in attempts to hedge against risk associated with inflation uncertainty and distortions in asset accumulation.
	4. Confusion about source of price movements: causes excessive relative price variability and a misallocation of resources.

some of the relevant effects given existing institutional arrangements in the United States.[3] These effects, as summarized in table 1, are organized by their source: the effects arising from anticipated (or expected) inflation and those arising from unanticipated inflation (or the difference between actual inflation and expected inflation) and the associated uncertainty about future inflation.

The Effects of Anticipated Inflation

Much of modern macroeconomic research has been devoted to examining how expectations affect economic decisions. In contrast to the idea that only "surprises" or unanticipated events can have real effects, economic theory suggests that even fully anticipated inflation can distort economic decisions. These "distortions" are said to be the costs of anticipated inflation. A useful way to focus solely on the effects of anticipated inflation is to assume that the future sequence of changes in the general price level is known in advance.[4]

Anticipated inflation influences the allocation of resources in the economy primarily through two types of tax effects. First, inflation effectively imposes a tax on money balances equal to the

---

[3]For a more exhaustive list and detailed analysis of the effects of inflation, see Fischer and Modigliani (1978). Also, Kessel and Alchian (1962) provide a useful discussion of inflation's consequences. For a survey of the earlier literature concerning the theory of inflation, see Laidler and Parkin (1975).

[4]This assumption is made purely for expositional ease. When uncertainty is introduced in the discussion, the effects of anticipated inflation mentioned in this section are simply added to those effects arising from the unanticipated component of inflation and those effects arising from uncertainty. It should be noted that the assumption of certainty does not preclude a variable inflation rate.

reduction of purchasing power of money holdings. For example, an individual holding $100 throughout 1988, when the inflation rate was around 4 percent, lost about $4 in purchasing power.[5]

Since inflation imposes a tax on money balances, it reduces individuals' demand for money.[6] Because individuals will attempt to economize on money holdings during periods of inflation by making extra trips to the bank or automatic teller machine, inflation is said to generate "shoe-leather costs." But the costs of the inflation tax are not merely the physical resources and time expended to avoid the inflation tax, as that term suggests. The total cost or the "gross burden" of the inflation tax more importantly includes the increase in the price paid to maintain real money balances and the value of lost services otherwise provided by money. Inflation, however, generates revenue to the government that indirectly accrues to individuals. The "excess burden" is the difference between the total costs and the government's revenues. Under some plausible assumptions, a rough estimate of this excess burden from a "small" inflation tax of 5 percent is about $13.4 billion or about 0.3 percent of gross national product (GNP) per year.[7]

The excess burden of the inflation tax on money balances is only part of the total welfare cost associated with inflation. The second type of tax effect arises as anticipated inflation interacts with the structure of the existing income tax system, exacerbating the distortions contained therein. Since the progressive income tax system is not completely indexed against increases in the price level, inflation will subject individuals' incomes to higher average and marginal tax rates. Even if wages fully adjust to inflation so that the real (before-tax) wage rate is approximately constant, an individual's real, after-tax income will decline.[8]

Although one would expect that, through the so-called "bracket-creep" effect, anticipated inflation would influence and distort individual's labor supply decisions, empirical evidence on the effects of marginal taxes suggests that anticipated inflation has little effect on aggregate

---

[5]Inflation as measured by the consumer price index for all urban consumers was 4.4 percent during 1988, while other measures indicate that inflation was between 3.0 percent and 4.5 percent. The current dollar loss of purchasing power of $100 is calculated by the following equation:

$$P_{t+1}\left(\frac{100}{P_t} - \frac{100}{P_{t+1}}\right), \text{ where } P_t \text{ is the general}$$

price level in time t. Since the rate of inflation, π_t, equals $\frac{P_{t+1} - P_t}{P_t}$, the loss in purchasing power in current dollar terms equals $100\,\pi_t$. As noted below, the tax on money balances generates revenue to the government.

[6]Another way to see why inflation reduces the demand for money is by noting that inflation increases the opportunity cost of holding those balances. The opportunity cost is the revenue forgone by holding money rather than securities yielding a nominal interest rate, R. (The assumption that money does not yield interest is not important here. As argued by Tatom (1979), among others, even checkable deposits that pay interest are subject to the inflation tax.) Suppose, for example, that there is no expected future inflation. Then the nominal rate paid on a security is its real yield, r. An individual holding $100 in cash balances for transaction services forgoes the real interest payment, $100r, that would have been obtained if he instead bought a $100 bond. In this case, the opportunity cost of holding money balances is r per dollar. Now suppose that inflation, π, in the next period is expected to be positive. The nominal yield on the bond R, will increase roughly by the amount of expected inflation to compensate lenders for the expected loss in purchasing power of the initial loan; the nominal yield will equal the real rate plus an expected inflation premium. (Strictly speaking, $R = (1 + r)(1 + \pi)-1$. Simply adding the real rate of interest and the rate of inflation will be a reasonable approximation provided that the product of the real rate of interest and the rate of inflation,

$r\pi$, is of a small order of magnitude.) The higher nominal rate forgone by holding money implies that the opportunity cost of holding money has increased.

[7]This estimate is intended to give only a rough order of magnitude of the excess burden of inflation. The estimate assumes that the current stock of money (M1) is about $780 billion and that the interest elasticity of the demand for money is -.15. This latter assumption means that when the opportunity cost of holding money increases 1 percent, the quantity of money demanded falls .15 percent. Thus, assuming the real rate of interest is 3 percent, the demand for money would increase by 25 percent to $975 billion if inflation were zero. It should be noted that the estimate of the welfare cost ignores the fact that total "tax" borne by the individual money holder does not go entirely to the government. Since the banking system receives part of the revenue from the inflation tax through money creation, the estimate above understates the excess burden. See Tatom (1976, 1979) and Fischer (1981b) for more detailed discussions of estimating the excess burden of the inflation tax on money balances.

[8]In a preliminary study, Baye and Black (1988) table II, p. 480, estimate that the "bracket-creep-induced inflation tax rate," defined as the difference between the rate of change in gross income necessary to keep utility constant and the associated rate of change in consumption expenditures, ranges from 0.2 percent to 2.4 percent between 1972 and 1981. Furthermore, they find that changes in the tax code during this period, intended to mitigate the bracket-creep effect, were largely offset by simultaneous increases in Social Security taxes (pp. 481-82).

labor supply.[9] Furthermore, to the extent that the current income tax system has become partially indexed by recent tax reform, the effects of inflation in terms of the bracket creep effect have been partially mitigated.[10]

Nonetheless, recent tax reform has not fully insulated individuals from the tax effects of anticipated inflation. Anticipated inflation produces an overstatement of interest income subject to taxation. The nominal interest rate required by lenders includes two components. The first component, r, is a payment to the lender for not consuming today and, hence, constitutes income. The second component, π, is a premium to compensate the lender for the anticipated lost purchasing power of the principal due to inflation. Because the latter component serves to preserve the value of the principal, it is not income in an economic sense. Yet, like income, it is taxed.

To see how an increase in anticipated inflation increases an individual's tax liability for a given before-tax real return, consider the following example. Suppose, first, that no inflation is expected and the marginal income tax rate is 25 percent. A one-year loan that yields a 3 percent (real) return to an individual before taxes generates an after-tax real return of 2.25 percent. If, instead, the anticipated rate of inflation were 2 percent, with the real interest rate on the one-year loan remaining at 3 percent, and the nominal yield rising to 5 percent (the real rate of interest plus the rate of inflation that would be required when abstracting from tax considerations), then the after-tax real rate of return to the lender would fall to 1.75 percent. A rise in the anticipated inflation rate to 5 percent would erode the expected (and actual) return dramatically to 1 percent.

Lenders will demand a nominal return higher than the original real interest rate plus the rate

of inflation to be compensated for the increased future tax liability arising from an increase in anticipated inflation. In the example above, for the lender to supply the same dollar amount of loans as when expected inflation was zero, the same after-tax real return of 2.25 percent would be required; this, in turn, would require a rise in the nominal return from 3 percent to 9.67 percent when expected inflation rises to 5 percent. Hence, the nominal rate of interest must rise by more than the rate of inflation to induce the lender to forgo the same amount of current consumption. If, however, nominal interest rates did not rise enough to keep the after-tax real rate the same when inflation rises, savings would be reduced. It has been estimated that the distortionary effect of a 10 percent rate of inflation on savings over a 20-year period produces a total welfare loss (total cost net of additional revenues to the government in present value terms) of about 7 percent of current savings or, assuming that savings is 10 percent of GNP, about 0.7 percent of current GNP.[11]

Tax incentives combined with anticipated inflation distort financial decisions. Because nominal interest payments on debt are tax-deductible and dividends are effectively taxed twice, anticipated inflation will induce corporations to finance an expansion of their operations by creating debt rather than issuing additional stock. If nominal interest rates do not adjust to anticipated inflation enough to maintain a fixed, after-tax real rate of return, then an increase in anticipated inflation can induce individuals to finance a greater proportion of their consumption and asset purchases with debt.[12] This bias for debt finance, which increases with anticipated inflation, could be costly if, by increasing future debt obligation as a fraction of expected future cash flows, it increases the chances of future default.

---

[9]See, for example, Hausman (1981), who finds that the tax-induced effects on wages do not significantly reduce aggregate labor supply. Inflation's effect on the marginal tax rate could similarly have an insignificant effect on labor supply.

[10]Tatom (1985) discusses the impact of the partial indexation of the income tax system on real tax liabilities. As discussed by Tatom, the currently used method of indexation does not fully mitigate the bracket creep effect because the indexation of tax brackets is calculated using past increases in the general price level. Furthermore, some deductions, credits and adjustments that can be made for tax purposes have maximum dollar limits or nominal ceilings that are not indexed. Even assuming a constant real income before taxes, an expected rise in the

price level implies that a larger portion of real income will be subject to taxes. Without increasing the marginal tax rate, anticipated inflation increases the average tax liability.

[11]Fischer (1981b), p. 23. As he notes, however, the estimate is rough and could be as large as 2 percent to 3 percent of GNP under slightly different, although still plausible, assumptions.

[12]Even if nominal rates fully adjusted to increases in anticipated inflation so as to not affect the after-tax real return, an increase in anticipated inflation decreases the cost of debt finance to firms provided that the corporate marginal tax rate exceeds the individual marginal tax rate.

The impact of anticipated inflation on economic behavior is not restricted solely to inflation-induced tax effects. Specifically, by changing prices, some firms incur lump-sum or "menu" costs. Even if these costs are small, real-world price adjustments occur at discrete times rather than continuously. Assuming that price changes are not sychronized, anticipated inflation (and deflation) can generate relative price changes in the short run. Since these inflation-induced relative price changes do not reflect real, fundamental changes in the economy, they can create a misallocation of resources, resulting in a welfare loss in addition to the explicit costs of changing prices.[13]

The Effects of Unanticipated Inflation and Uncertainty

Unanticipated inflation also can result in a misallocation of resources. Its impact on individuals' behavior, however, is less obvious. In particular, although unanticipated inflation primarily redistributes wealth among people, it is the uncertainty associated with these possible future redistributions that distorts economic behavior. Before discussing these distortionary effects, this section focuses on the distributional effects of unanticipated inflation.

To examine the distributional effects, while initially abstracting from the effects of uncertainty *per se*, suppose there is a one-time shock to the level of inflation. The shock is temporary in the sense that, after one period, the rate of inflation will return to the previously expected time path.[14] This unanticipated inflation influences the distribution of wealth through contracts that fix future nominal cash flows, especially debt contracts.

When debt contracts are fixed in nominal terms, the main effect of unanticipated inflation is to redistribute real wealth to net monetary debtors at the expense of net monetary creditors.[15] Not suspecting the possibility of a divergence between actual and expected inflation, a lender would demand a rate of return that compensates him only for not consuming today and for the lost purchasing power of the initial borrowings due to anticipated inflation. When actual inflation exceeds anticipated inflation, the lender unexpectedly suffers a loss on his loan; the purchasing power of the return on the loan falls below that expected at the time the loan was made.

For example, suppose an individual, who expects zero inflation over the next period, requires a 5 percent nominal (and real) return next period in exchange for lending $100 today. Regardless of next period's inflation, the lender will receive $105 in the next period. If there is a 5 percent (unanticipated) inflation, then the purchasing power of the $105 payment to the lender is identical to that of the $100 lent. In this case, the real net return is zero.

Just as unanticipated inflation erodes the real purchasing power of the return from the loan, it reduces the real liability of the debtor. Along the same lines, if nominal wages specified in labor contracts are fixed for an interval of time, unanticipated inflation reduces an individual's real wage while increasing an employer's income net of the wage bill in real terms.

Although the redistribution of wealth due to unanticipated inflation is important to the individual before and after the fact, it is not easy to say anything meaningful about the welfare implications of the realized or *ex post* redistrib-

---

[13]Mankiw (1985) demonstrates that, in the presence of even small price adjustment costs, optimizing behavior by price-setting firms can produce sticky prices that are inefficient from a social welfare perspective in a deflationary period. He shows, however, that sticky prices in an inflationary period could be more efficient than fully flexible prices. Since price-setting firms produce at lower-than-socially-optimal levels, sticky prices in an inflationary period reduce the wedge between actual and socially optimal output levels.

[14]If the level of inflation were permanently increased above its previously expected and actual level, but the possibility of a future shock were arbitrarily close to zero, the discussion to follow is virtually unchanged. It should be noted, however, that the discussion implicitly assumes that, when contracts are signed, individuals do not perceive the possibility of shock in the future. Hence, the discussion is about a counterfactual and can be misleading. Specifically, if individuals suspected that such a shock might occur

(with a positive probability), they would adjust their behavior, so that the terms of the contract reflect the possibility of a future shock. The implicit assumption is made for expositional purposes, and the possible adjustments in behavior are discussed in turn.

[15]A net monetary creditor's (debtor's) holdings of fixed nominally denominated assets are greater (less) than his holdings of nominally denominated liabilities. See, for example, Kessel and Alchian (1962). Alchian and Kessel (1959) present evidence that the market value of equity of firms classified as net monetary creditors tends to fall during inflationary periods. The converse holds for net monetary debtors.

utions.[16] The losses due to unanticipated inflation are matched by others' gains, so that there is no net change in wealth associated with the redistribution. In an expected or *ex ante* sense, however, the possible (and arbitrary) redistributions have aggregate welfare implications, because they distort behavior, especially that of individuals who dislike risk.

Uncertainty associated with inflation manifests itself quantitatively and qualitatively in both nominal and real contracts. In the presence of fixed nominal wage contracts, uncertainty associated with future inflation can depress the supply and demand for labor. As greater inflation uncertainty increases the difficulties and costs of forecasting future inflation, wage negotiations become more complex and costly. Consequently, without nominal wage indexation when future inflation becomes more uncertain, individuals and firms are less willing to lock themselves into fixed nominal contracts.

But the effects of inflation uncertainty will be partially alleviated as labor markets adjust. Greater uncertainty about future increases in the general price level gives risk-averse individuals and firms an incentive to increase the degree of indexation in wage contracts and to reduce the duration of the contract. The increased degree of indexation and the shortening of the length of the nominal contracts increases the responsiveness of nominal wages to unanticipated inflation.[17] Nevertheless, a recent empirical study, which accounts for the greater wage indexation induced by greater inflation uncertainty, indicates that an increase in inflation uncertainty similar to that which occurred

roughly between the 1960s and the 1970s would reduce growth in real GNP in the long term by approximately 2 percent.[18]

Inflation uncertainty also affects the demand and supply of nominally denominated debt of different maturities. Risk-averse lenders might be less willing to purchase a long-term nominal bond over short-term nominal bonds. As forecasting future inflation becomes more difficult with longer time horizons, the opportunity cost of holding a longer-term nominal bond is more uncertain. In addition, a given permanent unexpected movement in the rate of inflation will have a greater impact on the market value of the longer-term bond and, consequently, a greater impact on the realized rate of return from selling that bond. To compensate lenders for taking on additional risk, the required nominal yield on a bond with a longer maturity will embody a greater risk premium.

The uncertainty associated with future inflation creates an element of uncertainty about real, future rates of return on all investments whose returns are not fixed in real terms. The more uncertain are the future rates of inflation, holding all else constant, the greater the risk premia for all bonds of any given maturity.[19] As the required nominal yields on instruments of all maturities increase with greater inflation uncertainty, the cost of capital financed by nominal debt increases. Not all investments, however, are fixed in nominal terms. The risk-averse individual can hedge, at least partially, against unanticipated inflation by investing in projects or holding financial instruments whose actual and expected real returns are relatively

---

[16]Such a value judgment would depend on the specified social welfare function—in particular, the relative weights assigned to each individual's utility. Nonetheless, the decline in wealth experienced by some in a period of positive unanticipated inflation does not necessarily provide sufficient justification, in terms of a Pareto efficient criterion, for a "forced" transfer of resources to restore the initial distribution of wealth.

[17]When the economy is subject to real as well as to nominal disturbances, however, complete wage indexation is not desirable. See Gray (1976) for example. Also, see Holland (1984b) for a more detailed discussion of the effects of inflation uncertainty on labor markets.

[18]Holland (1988), p. 478-80. This is a cumulative effect over a number of years (e.g. 2 to 6 years). In general, however, there is mixed evidence about the effects of inflation uncertainty on output growth. For example, Jansen (1989) finds that the conditional variance of inflation as a measure of inflation uncertainty has no significant impact on real output growth.

[19]Taylor (1981), among others, finds a positive relation between the average rate of inflation and the variability of inflation across nations and through time. This stylized fact, however, does not imply any causal link between the two. Moreover, greater variability does not imply greater uncertainty. Nevertheless, preliminary evidence indicates that inflation variability is positively related to uncertainty, as measured by the variance of the forecast errors from survey data or from an econometric model for predicting future inflation, or as measured by the dispersion of inflationary expectations within a survey. But Jansen (1989) recently found no statistical relation between inflation and the conditional variance of inflation. See Taylor (1981) and Holland (1984a), who review the existing evidence on the relations between average inflation, the variability of inflation and uncertainty.

independent of future rates of inflation, such as human capital, homes and corporate stocks.[20]

Even a complete hedge against unanticipated inflation would not eliminate the welfare costs of uncertainty, however. Substantial transaction costs can be incurred by those who attempt to eliminate the risk associated with future inflation from their portfolios. In any case, as individuals and firms attempt to hedge against unanticipated movements in the general price level, inflation uncertainty can distort asset accumulation and the aggregate allocation of resources.[21]

Another distorting feature of the uncertainty associated with price movements arises when information about the source of price movements is not available without costs. If information were costless to obtain, the appropriate response to a given increase in prices is clear. For example, an unanticipated temporary increase in observed prices correctly attributed to monetary policy (a nominal factor), rather than to an increase in demand for some goods relative to others (a real factor), would not alter the decisions of producers in the absence of nominal rigidities. If it is costly, however, to distinguish between general price movements produced by nominal factors from those created by real factors, price movements will be "noisy." Confusion about the source of a given price movement and the appropriate response will produce excessive relative price

variability, resulting in a misallocation of resources.[22]

WHY NOT A ZERO RATE OF INFLATION?

While any positive inflation has a large number of distortionary effects, a zero inflation rate might not necessarily be desirable—even in the long run. First, the various measures of inflation (for example, the consumer price index and the GNP implicit price deflator) do not control perfectly for quality improvement of products over time. To the extent that the lower and higher quality versions of goods are treated as comparable, the difference in their prices will be measured as inflation; the resulting measure will tend to overstate the actual inflation rate. Given this positive bias in inflation measures, it has been suggested that a 2 percent inflation rate measured by the usual price indexes would be associated with roughly stable prices.[23] Moreover, some would contend that inflation also has some important benefits like providing a cheaper source of government revenue or creating higher output and employment, so that the long-run desirable rate of inflation is not zero, but positive.

Optimal Taxation

Some have argued that inflation is required for optimal taxation.[24] The inflation tax provides

---

[20]While homes appear to be good hedges against expected and unexpected inflation, the evidence for human capital is inconclusive, at least for the long run. Moreover, a puzzling negative relation between stock returns and expected as well as unexpected inflation has been widely documented, but not resolved. See, for example, Fama and Schwert (1977).

[21]See Jaffee and Kleiman (1977) for a more detailed discussion of the effects of inflation uncertainty on the allocation of resources.

[22]To be sure, relative price variability need not be a cost. To the extent that relative price movements signal real disturbances to the economy, those movements contain important information facilitating an efficient allocation of resources. Fischer (1981a) provides a summary of competing approaches to explaining the relation between the average inflation rate and relative price variability. Taylor (1981) and Fischer (1981b) do not find evidence indicating a causal relation between inflation and variability of relative prices. Rather, Taylor (1981) and Fischer (1981a) find evidence consistent with the notion that the positive relations between average inflation, the variability of inflation and relative price variability in the 1970s have been driven by supply shocks (for example, energy and food shocks). Taylor (1981) also finds that accommodative monetary policies aiming to stabilize output and employment in light of real disturbances to the economy contributed in a large part to the increased variability of inflation in the 1970s. Furthermore, Fischer (1981a) concludes that policy shocks that could have created confusion about

the source of price movements do not appear to be associated with lower aggregate economic activity.

[23]Friedman (1969), p. 47. According to Friedman (1969), however, a negative inflation rate (about 2 percent deflation) correctly measured would be optimal. In this case, a zero inflation rate, as measured by the various price indices would be a desirable target. (See Alchian and Klein (1973) for a critical assessment of the appropriateness of the price indexes for policy.)

[24]See, for example, Phelps (1973). The government's revenue from the production of money is the nominal rate of interest times the stock of the monetary base (total reserves plus currency). Using the fact that the ratio of the monetary base to the money stock (M1) is about 40 percent and assuming that the real interest rate is about 3 percent, the revenue with a 5 percent inflation tax on a stock of M1 of $780 billion is about $25 billion per year in current dollar terms. The inflation tax alone generates $15.6 billion per year. It is important to note that unanticipated inflation implicitly generates additional revenue to the government (a net monetary debtor) through its effect on the real value of public debt. By reducing the purchasing power of interest payments on outstanding debt, unanticipated inflation lowers the real liability of the government and the amount of revenue to be raised through income taxes.

the government an alternative source of revenue to other explicit and distorting taxes—for example, income taxes.[25] The theory of optimal taxation suggests that, to finance a given level of public expenditures, the government should trade off the costs of distortions arising from inflation against those arising from other taxes.[26] From this perspective, the optimal inflation tax rate equates the marginal cost per dollar of revenue from the inflation tax and from other distorting taxes.

Recent empirical evidence on the marginal costs of the inflation tax and other taxes, however, casts doubt on the relevance of the optimal taxation theory to justify a positive rate of inflation. These studies suggest that the marginal cost per dollar revenue of the inflation tax at any positive rate of inflation exceeds that for alternative taxes set at plausible rates.[27] In other words, inflation does not necessarily provide a cheaper source of government revenue. Furthermore, the interaction between inflation and the distortions produced by the tax system suggests that the marginal cost of income taxes could be positively related to the rate of inflation; thus, lowering the inflation tax not only would reduce the welfare losses associated with the inflation tax, but make income taxation a cheaper source of government revenue.[28]

The Inflation and Unemployment Trade-off

The older argument used to justify positive inflation hinges on the so-called Phillips curve trade-off between inflation and unemployment. Figure 1, which depicts the apparent trade-off that emerged in the 1960s, could be interpreted as suggesting that, by tolerating a higher level of inflation, society could benefit from lower levels of unemployment.

One possible story behind such an interpretation is that an expansionary monetary policy that increases the general price level can increase output if nominal wages are relatively fixed. With fixed nominal wages, a rise in inflation can induce firms to increase output. This incentive arises because the firm's marginal profit—that is, the change in real revenues net of the change in the real wage bill realized by expanding output—increases with unanticipated inflation. If nominal wages were not fixed, they would adjust quickly to the increase in prices to maintain a given real wage rate; output and unemployment would be essentially independent of inflation. But, according to the trade-off view, the existence of nominal wage contracts means that, by generating inflation, the government can decrease the rate of unemployment and thereby enhance social welfare.

The possibility of exploiting the trade-off between inflation and unemployment with monetary policy, however, depends on the way in which inflationary expectations are formed and incorporated into nominal wages. If inflation is correctly anticipated and incorporated into wage contracts, then real output will be independent of inflation in the long run. Even if the government were to generate inflation un-

[25]If there were non-distorting taxes, then the excess burden of the inflation tax discussed above would render inflation an "inefficient" tax. But, in the absence of non-distorting taxes as a source of revenue to the government, the optimal rate of inflation could be positive. Browning (1987), table 1, p. 16, estimates that in 1984 the total welfare cost associated with the distortionary effects of the labor tax ranged from $55.9 billion to $212.6 billion under various assumptions. As a percentage of tax revenues from labor, the welfare loss ranged from 7.5 percent to 28.5 percent, well below the inflation-induced welfare loss as a percentage of revenues from the inflation tax (about 86 percent).

[26]In recent studies, Mankiw (1987) and Poterba and Rotemberg (1988) test the implications of the hypothesis that the government optimally trades off the distortions from explicit income taxes and inflation. While Mankiw finds preliminary evidence supporting the hypothesis for the United States, Poterba and Rotemberg, who look at different nations, do not find conclusive evidence. That the hypothesis is not fully supported by the data might be a result of the maintained assumption that the distortionary effects of the explicit tax system are independent of the distortionary effects of the inflation tax. Given the discussion above, this assumption seems inappropriate.

[27]For example, Tatom (1976), p. 20, shows that marginal cost per dollar revenue of the inflation tax, assuming that the elasticity of demand for money is −.15, is 44 percent. This estimate is not conditional on the inflation rate, but it is highly sensitive to the assumed elasticity of demand for money. For example, an elasticity of −.25 would imply a marginal cost of 83.33 percent. Browning (1987), table 2, p. 21, shows that the marginal welfare cost from taxes on labor earnings ranges from 9.9 percent to 33.2 percent under the assumption that labor supply is not highly responsive to the marginal income tax rate (see footnote 9).

[28]It should be noted, however, that since the marginal cost of taxes on labor earnings is positively related to the marginal tax rate, the theory of optimal taxation in light of the evidence on marginal welfare costs does not necessarily imply a zero rate of inflation. Nevertheless, if the marginal cost of the inflation tax were positively related to inflation, the optimal rate of inflation would more likely be zero.

Figure 1
The Inflation-Unemployment Trade-off

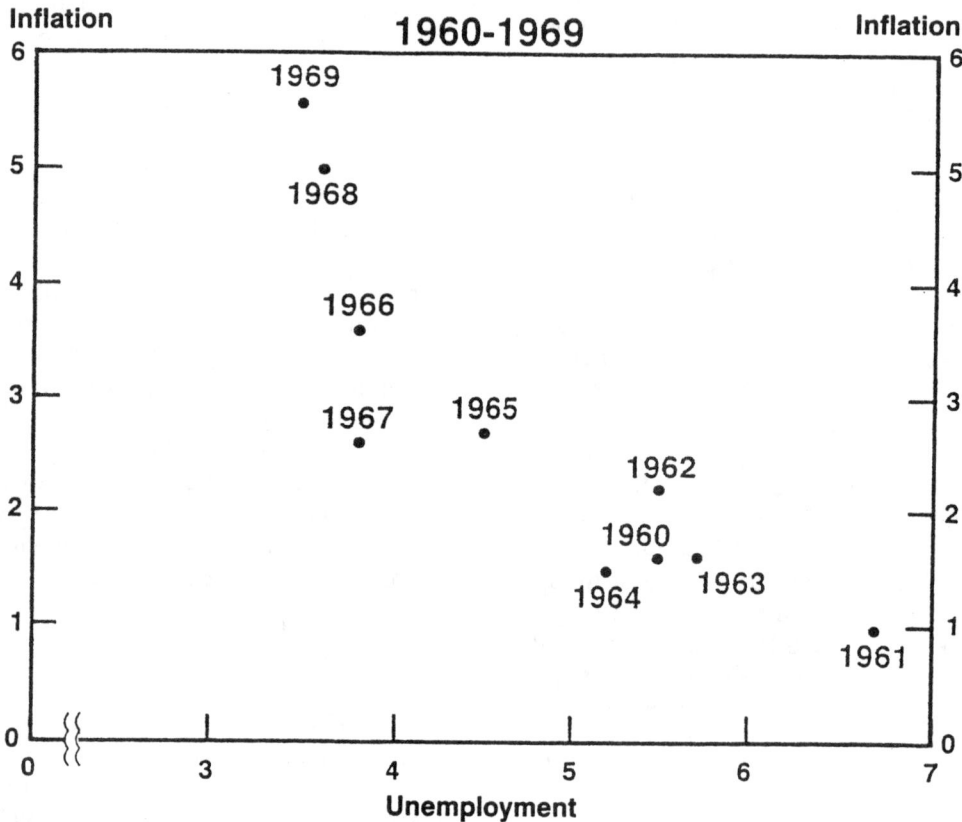

Inflation   **1960-1969**   **Inflation**

Unemployment

---

expectedly, the increase in output and decrease in unemployment would only be transitory. Subsequent wage changes would restore the original level of the real wage. As a consequence, the original profit rate would be restored, with output and unemployment returning to their original equilibrium or "natural" levels; the trade-off between unemployment and inflation would not exist in the long run.[29]

Indeed, figure 2, which plots the combinations of unemployment and inflation in the 1970s and the 1980s, does not support the existence of a long-run trade-off. While a short-run trade-off might exist, whether or not it is operative for the purpose of enhancing social welfare is un-

clear. Attempts to "fool" individuals systematically, by continuously creating surprise inflation so as to exploit the short-run trade-off, would not improve the welfare of all individuals because, although some individuals experience unexpected wealth gains, others suffer wealth losses. In addition, attempts to repeatedly fool individuals would increase the costs associated with inflation due to increased inflation uncertainty.

Moreover, as individuals and firms adjust to the higher inflation uncertainty, the trade-off becomes less favorable, because greater inflation uncertainty increases incentives for indexation. With greater wage indexation, a given

---

[29]See Fischer (1977), for example. The notion that real output and employment are independent of the inflation rate in the long run (a vertical Phillips curve) is known as the "Natural Rate Hypothesis."

Figure 2
The Inflation-Unemployment "Trade-off"

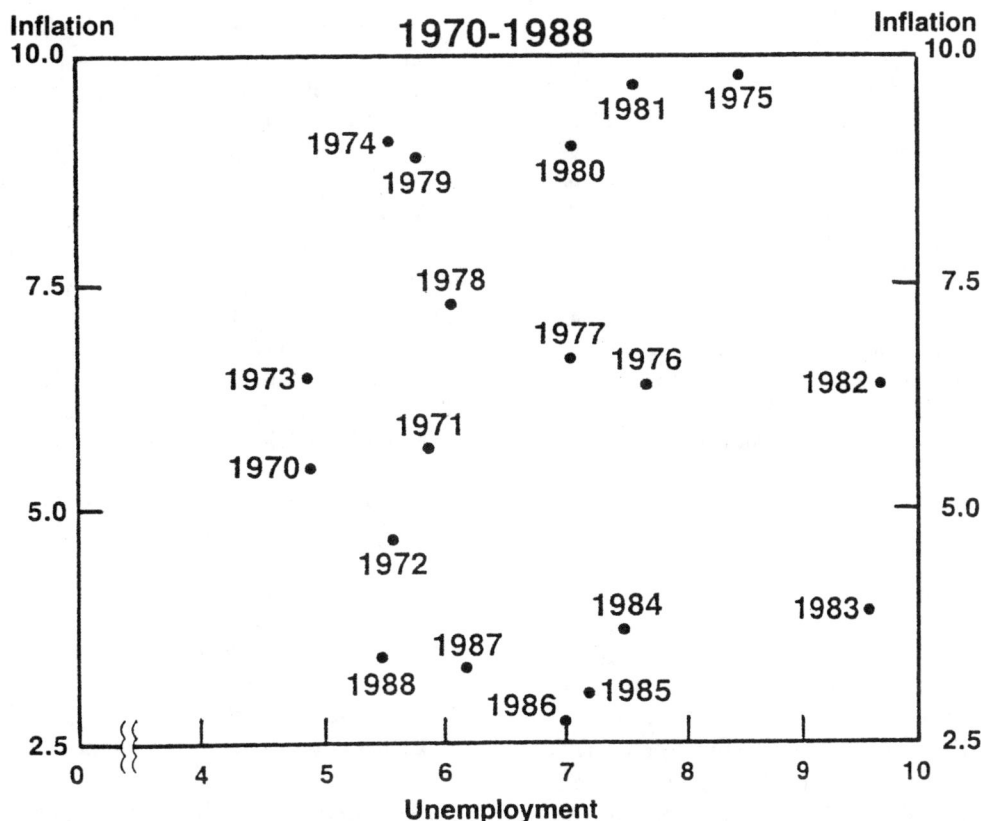

Inflation
10.0

1970-1988

Inflation
10.0

1974 • • 1981 • 1975
1979

1980

1978

1977
1976

1973 • 1982 •

1971

1970 •

1972

1984 1983 •

1987

1988 1986 • 1985

2.5 2.5
0 4 5 6 7 8 9 10

Unemployment

amount of surprise inflation will have a smaller transitory effect on output and employment as nominal wages become more responsive to actual inflation. Accordingly, the trade-off becomes steeper. If attempts to exploit the trade-off also increases average inflation, the trade-off shifts outward, so that a given rate of inflation will be associated with a higher rate of unemployment.

WHAT ARE THE COSTS OF REDUCING INFLATION?

The suggested benefits of inflation seem hardly compelling to justify any positive, sustained inflation. The long-run desirability of achieving stable prices, however, does not necessarily mean that the current rate of inflation is unac-

ceptable. Specifically, the latter discussion suggests that policies to reduce inflation and ultimately achieve the long-run desirable inflation rate can be costly. That is, any short-run trade-off between inflation and unemployment implies that anti-inflationary policies will produce temporary increases in unemployment.

Are The Costs Too High?

Table 2 shows the inflation rate, as measured by the GNP implicit price deflator, and the civilian unemployment rate; it indicates that the large reduction in inflation from 1979 to 1988 was accompanied by significantly large rates of unemployment. These observed high rates of unemployment, however, can overstate the costs of the anti-inflationary policy. Regardless of the current inflation rate or its prospective

Table 2

Unemployment and Inflation, 1979-88

Year	Civilian unemployment	Inflation[1]
1979	5.8%	8.9%
1980	7.1	9.0
1981	7.6	9.7
1982	9.7	6.4
1983	9.6	3.9
1984	7.5	3.7
1985	7.2	3.0
1986	7.0	2.7
1987	6.2	3.3
1988	5.5	3.4

SOURCE: *Economic Report of the President* (1989) and *Economic Indicators* (January 1989).

[1]Percentage change from the previous year in the GNP price deflator.

path, temporary unemployment is an efficient response to fundamental changes in the economy, as individuals search for new jobs. Consequently, the "natural" rate of unemployment (the rate of unemployment consistent with a steady inflation) can be positive. It has been estimated that, assuming the natural rate of unemployment is 6 percent, the decline in inflation from 9 percent in 1980 to 3.2 percent in the middle of 1987 was associated with about 2.4 percentage points of "excess" unemployment per percentage-point reduction in inflation.[30]

Similarly constructed estimates have been used to suggest that reducing inflation is unacceptable on efficiency grounds:

The damage that high unemployment does to economic efficiency is enormous and inadequately appreciated. By contrast, the harm that inflation inflicts on the economy is often exaggerated; and those costs which are not mythical can be minimized or even eliminated by indexing. Hard-headed devotion to the principle of efficiency thus argues for worrying less about inflation and running a high-pressure economy in which jobs are plentiful.[31]

By definition, excess unemployment is inefficient, because it implies that resources, otherwise available to increase consumption opportunities, have been wasted. But excess unemployment is only a transitional cost as the economy adjusts to the long-run desirable inflation rate. When the inflation goal is finally achieved and sustained, the excess unemployment will disappear. In contrast, the welfare costs associated with inflation are incurred indefinitely—that is, each year in which the economy's institutional features (for example, the explicit tax system) make the distortionary effects of inflation discussed above relevant.[32]

The Optimal Time Path of Reducing Inflation

Among the important questions that policymakers must face is the timing of anti-inflationary policy actions to reach the long-run desirable inflation rate. Given the initial inflation rate, the speed with which the desirable inflation rate is reached partly determines the cost of that policy.

One recent study shows that there are large differences in the costs of policies that vary with respect to their timing[33]. On the basis of various models, this study calculates the costs of several policies to bring inflation from 7.5 percent to zero. The costs of the policies are estimated in terms of output losses using a relationship known as Okun's law that translates each percentage point of excess unemployment into a 3.2 percent reduction in real output. For example, employing a Phillips curve model, this study

[30]Friedman (1988), p. 66. Each percentage point of unemployment above the natural rate (or that in a "fully employed" economy, with a steady inflation rate) constitutes a percentage point of "excess" unemployment. Of course, because the natural rate of unemployment is not observed and is subject to change during the evolution of the economy subject to permanent and transitory real shocks, one could argue that Friedman's estimate understates (or overstates, for that matter) the welfare loss associated with the reduction of inflation in the 1980s.

[31] Blinder (1987), p. 65.

[32]Of course, not all anti-inflationary policies can be justified. Rather, without a careful evaluation of the costs and benefits of reducing inflation, a monetary policy that pro-duces an inflation above (or below) the optimal rate does not easily follow from an efficiency criterion. As pointed out by Meyer and Rasche (1980, p. 14), among others, however, if the benefits from eliminating inflation (or identically, the costs of sustaining inflation) increase at the same rate of real potential output, then any anti-inflationary policy would be justified, irrespective of the policy's costs, provided that the costs are finite and that the initial gain from such a policy is positive.

[33]Meyer and Rasche (1980).

found that a gradual policy to eliminate inflation over a 23-year period could generate a discounted cumulative output loss of $1 trillion (in 1972 terms), whereas a policy that reached the inflation goal in 11 years could result in a discounted cumulative output loss of $1.5 trillion.[34]

The relation between the time path and the costs of the policy depends on the dynamic relation between unemployment and inflation. In addition to the degree to which the economy is indexed, this dynamic relation depends on the credibility of the anti-inflationary policy and expectations about future inflation. If, as assumed in the Phillips curve model, expectations depend on past inflation, a given inflation-reducing policy will be more costly; with nominal rigidities in the economy and a sluggish adjustment of expectations, the short-term trade-off between inflation and unemployment can be large. To achieve a specific reduction in inflation over a given time span can require higher levels of unemployment and greater output losses. If inflationary expectations are forward-looking and the policy is credible, however, the link between inflation and unemployment is weaker; in this case, unemployment is less responsive to movements in inflation. Accordingly, credible anti-inflationary policies will be less costly in terms of output losses than incredible ones.[35]

The time path of the anti-inflationary policy is also important because it determines the speed with which the gains from such a policy are realized fully. For example, a gradual policy that eliminates inflation over 50 years might not generate significant output losses, but the present discounted value of the benefits from that policy could be infinitesimally small.

CONCLUSION

Analyses of the acceptability of any particular positive inflation should start by asking what is the optimal rate of inflation. In reviewing the various effects and costs of inflation, this article questions the validity of the notion that any

positive inflation could be desirable as a long-run phenomenon. The surprisingly large number of distortionary effects resulting from inflation weakens the possible justifications for sustained positive inflation.

The long-run desirability of zero inflation need not imply, however, that a positive rate of inflation is never acceptable for any period. The transitional costs of reducing inflation over a short period could be considerably large relative to the benefits of quickly eradicating inflation. But the costs of fighting the current inflation do not preclude the desirability of an anti-inflationary policy, either. Indeed, the steady reduction in monetary aggregate growth since 1987 (measured by M1, M2 or the adjusted monetary base) suggests that the trade-off has been faced, at least implicitly. In any case, the acceptability of an inflation in excess of the long-run desirable rate depends on the appropriately measured net benefits of alternative paths to achieve the ultimate inflation goal.

REFERENCES

Alchian, Armen A., and Reuben A. Kessel. "Redistribution of Wealth Through Inflation," *Science* (September 4, 1959), pp. 535-39.

Alchian, Armen A., and Benjamin Klein. "On a Correct Measure of Inflation," *Journal of Money, Credit and Banking* (Part 1, February 1973), pp. 173-81.

Baye, Michael R., and Dan A. Black. "The Microeconomic Foundations of Measuring Bracket Creep and Other Tax Changes," *Economic Inquiry* (July 1988), pp. 471-84.

Blinder, Alan S. *Hard Heads, Soft Hearts: Tough-Minded Economics for a Just Society* (Addison-Wesley, 1987).

Browning, Edgar K. "On the Marginal Welfare Cost of Taxation," *American Economic Review* (March 1987), pp. 11-23.

Clark, Lindley H. Jr. "Why Don't We Aim for Zero Inflation?" *Wall Street Journal*, February 9, 1989.

Cukierman, Alex. "Central Bank Behavior and Credibility: Some Recent Theoretical Developments," this *Review* (May 1986), pp. 5-17.

Fama, Eugene F., and G. William Schwert. "Asset Returns and Inflation," *Journal of Financial Economics* (November 1977), pp. 115-46.

Fischer, Stanley. "Relative Shocks, Relative Price Variability, and Inflation," *Brookings Papers on Economic Activity* (1981a), pp. 381-431.

---

[34]Ibid., pp.7-8.

[35]Taylor (1983) shows that even if overlapping wage contracts temporarily fix nominal wages, a policy that gradually reduces inflation can be relatively costless provided that expectations about future inflation are rationally formed and everyone believes that the policy will actually be implemented. See Cukierman (1986) and references cited therein for analyses of the institutional and economic factors that tend to detract from the credibility of anti-inflationary policies. These analyses suggest that, without a perfect resolution of the credibility problem, the economy is likely to be characterized by an "inflationary bias." Fischer and Summers (1989) show how by decreasing the marginal costs of inflation, the government, recognizing the importance of its reputation, can reduce that bias. Without reputational considerations, however, reducing the costs of inflation can increase the inflationary bias.

_____. "Towards an Understanding of the Costs of Inflation: II," in Karl Brunner and Allan H. Meltzer, eds., *The Costs and Consequences of Inflation*, Carnegie-Rochester Conference Series on Public Policy (North-Holland, Autumn 1981b), pp. 5-42.

_____. "Long-Term Contracts, Rational Expectations, and the Optimal Money Supply Rule," *Journal of Political Economy* (February 1977), pp. 191-206.

Fischer, Stanley, and Franco Modigliani. "Towards an Understanding of the Real Effects and Costs of Inflation," *Weltwirtschaftliches Archiv* (Band 114, 1978), pp. 810-33.

Fischer, Stanley, and Lawrence H. Summers. "Should Governments Learn to Live With Inflation?" *American Economic Review* (May 1989), pp. 382-87.

Friedman, Benjamin M. "Lessons on Monetary Policy from the 1980s," *Journal of Economic Perspectives* (Summer 1988), pp. 51-72.

Friedman, Milton. "The Optimum Quantity of Money," *The Optimum Quantity of Money and Other Essays* (Aldine, 1969), pp. 1-50.

Gray, Jo Anna. "Wage Indexation: A Macroeconomic Approach," *Journal of Monetary Economics* (April 1976), pp. 221-35.

Greenspan, Alan. "1989 Monetary Policy Objectives," Testimony to the Congress (February 21, 1989) in *Federal Reserve Bulletin* (April 1989), pp. 272-77.

Hausman, Jerry A. "Labor Supply," in Henry J. Aaron and Joseph A. Pechman, eds., *How Taxes Affect Economic Behavior* (Brookings Institution, 1981), pp. 27-72.

Holland, A. Steven. "Indexation and the Effect of Inflation Uncertainty on Real GNP," *Journal of Business* (October 1988), pp. 473-84.

_____. "Does Higher Inflation Lead to More Uncertain Inflation?" this *Review* (February 1984a), pp. 15-26.

_____. "The Impact of Inflation Uncertainty on the Labor Market," this *Review* (August/September 1984b) pp. 21-28.

Jaffee, Dwight M., and Ephraim Kleiman. "The Welfare Implications of Uneven Inflation," in Erik Lundberg, ed., *Inflation Theory and Anti-Inflation Policy* (Macmillan, 1977), pp. 285-307.

Jansen, Dennis W. "Does Inflation Uncertainty Affect Output Growth? Further Evidence," this Review (July/August 1989), pp. 43-54.

Kessel, Reuben A., and Armen A. Alchian. "Effects of Inflation," *Journal of Political Economy* (December 1962), pp. 521-37.

Laidler, David E., and Michael Parkin. "Inflation: A Survey," *Economic Journal* (December 1975), pp. 741-809.

Mankiw, N. Gregory. "The Optimal Collection of Seigniorage: Theory and Evidence," *Journal of Monetary Economics* (September 1987), pp. 327-41.

_____. "Small Menu Costs and Large Business Cycles: A Macroeconomic Model of Monopoly," *Quarterly Journal of Economics* (May 1985), pp. 529-37.

Meyer, Laurence H., and Robert H. Rasche. "On the Costs and Benefits of Anti-Inflation Policies," this *Review* (February 1980), pp. 3-14.

Murray, Alan. "Fed's Goal is to Cut Inflation to Zero, Greenspan Says," *Wall Street Journal*, March 28, 1989.

Phelps, Edmund S. "Inflation in the Theory of Public Finance," *Swedish Journal of Economics* (March 1973), pp. 67-82.

Poterba, James M., and Julio J. Rotemberg. "Inflation and Taxation with Optimizing Governments," National Bureau of Economic Research Working Papers Series, 2567 (April 1988).

Stein, Herbert. "Inflation is Here, Still," *Wall Street Journal*, March 6, 1989.

Tatom, John A. "Federal Income Tax Reform in 1985: Indexation," this *Review* (February 1985), pp. 5-12.

_____. "The Marginal Welfare Cost of the Revenue From Money Creation and the 'Optimal' Rate of Inflation," *The Manchester School* (December 1979), pp.359-68.

_____. "The Welfare Cost of Inflation," this *Review* (November 1976), pp. 9-22.

Taylor, John B. "Union Wage Settlements During a Disinflation," *American Economic Review* (December 1983), pp. 981-93.

_____. "On the Relation Between the Variability of Inflation and the Average Inflation Rate," in Karl Brunner and Allan H. Meltzer, eds., *The Costs and Consequences of Inflation*, Carnegie-Rochester Conference Series on Public Policy (North-Holland, Autumn 1981), pp. 57-86.

Section II
Corporate Debt

Section II focuses on corporate debt. One of the most dominant trends in recent financial history is the explosion in corporate debt financing, not to mention the increase in federal financing requirements. The issuance of more debt has led to a dramatic altering in the mix between debt and equity in the financial structure of America's corporations. Much of this debt is fairly risky. Because of the low quality and credit ratings associated with this financing, the debt has become known as "junk bonds."

Some observers of the debt market believe that corporations rely too much on debt. Ben Bernanke examines this issue in his article "Is There Too Much Corporate Debt?" using an allegory of Goofus and Gallant, who start similar businesses, but use different levels of debt. Bernanke show how the higher level of debt financing can lead to the socially optimal allocation of resources. However, as Bernanke notes, the high leverage that keeps Gallant working while Goofus plays may also lead to financial distress for the economy as a whole.

The term "junk bond" is a pejorative term for "high-yield debt." In his paper, "The Case for Junk Bonds," Eric S. Rosengren accepts the pejorative (and quite common) name for the bonds and defends them. In essence, Rosengren argues that the junk bond market emerged as a partial replacement for commercial bank lending and is due to legitimate economic forces that are likely to continue. Therefore, Rosengren concludes, attempts to regulate the junk bond market will probably be unproductive and may impede the growth of small firms.

In "The Truth About Junk Bonds," Sean Becketti considers the three main criticisms raised against junk bonds: they fueled the merger boom, they are responsible for the rise in corporate debt levels, and they have increased financial market volatility. Becketti finds that the evidence does not support these charges. Instead, he argues that junk bonds are similar in character to other financing vehicles.

Article 5

Is There Too Much Corporate Debt?

*Ben Bernanke**

Borrowing by U.S. corporations has increased dramatically in recent years. The outstanding debt of nonfinancial corporations rose 70 percent between 1983 and 1988, more than two-thirds faster than growth of nominal GNP. Highly leveraged transactions, such as the $25 billion takeover of RJR Nabisco, routinely make the front pages.

Heavy borrowing such as this has raised the issue of whether corporate debt has become excessive. Congress has been considering whether changes should be made in the tax law to try to reduce the rate of corporate debt accumulation. The Federal Reserve has been studying the implications of debt growth for monetary policy and banking system oversight.

In evaluating the debt situation there are many issues to consider, but two questions lie at the heart of the debate. First is the "micro" issue: do high levels of debt increase the efficiency of firms, as some proponents of high leverage have claimed? Then there is the

*Ben Bernanke is a Professor of Economics at Princeton University. He wrote this article while he was a Visiting Scholar in the Research Department of the Federal Reserve Bank of Philadelphia.

"macro" issue: does increased corporate debt reduce the stability of the country's financial and economic system?

THE MICRO ISSUE:
DOES DEBT PROMOTE EFFICIENCY?

The traditional explanation for why corporations use debt as a source of finance is debt's tax advantage: interest payments made by a firm are tax-deductible, while dividend payments are not. Offsetting this advantage are the costs of bankruptcy and reorganization that may be incurred should the firm not be able to meet the stipulated interest payments. According to the traditional view, the optimal ratio of debt to equity is the one that just balances these two costs.

More recently, however, financial economists have gone beyond this traditional view to focus on the possibly beneficial effects of debt issuance on managerial performance.[1] This point can be illustrated by a simple example.

A Tale of Two Twins. Suppose that there are two potential entrepreneurs, who (like the two characters in a well-known children's magazine) are named Goofus and Gallant.[2] Goofus and Gallant plan to start ice cream stands on opposite sides of town. The necessary equipment for a stand costs $1,000, and since the entrepreneurs each have only $100, they must obtain some outside finance.

Goofus finances his ice cream stand through stock issuance: that is, he finds some friends to put up $900, in exchange for which he promises them 90 percent of the profits. Gallant issues debt instead; he gets a friend to lend him $900, for which Gallant promises to pay $100 in annual interest. Both boys thus have enough capital to get their businesses going.

---

[1]The classic article that introduced this approach is Jensen and Meckling (1976).

[2]The characters Goofus and Gallant are copyrighted by *Highlights for Children*, and their names are used with permission.

Things go along well enough at first for both entrepreneurs. But the summer days are hot, and scooping ice cream is hard work. Goofus says to himself, "I've made $100 profit at my stand already this week. If I were to keep working through the weekend, I could make another $100. But I have to share 90 percent with my partners—so that extra $100 really means only $10 for me! I'm not really willing to work the weekend for less than a $25 personal profit, so I think I'll quit and go fishing."

On the other side of town, Gallant is also having a crisis of conscience; he is developing scooper's elbow from serving so much ice cream. He loves to fish as much as Goofus does. Should he quit working? He says to himself, "The $100 I have earned so far is enough to cover the interest payment on my loan. From now on, any profits the ice cream stand earns are mine to keep. If I worked through the weekend, I could earn another $100; that's more than the $25 I would be willing to pay to knock off and go fishing." So Gallant goes back to work.

The two entrepreneurs have faced the same quandary, but have made different decisions. It is important to understand that, in both cases, it is economically efficient to keep the ice cream stand in operation through the weekend, in that the $100 in extra profit that could be earned is greater than the $25 value the proprietor of each stand places on his leisure. Yet, of the two, only Gallant does the "right" thing and keeps working.

Incentives to Do The Right Thing. In the children's magazine, Gallant's decisions to do the right thing stem from his superior moral character. In this example, morality has nothing to do with it; both boys make their decisions based on their calculations of personal gain. The difference between Goofus and Gallant is the way in which they have financed their ventures. By financing with equity, Goofus has created a situation in which his personal rewards are relatively insensitive to the profits of the company; a $100 increase in profits increases his personal return by only $10. This reduces Goofus's incentive to work hard and make decisions that are in the interest of the company. In contrast, once the interest payment is made, Gallant's personal returns fluctuate dollar for dollar with the profits of the company; he thus has a strong incentive to take actions that maximize the company's profits.

Indeed, in this particular example, Gallant would do the right thing (keep working) as long as he was financed at least 60 percent by debt. With 60 percent ($600) in debt, there would be 40 percent ($400) in total equity. Gallant's $100 in original capital would give him 25 percent of that equity, giving him a 25 percent share of the firm's profits. With a 25 percent share, Gallant would be just indifferent between working through the weekend (which nets him an extra .25 x $100 = $25) or going fishing (which is worth $25 to him). With anything above 60 percent debt finance, he would keep working.

Changing the Mode of Financing. We can add another chapter to the story of Goofus and Gallant. At the end of the summer, both boys notice that the debt-financed ice cream stand is more profitable than the equity-financed stand, and that this extra profitability is due entirely to the way in which the stands are financed. This implies that pure profits can be earned by a capital restructuring—a change in the mode of finance—of Goofus's operation. This restructuring can be accomplished if someone takes out a loan and uses the borrowed money to buy back the shares from Goofus's shareholders; this changes the stand's financing from equity to debt. The share buyback is particularly attractive at the current market price for Goofus's company's shares, which—because Goofus is always going fishing—is low. But the buyback would be profitable even if the acquirers had to pay the current stockholders some premium for their shares; the acquirers would simply be sharing with the current shareholders some of the profits expected to be produced by the restructuring.

The capital restructuring of Goofus's stand would work equally well if performed by Goofus, by Gallant, or by someone else.[3] In any case, the swapping of debt for equity is called a *leveraged buyout,* or LBO. If done by Goofus, the current manager of the operation, it could also be called a *management buyout*; if done by Gallant, it would be called a *takeover* (a hostile takeover, if Goofus resisted and tried to hold on to the company). The key point is that, in either case, the leverage of the company (its ratio of debt to equity) would increase, and this would lead to more efficient and profitable operations.

The Recent Explosion of Debt. The parable of Goofus and Gallant illustrates the idea that the financial structure of firms influences the incentives of "insiders" (managers, directors, and large shareholders with some operational interest in the business) and that, in particular, high levels of debt may increase the willingness of insiders to work hard and make profit-maximizing decisions. This incentive-based approach makes a valuable contribution to our understanding of a firm's capital structure. But while this theory might explain why firms like to use debt in general, does it explain why the use of debt has increased so much in recent years?

Michael Jensen, a founder and leading proponent of the incentive-based approach to capital structure, argues that it can.[4] Jensen focuses on a recent worsening of what he calls the "free cash flow" problem. Free cash flow is defined as the portion of a corporation's cash flow that

---

[3]This assumes, first, that Gallant has time to operate both stands and, second, that Gallant has enough profits from operating his own stand to buy out Goofus's share.

[4]For a summary of Jensen's views, see Jensen (1988). Jensen's article is part of a *Journal of Economic Perspectives* special symposium on takeovers, which provides an excellent and balanced introduction to this subject.

it is unable to invest profitably within the firm. Companies in industries that are profitable but no longer have much potential for expansion—the U.S. oil industry, for example—have a lot of free cash flow.

Why is free cash flow a problem? Jensen argues that managers are often tempted to use free cash flow to expand the size of the company, even if the expansion is not profitable. This is because managers feel that their power and job satisfaction are enhanced by a growing company; so given that most managers' compensation is at best weakly tied to the firm's profitability, Jensen argues that managers will find it personally worthwhile to expand even into money-losing operations. In principle, the board of directors and shareholders should be able to block these unprofitable investments; however, in practice, the fact that the management typically has far more information about potential investments than do outside directors and shareholders makes it difficult to second-guess the managers' recommendations.

How More Leverage Can Help. The problem of free cash flow is precisely analogous to the problem in the Goofus and Gallant example. Just as Goofus was willing to sacrifice company profits in order to pursue his personal goals (going fishing), so the company manager with lots of free cash flow may attempt to use that cash to increase his power and perquisites, at the expense of the shareholders. Jensen argues that the solution to the free-cash-flow problem is the same as the solution to the Goofus-Gallant problem: more leverage. For example, suppose that management uses the free cash flow of the company, plus the proceeds of new debt issues, to repurchase stock from the outside shareholders—that is, to do a management buyout. This helps solve the free-cash-flow problem in several ways. First, as in the Goofus and Gallant example, the personal returns of the managers are now much more closely tied to the profits of the firm, which gives them incentives to be more effi-

cient. Second, the re-leveraging process removes the existing free cash from the firm, so that any future investment projects will have to be financed externally; thus, future projects will have to meet the market test of being acceptable to outside bankers or bond purchasers. Finally, the high interest payments implied by re-leveraging impose a permanent discipline on the managers; in order to meet these payments, they will have to ruthlessly cut money-losing operations, avoid questionable investments, and take other efficiency-promoting actions.

According to Jensen, a substantial increase in free-cash-flow problems—resulting from deregulation, the maturing of some large industries, and other factors—is a major source of the recent debt expansion. Jensen also points to a number of institutional factors that have promoted increased leverage. These include relaxed restrictions on mergers, which have lowered the barriers to corporate takeovers created by the antitrust laws, and increased financial sophistication, such as the greatly expanded operations of takeover specialists like Drexel Burnham Lambert Inc. and the development of the market for "junk bonds."[5] Jensen's diagnosis is not controversial: it's quite plausible that these factors, plus changing norms about what constitutes an "acceptable" level of debt, explain at least part of the trend toward increased corporate debt.[6] However, the im-

---

[5]Junk bonds, more properly called below-investment-grade or high-yield bonds, have been used in a number of large corporate restructurings. For a discussion of the junk-bond market and the uses of junk bonds in takeovers, see Loeys (1986).

[6]One important piece of evidence in favor of this explanation is that net equity issues have been substantially negative since 1983. This suggests that much of the proceeds of the new debt issues is being used to repurchase outstanding shares. This is what we would expect if corporations are attempting to re-leverage their existing assets, rather than using debt to expand their asset holdings.

plied conclusion—that the debt buildup is beneficial overall to the economy—is considerably more controversial.

Criticisms of the Incentive-based Rationale for Increased Debt. Jensen and other advocates of the incentive-based approach to capital structure have made a cogent theoretical case for the beneficial effects of debt finance, and many architects of large-scale restructurings have given improved incentives and the promise of greater efficiency as a large part of the rationale for increased leverage. The idea that leverage is beneficial has certainly been embraced by the stock market: even unsubstantiated rumors of a potential LBO have been sufficient to send the stock price of the targeted company soaring, often by 40 percent or more. At a minimum, this indicates that stock market participants *believe* that higher leverage increases profitability. Proponents of restructuring interpret this as evidence that debt is good for the economy.

There are, however, criticisms of this conclusion. First, the fact that the stock market's expectations of company profitability rise when there is a buyout is not proof that profits *will* rise in actuality. It is still too soon to judge whether the increased leverage of the 1980s will lead to a sustained increase in profitability. One might think of looking to historical data for an answer to this question. But buyouts in the 1960s and 1970s were somewhat different in character from more recent restructurings, and, in any case, the profitability evidence on the earlier episodes is mixed.

Even if the higher profits expected by the stock market do materialize, there is contention over where they are likely to come from. The incentive-based theory of capital structure says they will come from improved efficiency. But some opponents have argued that the higher profits will primarily reflect transfers to the shareholders from other claimants on the corporation—its employees, customers, suppliers, bondholders, and the government. For example, Andrei Shleifer and Lawrence Summers, in a soon-to-be-published study, present evidence that the premium received by shareholders of Trans World Airlines, when it was taken over, was paid for twice over by the wage concessions wrested from three TWA unions. Customers may be hurt if takeovers are associated with increased monopolization of markets.[7] Bondholders have been big losers in some buyouts, as higher leverage has increased bankruptcy risk and thus reduced the value of outstanding bonds. The government may have lost tax revenue, as companies, by increasing leverage, have increased their interest deductions (although there are offsetting effects here, such as the taxes paid by bought-out shareholders on their capital gains). The perception that much of the profits associated with re-leveraging and buyouts comes from "squeezing" existing beneficiaries of the corporation explains much of the recent political agitation to limit these activities.[8]

Another possible explanation for the effect of LBOs on stock prices is that the announcement of a buyout provides information about, but does not directly affect, the firm's future prospects. Suppose that the management of a publicly owned pharmaceutical firm has secret information about a revolutionary new drug discovered in its laboratories. This highly profitable new opportunity, being secret, is not

---

[7]McAndrews and Nakamura (1989) present a model in which increased leverage by existing firms can help deter potential competitors from entering the market.

[8]Not much systematic empirical work on the "squeezing" hypothesis has been done to date. In a careful study of 76 companies' management buyouts, Kaplan (1988) found that most of the value gained from the buyout was due to increased operating income and tax benefits, and that the transfers from bondholders were small. However, the study considered only the first two years' experience of each firm after its buyout, and lack of data prevented measurement of the buyout's effects on employees, suppliers, and customers.

reflected in the firm's stock price. The management of this company has a strong incentive to do a buyout, because it knows the stock is currently underpriced relative to the firm's future profits. But if the managers attempt a buyout, this will reveal to the public that the management thinks the stock is underpriced—which will cause the stock price to be bid up. This means that the managers will have to share some of the profits from their inside information with the shareholders. Profits may indeed rise after the buyout—reflecting the introduction of the new drug—but this increase in profits would not be in any way caused by the increase in leverage associated with the buyout. Similar arguments apply if the buyout is initiated by a competitor or someone else who might have better information about the firm than do stock market investors.

The debt buildup can also be criticized from the perspective of incentive-based theories themselves. Two points are worth noting: first, the principal problem that higher leverage is supposed to address is the relatively weak connection between firms' profits and managers' personal returns, which reduces managers' incentives to take profit-maximizing actions. But if this is truly the problem, it could be addressed more directly—without subjecting the company to serious bankruptcy risk—simply by changing managerial compensation schemes to include more profit-based incentives. Robert Vishny and Andrei Shleifer (1988) argue that the approach of tying managers' pay to profits is limited by legal precedents that allow shareholders to sue if managerial compensation is "excessive"; however, if managerial incentives are really the problem, it does seem that more could be done in this direction.

The Downside of Debt Financing. A second point, made by the original Jensen-Meckling (1976) article and many since then, is that increased debt is not the optimal solution to all incentive problems. For example, it has been shown, as a theoretical proposition, that managers of debt-financed firms have an incentive to choose riskier projects over safe ones; this is because firms with fixed-debt obligations enjoy all of the upside potential of high-risk projects but share the downside losses with the debt holders, who are not fully repaid if bad investment outcomes cause the firm to fail.

That high leverage does not always promote efficiency can be seen when highly leveraged firms suffer losses and find themselves in financial distress. When financial problems hit, the need to meet interest payments may force management to take a very short-run perspective, leading them to cut back production and employment, cancel even potentially profitable expansion projects, and sell assets at fire-sale prices. Because the risk of bankruptcy is so great, firms in financial distress cannot make long-term agreements; they lose customers and suppliers who are afraid they cannot count on an ongoing relationship, and they must pay wage premiums to hire workers.

These efficiency losses, plus the direct costs of bankruptcy (such as legal fees), are the potential downside of high leverage. In terms of the ice cream stand, if Gallant does not earn enough to make his interest payment, he may be tempted to skimp on the ice cream or even serve the cracked cones, sacrificing future sales to increase short-run income and avoid bankruptcy. Or he may simply choose to stop working, letting the stand go into default. Maybe a highly leveraged Gallant isn't so gallant after all!

THE MACRO ISSUE: SPILLOVERS AND MULTIPLIERS

Most discussion of corporate debt has focused on the microeconomic efficiency issues. However, the macroeconomic implications of debt are also important. There are several possible (although speculative) scenarios under which high corporate debt could contribute to macroeconomic dislocations.

One scenario is a "liquidity crisis." In

1970, the bankruptcy of the Penn Central rail-road, and Penn Central's resulting default on its short-term borrowings, caused a tempo-rary, sharp decrease in new lending in the com-mercial-paper market. Prompt action by the Federal Reserve stabilized the situation. However, the potential for a similar episode, possibly on a larger scale, exists.

This potential arises from the fact that many firms count on being able to "roll over" their short-term debt (that is, re-borrow) as it comes due. If, for some reason, lenders became wor-ried about bankruptcy risk and refused to roll over maturing debt, then these firms (even though they might be fundamentally solvent) would find themselves illiquid—that is, short of cash to make promised payments.

In most cases, firms would respond to this by taking loans on lines of credit previously negotiated with banks; however, that would spread the illiquidity problem to the banking system, as banks suddenly were subjected to large demands for credit. To ease such a li-quidity crisis, the Federal Reserve would have to provide more funds to the financial system, either through the discount window, as it did during the Penn Central episode, or through open-market operations.

Perhaps a more disturbing scenario is a "solvency crisis." Suppose that, for reasons unrelated to financial structure, the economy were to enter a serious recession, leading to falling earnings and (perhaps) rising interest costs. Given high leverage inherited from the past, some firms might find it difficult to serv-ice their debt. Firms in financial distress are likely to retrench, cutting back employment, production, and investment. This would re-duce total demand, worsening the recession and leading to financial problems in other firms. Thus, the initial recessionary shock could be magnified by high leverage; in the language of traditional Keynesian macroeconomic analy-sis, the "multiplier" relating the size of the initial disturbance to the size of the resulting recession will have increased.

Distressed Firms Can Have Far-reaching Effects. The difference between the microeco-nomic and macroeconomic perspective is that in the macroeconomic approach, we are con-cerned not only with the effects of financial distress on the distressed firm itself, but with the effects of the distressed firm's actions on other firms. If there are "spillovers" from one firm to another (for example, if the shutdown of a large employer in a town affects the town's economy more generally), then financial dis-tress will increase the multiplier. Higher lever-age thus has the potential to increase the vul-nerability of the economy to destabilizing shocks. Importantly, the possible effects of spillovers and multipliers will not be taken into account by individual firms when they choose their preferred level of debt.

Are these scenarios likely? Nobody knows for sure, but there are several ways to argue that they are not very likely.

First, it should be pointed out that, despite the rapid increase in debt, corporate debt-to-equity ratios (measured in market-value terms) have not changed much during the 1980s. Indeed, Ben Bernanke and John Campbell (1988), using a sample of 1,400 large U.S. nonfinancial corporations, showed that debt-to-equity ra-tios in the 1980s remain well below their peaks, which occurred during the 1973-74 recession. The relative stability of the debt-to-equity ratio reflects the bull market in stocks of the 1980s, which allowed stock values to keep up with the high rate of debt issuance. From this perspec-tive, debt burdens have not really increased.

However, even though debt-to-equity ra-tios have not increased, another measure of debt burden—the ratio of interest payments to total cash flow—has grown significantly. Bernanke and Campbell found this measure of interest burden to be about 50 percent higher in the mid-1980s than in the 1970s; several studies report that this ratio is currently close to its 1981-82 recession high, despite the long expansion that has occurred since the end of 1982.

How do we reconcile the fact that the interest-payments-to-earnings ratios (and debt-to-earnings ratios) have grown while debt-to-equity ratios have not? Mechanically, the answer is that both debt and stock values have grown much faster than earnings. The high ratio of stock prices to current earnings—sometimes called the P/E ratio—implies optimism on the part of investors about future earnings.[9] The stock market can be interpreted as saying that, even though current interest burdens are high, earnings are likely to rise enough in the future for firms to meet their debt obligations.

If we take the stock market's prediction at face value, then, a liquidity crisis or solvency crisis cannot be called a likely event; a reasonable expectation is that the corporate debt will be serviced. This doesn't mean that macroeconomic problems due to debt are not possible, however; it only means that they should be thought of as a sort of worst-case scenario. Nevertheless, good policymaking requires attention to worst-case as well as average outcomes. Indeed, it is during crisis situations in which good policies are most important.

The Likelihood of Macroeconomic Debt Problems. To get an idea of what might happen in a worst-case situation, Bernanke and Campbell (1988) simulated the effects of a recession in their sample of large firms. They asked what would have happened if the changes in cash flow, stock prices, and interest rates that actually occurred in the recessions of 1973-74 and 1981-82 had occurred again in 1986, affecting the very same firms in their sample.

Those two recessions were found to have different effects in the simulations. In the 1973-74 scenario, the stock market declines sharply; the simulation shows that in this type of recession more than 10 percent of the large firms would become technically insolvent, in the sense that the market value of their assets would fall below the market value of their debt.[10] In the 1981-82 scenario the stock market is fairly stable, but cash flow falls and interest rates rise; in this case Bernanke and Campbell found that about 10 percent of their firms would be unable to meet interest obligations without further borrowing. In the terminology introduced above, a 1973-74-type recession would create the potential for a solvency crisis, while a 1981-82-type recession might lead to a liquidity crisis.

Overall, then, the high share prices of U.S. corporations—not to mention the willingness of lenders to accept the high leverage of borrowing corporations—suggest that knowledgeable investors consider a macroeconomic debt crisis unlikely. However, unlikely is not the same as impossible; the Bernanke-Campbell simulations suggest that macroeconomic debt problems could be triggered by recessionary shocks of a magnitude that has been experienced twice in the last decade and a half.[11] This risk could possibly be ameliorated in the short run by aggressively expansionary monetary and fiscal policies, but only at the cost of higher inflation and potentially greater instability in the long run.

---

[9]If the stock market is "efficient," then the price of a share should represent the present discounted value of current earnings and future expected earnings. If the P/E ratio is high, then either interest rates are low (which they currently are not), or future earnings are expected to be high relative to current earnings.

[10]If the value of assets is less than the value of debt, then the debt cannot be repaid; the firm must either eventually go bankrupt or be reorganized.

[11]Another quantitative objection to the possibility of a macroeconomic debt crisis is that much of the recent debt buildup has occurred in cyclically insensitive sectors, such as food processing and services (see Roach, 1988). While this is true, it is also true that debt burdens have increased in cyclically sensitive sectors, like durable goods, as well. The simulations reported in the text implicitly take into account any shifting sectoral composition of debt.

Has Debt Become Less Risky? An alternative way to question the possibility of a macroeconomic debt crisis is to argue that, because of changes in the financial environment, a given level of debt poses less risk in 1989 than it would have in, say, 1974. Here is a concrete example: a recent development is the use of what is called "strip financing," in which investors in a firm commit to holding a fixed combination of the firm's debt and equity instruments. The idea is to minimize conflict between debt holders and shareholders (who, under strip financing, are one and the same), thus reducing the potential cost of financial distress and reorganization. Another development, stressed by Jensen, is that financial firms involved in arranging buyouts are in some cases retaining some stake in the management of the LBO firm; thus, the financial firm will have an incentive to assist the reorganization process should the LBO fall into financial trouble.

It is certainly true that the safety of any given level of debt depends on the financial environment. Japanese corporations, for example, have borne much higher levels of debt than their U.S. counterparts without experiencing problems. This works because most Japanese corporate debt is in the form of bank loans, and the large banks take an active role in the management of the firms to which they lend. Should a firm experience difficulties, the bank assists in obtaining new finance or in reorganization; at the same time, the bank is well placed to oversee whatever management or strategy changes the firm must make. These sorts of practices, which contrast with traditional "arm's length" lending in the United States, make high debt burdens safer.

Whether the U.S. financial environment has in fact moved substantially in the Japanese direction is an open question. Oversight of corporate management by the financial firm that arranged the LBO is a step toward the Japanese model; however, it is not clear at this point how widespread this practice is. Working in the other direction is the fact that increasing corporate reliance on below-investment-grade (junk) bonds has come at the expense of corporate use of bank loans. Since junk bonds tend to be held by mutual funds, insurance companies, and other institutions not directly involved in the management of the firms to which they lend, the use of junk bonds (in place of bank loans) may strengthen the traditional "arm's length" tendency of U.S. capital markets. This may make negotiated avoidance of bankruptcy more difficult and increase potential bankruptcy costs.

The contention that the risks of leverage have been reduced by institutional changes also raises a theoretical question: according to the incentive-based approach, the whole point of increased leverage is to impose discipline on corporate management. If, because of changes in the financial environment, failure to make contracted interest payments becomes a minor concern, then it would seem that the disciplinary impact of debt on management will be much reduced.

CONCLUSION

The argument for higher leverage is that it imposes discipline on the managers of the corporation, leading to greater efficiency. Effectively, this greater discipline is achieved by means of a threat: if the firm does not perform up to expectations, it may well suffer insolvency and reorganization. As with the discipline of children, the advantage of a draconian threat is the good behavior it may promote; the disadvantage is that the threat may have to be carried out.

Here is an analogy often used in discussing the costs and benefits of high leverage. Suppose we want people to drive more carefully. One way to do this would be to require every car to have a dagger in the steering wheel, the point aimed directly at the chest of the driver. This would certainly promote more careful driving, since even a fender bender might have ghastly consequences. But suppose there was a sudden worsening in driving conditions—a freak snowstorm, for example—that unexpectedly put even the most careful drivers at risk of accidents. Under these circumstances, the dagger-in-the-wheel policy might well lead to more deaths and injuries than if this "discipline device" had never been used.

In this story, the dagger in the wheel is supposed to represent high corporate leverage—which under normal circumstances promotes profit maximization ("safe driving") by managers. The snowstorm is an economy-wide recession (or perhaps some other disturbance, like a sharp increase in interest rates). The concern is that high leverage, while possibly a boon in good times, might become a destructive force in bad times.

This trade-off poses a quandary for policymakers. Despite the criticisms and existing uncertainties, few economists would completely dismiss the claim that higher leverage can be used to improve incentives and promote efficiency. Given the importance of improving the performance of U.S. corporations in a competitive international marketplace, it would probably be a severe mistake for the government simply to ban buyouts or limit leverage. On the other hand, pro-debt biases in the tax code, the possibility that higher leverage can help shareholders "squeeze" employees and others, and the possibility of "spillovers" from financial distress all suggest that firms will take on more debt than is good for the economy as a whole.

Three types of policy responses might help the situation. First, the government should take actions to increase the accountability of managers to shareholders (for example, by eliminating legal barriers to paying managers profit-based compensation); this would reduce the need to improve incentives indirectly through high leverage. Second, banking, financial market, and antitrust regulators should carefully scrutinize highly leveraged deals that fall within their purview; it is particularly important that government-insured deposits not be the funding source for risky buyouts, unless the bank's capital is demonstrated to be adequate. Finally, biases in the tax code that favor buyouts and high leverage should be removed.

References

Bernanke, Ben, and John Campbell. "Is There a Corporate Debt Crisis?" Brookings Papers on Economic Activity (1988:1) pp. 83-125.

Jensen, Michael C. "Takeovers: Their Causes and Consequences," *Journal of Economic Perspectives*, vol. 2 (Winter 1988) pp. 21-48.

Jensen, Michael C., and William H. Meckling. "Theory of the Firm: Managerial Behavior, Agency Costs and Ownership Structure," *Journal of Financial Economics*, vol. 3 (1976) pp. 305-60.

Kaplan, Stephen. "Management Buyouts: Efficiency Gains or Value Transfers?" University of Chicago, unpublished (1988).

Loeys, Jan. "Low-Grade Bonds: A Growing Source of Corporate Funding," Federal Reserve Bank of Philadelphia *Business Review* (November/December 1986) pp. 3-12.

McAndrews, James J., and Leonard I. Nakamura. "Entry-Deterring Debt," Federal Reserve Bank of Philadelphia, Working Paper No. 89-15 (1989).

Roach, Stephen. "Living With Corporate Debt," *Economic Perspectives*, Morgan Stanley, November 11, 1988.

Shleifer, Andrei, and Lawrence Summers. "Breach of Trust in Hostile Takeovers," in Alan Auerbach, *Corporate Takeovers: Causes and Consequences*, Chicago: University of Chicago Press (forthcoming).

Vishny, Robert, and Andrei Shleifer. "Value Maximization and the Acquisition Process," *Journal of Economic Perspectives*, vol. 2 (Winter 1988) pp. 7-20.

Article 6

The Case for Junk Bonds

Eric S. Rosengren

Assistant Vice President and Economist, Federal Reserve Bank of Boston. This paper provides a defense of a controversial type of financing, junk bonds. It does not provide a comprehensive discussion of the opposing view. The author is grateful to Jessica Laxman, Adam Rosen, and Simeon Hyman for research assistance.

An important financial innovation of the 1980s was the emergence of original-issue junk bonds, securities of below investment grade with high initial yields to maturity. Such securities are not totally new. Fallen angels, securities that have lost their investment-grade rating, have been familiar since the inception of the corporate bond market because not all firms live up to the initial expectations of investors. Before the establishment of the original-issue junk bond market, firms that did not qualify initially as investment-grade borrowers could not issue long-term bonds. In the past these firms relied almost exclusively on short-term bank loans for debt financing, but now many such enterprises can obtain long-term financing in national credit markets.

Junk bonds are an extension of a trend to substitute publicly traded securities for bank loans, a process called disintermediation. Investment-grade firms, for example, substituted commercial paper for bank loans. As well-established firms found their credit ratings equaling or exceeding those of commercial banks, they were able to raise funds more economically by issuing instruments directly in the open market. Over time, such borrowers have become less dependent on depository institutions as a source of funds. While below-investment-grade firms have lower credit ratings than banks, by placing tradable securities directly with investors they can obtain debt with longer maturities than commonly available from banks.

Junk bonds nevertheless are under attack, with opponents arguing they facilitate excessive leverage. While junk bonds have substituted for some bank lending, both sources of debt financing have grown rapidly during the 1980s as firms have become more leveraged. Greater leverage reduces a firm's tax burden because of the tax deductibility of interest payments, but it also increases the probability of default. The recent increase in large corporate bankruptcies stems in part from firms' choice of riskier capital structure.

In response to the problems created by defaults or near defaults of highly leveraged firms, savings and loans are now prohibited from holding junk bonds. Bills before Congress would also limit other financial intermediaries' investments in junk bonds and eliminate corporate tax deductibility of interest payments on junk bonds. This article contends that such asset restrictions may be counterproductive, limiting access to public credit markets for below-investment-grade firms without reducing their demand for debt. As a result, they will turn to substitutes for junk bonds, such as bank loans, to meet their financing needs. This may limit the firms' ability to raise long-term funds, since bank loans generally have short maturities.

The first section of this article shows that junk bonds are a natural extension of the disintermediation occurring in other financial markets. The second section describes the evolution of the junk bond market. The third section argues that bank loans are close substitutes for junk bonds; therefore, regulating junk bonds alone will not prevent highly leveraged transactions. The final section concludes that further regulation of junk bonds could limit the ability of below-investment-grade firms to raise long-term funds.

I. Changing Corporate Borrowing Patterns

The major sources of debt financing for businesses are corporate bonds, commercial paper and bank loans. These instruments differ in maturity, number of borrowers, and quality of borrowers. While the corporate bond market and the commercial paper market have been major sources of debt financing, until the establishment of the junk bond market they were primarily available to large, credit-worthy companies. In 1988, about 1,000 investment-grade bonds were issued by nonfinancial corporations, with an average size of $44 million.[1] Similarly, the commercial paper market generally provides large denomination funds for firms with investment-grade ratings.

Most small and mid-sized firms are not large enough or financially strong enough to issue investment-grade debt and, therefore, depend on commercial banks for their debt financing. Table 1 shows the terms of commercial and industrial loans extended by commercial banks during the second week of November 1989, as surveyed by the Federal Reserve System.[2] As estimated from the survey, commercial

banks held approximately 142,000 loans with less than one year to maturity with an average size of $311,000, and approximately 20,000 loans with more than one year to maturity and an average size of $260,000. Thus, bank loans are generally smaller and of shorter maturity than corporate bond issues.

Only 12 percent of the commercial and industrial loans surveyed by the Federal Reserve had more than one year to maturity. Bank loans are predominantly short-term floating-rate instruments or fixed-rate loans with short maturities (the average fixed-rate short-term loan was only 30 days) because most bank

Table 1

Terms of Lending at Commercial Banks
Survey Conducted November 6–10, 1989

	Amount (Billions of Dollars)	Average Size (Thousands of Dollars)	Weighted Average Maturity
Short-Term	44.0	311	53 Days
Fixed	24.8	554	30 Days
Floating	19.3	199	117 Days
Long-Term	5.2	260	43 Months
Fixed	.9	114	49 Months
Floating	4.3	359	41 Months

Source: *Federal Reserve Bulletin*, March 1990.

liabilities are also both floating-rate and short-term. Banks can minimize their interest rate risk by issuing loans with characteristics that match those of their liabilities. While this strategy minimizes interest rate risk for banks, it increases the risks to borrowers who must fund long-term projects with short-term loans.[3]

Disintermediation

Before the development of the commercial paper market, most short-term funding for firms was provided by commercial banks. For firms that qualify for investment-grade ratings, issuing commercial paper has become a competitive alternative to bank financing. Firms have increasingly bypassed banks, with the commercial paper market expanding from $25 billion in 1979 to $85 billion by 1988. Banks have lost much of this business because they do not have a competitive advantage in providing funds, as commercial paper rates paid by investment-grade firms are virtually the same as certificate of deposit rates paid by banks. Banks specialize in evaluating and monitoring credit risk, a service not highly valued for firms where the risk of default is very low. For firms with the highest credit rating, investors are willing to supply funds at rates at or below those of banks.

Disintermediation has not been confined to corporate bonds and commercial paper issued by the most creditworthy firms. Mortgages, student loans, and consumer loans are frequently repackaged and issued directly to financial market participants. Banks have even promoted repackaging of financial assets by developing an active loan sale market, wherein commercial and industrial loans are sold without recourse to other banks in a manner similar to the underwriting services provided by investment banks. Although most of these loans have been short-term loans to investment-grade firms, they have included loans issued to firms with below-investment-grade ratings.

With so many borrowers seeking to extend their sources of credit beyond banks, the trend toward disintermediation naturally expanded to firms that sought long-term financing but did not qualify for investment-grade ratings. The breaking down of traditional banking relationships also encouraged the substitution of junk bonds for bank loans. Banks typically have provided funds to below investment-grade firms, because banks specialized in gathering and analyzing credit risks of firms. Banks frequently supplemented their lending services with cash management, payroll, and other financial services that solidified the banking relationships. Greater competition among financial intermediaries and a trend towards separate pricing of banking services have enabled firms to unbundle these activities. Thus, firms could seek long-term financing from other sources without sacrificing the banking services that firms required.

Changes in the Composition of Corporate Debt

The changing composition of corporate financing is shown in table 2. Two major trends appear in the table. First, all forms of debt financing have grown rapidly. Second, disintermediation has been important: commercial paper and high-yield debt have grown more rapidly than bank loans to businesses.

As investment-grade firms successfully bypassed banks for both their short-term and their long-term financing needs, it was inevitable that firms with lower ratings should try to do the same. While some below-investment-grade firms have issued commercial paper, most still obtain their financing from banks. However, the long-term financing needs of below-investment-grade firms have not been met by banks. Since 1979, these firms have increasingly turned to long-term financing through the high-yield bond market.

Evolution of the Junk Bond Market

The junk bond market has followed the trends occurring in bank financing. During the past decade banks have increasingly financed highly leveraged transactions such as takeovers and recapitalizations. By the end of the 1980s, these transactions represented a significant portion of commercial and industrial loans for some banks.

Table 2
Corporate Debt Outstanding

	1979		1988	
	Billions of Dollars	Percent	Billions of Dollars	Percent
Investment-Grade Corporate Bonds and Private Placements	310	55	702	48
Commercial Paper	25	4	85	6
High-Yield Bonds	28	5	183	12
Bank Loans	204	36	502	34

Source: Board of Governors of the Federal Reserve System, *Flow of Funds.*

Most junk bonds issued in 1979 financed working capital, in place of bank loans. Table 3 describes the junk bonds issued in 1979, the first year with a significant number of new issues. Of the ninety-three issues, we were able to examine prospectuses for fifty-three. An analysis of the prospectuses in conjunction with news releases and other financial reports showed that only 11 percent of the issues (10 percent of dollar value) was used exclusively for acquisitions. Proceeds of most issues were used for working capital, consistent with the trend toward greater securitization in financial markets.

In 1988, junk bond financing of acquisitions was much greater. Of the $23 billion in junk bonds categorized in this study, only 20 percent of the new issues (9 percent of dollar value) was not planned for use in acquisition financing, while 64 percent was to be used exclusively for new acquisitions or to retire debt from previous acquisitions. The number of issues to be used for investments not related to acquisitions actually dropped. The amount of proceeds increased, however, reflecting the larger average size of junk bond issues. Most of the largest issuers in 1988 used the proceeds to finance takeovers.

Junk bonds are attractive as a financing vehicle for takeovers. Bank loans frequently have stringent underwriting standards and collateralization requirements that junk bond investors may not require if they receive a higher return. National banks and many state-chartered banks are not permitted to hold equity positions in firms, while junk bond investors may receive equity positions that enable them to share the benefits of successful ventures. To eliminate this advantage, many bank holding companies acquire equity and mezzanine financing similar to junk bonds in their nonbank subsidiaries, enabling the holding company to maintain a stake in all tiers of the transaction. Banks traditionally have been unwilling to acquire a takeover loan that represents a significant portion of their capital. However, as will be discussed later, banks are becoming more willing and able to finance takeovers.

Table 3

Amount and Purpose of Junk Bond Issues, 1979 and 1988

	Number of Issues	Amount (Millions of Dollars)
1979 Junk Bond Issues		
All Junk Bonds	93	2,653
All Junk Bonds Categorized	53	1,733
Percent of Category:		
Proceeds used exclusively to finance takeovers	11%	10%
Portion of proceeds to finance takeover or possible future takeovers	11%	25%
Proceeds not used to finance takeovers	78%	65%
1988 Junk Bond Issues		
All Junk Bonds	223	39,182
All Junk Bonds Categorized	137	22,858
Percent of Category:		
Proceeds used exclusively to finance takeovers	64%	76%
Portion of proceeds to finance takeover or possible future takeovers	16%	15%
Proceeds not used to finance takeovers	20%	9%

Source: IDD Information Services and company prospectuses.

Credit Rating Deterioration

Both the credit rating of junk bond issues and their importance to takeovers have changed substantially from 1979. Table 4 shows Standard & Poor's initial credit ratings for junk bonds issued in 1979 and in 1988: BB, B, or CCC, with BB the rating for a junk bond with the lowest probability of default and CCC the rating for a junk bond with the highest probability of default.

The proportion of rated junk bonds issued in 1979 in the higher rating categories is greater than for junk bonds issued in 1988. In 1979 only 5 percent of the total value of junk bonds issued had the lowest rating, CCC, and those issues were smaller than the average issue. None of the categorized issues whose proceeds were used to finance takeovers in 1979 had a CCC rating. In contrast, 17 percent of the total value of junk bonds issued in 1988 had the lowest credit rating and they were the largest issues. All five of the largest issues in 1988 were used to finance takeovers or restructuring to forestall a takeover attempt. Where the proceeds could be categorized, 25 percent of the issues devoted exclusively to finance takeovers had a CCC rating, while only 9 percent of the issues not used in takeovers had a CCC rating. Furthermore, securities in the largest category, B, are now of

Table 4
Standard & Poor's Initial Ratings for Junk Bonds, 1979 and 1988

Category	Amount (Millions of Dollars)	S & P Rating (Percent)			Not Rated
		BB	B	CCC	
1979 Junk Bond Issues					
All Junk Bonds	2,652.5	14.1	43.3	4.9	37.7
All Junk Bonds Categorized	1,732.8	16.1	32.5	7.6	43.8
Proceeds used exclusively to finance takeovers	165	24.2	54.5		21.2
Portion of proceeds used to finance takeovers or possible future takeovers	425	14.1	37.6		48.2
Proceeds not used to finance takeovers	1,142.8	15.7	27.4	11.5	45.5
1988 Junk Bond Issues					
All Junk Bonds	39,181.5	8.4	66.7	17.4	7.5
All Junk Bonds Categorized	22,858.2	8.3	64.9	21.7	5.0
Proceeds used exclusively to finance takeovers	17,390.7	6.8	64.3	24.6	4.4
Portion of proceeds used to finance takeovers or possible future takeovers	3,393.7	5.9	77.0	14.7	2.4
Proceeds not used to finance takeovers	2,073.8	25.3	50.6	9.4	14.7

Source: IDD Information Services and company prospectuses.

lower quality. Since 1982, Standard & Poor's has augmented the general rating with + or − to differentiate issues further. Since 1982 an increasing share of the B category has been designated B−. The higher proportion of securities with a CCC or B− rating shows that the rating agencies believe that the quality of original junk bond issues has been declining.

Given the lower credit ratings for recently issued junk bonds, one can probably expect a default rate higher than in the 1979 sample, particularly if the economy does not continue to perform as well as it has over the past ten years. A significant proportion of junk bonds issued in 1979 defaulted, despite their better initial credit ratings (table 5). Of the issues whose status could be verified, 23 percent have defaulted or have been converted under distressed conditions. This is consistent with findings by Asquith, Mullins and Wolff (1989), who analyzed a smaller sample of junk bonds from 1979. None of the bonds initially used to finance takeovers defaulted, however. Table 6 shows the defaults, classified by initial rating. No clear relationship emerges between

initial ratings and defaults, with bonds with the lowest rating having the lowest default rates. In a larger sample, however, lower initial ratings might indicate a higher probability of default.

The trend toward more acquisition-related financing and lower credit standards is not unique to junk bonds. Banks have also become increasingly aggressive lenders for takeovers and restructuring. The number of highly leveraged transactions financed by banks, and the number of highly leveraged loans past due, have been increasing. Despite the loss potential of highly leveraged debt, both for holders of junk bonds and for banks, these loans can be profitable. Defaults do not mean that all the principal is lost, only that the timely payment of interest is not made. Most troubled firms restructure, resulting in some losses to debt holders but still paying a significant proportion of the principal value. When creditors cannot reach agreement, the firm is forced into bankruptcy. Altman (1989) estimates that even in bankruptcy junk bonds sell for 45 percent of their face value one month after default. Banks that

Table 5

Status of Junk Bond Issues of 1979, Classified by Use

	Still Outstanding	Called	Converted or Defaulted	Status Not Verified
Total Number of Junk Bond Issues	27	29	17	20
Issues Categorized	17	17	6	13
Proceeds used exclusively to finance takeovers	4	0	0	2
Portion of proceeds used to finance takeovers	1	1	1	3
Proceeds not used to finance takeovers	12	16	5	8

Source: IDD Information Services and company prospectuses.

hold more senior debt positions would expect substantially higher payments from firms in default. Despite defaults, with the very high interest rates that these loans and junk bonds pay, lenders that carefully monitor the risks of their portfolios can earn high profits.

III. Regulating Junk Bonds

Recent legislation prohibits financial intermediaries such as national banks and savings and loans from holding junk bonds after an adjustment period to liquidate existing positions. Proposals to eliminate the tax deductibility of interest paid on junk bonds would further discourage the issuance of these securities. These asset restrictions have been focused on junk bonds because of their use in highly leveraged transactions and their association with takeovers,

particularly hostile takeovers. Alternative debt financing is available, however, and few highly leveraged transactions will be prevented by legislation narrowly focused to discourage investors from holding junk bonds. This section argues that such asset restrictions are not effective because bank loans are close substitutes for junk bonds and these restrictions do not alter the incentives firms have to assume more leverage.

The importance of junk bonds for financing takeovers is often overstated. Table 7 provides the number and value of junk bond issues, corporate acquisitions and hostile takeovers from 1985 to 1988. The total value of junk bonds issued includes those issued for other purposes as well as those issued for takeovers and restructuring. The value of acquisitions includes publicly announced takeover values as ascertained by *Mergerstat Review*. The table overstates the role of junk bonds in acquisitions, since other

Table 6

Status of Junk Bond Issues of 1979, Classified by Initial S & P Credit Rating

Initial Credit Rating	Still Outstanding	Called	Converted or Defaulted	Status Not Verified
BB	4	3	2	0
B	15	10	8	8
CCC	1	4	1	2
NR	7	12	6	10
TOTAL	27	29	17	20

Source: IDD Information Services.

Table 7

Number and Value of Junk Bond Issues, Net Merger Announcements, and Hostile Takeovers

| Year | Junk Bonds | | | Net Merger Announcements | | Successful Hostile Takeovers | |
	Number of Junk Issuers	Number of Junk Issues	Value (Millions of Dollars)	Number	Value (Millions of Dollars)	Number	Value (Millions of Dollars)
1988	169	223	39,181.5	2,258	246,875.1	27	38,474.4
1987	263	321	37,801.2	2,032	163,686.3	18	18,630.3
1986	369	442	45,604.2	3,336	173,136.9	15	7,613.7
1985	257	328	20,694.5	3,001	179,767.5	14	8,232.3

Source: *Mergerstat Review*, IDD Information Services.

junk bonds are included and those acquisitions whose value could not be ascertained are not included. In 1988, net merger announcements totaled $247 billion, while junk bonds issued for all purposes totaled $39 billion: the value of junk bonds relative to the total value of acquisitions had dropped to 16 percent in 1988 from a high of 26 percent in 1986.[4] The data suggest that most takeovers are financed by sources other than junk bonds.

Acquisitions are financed mostly by bank loans, internal funds and investment-grade debt. Of the ten most active acquirers from 1978 through 1985 (*Mergerstat Review* 1986), one firm had no debt outstanding and the other nine all qualified for investment-grade rating. These acquirers included Merrill Lynch & Co., General Electric, and W.R. Grace & Co. Junk bond restrictions will not diminish other important sources of acquisition financing, such as bank lending or investment-grade debt issues.

Hostile Takeovers and Junk Bonds

Successful hostile takeovers comprise less than 1 percent of the total number of takeovers, yet they have been the source of much policy debate. They are also frequently associated with junk bonds, even though hostile takeovers are usually financed by other sources of funds.[5] Table 8 shows the initial financing for nineteen successful hostile takeovers from 1985 through 1987 (40 percent of the successful hostile takeovers during this period) for which financial information was available. Sixteen of the nineteen hostile acquisitions used no junk bonds initially. Investment-grade bonds and internal funds were used in seven. The primary source of initial financing

was bank loans, used in thirteen of the cases and accounting for over 50 percent of the total amount raised for initial financing. Recently the importance of bank loans has increased further as a number of large takeovers have been structured to avoid using junk financing. As was shown in table 7, the total value of newly issued junk bonds in 1988 was $6 billion less than in 1986, while the value of acquisitions in 1988 was $73 billion more than in 1986.

In the case of the hostile takeovers shown in table 8, many of the bank loans were liquidated quickly, either through asset sales or issuance of new debt or equity. At the end of one year, however, junk bonds and non-rated debt accounted for only 20 percent of the initial price of the successful takeovers. Junk bonds are a significant source of funds, but a majority of successful hostile takeovers are financed by other means.

In hostile takeovers, bank loans and junk bonds are very close substitutes as a source of financing. Almost 50 percent of initial issues of junk bonds in table 8 were retired by the following year, in a manner very similar to bridge loans. While many bank loans are converted to junk bonds in the year following the acquisition, investment-grade debt, asset sales, and internal funds are also major ways of retiring bank loans.

Effects of Discouraging Junk Bond Financing

Restrictions on junk bonds will change the composition of debt financing without necessarily reducing acquisitions significantly. Bank loans and investment-grade debt will still be available to finance takeovers, and the incentives for firms to acquire

Table 8

Financing of Nineteen Successful Hostile Takeovers between 1985 and 1987[a]

	At Time of Transaction	One Year After Transaction			Percent of Total Cost of Transaction[b]
		Newly Issued	Retired	Net Total	
Junk Bonds					
Total Dollars	595.5	1,355	281.8	1,668.7	11.86
Number of Takeovers	3	4	2		
Investment-Grade Bonds					
Total Dollars	1,875	604	1.1	2,477.9	17.19
Number of Takeovers	3	3	1		
Bank Loans					
Total Dollars	7,747.9	160	5,531.5	2,376.4	16.49
Number of Takeovers	13	2	13		
Privately Placed and Nonrated Debt					
Total Dollars	1,252.83	675.5	550.4	1,377.9	9.56
Number of Takeovers	6	2	4		
Commercial Paper					
Total Dollars	500		500		
Number of Takeovers	1	0	1	0	
Stock Sales					
Total Dollars	1,760		200	1,560	10.83
Number of Takeovers	5	0	1		
Internal Funds					
Total Dollars	330	560	60	830	5.76
Number of Takeovers	4	5	1		
Asset Sales					
Total Dollars		3,417		3,417	23.71

[a]Complete information was available for only 19 of the 47 successful hostile takeovers from 1985 to 1987.
[b]Total cost of transactions was $14.4 billion.
Source: IDD Information Services and bond prospectuses.

other firms will remain. Enterprising lawyers, accountants, and investment bankers will find substitutes for junk bond financing.

If the purpose of restricting junk bonds is to reduce corporate leverage, it is unlikely to achieve its goal. From the mid 1970s to the present, corporate leverage rose with banks, commercial paper, and investment-grade bonds providing most of the debt. Leverage today is comparable to that of the late 1960s and early 1970s, a period when all debt consisted of bank loans and investment-grade bonds, and original-issue junk bonds were unknown. The availability of junk bond financing is not a major reason for higher leverage.

If the purpose of restricting financial intermediaries from holding junk bonds is to limit their exposure to risk, it is not likely to be effective. "Safe" assets such as government bonds and real estate loans can cause an intermediary to fail if the institution is not appropriately diversified. First Pennsylvania failed because of capital losses on government securities. Banks in Texas and New England have learned that large losses can occur on real estate loans. Despite these losses, one would not advocate prohibiting banks from holding government bonds and real estate loans. Instead, banks should carefully monitor the risk inherent in their portfolios of assets relative to their capital positions, and if they are overexposed, seek further diversification.

In commercial and industrial lending, banks essentially provide debt financing for businesses lacking investment-grade ratings. Historically, banks have profited from such lending despite the high risk of default, by monitoring their credit risk and diversifying their portfolios. Similarly, junk bonds, if appropriately monitored, can compensate investors for their higher default risk. They provide access to public capital markets for firms that previously relied solely on banks and other financial intermediaries for their external financing. In addition, junk bond financing is longer-term than that commonly available from bank loans.

Junk bonds can improve the diversity of a bank's portfolio. Most bank lending is tied to the region where the bank is located. Diversification outside the region requires setting up expensive loan offices or purchasing loans that other banks do not want to keep in their portfolios. Just as the development of the secondary mortgage market made mortgage loans more liquid, junk bonds make commercial and industrial loans more liquid. The secondary mortgage market was actively promoted by public policy, however, while public policy if anything has deterred the growth of the junk bond market. Regulators frequently restrict the investments of institutions. Not allowing poorly capitalized institutions to purchase junk bonds may be advisable, but not allowing well capitalized institutions to purchase junk bonds may limit their ability to diversify.

IV. Conclusion

Disintermediation, whereby firms obtain funds directly in financial markets rather than from banks, can encourage a more efficient transfer of funds from lenders to borrowers. For example, the secondary market for mortgage loans insulated the housing market from many of the recent problems in the savings and loan industry. The purchasing of liquid mortgage instruments permitted mutual funds, pension funds, and insurance firms to increase their participation in home financing.

Until recently, only firms with investment-grade credit ratings could raise funds directly from credit markets. These firms have such low default risk that they can obtain funds at or below the rates on certificates of deposit. As a result, they rely much more heavily on commercial paper and corporate bonds than on bank loans. Less established companies have not had such access, relying instead on short-term, floating-rate bank loans. The original-issue junk bond market has provided below-investment-grade firms an opportunity to raise long-term funds in national credit markets. By issuing "junk" debt instruments, these firms are able to attract investors who previously had not actively financed commercial activities by relatively small firms.

Despite the advantages to below-investment-grade firms of disintermediating loans, opponents have sought to discourage investors by limiting which intermediaries can hold junk bonds and by eliminating the tax deductions for interest paid on junk bonds. Such asset restrictions do not discourage leverage or takeovers. However, they will encourage firms to substitute bank loans for junk bonds, because bank loans and junk bonds are close substitutes. These restrictions will not alter the motives for holding debt but will limit access by below-investment-grade firms to long-term financing through national credit markets.

---

[1] These figures are approximations from the U.S. Securities and Exchange Commission, *SEC Monthly Statistical Review*, vol. 48, no. 2, February 1989, as follows:

Public Non-Convertible Bond Offerings

	Amount $ billions	Number
Total Business	$ 224.5	3927
Less: Financial and Real Estate	−139.1	−2625
Foreign	−4.5	−36
Junk Bonds	−37.1	−214
Total Nonfinancial Investment-Grade Bonds	$ 43.8	1052

[2] The survey does not include mortgage loans or foreign loans. Construction and land development loans are included in the survey but not reported in the table because they are not available by maturity.

[3] Borrowers can reduce this interest rate risk by hedging with interest rate futures or interest rate swaps (Felgran 1987). If borrowers can get long-term commitments from banks, with the aid of swaps they can create, at some transactions cost, an instrument that mimics long-term bonds. The Federal Reserve lending survey (table 1) shows, however, that long-term fixed or floating-rate agreements by banks are still relatively uncommon.

[4] "Net merger announcements" is calculated as total announcements in the year minus cancelled transactions in the year. As long as cancellations are stable over time, acquisition announcements should be a reasonable approximation for completions. Cancellations as a percent of gross announcements were 7 percent in 1985, 1987 and 1988 and 6 percent in 1986.

[5] The term "successful hostile takeovers" refers to tender offers by acquirers who successfully purchased the firm despite opposition of incumbent management. The list of successful hostile takeovers is taken from *Mergerstat Review*.

References

Altman, Edward. 1989. "Measuring Corporate Bond Mortality and Performance." *Journal of Finance*, vol. 44, September, pp. 909–921.

Asquith, Paul, David Mullins, Jr. and Eric Wolff. 1989. "Original Issue High Yield Bonds: Aging Analyses of Defaults, Exchanges and Calls." *Journal of Finance*, vol. 44, September, pp. 923–954.

Blume, Marshall. 1987. "Risk and Return Characteristics of Lower Grade Bonds," *Financial Analysts Journal*, vol. 43, July/August, pp. 26–33.

Drexel Burnham Lambert. 1989. *High Yield Market Report*.

Felgran, Steven D. 1987. "Interest Rate Swaps: Use, Risk, and Prices." *New England Economic Review*, November/December, pp. 22–32.

Kopcke, Richard W. and Eric S. Rosengren. 1989. "Regulation of Debt and Equity." In *Are the Distinctions Between Debt and Equity Disappearing?* Kopcke and Rosengren, eds., Federal Reserve Bank of Boston Conference Series No. 33.

Mergerstat Review. Various Years. Merrill Lynch Business Brokerage & Valuation, Inc.

Article 7

The Truth about Junk Bonds

By Sean Becketti

Junk bonds have been a common element in some of the country's worst financial wrecks this year. The Campeau retailing conglomerate collapsed in January under a heavy debt burden, much of it junk bonds. First Executive Corporation, one of the nation's largest insurance companies, announced a fourth-quarter 1989 loss of $859 million on its junk bond holdings. And Drexel, Burnham, Lambert, the investment bank responsible for the growth of the junk bond market, filed for bankruptcy in February 1990.

These corporate casualties are only the most recent of the problems blamed on junk bonds. For years, some critics have claimed junk bonds are responsible for a host of broader financial market ills. According to these critics, junk bonds fueled the merger mania of the 1980s, caused the rapid growth in the level of corporate debt in recent years, and more generally increased financial market volatility.

If these serious charges are accurate, it may be time for laws or regulations to restrict the use of junk bonds. But if the charges are not accurate, restricting the use of junk bonds would unnecessarily increase the cost of funds for many businesses.

The truth is that the evidence does not support these extreme charges against junk bonds. To be sure, there may be other concerns about junk bonds, such as whether junk bonds are suitable investments for banks and thrifts. This article does not address concerns such as these. Instead, the article examines whether junk bonds should be blamed for the rise in corporate mergers, corporate debt, and financial market volatility. The first section of the article defines junk bonds. The second section explains why some critics make these accusations against junk bonds, and the third section shows why these charges are not well-founded.

I. What Are Junk Bonds?

A corporation can obtain funds in many ways. It can raise funds by retaining earnings, issuing equity, or floating debt. If it chooses to take on debt, the corporation faces further choices. For short-term finance, it can issue commercial paper or take out bank loans. For intermediate and long-term finance, it can take out

Sean Becketti is a senior economist at the Federal Reserve Bank of Kansas City. Dan Roberts, a research associate at the bank, assisted in the preparation of the article.

bank loans, mortgage property, privately place bonds, or issue marketable corporate bonds. If the corporation chooses to issue marketable bonds, the bonds might be junk bonds.

Junk bonds are corporate bonds with low ratings from a major ratings service. Bond ratings are letter grades that indicate the rating services' opinions of the likelihood of a default. High-rated bonds are called investment-grade bonds, low-rated bonds are called speculative-grade bonds or, less formally, junk bonds.

A bond may receive a low rating for a number of reasons. If the financial condition or business outlook of the company is poor, bonds are rated speculative-grade. Bonds also are rated speculative-grade if the issuing company already has large amounts of debt outstanding. Some bonds are rated speculative-grade because they are subordinated to other debt—that is, their legal claim on the firm's assets in the event of default stands behind the other claims, so-called senior debt.

Junk bonds are traded in a dealer market rather than being listed on an exchange. A small group of investment banks makes a market in these securities; that is, they stand ready to buy or sell junk bonds.[1] Participating investment banks typically make a market in the issues they underwrite and in a limited number of relatively heavily traded issues considered "good credits."

Institutional investors hold the largest share of junk bonds. At the end of 1988, insurance companies, money managers, mutual funds, and pension funds held three-quarters of the face value of the outstanding junk bonds (SEC 1990, p. 22). Individual investors held only 5 percent of the outstanding bonds.

II. Why Are Junk Bonds Criticized?

Junk bonds have been blamed for three financial market ills in recent years: the merger boom, the rise in corporate debt, and the increase in financial market volatility. Critics connect junk bonds with these developments because they occurred simultaneously during the 1980s.

The market for junk bonds was revitalized in the late 1970s and the 1980s after decades of inactivity.[2] In 1977, the investment banking firm of Drexel, Burnham, Lambert began underwriting original-issue junk bonds. From 1977 through 1981, new issues never exceeded $1.5 billion (Chart 1). Then, starting in 1982, junk bond issues enjoyed five years of explosive growth. New issues peaked in 1986 and receded slightly in the last few years to between $25 billion and $30 billion a year. The face value of outstanding junk bonds is currently in the neighborhood of $200 billion, up almost twentyfold over ten years ago.[3]

As the junk bond market flourished during the last decade, mergers, corporate debt, and financial market volatility also grew. From the end of 1979 through the end of 1989, the value of U.S. mergers grew more than 300 percent.[4] Corporate debt grew over 270 percent.[5] Volatility in U.S. bond markets reached an all-time high in the 1980s. In addition, notable episodes of financial market volatility were the stock market collapses of October 1987 and October 1989.

More than mere coincidence, however, is needed to blame the financial market ills of the 1980s on the growth of the junk bond market. The decade of the 1980s saw the rise of many financial market innovations besides junk bonds—financial futures, program trading, portfolio insurance, and asset-backed securities to name just a few.[6] Why single out junk bonds as the cause of the merger boom, the growth in corporate debt, and financial market volatility?

Some observers suggest that junk bonds caused both the merger boom and the growth in corporate debt by extending credit too freely. According to this argument, corporations unable to borrow in traditional debt markets obtained funds by issuing junk bonds. Some potential acquirers found it easy to float junk bonds to raise

Chart 1
New Issues of Junk Bonds

Billions of dollars

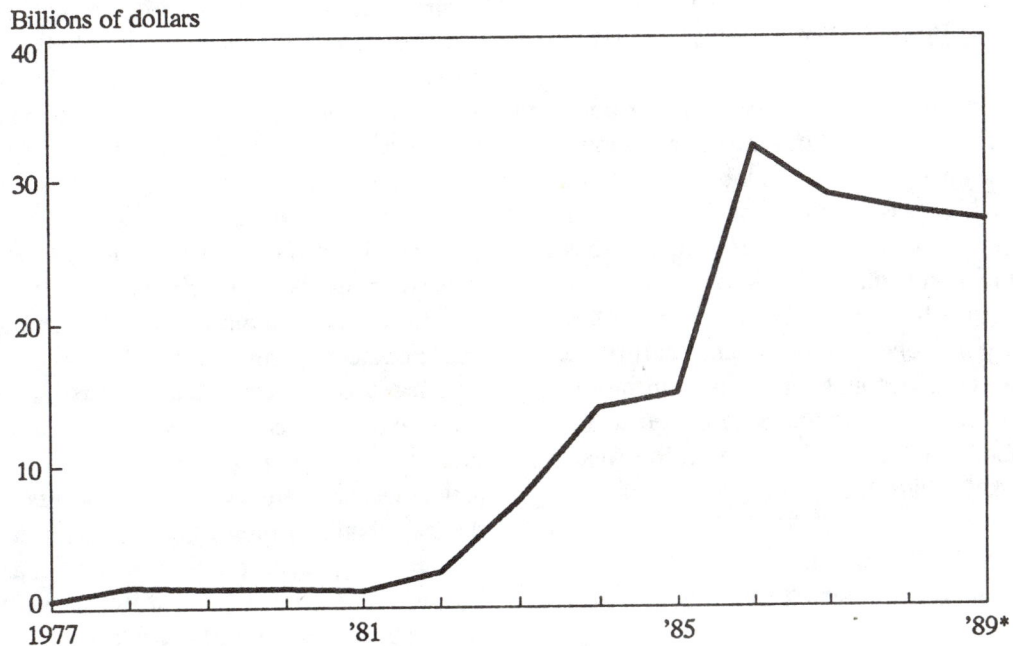

*Annualized estimate from data for the first nine months of 1989.

Sources: Perry and Taggart, Jr. 1990 (1977-80); SEC 1990 (1981-89).

the funds for their corporate takeovers. Similarly, some corporate borrowers took advantage of lower credit standards in the junk bond market to go on a debt "binge."[7]

Observers also suggest that the unusual volatility and unpredictability of junk bonds led to higher financial market volatility. This argument is related to the previous one. If, as some critics believe, junk bonds are the result of declining credit standards, then the market for junk bonds is prone to collapse. Investors may initially enjoy high returns, but the borrowers' failure to generate enough earnings to redeem the bonds leads inevitably to defaults. The prospect of these defaults causes frequent shifts in investor portfolios, from junk bonds to safer assets and back again, as investor confidence in junk bonds ebbs and flows with every change in the financial news. These shifts into and out of junk bonds increase the volatility of returns in other markets, such as the market for investment-grade corporate bonds and the market for equities.[8]

These arguments about the links between junk bonds and other financial market developments imply that junk bonds are qualitatively different from other securities and forms of debt. No one claims that such conventional securities as investment-grade bonds or equity extend funds too freely. Nor are these conventional forms of finance accused of causing excessive financial market volatility. Thus, if junk bonds are responsible for the growth in corporate debt, the merger boom, and the increase in financial market volatility, they must have some special characteristic that sets their behavior very much apart from that of other forms of finance.

III. The Truth about Junk Bonds

This section disputes the idea that junk bonds have special characteristics—the key assumption behind the charges against junk bonds. The section then discusses specific flaws in each of the claims and draws the following conclusions: First, junk bonds played a relatively small role in financing the merger boom of the 1980s. Second, junk bonds are too small a part of the debt market to account for the growth in corporate debt. Third, the timing of the growth in junk bond issues is not closely related to financial market volatility.

Junk bonds are similar to conventional investments

Junk bonds are similar to other, familiar investments with respect to the four principal characteristics of investments: risk, return, liquidity, and control over corporate management.[9] When measuring investments along each of these four dimensions, junk bonds lie between such conventional investments as equities, investment-grade bonds, bank loans, and private placements.[10]

Junk bonds are *riskier* than investment-grade bonds but less risky than equities. Altman (1988) finds that the junk bond default rate, a key component of risk, was 2.2 percent for the years 1970 through 1986, compared with just 0.2 percent for all publicly issued corporate bonds.[11] A more comprehensive measure of risk is the standard deviation of returns. Perry and Taggart (1990) find the standard deviation of monthly returns of junk bonds is greater than that of investment-grade bonds but less than that of equities and of the capital market as a whole.

Junk bond *returns* lie between those of

investment-grade bonds and equities. Blume and Keim (1990) find that from January 1977 through December 1988 average monthly junk bond returns were 0.89 percent, higher than the 0.71 percent earned by investment-grade bonds and lower than the 1.14 percent earned by stocks. Perry and Taggart examined the relative performance of various portfolios in the quarters just preceding, during, and just after the seven post-World War II recessions. They found, again, that junk bond returns were intermediate between those of investment-grade bonds and equities.[12]

Junk bonds are more *liquid* than bank loans and private placements but less liquid than equities. Loan contracts and private placements typically contain customized clauses protecting the rights of the investors and restricting the actions of the borrowers. These clauses reduce the marketability of loans and private placements by increasing the cost to third parties of analyzing and valuing the debts and by increasing the frequency of renegotiation. Junk bonds, in contrast, are relatively standardized securities with an established secondary market. Even issues in default have a limited secondary market allowing investors to cut their losses and avoid protracted bankruptcy proceedings.[13] Recent disruptions in the junk bond market, however, are a reminder that the junk bond secondary market is neither as developed nor as liquid as the secondary market for equities.

Junk bonds offer investors more *control over corporate management* than investment-grade bonds but less control than bank loans, private placements, and equities. Some junk bonds contain "equity kickers," that is, options or conversion privileges that let investors obtain an equity share in the borrowing firm. These features give investors the option to participate in the management of the firm.[14] In addition, some junk bonds are sold in strip financing deals, where both bonds and stocks are sold in fixed proportions to investors. In this case, bond holders have voting rights in the management of the firm.[15]

Since junk bonds are not markedly different from other securities, it is hard to understand why they should have any special ability to trigger corporate borrowing sprees. Junk bonds may have cost or tax advantages that allow for some marginal increase in debt. But these advantages are not likely to induce bondholders to invest in junk bonds more recklessly than they do in other debt instruments that are not materially different from junk bonds. Indeed, the bulk of junk bonds are purchased by the same institutional investors who purchase the bulk of private placements, investors who presumably apply the same credit standards to both types of investment.

Again, because junk bonds are similar to traditional financial instruments, it is doubtful they have any special ability to disrupt financial markets. As in any new financial market, the junk bond market may endure brief periods of somewhat greater volatility than average as the market matures and as investors learn how to analyze the investment characteristics of junk bonds. This extra volatility in the junk bond market may be transmitted to other markets as investors adjust their holdings of junk bonds and other securities. However, the fundamental investment characteristics of junk bonds are similar to those of other well-understood securities, such as equities and investment-grade bonds. All of these markets endure episodes of turbulence: the junk bond market does not stand alone in this regard.

In sum, the similarity of junk bonds to conventional financial instruments casts doubt on claims that junk bonds are responsible for the financial market ills of the 1980s. Furthermore, there are specific reasons why junk bonds should not be blamed for these events.

Junk bonds and the merger boom of the 1980s

The junk bond market is too small to have caused the 1980s merger boom. Although a large fraction of the junk bonds issued in the late 1980s were used to finance corporate takeovers, junk bonds accounted for only a small share of merger finance.[16] Even if all junk bonds issued had been used to finance mergers, junk bonds would have accounted for less than 8 percent of the value of U.S. mergers each year. Because not all junk bonds are used to finance mergers, this ratio is a generous upper bound on the junk bond share of merger finance. Moreover, a General Accounting Office study (1988) found that the bulk of the initial financing for tender offers came not from junk bonds but from bank loans. Thus, junk bonds appear to have played a minor role in financing mergers in the 1980s.

Some critics argue that junk bonds were the catalyst for many mergers and, in this way, caused the merger boom despite their small share in merger finance. It is true that junk bonds played a prominent role in several well-publicized mergers, and it is likely that the availability of junk bonds made a few more mergers possible than would have been the case without junk bonds. However, there are many ways to finance a merger. If junk bonds had not been available, mergers that made economic sense would probably have found other forms of finance. Indeed, previous merger booms have occurred without the aid of junk bonds. For example, during the merger wave of the late 1960s—the most recent merger wave prior to the current one and by some measures as significant as the wave of the 1980s—there was no market for original-issue junk bonds. This lack of junk bond financing in no way restrained the 1960s merger wave.

In fact, the merger boom of the 1980s may have helped establish the junk bond market rather than the other way around. The surge in new issues of junk bonds in the late 1980s coincided with the peak in the merger boom. Some part of the demand for debt generated by the merger boom may have increased interest in junk bonds and other innovative debt instruments.

Chart 2

Junk Bond Issues and Stock Market Volatility

Standard deviation   Billions of dollars

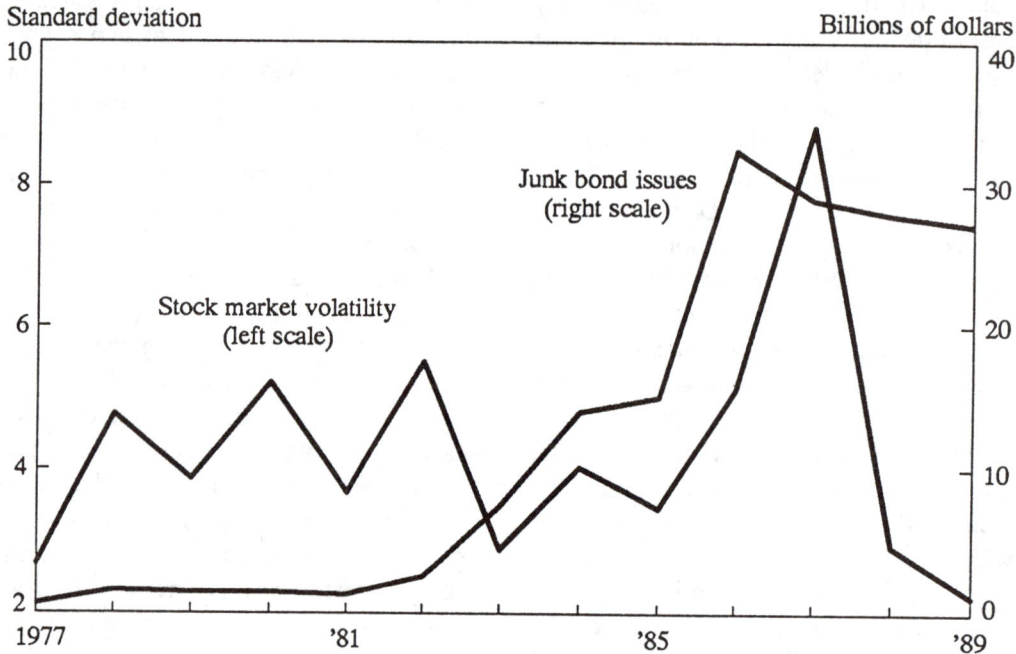

Note: In this chart, volatility is measured by the annual standard deviation of monthly stock returns of the Standard & Poor's index of 500 stocks.

Sources: See chart 1 (junk bond issues); Center for Research in Security Prices (stock market volatility).

Junk bonds and corporate debt

There is a striking coincidence in the growth of corporate debt and the revitalization of the junk bond market. However, the growth in outstanding junk bonds in the 1980s is not large enough to account directly for the growth in corporate debt. Junk bonds outstanding increased $189 billion from the end of 1979 to the end of 1989. Over the same period, corporate debt increased $1,322 billion. Thus, junk bonds accounted for only 14 percent of the growth in corporate debt.

Furthermore, it is difficult to say that junk bonds were more responsible for the growth in total corporate debt than any another component. During the 1980s, investment-grade bonds

increased more than 100 percent, bank loans grew more than 150 percent, and commercial paper outstanding increased more than 300 percent (Board of Governors of the Federal Reserve System 1990, pp. 35-36). These three forms of debt account for two-thirds of the growth in corporate debt. Clearly, all of these forms of debt played a part in the growth.

Indeed, it is possible that the growth in corporate debt contributed to the growth of the junk bond market, rather than the other way around. A prominent trend in financial markets in the 1980s was the move toward securitization of debt, that is, a move away from intermediated, nonmarketable forms of debt, such as bank loans, and toward marketable securities, such as corporate bonds.[17] Many of the financial innova-

Chart 3
Junk Bond Issues and Bond Market Volatility

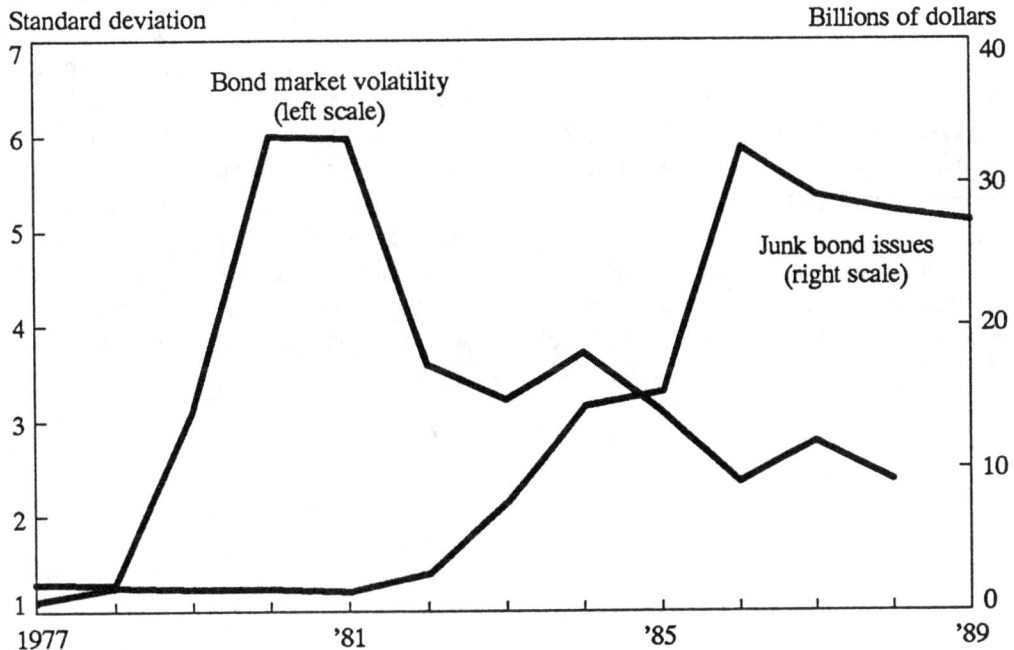

Note: In this chart, volatility is measured by the standard deviation of monthly returns of the Salomon Brothers' Long-Term High-Grade Corporate Bonds Index.

Sources: See chart 2.

tions of the 1980s came to popularity as part of this trend. Junk bonds may be just another reflection of the securitization phenomenon.

Junk bonds and financial market volatility

Financial markets in the late 1980s endured some difficult times—particularly the stock market collapse of October 1987. Some observers claim the growth of the junk bond market increased financial market volatility.

One problem with this claim is the lack of an apparent relationship between the growth of the junk bond market and stock market volatility. Chart 2 shows new issues of junk bonds and stock market volatility from 1981 through

1989.[18] Junk bond issues grew rapidly through 1986 and then leveled off. Stock market volatility was very high in 1987, thanks to the October market collapse, but was unexceptional otherwise.[19] If there were a connection between stock market volatility and the growth of the junk bond market, stock volatility would be high throughout the late 1980s instead of just in 1987.

Furthermore, the growth of the junk bond market and volatility in high-grade corporate bond returns are inversely related. Chart 3 shows new issues of junk bonds again, but this time with the volatility of the Salomon Brothers index of long-term, high-grade corporate bonds.[20] Bond market volatility began the 1980s at record levels and was lower thereafter. If there were a connection between bond market volatility and the growth of the junk bond market, bond volatility would have risen rather than fallen in the late 1980s.[21]

IV. Conclusion

For years, critics have blamed junk bonds for a variety of financial market ills. The merger boom of the 1980s, the rise in corporate debt, and financial market volatility in the 1980s are all traced, by some observers, to junk bonds.

The truth is that the evidence does not support these charges against junk bonds. The key premise in the case against junk bonds—the belief that junk bonds have special properties that upset financial markets—is questionable. While the junk bond market grew at the same time that financial market problems surfaced, this circumstantial link turns out to be unpersuasive. The junk bond market has accounted for only a small part of the merger boom and of the growth in corporate debt, and the growth in the junk bond market is not closely associated with the trends in financial market volatility. Of course, there may be other concerns over junk bonds; for example, it may be inappropriate for banks and thrifts to hold junk bonds. Nevertheless, the three charges against junk bonds examined in this article are not supported by the evidence.

Endnotes

[1] A small number of junk bonds, including some RJR Nabisco issues, are listed on the New York Stock Exchange (SEC 1990, p. 1).

[2] Junk bonds are just low-rated bonds, and low-rated bonds have always been a component of debt markets. In fact, in the 1920s and 1930s, junk bonds accounted for about 17 percent of new issues of corporate bonds on average (Hickman 1958, p. 153). However, the high default rates of the 1930s soured investors on junk bonds, and the market languished until the late 1970s.

[3] The SEC estimates that $204 billion par value registered securities were outstanding as of September 30, 1989. There are no reliable estimates of the market value of these securities (SEC 1990, p. 1). Altman (1987) gives estimates of the value of outstanding junk bonds for earlier years.

[4] This figure is from the database maintained by *Mergers & Acquisitions* magazine. This database tracks mergers of domestic firms with at least $1 million in assets. The value of each merger is recorded as the estimated value of all forms of consideration paid—cash, stocks, bonds, options, etc.—for the acquired company.

[5] There are many ways to measure the increase in corporate indebtedness in the 1980s. Two thorough examinations of this issue are Bernanke and Campbell 1988 and Faust 1990.

[6] Links have been suggested between financial market problems and some of these innovations. For example, program trading and portfolio insurance have been blamed for financial market volatility. However, none of these innovations has been connected with all three financial market developments.

[7] A number of observers make these or similar claims. For examples on the connections between junk bonds and the merger boom, see the comments of Gail I. Hessol, Managing Director for Standard & Poor's, a major securities rating service (Hessol 1988 and *Wall Street Journal* 1990).

To the extent junk bonds caused the merger boom, they also contributed to the growth in corporate debt, since a part of the growth in debt represents the financing of mergers (Clark and Malabre 1988).

[8] Hessol (1988) testified both to the current and prospective risk of junk bonds. In addition, if junk bonds caused the merger boom and the growth of corporate debt, then junk bonds may also have indirectly increased financial market volatility, because some analysts believe that both the merger boom and higher debt affected financial market performance. This point was made in a speech by Rand Araskog, the chairman of ITT Corporation (Clark and Malabre 1988). More recently, some market participants attributed the stock market disruptions of October 1989 to the collapse of the United Airlines buyout.

[9] The similarity of junk bonds to conventional investments does *not* imply that junk bonds are appropriate investments for all investors. For example, junk bonds may not be appropriate for banks and thrifts, just as some other conventional investments—equities, for example—are considered inappropriate investments for banks and thrifts.

[10] Private placements are essentially loans made by non-banks, typically such institutional investors as insurance companies. They may take the form of either loan contracts or bonds. However, if they are bonds, they are not offered for sale on the public market. Private placements are underwritten by commercial and investment banks.

[11] Junk bonds are, of course, expected to have a higher default rate than investment-grade bonds. That is why they are rated lower than investment-grade bonds. A number of studies attempt to quantify the default risk of junk bonds. Most report annual default rates in the 1 to 3 percent range. Asquith, Mullins, and Wolff (1989) find much higher annual default rates, in the 3 to 9 percent range.

[12] Some observers argue that changes in the nature of junk bond issues make historical evidence on the risk and return of junk bonds an unreliable guide to their future behavior. If these observers are correct, junk bonds could be much riskier and could earn lower returns in the future.

[13] Altman (1989) reports that, on average, junk bonds sell for slightly less than 40 percent of face value at the end of the month in which default takes place.

[14] Equity kickers also allow investors to share in any unexpectedly high profits the firm might earn. This characteristic stands in contrast to traditional bonds where returns are limited to the coupons explicitly offered by the bond. These features not only increase the expected return to bondholders but also serve as a form of call protection since borrowers are more likely to call bonds when profits increase.

[15] Some observers argue that strip financing, along with other forms of junk bond finance, is chosen to reduce the double taxation of corporate dividends while retaining an equity relationship with investors. In other words, according to this view, junk bonds in strip financing function as though they were common stock. The interest paid on the junk bonds is tax deductible to the corporation, in contrast to any dividends paid. Since bondholders and stockholders are the same entities, the net tax burden can be decreased by paying out earnings as coupon payments on the junk bonds rather than as dividends on the common shares.

[16] Drexel, Burnham, Lambert estimated that all forms of acquisition financing accounted for 79 percent of junk bond issues in 1987 and 83 percent in 1988. First Boston found that acquisition financing accounted for 76 percent of junk bond issues in 1989 (SEC 1990, p. 20).

[17] All forms of corporate debt grew in the 1980s. However, bank loans grew more slowly than bonds, causing them to lose market share to corporate bonds.

[18] New issues of junk bonds are compared with the annual standard deviation of monthly returns to see if the growth of the junk bond market increased financial market volatility generally. It might be the case that very short-lived disruptions in the junk bond market caused similarly brief disruptions in other financial markets. That is not the kind of volatility considered here.

The rate of new issues is used to measure the size of the junk bond market in this chart. Essentially the same picture would be produced by using the value of outstanding junk bonds to measure the size of the market.

[19] For the post-World War II period, the annual standard deviation of monthly stock returns averaged 3.9 percent. Excluding 1987, the annual standard deviation of monthly stock returns in the 1980s was again 3.9 percent.

[20] The Salomon Brothers index includes AAA and AA corporate bonds with maturities of ten years or more. These data end in 1988. In the post-World War II era, the annual standard deviation of this index averaged 1.8 percent. In the 1980s, the annual standard deviation averaged 3.7 percent.

[21] Although bond market volatility fell during the 1980s, it remained above its post-World War II average throughout the decade. Some observers maintain that increased corporate leverage in the 1980s, that is, higher ratios of corporate debt to equity, is responsible for this generally higher bond market volatility. Even if this claim is correct, all forms of corporate debt grew in the 1980s, and there is no reason to single out junk bonds as the sole or most important debt component responsible for increased volatility.

References

Altman, Edward I., ed. 1987. "The Anatomy of the High-Yield Bond Market," *Financial Analysts Journal*, July/August.

_____. 1988. "Analyzing Risks and Returns in the High-Yield Bond Market," *Financial Markets and Portfolio Management*.

_____. 1989. "The 'Junk Bond' Default Rate Debate," Working Paper 539, Salomon Brothers Center for the Study of Financial Institutions, New York University, November.

Asquith, P., D. Mullins, and E. Wolff. 1989. "Original Issue High Yield Bonds: Aging Analyses of Defaults, Exchanges, and Calls," *Journal of Finance*. September.

Bernanke, Ben S., and John Y. Campbell. 1988. "Is There a Corporate Debt Crisis?" *Brookings Papers on Economic Activity*.

Blume, Marshall E., and Donald B. Keim. 1990. "Risk and Return Characteristics of Lower-Grade Bonds, 1977-1987," in Edward I. Altman, ed., *The High-Yield Debt Market: Investment Performance and Economic Impact*. Homewood, Ill.: Dow Jones-Irwin.

Board of Governors of the Federal Reserve System. 1990. Balance Sheets for the U.S. Economy 1945-89.

Clark, Jr., Lindley H., and Alfred Malabre, Jr. 1988. "Takeover Trend Helps Push Corporate Debt and Defaults Upward," *Wall Street Journal*. March 15.

Faust, Jon. 1990. "Will Higher Corporate Debt Worsen Future Recessions?" *Economic Review*, Federal Reserve Bank of Kansas City, March/April.

General Accounting Office. 1988. *Financial Markets: Issuers, Purchasers, and Purposes of High Yield, Non-investment Grade Bonds*. Washington: Government Printing Office. February.

Hessol, Gail. 1988. *United States General Accounting Office Hearing on High Yield Bonds*, comments in appendix. General Accounting Office. May, p. 177.

Hickman, W. Braddock. 1958. *Corporate Bond Quality and Investor Experience*. Princeton, N.J.: Princeton University Press.

Perry, Kevin J., and Robert A. Taggart, Jr. 1990. "Development of the Junk Bond Market and Its Role in Portfolio Management and Corporate Finance," in Edward I. Altman, ed., *The High-Yield Debt Market: Investment Performance and Economic Impact*. Homewood, Ill.: Dow Jones-Irwin.

U.S. Securities and Exchange Commission. 1990. *Recent Developments in the High Yield Market*. Staff report, March.

Wall Street Journal. 1990. "Reactions to Milken: Villain or Victim?" April 25.

Section III
Capital Structure

As we have seen in the preceding sections, there has been a great increase in corporate debt in the 1980s. This has naturally led to an increased role for debt in the capital structure of America's corporations. Not surprisingly, the changing capital structure of today's corporations has helped fuel continuing interest in the capital structure debate.

In 1990, the importance of the capital structure issue was formally recognized by the Nobel prize committee when it awarded its prize to Merton Miller, largely for his work on capital structure. In 1958, Merton Miller and Franco Modigliani published a paper containing the now famous Miller–Modigliani propositions. In essence, M&M were able to show that capital structure in a perfect market was irrelevant. This proof was also tantamount to showing that any importance that capital structure might have in the real world stemmed from market imperfections, such as taxes or costs associated with trading securities. In his paper, "The Modigliani–Miller Propositions After Thirty Years," Merton H. Miller assesses the importance of that earlier work and the refinements that have extended the original M&M propositions.

"Still Searching for Optimal Capital Structure," by Stewart C. Myers, assesses the continuing debate about the best capital structure for the corporation. Faced with the airtight logic of the M&M propositions and the continuing practical importance of capital structure, theorists have attempted to devise alternative theories to explain capital structure. Myers describes these theories in a non-technical way and evaluates their adequacy.

J. Michael Pinegar and Lisa Wilbricht reveal the opinions of front-line financial managers in their paper, "What Managers Think of Capital Structure Theory: A Survey." Pinegar and Wilbricht found that managers most prefer to use internally generated funds, retained earnings, as a source of new financing. Their second choice was straight (non-convertible) debt. Among their various interesting results, Pinegar and Wilbricht found that managers generally gave a fairly low weight to maintaining a pre-determined capital structure.

Article 8

THE MODIGLIANI-MILLER PROPOSITIONS AFTER THIRTY YEARS

by Merton H. Miller, University of Chicago*

I t has now been 30 years since the Modigliani-Miller Propositions were first presented in "The Cost of Capital, Corporation Finance and the Theory of Investment," which appeared in the *American Economic Review* in June 1958. I have been invited, if not to celebrate, at least to mark, the event with a retrospective look at what we set out to do on that occasion and an appraisal of where the Propositions stand today after three decades of intense scrutiny and often bitter controversy.

*This article is a shortened version of an article that appeared in the *Journal of Economic Perspectives* (Fall 1988) and is reprinted here with permission of the American Economic Association, the journal's publisher. The author would like to acknowledge helpful comments on an earlier draft made by George Constantinides, Melvin Reder, Lester Telser, Hal Varian, Robert Vishny, and by the editors of the *Journal of Economic Perspectives*, Carl Shapiro, Joseph Stiglitz, and Timothy Taylor.

82   Section III   Capital Structure

Some of these controversies can by now be regarded as settled. Our Proposition I, which holds the value of a firm to be independent of its capital structure (its debt/equity ratio), is accepted as an implication of equilibrium in perfect capital markets. The validity of our then novel arbitrage proof of that proposition is also no longer disputed, and essentially similar arbitrage proofs are now common throughout finance.[1] Propositions analogous to, and often even called, M and M propositions have spread beyond corporation finance to the fields of money and banking, fiscal policy, and international finance.[2]

Clearly Proposition I, and its proof, have been accepted into economic theory. Less clear, however, is the empirical significance of the MM value-invariance Proposition I in its original sphere of corporation finance.

Skepticism about the practical force of our invariance proposition was understandable given the almost daily reports in the financial press, then as now, of spectacular increases in the values of firms after changes in capital structure. But the view that capital structure is literally irrelevant or that "nothing matters" in corporate finance, though still sometimes attributed to us (and tracing perhaps to the very provocative way we made our point), is far from what we ever actually said about the real-world applications of our theoretical propositions. Looking back now, perhaps we should have put more emphasis on the other, upbeat side of the "nothing matters" coin: showing what *doesn't* matter can also show, by implication, what *does*.

This more constructive approach to our invariance proposition and its central assumption of perfect capital markets has now become the standard one in teaching corporate finance. We could not have taken that approach in 1958, however, because the analysis departed too greatly from the then accepted way of thinking about capital structure choices. We first had to convince people (including ourselves!) that there could be *any* conditions, even in a "frictionless" world, where a firm would be indifferent between issuing securities as different in legal status, investor risk, and apparent cost as debt and equity. Remember that interest rates on corporate debts were then in the 3 to 5 percent range, with equity earnings/price ratios—then the conventional measure of the "cost" of equity capital—running from 15 to 20 percent.

The paradox of indifference in the face of such huge spreads in the apparent cost of financing was resolved by our Proposition II, which showed that when Proposition I held, the cost of equity capital was a linear increasing function of the debt/equity ratio. Any gains from using more of what might seem to be cheaper debt capital would thus be offset by the correspondingly higher cost of the now riskier equity capital. Our propositions implied that the *weighted average* of these costs of capital to a firm would remain the same no matter what combination of financing sources the firm actually chose.

Though departing substantially from the then conventional views about capital structure, our propositions were certainly not without links to what had gone before. Our distinction between the real value of the firm and its financial packaging raised many issues long familiar to economists in discussions of "money illusion" and money neutrality. . .

In the field of corporate finance, however, the only prior treatment similar in spirit to our own was by David Durand in 1952 (who, as it turned out, also became our first formal critic).[3] Durand had proposed, as one of what he saw as two polar approaches to valuing shares, that investors might ignore the firm's then-existing capital structure and first price the whole firm by capitalizing its operating earnings *before* interest and taxes. The value of the shares would then be found by subtracting out the value of the bonds. But he rejected this possibility in favor of his other extreme, which he believed closer to the ordinary real-world way of valuing corporate shares. According to this conventional view, investors capitalized the firm's net income *after* interest and taxes with only a loose, qualitative adjustment for the degree of leverage in the capital structure.

That we too did not dismiss the seemingly unrealistic approach of looking through the momentary capital structure to the underlying real flows may

---

1. Examples include Cornell and French (1983) on the pricing of stock index futures, Black and Scholes (1973) on the pricing of options, and Ross (1976) on the structure of capital asset prices generally. For other, and in some respects, more general proofs of our capital structure proposition, see among others, Stiglitz (1974) for a general equilibrium proof showing that individual wealth and consumption opportunities are unaffected by capital structures; Hirshleifer (1965) and (1966) for a state preference, complete-markets proof; Duffie and Shafer (1986) for extensions to some cases of incomplete markets; and Merton (forth-

coming) for a spanning proof.

Full citations for all articles mentioned are listed in the References section at the end of this article.

2. See, for example, Wallace (1981) on domestic open-market operations; Sargent and Smith (1986) on central bank foreign-exchange interventions; Chamley and Polemarchakis (1984) on government tax and borrowing policies; and Fama (1980),(1983) on money, banking, and the quantity theory.

3. Durand (1959).

well trace to the macroeconomic perspective from which we had approached the problem of capital structure in the first instance. Our main concern, initially, was with the determinants of *aggregate* economic investment by the business sector. The resources for capital formation by firms came ultimately from the savings of the household sector, a connection that economists had long found convenient to illustrate with schematic national income and wealth T-accounts, including, of course, simplified sectoral balance sheets such as:

BUSINESS FIRMS		HOUSEHOLDS	
Assets	**Liabilities**	**Assets**	**Liabilities**
Productive Capital	Debts owed to households	Debts of firms	Household net worth
	Equity in firms owned by households	Equity in firms	

Consolidating the accounts of the two sectors leads to the familiar national balance sheet in which the debt and equity securities no longer appear:

Assets	**Liabilities**
Productive Capital	Household Net worth

The value of the business sector to its ultimate owners in the household sector is thus seen clearly to lie in the value of the underlying capital. And by the same token, the debt and equity securities owned by households can be seen not as final, but only as intermediate, assets serving to partition the earnings (and their attendant risks) among the many separate individual households within the sector.

Our value-invariance Proposition I was in a sense only the application of this macroeconomic intuition to the microeconomics of corporate finance; and the arbitrage proof we gave for our Proposition I was just the counterpart, at the individual investor level, of the consolidation of accounts and the washing out of the debt/equity ratios at the sectoral level. In fact, one blade of our arbitrage proof had the arbitrager doing exactly that washing out. If levered firms were undervalued relative to unlevered firms, our arbitrager was called on to "undo

the leverage" by buying an appropriate portion of both the levered firm's debt and its shares. On a consolidated basis, the interest paid by the firm cancels against the interest received and the arbitrager thus owned a pure equity stream. Unlevered corporate equity streams could in turn be relevered by borrowing on individual account if unlevered streams ever sold at a discount relative to levered corporate equity. That possibility of "homemade leverage" by individual investors provided the second and completing blade of our arbitrage proof of value invariance.

Our arbitrage proof drew little flak from those who saw it essentially as a metaphor—an expository device for highlighting hidden implications of the "law of one price" in perfect capital markets. But whether the operations we called arbitrage could *in fact* substitute for consolidation when dealing with real-world corporations was disputed. Could investors, acting on their own, really replicate and, where required, wash out corporate capital structures—if not completely, as in the formal proof, then by enough, and quickly enough, to make the invariance proposition useful as a description of the central tendency in the real-world capital market? These long-standing and still not completely resolved issues of the empirical relevance of the MM propositions will be the primary focus of what follows here.

Three separate reasons (over and above the standard complaint that we attributed too much rationality to the stock market) were quickly offered by our critics for believing that individual investors could not enforce the corporate valuations implied by Propositions I and II. These lines of objection, relating to dividends, debt defaults, and taxes, each emphasized a different, distinctive feature of the corporate form of business organization. And each in turn will be reexamined here, taking full advantage this time, however, of the hindsight of thirty years of subsequent research and events. . .

■ ARBITRAGE, DIVIDENDS, AND THE CORPORATE VEIL

The law of one price is easily visualized in commodity settings where market institutions deliberately provide the necessary standardization and interchangeability of units. But to which of the many features of an entity as complex as an operating business firm would our financial equilibration extend?

We opted for a Fisherian rather than the

standard Marshallian representation of the firm. Irving Fisher's view of the firm—now the standard one in finance, but then just becoming known—impounds the details of technology, production, and sales in a black box and focuses on the underlying net cash flow. The firm for Fisher was just an abstract engine transforming current consumable resources, obtained by issuing securities, into future consumable resources payable to the owners of the securities. Even so, what did it mean to speak of firms or cash flow streams being different, but still "similar" enough to allow for arbitrage or anything close to it?

Some of the answers would be provided, we hoped, by our concept of a "risk class," which was offered with several objectives in mind. At the level of the theory, it defined what today would be called a "spanning" set; the uncertain underlying future cash flow streams of the individual firms within each class could be assumed perfectly correlated, and hence perfect substitutes. But the characteristics of those correlated streams could be allowed to differ from class to class. Hence, at the more practical level, the risk class could be identified with Marshallian industries— groupings around which so much academic and Wall Street research had always been organized.[4] We hoped that the earnings of firms in some large industries such as oil or electricity generation might vary together closely enough not just for real-world arbitragers to carry on their work of equilibration efficiently, but also to offer us as outside observers a chance of judging how well they were succeeding. Indeed, we devoted more than a third of the original paper (plus a couple of follow-up studies) to empirical estimates of how closely real-world market values approached those predicted by our model. Our hopes of settling the empirical issues by that route, however, have largely been disappointed.[5]

INVESTOR ARBITRAGE WHEN DIVIDENDS DIFFER: THE DIVIDEND-INVARIANCE PROPOSITION

Although the risk class, with its perfect correlation of the underlying real cash streams may have provided a basis for the arbitrage in our formal proof, there remained the sticking point of how real-world market equilibrators could gain access to a firm's operating cash flows, let alone to two or more correlated ones. As a matter of law, what the individual equity investor actually gets on buying a share is not a right to the firm's underlying cash flow but only to such cash dividends as the corporation's directors choose to declare. Must these man-made payout policies also be assumed perfectly correlated along with the underlying cash flows to make the equilibration effective? If so, the likely empirical range of the value-invariance proposition would seem to be narrow indeed.

A second MM-invariance proposition—that the value of the firm was independent of its dividend policy—was developed in part precisely to meet this class of objections. The essential content of the dividend-"irrelevance" argument was already in hand at the time of the original leverage paper and led us there to dismiss the whole dividend question as a "mere detail" (not the last time, alas, that we may have overworked that innocent word "mere"). We stated the dividend-invariance proposition explicitly, and noted its relation to the leverage proof in the very first round of replies to our critics.[6] But because dividend decisions were controversial in their own right, and because considering them raised so many side issues of valuation theory and of practical policy, both private and public, we put off the fuller treatment of dividends to a separate paper that appeared three years after the first one.[7]

That the close connection in origin of the two invariance propositions has not been more widely appreciated traces not only to their separation in time, but probably also to our making no reference to arbitrage (or even to debt or equity) in the proof of the dividend-invariance proposition. Why bring in arbitrage, we felt, when an even simpler line of proof would serve? The dividend invariance proposition stated only that, *given* the firm's investment decision, its dividend decision would have no effect on the value of the shares. The added cash to fund the higher dividend payout must come from somewhere, after all; and with investment fixed, that somewhere could only be from selling off part of the firm. As long as

4. Remember, in this connection, that the capital asset pricing models of Sharpe (1964) and Lintner (1965) and their later extensions that now dominate empirical research in finance had yet to come on the scene. For some glimpses of how more recent asset pricing frameworks can accommodate the MM propositions without reference to MM risk classes or MM arbitrage, see Ross (1988).

5. Direct statistical calibration of the goodness of fit of the MM value-invariance propositions has not so far been achieved by us or others for a variety of reasons, some of which will be noted further in due course below.
6. See Modigliani and Miller (1959), especially pages 662-668.
7. See Miller and Modigliani (1961).

the securities sold off could be presumed sold at their market-determined values, then, whether the analysis was carried out under conditions of certainty or uncertainty, the whole operation of paying dividends, again holding investment constant, could be seen as just a wash—a swap of equal values not much different in principle from withdrawing money from a pass-book savings account.

The Informational Content of Dividends

Managerial decisions on dividends thus might affect the cash component of an investor's return; but they would not affect the *total* return of cash plus appreciation, and the total is what mattered. In practice, of course, even changing the cash-dividend component often seemed to matter a great deal, at least to judge by the conspicuous price jumps typically accompanying announcements of major boosts or cuts in dividends. These highly visible price reactions to dividend announcements were among the first (and are still the most frequently mentioned) of the supposed empirical refutations of the MM value-invariance principle. By invoking the dividend-invariance proposition to support the leverage-invariance proposition, we seemed to have succeeded only in substituting one set of objections for another.

But, as we suggested in our 1961 dividend paper, these price reactions to dividend announcements were not really refutations. They were better seen as failures of one of the key assumptions of both the leverage and dividend models, *viz.* that all capital market participants, inside managers and outside investors alike, have the same information about the firm's cash flows. Over long enough time horizons, this all-cards-on-the-table assumption might, we noted, be an entirely acceptable approximation, particularly in a market subject to S.E.C. disclosure rules. But new information is always coming in; and over shorter runs, the firm's inside managers were likely to have information about the firm's prospects not yet known to or fully appreciated by the investing public at large. Management-initiated actions on dividends or other financial transactions might then serve, by implication, to convey to the outside market information not yet incorporated in the price of the firm's securities.

Although our concern in the 1961 dividend paper was with the observed announcement effects of dividend decisions, informational asymmetry also raised the possibility of strategic behavior on the part of the existing stockholders and/or their management agents. Might not much of the price response to dividend (and/or other capital structure) announcements simply be attempts by the insiders to mislead the outsiders; and if so, what point was there to our notion of a capital market equilibrium rooted solely in the fundamentals? Our instincts as economists led us to discount the possibility that firms could hope to fool the investing public systematically. But, at the time, we could offer little more support than a declaration of faith in Lincoln's Law—that you can't fool all of the people all of the time.

By the 1970s, however, the concept of an information equilibrium had entered economics, and came soon after to the field of corporate finance as well.[8] In 1978, for example, Stephen Ross showed how debt/equity ratios might serve to signal, in the technical sense, managements' special information about the firm's future prospects.[9] But the extent to which these and subsequent asymmetric information models can account for observed departures from the "invariance" propositions has not so far been convincingly established.[10]

The Interaction of Investment Policy and Dividend Policy

The dividend-invariance proposition, as we initially stated it, highlights still another way in which the corporate form of organization, and especially the separation it permits between ownership and management, can have effects that at first sight at least seem to contradict the MM value-invariance predictions. Recall that the dividend-invariance proposition takes the firm's investment decision as given—which is just a strong way of saying that the level of investment, whatever it might be, is set by management *independently* of the dividend. Without imposing such an "other-things-equal" condition, there would, of course, be no way of separating

---

8. Bhattacharya (1979) noted the formal similarity between Spence's (1973) job-market signalling model and the MM dividend model with asymmetric information.

9. Ross (1977).

10. For a recent survey of results on dividend signalling, see Miller (1987). For a more general survey of asymmetric information models in finance, see Stiglitz (1982).

the market's reaction to real investment events from reactions to the dividend and any associated, purely financial events.

In the real world, of course, the financial press reports single-company stories, not cross-sectional partial regression coefficients. In these single-company tales, the investment decision and the dividend/financing decisions are typically thoroughly intertwined. But if the tale is actually one of cutting back unprofitable investments and paying out the proceeds as dividends, followed by a big run-up in price, then the MM invariance proposition may seem to be failing, but is really not being put to the test. Nor is this scenario only hypothetical. Something very much like it appears in a number of the most notorious of recent takeover battles, particularly in the oil industry where some target firms had conspicuously failed to cut back their long-standing polices of investment in exploration despite the drastic fall in petroleum prices.

In a sense, as noted earlier, these gains to shareholders from ending a management-caused undervaluation of the firm's true earning power can also be viewed as a form of capital-market arbitrage, but not one that atomistic MM investors or arbitragers can supply on their own. Once again, the special properties of the corporate form intrude, this time the voting rights that attach to corporate shares and the majority-like rules (and sometimes supermajority rules) in the corporate charters that determine the control over the firm's decisions. Much of the early skepticism, still not entirely dispelled, about the real empirical force of inter-firm arbitrage (MM-arbitrage included) traces to these properties of corporate shares beyond their purely cash-flow consequences. A particular example of the obstacle they offered to effective capital market equilibrium was that of closed-end investment funds. In 1958, as still today, closed-end funds often sold at a substantial discount to net asset value—a discount that could be recaptured only by the shareholders merely (that word again) by getting enough of them to vote to convert to open-end fund status . . .

[Omitted here from the original is a section entitled "MM Invariance with Limited Liability and Risky Debt."]

THE MM PROPOSITIONS IN A WORLD WITH TAXES

We have no shortage of potential candidates for forces that might well lead the market to depart systematically and persistently from the predictions of the original MM value-invariance propositions. One such likely candidate, the third of the original lines of objection, has loomed so large in fact as to have dominated academic discussions of the MM propositions, at least until the recent wave of corporate takeovers and restructurings became the new focus of attention. That candidate is the corporate income tax, the one respect in which everyone agreed that the corporate form really did matter.

The U.S. Internal Revenue Code has long been the classic, and by now is virtually the world's only, completely unintegrated tax system imposing "double taxation" of corporate net income. A separate income tax is first levied directly on the corporation; and, except for certain small and closely held corporations, who may elect to be taxed as partnerships under Subchapter S of the Code, a second tax is then levied at the personal level on any income flows such as dividends or interest generated at the corporate level. Double taxation of the interest payments is avoided because interest on indebtedness is considered a cost of doing business and hence may be deducted from corporate gross income in computing net taxable corporate earnings. But no such allowance has been made for any costs of equity capital.[11]

If the separate corporate income tax were merely a modest franchise tax for the privilege of doing business in corporate form, as was essentially the case when it was introduced in the early years of this century, the extra burden on equity capital might be treated as just one more on the long list of second-order differences in the costs of alternative sources of capital for the firm. But, at the time of our 1958 article, the marginal tax rate under the corporate income tax had been close to and sometimes over 50 percent for nearly 20 years, and it remained there for almost another 30 years until dropped to 34 percent by the recent Tax Reform Act of 1986. The cost differentials of this size were just too big to be set aside in any normative or empirical treatments of real-world capital structure choices.

---

11. Two exceptions should be noted for the record. An undistributed profits tax from which dividends were deductible was in force for two years in the late 1930s. The excess-profits tax during World War II also allowed a deduction not for dividends, but for the "normal profits" of the firm.

Strictly speaking, of course, there is one sense, albeit a somewhat strained one, in which the basic value-invariance does go through even with corporate taxes. The Internal Revenue Service can be considered as just another security holder, whose claim is essentially an equity one in the normal course of events (but which can also take on some of the characteristics of secured debt when things go badly and back taxes are owed). Securities, after all, are just ways of partitioning the firm's earnings: the MM propositions assert only that the sum of the values of all the claims is independent of the number and the shapes of the separate partitions.

However satisfying this government-as-a-shareholder view may be as a generalization of the original model, the fact remains that the government, though it sometimes gives negative taxes or subsidies for some kinds of investment, does not normally buy its share with an initial input of funds that can serve to compensate the other stockholders for the claims on income they transfer to the Treasury. Nor are we talking here of taxation-according-to-the-benefits or of the rights of eminent domain, or even of whether the corporate tax might ultimately be better for the shareholders, or for the general public, than alternative ways of raising the same revenue. For the nongovernment equity claimholders, the government's claim to the firm's earnings is a net subtraction from their own.

THE MM TAX-ADJUSTED LEVERAGE PROPOSITION

Allowing for that subtraction can lead to a very different kind of MM Proposition, though one, as we showed in our Tax Correction article (1963), that can still be derived from an arbitrage proof along lines very similar to the original.[12] This time, however, the value of the firm (in the sense of the sum of the values of the private, nongovernmental claims) is *not* independent of the debt/equity division in the capital structure. In general, thanks to the deductibility of interest, the purely private claims will increase in value as the debt ratio increases. In fact, under conditions which can by no means be dismissed out of hand as implausible, we showed that the value of the private claims might well have no well-defined interior maximum. The optimal capital structure might be all debt!

In many ways this tax-adjusted MM proposition provoked even more controversy than the original invariance one—which could be, and often was, shrugged off as merely another inconsequential paradox from some economists' frictionless dream-world. But this one carried direct and not very flattering implications for the top managements of companies with low levels of debt. It suggested that the high bond ratings of such companies, in which the management took so much pride, may actually have been a sign of their incompetence; that the managers were leaving too much of their stockholders' money on the table in the form of unnecessary corporate income tax payments—payments which in the aggregate over the sector of large, publicly-held corporations clearly came to many billions of dollars.

We must admit that we too were somewhat taken aback when we first saw this conclusion emerging from our analysis. The earlier modeling of the tax effect in our 1958 paper, which the 1963 paper corrected, had also suggested tax advantages in debt financing, but of a smaller and more credible size. By 1963, however, with corporate debt ratios in the late 50s not much higher than in the low tax 1920s,[13] we seemed to face an unhappy dilemma: either corporate managers did not know (or perhaps care) that they were paying too much in taxes; or something major was being left out of the model. Either they were wrong or we were.

The Offsetting Costs of Debt Finance

Much of the research effort in finance over the next 25 years has been spent, in effect, in settling which it was. Since economists, ourselves included, were somewhat leerier then than some might be now in offering mass ineptitude by U.S. corporate management as an explanation for any important and long-persisting anomalies, attention was naturally directed first to the possibly offsetting costs of leveraging out from under the corporate income tax. Clearly, leveraging increased the riskiness of the shares, as we ourselves had stressed in our original Proposition II and its tax-adjusted counterpart. A sequence of bad years, moreover, might wipe out the firm's taxable income and, given the very ungenerous treatment of losses in our tax law, that

---

12. Modigliani and Miller (1963).
13. See Miller (1963).

could reduce, possibly quite substantially, any bene-fits from the interest tax shields. A run of very bad years might actually find a highly-levered firm una-ble (or, as the option theorists might prefer, unwil-ling) to meet its debt-service requirements, precipi-tating thereby any of the several processes of recon-tracting that go under the general name of bankrupt-cy. These renegotiations can be costly indeed to the debtor's estate, particularly when many separate classes of creditors are involved.[14]

The terminal events of bankruptcy are not the only hazards in a high-debt strategy. Because the in-terests of the creditors and the stockholders in the way the assets are managed need not always be con-gruent, the creditors may seek the additional protec-tion of restrictive covenants in their loan agreement. These covenants may not only be costly to monitor but may foreclose, if only by the time delay in renegotiating the original terms, the implementa-tion of valuable initiatives that might have been seized by a firm less constrained. Nor should the transaction and flotation costs of outside equity fi-nancing be neglected, particularly in the face of in-formation asymmetries. Prudence alone might thus have seemed to dictate the maintenance of a substan-tial reserve of untapped, quick borrowing power, es-pecially in an era when those managing U.S. corpo-rations (and the financial institutions buying their debt securities) still had personal memories of the debt refinancing problems in the 1930s.

We dutifully acknowledged these well-known costs of debt finance, but we were hard put at the time to see how they could overweigh the tax savings of up to 50 cents per dollar of debt that our model implied. Not only did there seem to be potentially large amounts of corporate taxes to be saved by con-verting equity capital to tax-deductible interest debt capital, but there appeared to be ways of doing so that avoided, or at least drastically reduced, the sec-ondary costs of high-debt capital structures. The bankruptcy risk exposure of junior debt could have been blunted with existing hybrid securities such as income bonds, to take just one example, under which deductible interest payments could be made in the good years, but passed or deferred in the bad years without precipitating a technical default.

For reducing the moral hazards and agency costs

in the bondholder-stockholder relation, the undo-ing-of-leverage blade in the original MM proof offered a clue: let the capital suppliers hold some of each—equity as well as debt—either directly or through convertible or exchangeable securities of any of a number of kinds. In sum, many finance spe-cialists, myself included, remained unconvinced that the high-leverage route to corporate tax savings was either technically unfeasible or prohibitively expen-sive in terms of expected bankruptcy or agency costs.

JUNK BONDS, LEVERAGED BUY-OUTS AND THE FEASIBILITY OF HIGH-LEVERAGE STRATEGIES

A number of recent developments in finance can be seen as confirming the suspicions of many of us academics in the early 1960s that high-leverage strategies to reduce taxes were indeed entirely feasi-ble. Among these, of course, is the now large out-standing volume of what are popularly known as "junk bonds." The very term is a relic of an earlier era in which the distinguishing characteristic of bonds as investments was supposedly their presence at the low-risk end of the spectrum. High-risk, high-yield bonds did exist, of course, but were typically bonds issued initially with high ratings by companies that had subsequently fallen on hard times. The signifi-cant innovation in recent years—and it is still a puz-zle as to why it took so long—has been in the show-ing that, contrary to the conventional wisdom, junk bonds could in fact be issued and marketed success-fully by design, and not just as "fallen angels."

The designs utilizing new risky-debt securities have often taken the very conspicuous form of "leveraged buyouts" of the outside shareholders by a control group typically led by the existing top man-agement. The device itself is an old one, but had been confined mainly to small firms seeking both to assure their continuity after the death or retirement of the dominant owner-founder, and to provide more liquidity for the entrepreneur's estate. The new development of recent years has been the abili-ty, thanks in part to the market for junk bonds, to ap-ply the technique to a much wider range of publicly-held, big businesses with capitalizations now routinely in the billions, and with new size records

---

14. The perceived complexity of the present bankruptcy code (and perhaps even the very reason for having such a code) reflect mainly the need for resolving conflicts within and between the various classes of creditors. The difficulties parallel those encountered elsewhere in "common pool" problems. (See Jackson (1987)).

being set almost every year.

The debt/equity ratios in some recent LBOs have reached as high as 9 to 1 or 10 to 1 or even more—far beyond anything we had ever dared use in our numerical illustrations of how leverage could be used to reduce taxes. The debtor/creditor incentive and agency problems that might be expected under such high leverage ratios have been kept manageable partly by immediate asset sales, but over the longer term by "strip financing"—trendy investment banker argot for the old device of giving the control and most of the ownership of the equity (except for the management incentive shares) to those providing the risky debt (or to the investment bankers they have designated as monitors). The same hold-both-securities approach, as in our arbitrage proof, has long been the standard one in Japan where corporate debt ratios are, or are at least widely believed to be, substantially higher than for their U.S. counterparts.

Some Possible Non-tax Gains from Leveraging

The recent surge of leveraged buyouts not only shows the feasibility of high-leverage capital structures for reducing corporate income taxes, but also suggests at least two other possible sources for the gains to the shareholder that may accompany a major recapitalization with newly-issued debt. The firm may, for example, already have had some long-term debt outstanding when the additional debt needed to accomplish the buyout was arranged. Even in a world without taxes, the no-gain-from-leverage implication of the original MM invariance proposition might fail if the new debt was not made junior in status to the old, if the old bond covenant was "open ended," as many still are, and if the new bonds were issued under it. Assuming no change in the underlying earning power from the recapitalization, the original creditors would then find the value of their claim diluted. The benefits of this dilution of the old bondholders accrue, of course, to the stockholders, which is why it has often been labeled "theft," particularly by the adversely affected bondholders. (Finance specialists prefer the less emotionally charged term "uncompensated wealth transfer.")

The high debt ratios in LBOs also redirect attention to the assumption, shown earlier to be crucial to the MM dividend-invariance proposition, that the firm's financial decisions can be taken as independent of its real operating and investment decisions. That assumption never sits well and certainly the notion that heavy debt burdens might indeed lead to overcautious business behavior has long been part of the folk wisdom on the dangers of debt. The new wrinkle to the interdependence argument brought in recently by the defenders of LBOs has been to stress the positive *virtues* of having managers face large debt obligations. Managements in such firms must work hard and diligently indeed to achieve any earnings above interest to enhance the value of the residual equity they hold in the firm. By accepting such heavy debt-service burdens, moreover, the managers are making a binding commitment to themselves and to the other residual equity holders against yielding to the temptations, noted earlier, to pour the firm's good money down investment ratholes.[15]

Voluntary Recapitalizations and the MM Dividend Proposition

High debt ratios have been installed in some U.S. firms in recent years, not just by outside-initiated LBOs but through voluntary recapitalizations— sometimes, it is true, merely for fending off an imminent hostile takeover, but sometimes also with the tax benefits very clearly emphasized. Even apart from the tax angles, nothing in the practice of finance these days could be more quintessentially MM than these often highly visible "self takeovers," as some wag has dubbed them. Leverage-increasing recapitalizations of this kind do indeed raise the firm's debt/equity ratio, but because the proceeds of the new bonds floated are turned over to the shareholders, the self takeovers also reunite in a single operation the two Siamese-twin MM propositions, the leverage proposition and the dividend proposition (joined together originally at birth, but soon parted and living separate lives thereafter).

The dividend proposition, as noted earlier, was put forward initially to overcome a line of objection to the leverage proof. But how dividends might actually affect real-world prices raises other issues which in turn have led to as much controversy, and to an

---

15. This view of debt service as a device for reining in managerial discretion is a major strand in what has come to be called the "free cash flow" theory of corporate finance. For an account of that theory, see Jensen (1988).

even larger number of discordant empirical findings, than for the leverage propositions. Once again, moreover, major tax differentials intruded, this time the gap between rates on dividends and capital gains under the personal income tax, with again what seemed in the late 50s and early 60s to be strikingly unorthodox policy implications. Some high-income stockholders clearly would have been better off if the firm paid no dividends and simply reinvested its earnings or bought shares in other corporations. That much every real-world conglomerator and every public finance specialist surely knew.

But the value-for-value presumption of the MM dividend proposition carried within it some further advice. There were better ways to avoid taxes on dividends than pouring the firm's money down ratholes: use the money to buy back the firm's shares! For the taxable shareholders, buybacks at market-determined prices could transform heavily-taxed dividends into less-heavily taxed capital gains and, better yet, into unrealized capital gains for shareholders who choose not to sell or trade their shares. Unlike a declared regular dividend, moreover, an announced share repurchase, whether by tender or by open market purchases, carried no implied commitments about future payouts.

PERSONAL-CORPORATE TAX INTERACTIONS AND CAPITAL MARKET EQUILIBRIUM

These tax-advantaged dividend-substitution properties of share repurchase may also offer a clue as to why the leveraging of corporate America out from under the corporate income tax may have been so long delayed. The point is not so much that share repurchase by itself has been a major vehicle deliberately invoked by corporations to reduce the personal income taxes of their shareholders, though its potential for that purpose certainly has not been lost on corporate treasurers and directors.[16] But the very presence of such a possibility at the corporate level serves as a reminder that the U.S. tax system has not one but two distinct taxes that bear on capital structure choices. Any model of capital market equilibrium must allow for both, and for their interactions.

In particular, under reasonable assumptions, the joint corporate-personal tax gains from corporate leverage, G_L, can be expressed in the following relatively transparent formula:

$$G_L = [1 - \frac{(1 - t_c)(1 - t_{PS})}{(1 - t_{PB})}] B_L$$

where B_L is the value of the levered firm's interest-deductible debts, t_c is the marginal corporate tax rate, and t_{PS} and t_{PB} are the marginal investor's personal marginal tax rates on, respectively, income from corporate shares and income from interest-bearing corporate debts.[17] In the special case in which the personal income tax makes no distinction between income from debt or from equity (i.e., $t_{PS} = t_{PB}$), the gain from leverage reduces to $t_c B_L$, which is precisely the expression in the MM tax model.[18] But in the contrasting extreme special case in which (a) the capital gains provisions or other special reliefs have effectively eliminated the personal tax on equity income, (b) full loss offsets are available at the corporate level, and (c) the marginal personal tax rate on interest income just equals the marginal corporate rate ($t_{PB} = t_c$), the purely tax gains from corporate leverage would vanish entirely. The gains from interest deductibility at the corporate level would be exactly offset by the added burden of interest includability under the personal tax—an added burden that, in equilibrium, would be approximated by risk-adjusted interest rate premiums on corporate and Treasury bonds over those on tax-exempt municipal securities.

This somewhat surprising special case of zero net gain from corporate leverage has inevitably received the most attention, but it remains, of course, only one of the many potentially interesting configurations for market equilibrium. Stable intermediate cases are entirely possible in which some gains to corporate leverage still remain, but thanks to the capital gains or other special provisions driving t_{PS} below t_{PB}, or to limitations on loss offsets, those gains at the corporate level are substantially below those in the original MM tax model. The tax gains from lev-

---

16. Most economists, upon first hearing about share repurchase as an alternative to dividend payments, assume that the Internal Revenue Service must surely have some kind of magic bullet for deterring so obvious a method of tax avoidance. It doesn't, or at least not one that will work in the presence of even minimally-competent tax lawyers.

17. See Miller (1977).

18. That special case assumes, among other things, that debt, once in place, is maintained or rolled over indefinitely. For valuing the tax savings when debts are not perpetuities, see the comment on this paper by Franco Modigliani that appears in the same issue of *Journal of Economic Perspectives* (Fall 1988) as this article originally appeared in.

erage might, in fact, even be small enough, when joined with reasonable presumed costs of leverage, to resolve the seeming MM anomaly of gross under-leveraging by U.S. corporations.[19]

THE MM PROPOSITIONS AND THE RECENT TAX REFORM ACT

Any such "Debt and Taxes" equilibrium, however, that the corporate sector might have reached in the early 1980s by balancing costs of debt finance against MM tax gains from leverage must surely have been shattered by the Tax Reform Act of 1986. That act sought, among other things, to reverse the long steady slide, accelerating in the early 1980s, in the contribution of corporate income taxes to total federal tax revenues. But, in attempting to increase the load on corporations, Congress seemed to have overlooked some of the interactions between corporations and individual investors that lie at the heart of the MM propositions and their later derivatives. For shareholders taxable at high marginal rates on interest or dividends under the personal income tax, for example, maintaining assets in corporate solution and suffering the corporate tax hit might make sense, provided enough of the after-corporate tax earnings could be transmuted into long-deferred, low-taxed capital gains by profitable reinvestment in real assets. In fact, over much of the life of the income tax, when shares were held largely by wealthy individuals and hardly at all by pension funds or other tax-exempt holders, the corporate form of organization for businesses with great growth potential may well have been the single most important tax shelter of all.

But the pattern of tax advantages that encouraged the accumulation of wealth in corporate form appears to have been altered fundamentally by the Tax Reform Act of 1986. The Investment Tax Credit and related tax subsidies to fixed investment have been phased out. The marginal rate on the highest incomes under the personal income tax has now been driven to 28 percent and, hence, below the top corporate rate of 34 percent. The long-standing personal income tax differential in favor of long-term realized capital gains has been eliminated, though

income in that form still benefits from a variety of timing options and from the tax-free write-up of any accumulated gains when the property passes to heirs. The analogous tax free write-up privileges for corporate deaths or liquidations, however, formerly allowed under the so-called *General Utilities* doctrine, have now been cut back by the TRA and some of its recent predecessors, reducing still further the tax benefits of the corporate form.

To finance specialists familiar with the MM propositions, these combined changes suggest that Congressional hopes of substantially increasing the yield of the corporate income-tax—that is to say, their hopes of reinstating the double taxation of corporate profits—may well be disappointed.[20] Our capital markets and legal institutions offer too many ways for averting the double hit. Corporations can split off their cash-cow properties into any of a variety of non-corporate "flow-through" entities such as master limited partnerships or royalty trusts. And, as has been the running theme of this entire section, firms retaining corporate form can always gut the corporate tax with high-leverage capital structures. In fact, under not entirely implausible conditions (notably that the marginal bondholder is actually a tax-exempt pension fund rather than a taxable individual investor, implying that the t_{PB} is zero) the incentive to leverage out from under the corporate tax may now actually be as high or higher than it was back in 1963. The statutory top corporate tax rate has indeed been cut; but with the Investment Tax Credit and Accelerated Depreciation also blown away by the Tax Reform Act of 1986, many capital-intensive corporations may now, for the first time in a very long while, be facing the unpleasant prospect of actually paying substantial corporate taxes.

And perhaps that observation can serve as a fitting note of uncertainty, or at least of unfinished business, on which to close this look back at the MM propositions. The open questions about those propositions have long been the empirical ones, as noted here at many points. Are the equilibria the propositions imply really strong enough attractors to demand the attention of those active in the capital markets either as practitioners or as outside observers? In the physical or biological sciences, one

---

19. For some recent empirical tests of such an intermediate equilibrium using the premium over municipals, see Buser and Hess (1986). Kim (1987) offers a wide-ranging survey of recent theoretical and empirical research on capital market

equilibrium in the presence of corporate-personal income tax interactions.

20. For some recent signs of Congressional concerns on this score, see Brooks (1987) and Canellos (1987).

can often hope to answer such questions by deliberately shocking the system and studying its response. In economics, of course, direct intervention of that kind is rarely possible, but nature, or at least Congress, can sometimes provide a substitute. The U.S. tax system is a pervasive force on business decisions of many kinds, but especially so on the class of financial decisions treated in the MM propositions. Tax considerations have for that reason always figured prominently in the field of finance. Occasionally, the profession may even see changes in the tax regime drastic enough for the path of return to a new equilibrium to stand out sharply against the background of market noise. Whether the Tax Reform Act of 1986 is indeed one of those rare super shocks that can validate a theory remains to be seen.

REFERENCES

Bhattacharya, Sudipto, "Imperfect Information, Dividend Policy and the 'Bird in the Hand' Fallacy." *Bell Journal of Economics* 10.1 (Spring 1979): 259-70.

Black, Fischer, and Cox, John, "Valuing Corporate Securities: Some Effects of Bond Indenture Provisions." *Journal of Finance* 31.2 (May 1976): 351-67.

Black, Fischer, and Scholes, Myron, "The Pricing of Options and Corporate Liabilities." *Journal of Political Economy* 81.3 (May-June 1973): 637-54.

Brooks, Jennifer J. S., "A Proposal to Avert the Revenue Loss from 'Disincorporation.'" *Tax Notes* 36.4 (July 27 1987): 425-428.

Buser, Stephen A., and Hess, Patrick J., "Empirical Determinants of the Relative Yields on Taxable and Tax-exempt Securities." *Journal of Financial Economics* 17 (May 1986): 335-56.

Canellos, Peter C., "Corporate Tax Integration: By Design or by Default?" *Tax Notes* 35.8 (June 8 1987): 999-1008.

Chamley, Christopher, and Polemarchakis, Heraklis, "Assets, General Equilibrium and the Neutrality of Money." *Review of Economic Studies* 51.1 (January 1984): 129-38.

Cornell, Bradford, and French, Kenneth, " Taxes and the Pricing of Stock Index Futures." *Journal of Finance* 38.3 (June 1983): 675-94.

Duffie, Darrell, and Shafer, Wayne, "Equilibrium and the Role of the Firm in Incomplete Markets." Manuscript, (August 1986).

Durand, David, "Costs of Debt and Equity Funds for Business: Trends and Problems of Measurement." In Conference on Research in Business Finance. National Bureau of Economic Research. New York. (1952): 215-47.

Durand, David, "The Cost of Capital. Corporation Finance and the Theory of Investment: Comment." *American Economic Review* 49.4 (September 1959): 639-55.

Fama, Eugene, "Banking in the Theory of Finance." *Journal of Monetary Economics* 6.1 (January 1980): 39-57.

Fama, Eugene, "Financial Intermediation and Price Level Control." *Journal of Monetary Economics* 12.1 (January 1983): 7-28.

Hirshleifer, Jack, "Investment Decision under Uncertainty: Choice Theoretic Approaches." *Quarterly Journal of Economics* 79 (November 1965): 509-36.

Hirshleifer, Jack, "Investment Decision under Uncertainty: Applications of the State Preference Approach." *Quarterly Journal of Economics* 80 (May 1966): 611-17.

Jackson, Thomas H., *The Logic and Limits of Bankruptcy Law.* Cambridge. Mass.: Harvard University Press. 1986.

Jensen, Michael C., "Takeovers: Their Causes and Consequences." *Journal of Economic Perspectives* 2 (Winter 1988): 21-48.

Kim, E. Han, "Optimal Capital Structure in Miller's Equilibrium." in *Frontiers of Financial Theory.* Edited by Sudipto Bhattacharya and George Constantinides [Totowa. N.J.: Renan and Littlefleld. 1987]. forthcoming.

Lintner, John. "The Valuation of Risk Assets and the Selection of Risky Investments in Stock Portfolios and Capital Budgets." *Review of Economics and Statistics* 47 (February 1965): 13-37.

Merton, Robert C., "Capital Market Theory and the Pricing of Financial Securities." in *Handbook of Monetary Economics* edited by Benjamin Friedman and Frank Hahn. Amsterdam: North Holland. forthcoming.

Merton, Robert C., "On the Pricing of Corporate Debt: The Risk of Interest Rates." *Journal of Finance* 29.3 (May 1974): 449-70.

Miller, Merton H., "The Corporate Income Tax and Corporate Financial Policies." In *Stabilization Policies,* The Commission on Money and Credit, Prentice-Hall. Inc., New Jersey. (1963): 381-470.

Miller, Merton H., "Debt and Taxes." *Journal of Finance* 32.2 (May 1977): 261-75.

Miller, Merton H., "The Informational Content of Dividends." In *Macroeconomics and Finance: Essays in Honor of Franco Modigliani.* Editors Rudiger Dornbusch. Stanley Fischer and John Bossons. MIT Press. Cambridge. MA. (1987): 37-58.

Miller, Merton H., and Modigliani, Franco, "Dividend Policy. Growth and the Valuation of Shares." *Journal of Business* 34.4 (October 1961): 411-33.

Miller, Merton H., and Modigliani, Franco, "Some Estimates of the Cost of Capital to the Utility Industry, 1954-7." *American Economic Review* 56. 3 (June 1966): 333-91.

Miller, Merton H., and Scholes, Myron S, "Dividends and Taxes." *Journal of Financial Economics* 6.4 (December 1978): 333-64.

Modigliani, Franco, "Debt, Dividend Policy, Taxes, Inflation and Market Valuation." *Journal of Finance* 37.2 (May 1982): 255-73.

Modigliani, Franco, and Miller, Merton H., "The Cost of Capital. Corporation Finance and the Theory of Investment." *American Economic Review* 48.3 (June 1958): 261-97.

Modigliani, Franco, and Miller, Merton H., "The Cost of Capital, Corporation Finance and the Theory of Investment: Reply." *American Economic Review* 49.4 (September 1959): 655-69.

Modigliani, Franco, and Miller, Merton H., "Corporate Income Taxes and the Cost of Capital: A Correction." *American Economic Review* 53.3 (June 1963).

Ross, Stephen, "The Determination of Financial Structure: The Incentive Signalling Approach." *Bell Journal of Economics* 8.1 (Spring 1977): 23-40.

Ross, Stephen, "Return, Risk and Arbitrage." In *Risk and Return in Finance.* Editors Irwin Friend and James Bicksler. Vol. 1. Ballinger. Cambridge MA.(1976): 189-219.

Rubinstein, Mark, "Derivative Assets Analysis." *Journal of Economic Perspectives* 1 (Fall 1987): 73-93.

Sargent, Thomas J., and Smith, Bruce D., "The Irrelevance of Government Foreign Exchange Operations." Manuscript, 1986.

Sharpe, William F., "Capital Asset Prices: A Theory of Market Equilibrium under Conditions of Risk." *Journal of Finance* 19 (September 1964): 425-42.

Spence, Michael, "Job-Market Signalling." *Quarterly Journal of Economics* 87.3 (August 1973): 355-79.

Stiglitz, Joseph, "A Re-Examination of the Modigliani-Miller Theorem." *American Economic Review* 59, 5 (December 1969): 784-93.

Stiglitz, Joseph, "On the Irrelevance of Corporate Financial Policy." *American Economic Review* 64.6 (December 1974): 851-66.

Stiglitz, Joseph, "Information and Capital Markets." In *Financial Economics: Essays in Honor of Paul Cootner.* Editors William F. Sharpe and Cathryn Gootner, Prentice Hall, New Jersey (1982): 118-58.

Stoll, Hans R. "The Relationship Between Put and Call Option Prices," *Journal of Finance* 24 (December 1969): 801-24.

Wallace, Neil, "A Modigliani-Miller Theorem for Open Market Operations." *American Economic Review* 71.5 (June 1981): 267-74.

■ MERTON MILLER

is Robert R. McCormick Distinguished Service Professor at the Graduate School of Business, University of Chicago. He is a past president of the American Finance Association. He is one of three co-editors of the *Journal of Business.* Dr. Miller has co-authored two well-known textbooks: *The Theory of Finance* (with Eugene Fama also of the University of Chicago) and *Macroeconomics: A Neoclassical Introduction* (with Charles Upton of Rutgers).

Article 9

Still Searching for Optimal Capital Structure

*Stewart C. Myers**

The optimal balance between debt and equity financing has been a central issue in corporate finance ever since Modigliani and Miller (1958) showed that capital structure was irrelevant. Thirty years later their analysis is textbook fare, not in itself controversial. Yet in practice it seems that financial leverage matters more than ever. I hardly need document the aggressive use of debt in the market for corporate control, especially in leveraged buyouts, hostile takeovers, and restructurings. The notorious growth of the junk bond market means by definition that firms have aggressively levered up. In aggregate there appears to be a steady trend to more debt and less equity.

Of course none of these developments disproves Modigliani and Miller's irrelevance theorem, which is just a "no magic in leverage" proof for a taxless, frictionless world. Their practical message is this: if there is an optimal capital structure, it should reflect taxes or some specifically identified market imperfections. Thus, managers are often viewed as trading off the tax savings from debt financing against costs of financial distress, specifically the agency costs generated by issuing risky debt and the deadweight costs of possible liquidation or reorganization. I call this the "static trade-off" theory of optimal capital structure.

My purpose here is to see whether this or competing theories of optimal capital structure can explain actual behavior and current events in financial markets, particularly the aggressive use of debt in leveraged buyouts, takeovers, and restructurings. I will consider the static trade-

*Gordon Y Billard Professor of Finance, Sloan School of Management, Massachusetts Institute of Technology.

Article 9   Still Searching for Optimal Capital Structure—*Myers*   95

off theory, a pecking order theory emphasizing problems of asymmetric information, and a rough, preliminary organizational theory that drops the assumed objective of market value maximization.

In the end, none of these theories is completely satisfactory. However, the exercise of trying to apply them forces us to take the firm's point of view and to think critically about the factors that may govern actual decisions.

I will not describe or document current events in detail here. The tendency to substitute debt for equity, at least by mature, cash-cow public firms, is evident from casual observation. The gains to investors from leveraged buyouts, restructurings, and leveraged takeovers have been summarized by Jensen (1986) and others. Taggart (1985) describes the trend to higher debt ratios for nonfinancial corporations generally.

Nor will I worry about the dividing line between debt and equity. That line is obviously important for tax or legal purposes, but it does not exist in finance theory. Every corporate debt security is part equity if there is any chance at all of default; it is (locally) equivalent to a weighted average of a default-risk-free debt and a pure equity claim on the firm's assets. The more debt the firm issues, holding assets, earnings, and future opportunities constant, the greater the equity content. Thus, "How much should the firm borrow?" is the same as asking how much implicit equity lenders should be induced to hold. When this conference's title asks, "Are distinctions between equity and debt disappearing?" finance theory answers, "Of course. Riskier debt is more like equity. Now let's get on to the real issue: Why are companies borrowing more?"

The following sections of the paper are devoted to the static trade-off, pecking order, and organizational theories.[1] The final section briefly summarizes what these theories can say about actual firm behavior and offers a few comments on "current events."

The Static Trade-off Theory

Figure 1 summarizes the static trade-off theory. The horizontal base line expresses Modigliani and Miller's idea that V, the market value of the firm—the aggregate market value of all its outstanding securities—should not depend on leverage when assets, earnings, and future investment opportunities are held constant. But the tax deductibility of

---

[1] Please understand that this is not a self-contained survey article. I have stated theories intuitively and have not attempted to derive them. I have attempted to cite interesting and representative research by others but have nevertheless skipped over many useful empirical and theoretical contributions. See Masulis (1988) for an extensive survey and bibliography.

Figure 1

The Static Trade-Off Theory of
Capital Structure

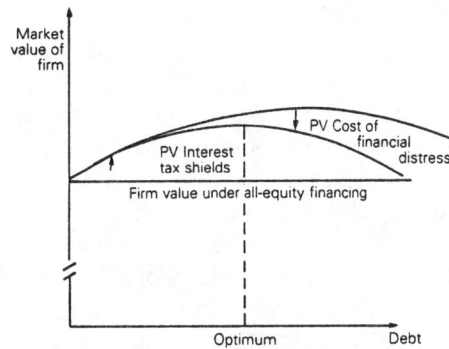

interest payments induces the firm to borrow to the margin where the present value of interest tax shields is just offset by the value loss due to agency costs of debt and the possibility of financial distress.

The static trade-off theory has several things going for it. First, it avoids corner solutions and rationalizes moderate borrowing with a story that makes easy common sense. Most business people immediately agree that borrowing saves taxes and that too much debt can lead to costly trouble.

Second, closer analysis of costs of financial distress gives a testable prediction from the static trade-off story; since these costs should be most serious for firms with valuable intangible assets and growth opportunities, we should observe that mature firms holding mostly tangible assets should borrow more, other things constant, than growth firms or firms that depend heavily on R & D, advertising, and the like. Thus, we would expect a pharmaceutical company to borrow less than a chemical manufacturer, even if the business risks of the two firms (measured by asset beta, for example) are the same. This predicted inverse relationship between (proxies for) intangible assets and financial leverage has been confirmed by Long and Malitz (1985).

The static trade-off theory may also seem to draw support from studies of the reaction of stock prices to announcements of security issues, retirements, or exchanges. Smith's (1986) summary of this research shows that almost all leverage-increasing transactions are good news, and leverage-decreasing transactions bad news. Thus, announcements of common stock issues drive down stock prices, but repurchases push them up; exchanges of debt for equity securities drive up stock prices, but equity-for-debt exchanges depress them. These impacts are often striking and generally strong enough to bar quibbles about statistical significance.

These "event studies" could be interpreted as proving investors' appreciation of the value of interest tax shields, thus confirming the practical importance of the static trade-off theory's chief motive for borrowing. But on balance this evidence works against the theory. First, the competing pecking order theory can explain the same facts as the market's rational response to the issue or retirement of common equity, even if investors are totally indifferent to changes in financial leverage. This point is discussed further in the next section.

Second, the simple static trade-off theory does not predict what the event studies find. If the theory were true, managers would be diligently seeking optimal capital structure, but find their firms bumped away from the optimum by random events. A couple of years of unexpectedly good operating earnings or the unanticipated cash sale of a division might leave a firm below its optimum debt ratio, for example; another firm suffering a string of operating losses might end up too highly levered.

Thus we would expect to observe some firms issuing debt and/or retiring equity to regain the optimal debt ratio; they would move to the right, up the left-hand side of Figure 1. But other firms would be reducing leverage and moving to the left, up the right-hand slope of the figure. The movement should be value-increasing in both cases, and good news if it is news at all.

It is possible, of course, that the leverage-increasing transactions reflect reductions in business risk and increases in target debt ratios. If investors cannot observe these changes directly, then a debt-for-equity exchange is good news; it demonstrates management's confidence in the level and safety of future earnings.

It is also possible that managers are not value-maximizers and do not attempt to lever up to the optimum. If most firms are sitting comfortably but inefficiently on the left of the upward-sloping "V curve" in Figure 1, then any increase in leverage is good news, and any decrease bad news. However, we cannot just explain away the event study results without thinking more carefully about how a "managerial" firm would want to arrange its financing. This too is left to a later section of the paper.

The most telling evidence against the static trade-off theory is the strong inverse correlation between profitability and financial leverage.

Within an industry, the most profitable firms borrow less, the least profitable borrow more. Kester (1986), in an extensive study of debt policy in United States and Japanese manufacturing corporations, finds that return on assets is the most significant explanatory variable for actual debt ratios. Baskin (1989) gets similar results and cites about a dozen other corroborating studies.

To repeat: high profits mean low debt. Yet the static trade-off story would predict just the opposite relationship. Higher profits mean more dollars for debt service and more taxable income to shield. They should mean higher target debt ratios.

Could the negative correlation between profitability and leverage reflect delays in firms' adjustments to their optimum debt ratios? For example, a string of unexpectedly high (low) profits could push a firm's actual debt ratio below (above) the target. If transaction costs prevent quick movements back to the optimum, a negative correlation is established—a negative correlation between profitability and deviations from target debt ratios.

This explanation is logically acceptable but not credible without some specific theory or evidence on how firms manage capital structures over time. Expositions of the static trade-off story rarely mention transaction costs;[2] in fact they usually start by accepting Proposition I of Modigliani and Miller (the flat base line in Figure 1), which assumes that transaction costs are second-order.

None of the evidence noted so far justifies discarding the static trade-off theory. However, it is foolish not to be skeptical. The theory sounds right to financial economists, and business people will give it lip service if asked. It may be a weak guide to average behavior. It is not much help in understanding any given firm's decisions.

The Pecking Order Theory

The pecking order theory of capital structure says that:

(1) Dividend policy is "sticky."

---

[2] One exception is the target adjustment models used in empirical studies of capital structure choice, for example by Jalilvand and Harris (1984). In these models, random events change actual capital structures, but transaction costs force firms to work back only gradually towards actual capital structures. Actual capital structures revert toward the mean.

These models work fairly well if one assumes that the static trade-off theory holds and that each firm has a well-defined target debt ratio. Unfortunately, the models work equally well when the firm has no target and follows a pure pecking order strategy. See Shyam-Sunder (1988). In other words, the models offer no support for the static trade-off theory against that competitor.

(2) Firms prefer internal to external financing. However, they seek external financing if necessary to finance real investments with a positive net present value (NPV).

(3) If firms do require external financing, they will issue the safest security first; that is, they will choose debt before equity financing.[3]

(4) As the firm seeks more external financing, it will work down the pecking order of securities, from safe to risky debt, perhaps to convertibles and other quasi-equity instruments, and finally to equity as a last resort.

In the pecking order theory, no well-defined target debt ratio exists. The attraction of interest tax shields and the threat of financial distress are assumed to be second-order. Debt ratios change when an imbalance of internal cash flow occurs, net of dividends, and real investment opportunities arise. Highly profitable firms with limited investment opportunities work down to a low debt ratio. Firms whose investment opportunities outrun internally generated funds are driven to borrow more and more.

This theory gives an immediate explanation for the negative intra-industry correlation between profitability and leverage. Suppose firms generally invest to keep up with industry growth. Then rates of real investment will be similar within an industry. Given sticky dividend payout, the least profitable firms in the industry will have less internal funds for new investment and will end up borrowing more.

The pecking order story is not new. There are long-standing concerns about corporations that rely too much on internal financing to avoid the "discipline of capital markets." Donaldson (1984) has observed pecking order behavior in careful case studies. But until Myers and Majluf (1984) and Myers (1984), the preference for internal financing and the aversion to new equity issues were viewed as "managerial" behavior contrary to shareholders' interests. These papers showed that managers who act solely in (existing) shareholders' interests will rationally prefer internal finance and will issue the least risky security if forced to seek outside funds.

The pecking order theory reflects problems created by asymmetric information, a fancy way of saying that managers know more about their firms than outside investors do. How do we know managers have superior information? Well, outside investors clearly think they do because stock prices react to firms' announcements of earnings, major

---

[3] Warrants would be even lower on the pecking order. However, warrants are usually issued in a package with debt—roughly equivalent to a convertible bond.

capital expenditures, exchange offers, stock repurchases, and the like. The market learns from managers' actions because the managers are believed to have better or earlier information.

Consider the following story:

(1) Because managers know more about their firms than outside investors do, they are reluctant to issue stock when they believe their shares are undervalued. They are more likely to issue when their shares are fairly priced or overpriced.

(2) Investors understand that managers know more and that they try to "time" issues.

(3) Investors therefore interpret the decision to issue as bad news; therefore, firms that issue equity can do so only at a discount.

(4) Faced with this discount, firms that need external equity may end up passing by good investment opportunities (or accepting "excessive" leverage) because shares cannot be sold at what managers consider a fair price.

This story has three immediate implications. First, internal equity is better than external equity. (Note that the static trade-off theory makes no distinction between equity from retained earnings and equity from stock issues.) Because dividends are sticky and debt service predetermined, retention of any excess operating cash flow is more or less automatic and does not convey information to investors.

Second, financial slack is valuable. It relieves managers' fear of passing by an outlay with positive net present value (NPV) when external equity finance is required, but shares can only be issued at a substantial discount to intrinsic value.

Financial slack means cash, marketable securities, and readily saleable real assets. It also means the capacity to issue (nearly) default-risk-free debt. If a new debt issue carries no default risk, potential investors do not have to worry about whether the firm as a whole is overvalued or undervalued by the market.

Third, debt is better than equity if external financing is required, simply because debt is safer than equity. Asymmetric information drives the firm to issue the safest possible security. This establishes the pecking order.

Why are safer securities better? Not because the manager always wants to issue them. On the contrary, when the market overvalues the firm, the manager would like to issue the most overvalued security: not debt, but equity. (Warrants would be even better.) If the market undervalues the firm, the manager would like to issue debt in order to minimize the bargain handed to investors.

But no intelligent investor would let the manager play this game. Suppose you are a potential buyer of a new security issue, either debt or equity. You know the issuer knows more than you do about the securities' true values. You know the issuer will want to offer equity only when it is overvalued—that is, when the issuer is more pessimistic than you are. Would you ever buy equity if debt were an alternative? If you do, the issuer is guaranteed to win and you to lose. Thus you will refuse equity and only accept debt. The firm will be forced to issue debt, regardless of whether the firm is overvalued or undervalued.

Issuing safer securities minimizes the manager's information advantage. Any attempt to exploit this information advantage more aggressively will fail because investors cannot be forced to buy a security they infer is overvalued. An equity issue becomes feasible in the pecking order only when leverage is already high enough to make additional debt materially expensive, for example, because of the threat of costs of financial distress. If the manager is known to have a good reason to issue equity rather than debt and is willing to do so in some cases where the equity is actually underpriced, then purchase of new equity can be a fair game for investors, and issue of new equity becomes feasible despite the manager's information advantage.

In practice, the pecking order theory cannot be wholly right. A counterexample is generated every time a firm issues equity when it could have issued investment-grade debt. Nevertheless, the theory immediately explains otherwise puzzling facts, such as the strong negative association between profitability and leverage. It also explains why almost all corporate equity financing has come from retention rather than new issues.[4]

The pecking order model also explains why stock price falls when equity is issued. Myers and Majluf show that if the firm acts in the interest of its existing shareholders, the announcement of an equity issue is always bad news. So is an equity-for-debt exchange offer—not because the exchange reduces financial leverage, but because it amounts to a new issue of common stock. The fact that investors pay for the issue with an unusual currency (the issuing firm's previously outstanding debt securities) is irrelevant.

Conversely, a debt-for-equity exchange is good news not because it increases outstanding debt, but because it amounts to a repurchase of equity. If investors believe managers have superior knowledge, then their decision to repurchase signals optimism and pushes the stock price up.

Thus the pecking order theory neatly explains why equity issues reduce stock price, but plain-vanilla debt issues do not. If the probability of default is low, then managers' information advantage is not a major

---

[4] See Brealey and Myers (1988), Table 14-3, p. 313.

concern to potential buyers of a debt issue. The smaller the managers' advantage, the less information is released by the decision to issue. The pecking order theory would predict a small negative impact when a debt issue is announced (all corporate debt carries some default risk), but for most public issues the effect should be very small and likely to be lost in the noise of the market.

An Organizational Theory of Capital Structure

Both of the theories reviewed so far assume that managers act in their current stockholders' interests. This is a useful convention of modern corporate finance theory but hardly a law of nature.

Current events in the market for corporate control have revived analysis of the conflicts between managers and stockholders. Consider Jensen's "free cash flow" problem, the alleged natural tendency of firms with excess cash flow to waste it rather than pay it out to investors. "The problem," as Jensen says, "is how to motivate managers to disgorge the cash rather than investing it below the cost of capital or wasting it on organizational inefficiencies" (1986, p. 323).

Competition tends to punish such waste. We would not expect to find it in toughly competitive industries. But if product market competition does not do the job, then competition in the market for corporate control may take its place. U.S. automobile companies were forced to slim down their organizations by their Japanese competitors. However, the Japanese do not pump oil, and so U.S. oil companies were forced to diet by (actual or threatened) takeovers.

Suppose we accept for sake of argument that important divergences exist between organizations' and investors' interests. What does that say about the role financing decisions play in "current events"? Second, what help does it give us in understanding financing decisions made by corporations that are not "in play" or under threat in the market for corporate control? Let me address the second question now and return to the first in the next section. Here is a sketch of an organizational theory of capital structure.[5]

Table 1 presents an organizational balance sheet. This has no necessary, direct connection with the firm's books. It is just a way of expressing the identity between the market value of assets and liabilities.

---

[5] I say "organizational" rather than "managerial" to emphasize my interest in the interests and behavior of the organization as a whole rather than the personal motives and decisions of a few people at the top of the corporate hierarchy.

Table 1
Organizational Balance Sheet
All Entries at Market Value

Present value (PV) of existing assets, pre-tax	PVA	Existing debt	D
PV growth opportunities, pre-tax	PVGO	Employees' surplus	S
Less: PV future taxes	−PVTAX	Existing equity	E
After-tax value	V	After-tax value	V

Corporate wealth = employees' surplus + equity
W = S + E

On the left is PVA, the present value of future cash flows from existing assets, plus PVGO, the present value of growth opportunities, less the present value of the government's tax claim, PVTAX. Note that PVGO can be negative if the firm is expected to waste money on negative-NPV capital investments or to overpay for acquisitions.

On the right are D, existing debt, E, equity, plus S, the present value of "employees' surplus." This surplus reflects the present value of perks, overstaffing, and above-market wages. (Note that PVA and PVGO are defined before this surplus is subtracted.)

Treynor (1981, p. 70) suggests that "the financial objective of the corporation is to conserve, and when possible, to enhance the corporation's power to distribute cash," which depends on the net market value of the firm. For a public corporation traded in well-developed capital markets, market value is fungible. Therefore the "power to distribute cash" is strictly proportional to net corporate wealth. This is the sum of equity and employee surplus, W = E + S.

Donaldson concluded from extensive case studies of mature public corporations that "the financial objective that guided the top managers of the companies studied [was] maximization of corporate wealth. Corporate wealth is *that wealth over which management has effective control and is an assured source of funds . . . .*" (1984, p. 22, emphasis in original).

Of course standard corporate finance theory also assumes the firm maximizes wealth. But it is shareholders' wealth. Standard theory says that dividend policy is irrelevant in perfect, frictionless markets because paying a dollar per share dividend reduces the share price by exactly a dollar; shareholders' wealth is unchanged. However, corporate wealth declines by a dollar per share. The dollar is no longer under the effective control of management.

I will briefly describe how several common financial decisions would be analyzed by a firm seeking to maximize corporate wealth. For simplicity I will assume the manager has no information advantage and also that existing debt is (close to) default-risk-free, so no temptation arises to undertake transactions to undercut existing creditors.

Because corporate wealth is measured in terms of market value, rules for ranking capital investments are exactly the same as in standard finance theory. The firm always seeks positive net present value (NPV) and prefers more NPV to less.

Suppose the firm issues debt to finance additional capital investment projects that happen to have NPV = 0.[6] Then corporate wealth does not change: the market value of additional real assets is offset by the new debt liability. Thus debt financing would provide no incentive to overinvest in negative-NPV projects. Outside investors should see no bad signals in a debt issue earmarked for additional assets. This is consistent with the lack of response of stock prices to announcements of new debt issues.

However, an issue of debt that replaces equity, holding PVA and PVGO constant, decreases corporate wealth. As debt increases, corporate wealth, which is the sum of equity and employees' surplus, must go down. This could be good news for stockholders. First, PVTAX, the government's claim on the firm, could be significantly decreased by interest tax shields.

Second, employees' surplus would decrease, transferring value to the equity account. Employees' surplus is similar to a subordinated debt claim, whose market value falls when more senior debt is issued and inserted between the junior debt and the firm's assets. The employees' surplus is junior because creditors can usually force the firm to "go on a diet" if debt service is threatened. The diet squeezes out the perks, overstaffing and above-market wages that constitute employees' surplus.

Thus the organizational theory can explain why debt-for-equity changes are good news for stockholders. (Of course one has to accept that interest tax shields have significant value and that employees' surplus is an important entry on the organizational balance sheet.) The theory also predicts that firms will not undertake debt-for-equity exchanges except, say, under threat of a takeover.

An issue of equity that replaces debt would be bad news for investors. The reasoning is just as for a debt-for-equity exchange, with signs of course reversed. But would a new equity issue, or unanticipated retention of earnings, be bad news if the money is put to use on the asset side of the balance sheet? Yes, because employees' surplus increases.

---

[6] The present value of interest tax shields on debt supported by the project is included in the project's NPV.

Remember that this surplus resembles a junior debt, whose value increases when the firm adds equity-financed assets. New equity investors anticipate this and adjust the purchase price of the new shares accordingly. The increase in surplus must therefore be extracted from existing equity.

The equity issue may be even worse news if the proceeds are not productively invested. If $10 million is raised and invested in a project with a value of only $6 million, existing shareholders lose $4 million (and also lose whatever the employees gain from appreciation in the value of their junior claim). Other things constant, corporate wealth nevertheless increases by $6 million.

Thus, the negative stock market reaction to equity issues is guaranteed if one assumes that marginal investments are negative-NPV. But why should the corporate-wealth-maximizing firm ever accept a negative-NPV project? Why not issue equity and buy marketable securities, which presumably have NPV = 0? Then a $10 million equity issue should add $10 million to corporate wealth.

This is not an easy question for the organizational theory, but some answers are possible. First, buying marketable debt securities amounts to lending money. If borrowing has a significant tax advantage, there must be a corresponding disadvantage to lending. Thus investment in a Treasury bill should have NPV < 0 after tax. Second, if another company's equity securities are purchased, an additional layer of taxation is created, which should drive NPV negative. This layer of tax is eliminated if the other company is taken over, but takeovers not motivated by real economic gains are also likely to be negative-NPV once transaction costs and takeover premiums are recognized.

Assume, then, that outlets for investment with at least zero NPV are limited. That limit defines the maximum scale of a shareholder-value-maximizing firm. What limits the scale of a firm that maximizes corporate wealth? It seems that any new equity issue inevitably increases corporate wealth, regardless of whether the proceeds are used to repay debt or add to assets. (Corporate wealth is also increased if earnings are retained rather than paid out as dividends.) This is so even if the assets' NPVs are negative, so long as they have any value at all. Why doesn't the firm issue more and more equity, expanding and generating practically unlimited corporate wealth? If corporate wealth is the objective, the firm does not care about the price of new shares.

This, too, is not an easy question. One can appeal to the threat of takeover by other firms seeking to maximize their own corporate wealth by preying on other firms with large employee surpluses or substantial negative-NPV investments. However, takeovers did not appear as a significant threat to large public corporations until relatively recently. One can also note the compensation schemes of top management, whose fortunes are tied more closely to equity earnings and stock prices than those of most of their employees.

The deeper answer is that corporate wealth is in the end not determined by the corporation but by investors. Only market value can be translated into "the power to distribute cash." That depends on what investors are willing to pay.

The only reason they are willing to pay anything at all, absent the threat of takeover, is that the firm has somehow bonded itself to distribute cash to shareholders. Obviously the bond is not contractual, as it is with debt, but implicit. Presumably this is the reason why firms have fairly well-defined, sticky dividend policies, and also why top managers accept compensation schemes linked to stock prices, despite the otherwise diversifiable risk this forces them to carry.

A stock issue increases equity value only if this bonded or "promised" future payout increases. Consider the two extreme cases. First, suppose that the firm issues $10 million in new equity but does not "promise" to pay out any additional future dividends. Then existing shareholders must absorb a $10 million capital loss. In other words, the decision to issue new stock breaks the firm's "promise" to old shareholders. But having just broken that promise, it is not clear where the firm would find any rational new shareholders. In other words, an equity issue would probably be infeasible.

At the other extreme, the firm could accept an implicit obligation to pay out additional future dividends with a present value of $10 million. This fully "covers" the newly issued shares, so existing shares maintain their value. Total equity value increases by $10 million.

Corporate wealth also increases by $10 million. However, not much of this goes to employees. The firm has $10 million more in assets but has also promised $10 million to new shareholders. Nothing is left over for employees' surplus, except for the transfer to surplus from existing equity, which occurs because employees now hold better-protected junior claims on the firm's assets. (Note that this transfer could explain the markets' negative reaction to stock issues.)

Perhaps this tells us why firms prefer to accumulate retained earnings rather than to issue shares. Suppose the firm has "promised" to pay out dividends according to some sticky rule. Then if earnings are higher than anticipated, much of the increase is free for employees to deploy; it has not been promised to shareholders. On the other hand, if an unanticipated shortfall occurs, dividends are to some extent protected, and the firm may have to turn to outside financing for real investment.

This begins to look like a pecking order, at least with respect to a preference for internal versus external financing. Thus the organizational theory of capital structure may be able to explain why the most profitable firms typically borrow the least. Their higher than "normal" or expected earnings are retained because their contract with stockholders does not require them to be paid out. If real investment opportunities do not increase proportionally to earnings—as is likely for mature firms—then high earnings mean greater retention, less reliance on external financing, and presumably a lower debt ratio.[7]

The organizational theory also seems to explain stock market reactions to announcements of security issues, retirements, and exchanges. Overall it is a promising alternative to capital structure theories based on shareholder wealth maximization.

Yet caution is called for. I have not been able to develop the theory fully and formally in this paper. I have not analyzed the implicit contract between the firm and its shareholders or attempted a link-up to the literature on dividend policy. I have compared employees' surplus to a junior debt liability without giving a detailed description of the properties of this claim, and I have implicitly treated employees' surplus as a kind of tax that does not reduce the potential value of existing assets and growth opportunities. This is almost certainly oversimplified.

Finally, I have accepted Treynor's and Donaldson's suggested objective of maximizing corporate wealth. The discussion above of equity issues and the firm's implicit contract with shareholders suggests that maximizing corporate wealth may not always be in the employees' interest, even if all employees could act as one.

Conclusions

This paper has briefly reviewed three theories—perhaps I should say stories—of capital structure. I have tried to match them to firms' actual behavior and to judge their ability to explain the two most striking facts about corporate financing.

The first fact is that investors regard almost all leverage-increasing security issues or exchanges as good news, and leverage-decreasing transactions as bad news. The only exception is plain-vanilla debt issues, which apparently are no news at all. The second fact is the strong negative correlation between profitability and financial leverage.

The widely cited static trade-off theory, taken literally, explains neither fact. It is at best a weak guide to average behavior.

The pecking order theory is a minority view that seems to explain the two striking facts.

---

[7] I admit that the organizational theory does not fully explain why firms should prefer debt to equity if external financing is sought.

The organizational theory described in this paper is a first try at restating Jensen's free cash flow theory of the market for corporate control as a general theory of capital structure choice. It also explains the two striking facts, though its predictions are not as clear and definite as those of the pecking order model. A more thorough and formal development of the organizational theory is obviously needed.

The initial plausibility of the organizational theory derives from current events, particularly the aggressive use of leverage in leveraged buyouts, takeovers, and restructurings. The leading explanation for this is that high debt ratios are necessary to force mature companies on a diet and to prevent them from making negative-NPV capital investments or acquisitions. The debt is viewed as a contractual bond that forces the firm to distribute cash to investors.

The organizational theory is an extension of this argument, and therefore broadly consistent with current events. The static trade-off theory gives no help with current events unless it is assumed that target firms are systematically underleveraged and therefore not maximizing market value. But in that case the static trade-off theory is no more than an open invitation to develop an organizational theory.

Thus, the race to explain capital structure really has only two contenders: models such as the pecking order theory that assert asymmetric information as the chief underlying problem, and models that start from the proposition that organizations act in their own interests.

References

Baskin, J. 1989. "An Empirical Investigation of the Pecking Order Hypothesis." *Financial Management*, vol. 18, no. 1, Spring, pp. 26-35.

Brealey, R.A. and S.C. Myers. 1988. *Principles of Corporate Finance*. 3rd ed. New York: McGraw-Hill Book Co.

Donaldson, G. 1984. *Managing Corporate Wealth: The Operation of a Comprehensive Financial Goals System*. New York: Praeger.

Jalilvand, A. and R.S. Harris. 1984. "Corporate Behavior in Adjusting to Capital Structure and Dividend Targets: An Econometric Study." *Journal of Finance*, vol. 39, no. 1, March, pp. 127-144.

Jensen, Michael C. 1986. "Agency Costs of Free Cash Flow, Corporate Finance, and Takeovers. "*The American Economic Review*, vol. 76, no. 2, May, pp. 323-329.

Jensen, Michael C. and W.H. Meckling. 1976. "Theory of the Firm: Managerial Behavior, Agency Costs and Ownership Structure." *Journal of Financial Economics*, vol. 3, pp. 305-360.

Kester, W.C. 1986. "Capital and Ownership Structure: A Comparison of United States and Japanese Manufacturing Corporations." *Financial Management*, Spring, pp. 5-16.

Long, M. and I. Malitz. 1985. "Investment Patterns and Financial Leverage." In *Corporate Capital Structure in the United States*, B. Friedman, ed., pp. 325-348. Chicago: University of Chicago Press.

Masulis, R.W. 1988. *The Debt-Equity Choice*. New York: Ballinger Publishing Co.

————. 1989. "The Effects of Capital Structure Change on Security Prices: A Study of Exchange Offers." *Journal of Financial Economics*, vol. 8, no. 2, June, pp. 139-177.

Modigliani, Franco and Merton H. Miller. 1958. "The Cost of Capital, Corporation Finance and the Theory of Investment." *The American Economic Review*, vol. 48, pp. 261-297.

Myers, Stewart C. 1977. "Determinants of Corporate Borrowing." *Journal of Financial Economics*, vol. 5, November, pp. 147-175.

————. 1983. "The Search for Optimal Capital Structure." *Midland Corporate Finance Journal*, vol.1, no.1, Spring, pp. 6-16.

————. 1984. "The Capital Structure Puzzle." *Journal of Finance*, vol. 39, July, pp. 575-592.

Myers, Stewart C. and Majluf, N.S. 1984. "Corporate Financing and Investment Decisions When Firms Have Information That Investors Do Not Have." *Journal of Financial Economics*, vol. 13, June, pp. 187-221.

Shyam-Sunder, L. 1988. "Essays in Corporate Financing." Ph.D. dissertation, Massachusetts Institute of Technology.

Smith, C.W. 1986. "Investment Banking and the Capital Acquisition Process." *Journal of Financial Economics*, vol. 15, pp. 3-29.

Taggart, Robert A. 1985. "Secular Patterns in the Financing of Corporations." In *Corporate Capital Structures in the United States*, B.M. Friedman, ed. Chicago: University of Chicago Press.

Treynor, Jack L. 1981. "The Financial Objective in the Widely Held Corporation." *Financial Analysts Journal*, March-April, pp. 68-71.

Williamson, S. 1981. "The Moral Hazard Theory of Corporate Financial Structure: An Empirical Test." Ph.D. dissertation, Massachusetts Institute of Technology.

Article 10

Survey

What Managers Think of Capital Structure Theory: A Survey

J. Michael Pinegar and Lisa Wilbricht

J. Michael Pinegar is an Associate Professor of Finance, Marriott School of Management, Brigham Young University, Provo, UT. Lisa Wilbricht is an honors graduate from the College of Business, University of Iowa, Iowa City.

■ This survey examines the extent managers use the assumptions and/or inputs of capital structure models generated by academicians in making financing decisions. Modigliani and Miller [14] showed that capital structure decisions do not affect firm value when capital markets are perfect, corporate and personal taxes do not exist, and the firm's financing and investment decisions are independent. However, when one or more of the MM assumptions are relaxed, many authors demonstrate how firm value may vary with changes in the debt-equity mix. Most frequently, the optimal capital structure maximizes firm value by simultaneously minimizing external claims to the cash flow stream flowing from the firm's assets. Such claims include

We appreciate the many useful comments made by James Ang. Barbara Yerkes, and the referees of this journal.

taxes paid to the government by the firm and its security holders; bankruptcy costs paid to accountants, lawyers, and the firm's vendors; and/or agency costs incurred to align managerial interests with the interests of capital suppliers.

Until recently, the capital structure debate was mainly a theoretical one, with the relevance or irrelevance of financing decisions turning on the modeler's willingness to accept the existence of significant market imperfections. (See Miller [12], DeAngelo and Masulis [2], Kim [9], Haugen and Senbet [6], Titman [25], Jensen and Meckling [8], Fama [5], and Smith and Warner [22] for different perspectives on the relevance of the market imperfections in the preceding paragraph.) However, empirical evidence, summarized nicely by Smith [21], now strongly indicates that changes in a firm's capital structure can affect firm value. Thus, the focus of the debate has shifted from whether capital structure decisions matter to why they matter.

One explanation of why security prices respond to announcements of capital structure change is that firms are moving closer to (or farther from) their optimal or target capital structures, as defined by the models alluded to above. A second explanation is that capital structure decisions are irrelevant but that the information they convey concerning the firm's investment opportunities causes security holders to revise their expectations of the firm's prospects.

This study augments market studies of capital structure change that seek to disentangle the above two interpretations by reporting results of a survey that was sent to chief financial officers of each of the Fortune 500 firms for 1986. Although this is not the first to report survey results on capital structure issues, it makes important extensions to its precursors. In contrast to Donaldson's [4] classic study which analyzed the financing practices of 25 major firms, this study reports results for 176 firms from the Fortune 500 list. Further, this survey deals more extensively with capital structure theory than did the survey of Scott and Johnson [19].

I. Capital Structure Theories

The capital structure models considered here can be classified conveniently into three groups: models that imply an optimal combination of long-term funds, models that imply an optimal hierarchy in raising funds, and models that imply neither of these approaches. Myers [16] labels models in the first and second categories as "static tradeoff" and "pecking order" models, respectively. Those terms are adopted in the brief discussion below.

A. Static Tradeoff Models

In general, static tradeoff models predict that firms maintain a target debt-equity ratio that maximizes firm value by minimizing the costs of prevailing market imperfections. The earliest of these models (e.g., Kraus and Litzenberger [11], Scott [20], and Kim [9]) balance the corporate tax advantages of debt against the cost disadvantages of bankruptcy. Later refinements also incorporate personal taxes and non-debt tax shields (e.g., Miller [12] and DeAngelo and Masulis [2]).

Agency cost theories, though not categorized by Myers, share many of the features of the tax-cum-bankruptcy cost models. In Jensen and Meckling [8], for example, the value of the firm is maximized when total agency costs of debt and external equity are min-

imized. To minimize total agency costs, managers issue both debt and equity and agree to restrictive covenants written into bond indentures (as in Smith and Warner [22]). Hence, firms' unique optimal capital structures involve a balance of debt and equity, even though neither corporate nor personal taxes are assumed to exist.

B. Pecking Order Hypothesis

Myers and Majluf [17] extend Donaldson [4] by assuming that the firm is undervalued because managers have, but cannot reveal, information that the market lacks concerning new and existing investment opportunities. Managers avoid issuing undervalued securities by financing first with internal equity and then with external claims that are least likely to be mispriced. Internal equity is the most preferred source, external equity is the least, and straight and convertible debt are in the middle.[1]

C. Other Models

Like Myers and Majluf, Miller and Rock [13] develop a model in which internal funding strictly dominates external sources. However, unlike Myers and Majluf, Miller and Rock make no distinction between the types of external funds raised because all such sources signal to the market that internal sources have fallen short of projections. Hence, the Miller-Rock model represents the capital structure category in which neither an optimal combination nor an optimal hierarchy of external sources is implied.

The predictions of the foregoing models follow directly from the assumptions used to develop them. The Myers-Majluf and Miller-Rock models assume that corporate taxes do not exist; static tradeoff models assume that investors and managers have equal information about real growth opportunities. Although such assumptions make the models tractable, they oversimplify the conditions under which managers make

---

[1]Hierarchies also could be derived using the Jensen [7] free cash flow hypothesis or the Ross [18] signaling model. The hierarchies in the Jensen and Ross models would run from debt (and preferred stock) to common stock. The assumptions about investment opportunities in Ross [18], Myers and Majluf [17] and Jensen [7] are not the same, however. Ross assumes that the investment decision has already been made but that the market does not understand the true value of the firm; Myers and Majluf assume that because the firm is undervalued managers may refuse to undertake even positive NPV projects; and Jensen assumes the market knows that all positive NPV projects have already been undertaken and that managers must be monitored to keep them from wasting free cash flows.

financing decisions. Thus, the results reported below are unlikely to support any of the models above to the exclusion of the others. Nevertheless, the survey responses indicate that the pecking order hypothesis is more descriptive of how financing decisions are made in practice than are either of the other two alternatives. More descriptive still, however, are conventional financial planning principles.

II. Sampling Procedures

A list of the Fortune 500 firms for 1986 was obtained from the April 27, 1987 edition of *Fortune* magazine. *Standard and Poor's Register of Directors and Executives* was then used to find the names and addresses of the chief financial officer of each firm. A cover letter was enclosed with each questionnaire requesting that the chief financial officer or the officer most familiar with financing procedures answer the nine-question survey.[2]

No attempt was made to identify specific firms that participated. Thus, cross-classifying financing preferences with firm size, industry, or ownership structure is not possible. The reason for proceeding in this manner was to protect the anonymity of the respondents. Conceivably, the decision improved the candor with which the questions were answered and increased the number of usable responses (176) received.[3]

Moreover, some generalizations are possible even if specific firms that participated in the survey are not identified. First, since the Fortune 500 list includes only industrials, there are no utilities and no financial corporations in the sample. Thus, firms that are most heavily regulated and whose financing decisions are least likely to convey new information to the market are excluded. Second, most firms in the sample are large. Only 15 of the entire Fortune 500 list for 1986 had market values of $100 million or lower. Therefore, although financing preferences may differ by firm size,

the sample essentially eliminates the variation attributable to the smallest market value firms.

The bias toward large, successful firms in the sample does limit the inferences that can be drawn. Sampling from a single point in time may impose further restrictions. However, the bias that exists may make the permissible inferences more interesting. For example, large successful firms should have more flexibility than smaller firms to alter their financing mix in response to the enactment of the Tax Reform Act of 1986. Hence, if tax laws are dominant determinants of a firm's capital structure, successful firms will alter their financing mix to increase after-tax cash flows. Similarly, because ownership of the sample firms is likely to be disperse, managers should have incentives to limit the agency costs they bear. Thus, both the tax and the agency cost biases favor a target capital structure over a financing hierarchy.[4]

IV. Sample Results
A. Static Tradeoff vs. Pecking Order and Other Models

Despite the aforementioned biases, 68.8% (121/176) of our survey respondents indicated a preference for the financing hierarchy.[5] Rankings of six sources of long-term funds by respondents who expressed this preference are summarized in Exhibit 1. For each source, the percentage of responses within each rank, the percentage of respondents who did not rank the source, and the mean of the rankings are given. Higher means imply higher preferences.

As indicated, 84.3% of the respondents ranked internal equity as their first choice, while 39.7% ranked external equity as their last choice. The respective mean

---

[2]A copy of the survey is given in the appendix. Respondents were not specifically asked to state their positions with the firms. Consequently, actual decision makers may not have responded in some cases. To the extent that is true, respondents may have answered according to what they think financing policies should be rather than what they are. However, given the inconclusiveness of capital structure theory, it is not clear what the policy should be. Hence, how this potential bias affects the results is unknown.

[3]In total, 203 responses were received. However, 17 firms explained that they no longer respond to survey requests because of increased demands on managerial time, and 10 firms were not publicly traded.

[4]Although agency cost arguments can support either a target capital structure (Jensen and Meckling [8]) or a financing hierarchy (Jensen [7]), the success of the Fortune 500 firms suggests that positive NPV opportunities still exist. Therefore, the costs of free cash flow discussed by Jensen should be less important than the costs discussed in Jensen and Meckling.

[5]Some of the answers were inferred from the responses to question 2. Respondents who expressed a preference for maintaining a target debt-equity ratio were instructed not to answer question 2. Therefore, when question 2 was answered but question 1 was not, an 'intended' response to question 1 was assumed. When only direct answers to question 1 are used, 66.7% (80/120) of the respondents indicated that they follow a financing hierarchy. Because the results for this and other questions are insensitive to these inferences, both direct and inferred answers are reported.

Exhibit 1. Preference Rankings of Long-Term Sources of Funds Among U.S. Industrial Firms that Follow a Financing Hierarchy[a]

Sources by Order of Preference	Percentage of Responses Within Each Rank							Mean[b]
	First	Second	Third	Fourth	Fifth	Sixth	Not Ranked	
1. Internal Equity (Retained Earnings)	84.3	7.4	2.5	0.8	2.5	0.8	1.7	5.61
2. Straight Debt	14.9	71.9	5.0	5.0	1.7	0.8	0.8	4.88
3. Convertible Debt	0.0	2.5	43.0	31.4	9.9	3.3	9.9	3.02
4. External Common Equity	0.0	9.9	23.1	19.0	1.7	39.7	6.6	2.42
5. Straight Preferred Stock	0.0	4.1	16.5	15.7	37.2	14.0	12.4	2.22
6. Convertible Preferred Stock	0.0	2.5	3.3	15.7	33.1	33.1	12.4	1.72

[a]In total, 121 firms indicated they follow a financing hierarchy, while 47 indicated they seek to maintain a target capital structure. These estimates include both direct and inferred answers. When only direct answers are used, the numbers following the financing hierarchy and target capital structure are 80 and 40, respectively. The percentages given in the table are immaterially different from the percentages that obtain for the 80 firms.

[b]Means are calculated by assigning scores of 6 through 1 for rankings from 1 through 6, respectively, and by multiplying each score by the fraction of responses within each rank. A score of 0 is assigned when a source is not ranked.

rankings for the common equity alternatives are 5.61 and 2.42. Similarly, straight debt dominates convertible debt. The mean ranks are 4.88 and 3.02. For debt and common equity, therefore, the pattern depicted in Exhibit 1 conforms to the Myers-Majluf [17] predictions—managers who follow a financing hierarchy prefer internal equity, then straight debt, then convertible debt, and finally new common stock.[6]

On the other hand, the rankings of straight and convertible preferred stock are more difficult to interpret. Straight preferred is more popular than convertible preferred, as the respective mean ranks of 2.22 and 1.72 indicate. But, judging from those means, preferred stock financing of any sort is less appealing than financing with external common stock. This finding is inconsistent with the pecking order hypothesis as it currently stands.[7]

B. Specific Capital Structure Models and Planning Principles

A better understanding of the relative significance of specific capital structure theories can be gained by examining managers' rankings of 11 inputs and/or assumptions often found in theoretical models. Exhibit 2 summarizes those rankings. The format is the same as the format for Exhibit 1; the percentages here, however, are based on the full sample.

Information Conveyance Models Of all the inputs in Exhibit 2, the projected cash flow of the assets to be financed (4.41), avoiding dilution of common shareholders' claims (3.94), and the risk of the new asset (3.91) have the highest mean ranks. Since two of these factors relate to the new project, the findings strongly suggest that corporate managers evaluate investment and financing decisions simultaneously. Hence, these decisions are not independent and security price reactions to capital structure changes may reflect a

---

[6]If managers move to the target capital structure by following a hierarchy, these two concepts need not be mutually exclusive. However, the process envisioned by Myers [16] and the responses above seem to imply that most managers do not even seek the target capital structure because the process is dynamic, not static.

[7]This finding may indicate that industrial managers resort to preferred stock mainly for specialized needs, such as acquisition or reorganization. (See Dewing [3, pp. 131–134].)

Exhibit 2. Relative Importance of Capital Structure Model Inputs and/or Assumptions in Governing Financing Decisions of Major U.S. Industrial Firms

	Percentage of Responses Within Each Rank[a]						
Inputs/Assumptions by Order of Importance	Unimportant	2	3	4	Important	Not Ranked	Mean[b]
1. Projected cash flow from asset to be financed	1.7	1.1	9.7	29.5	58.0	0.0	4.41
2. Avoiding dilution of common shareholders' claims	2.8	6.3	18.2	39.8	33.0	0.0	3.94
3. Risk of asset to be financed	2.8	6.3	20.5	36.9	33.0	0.6	3.91
4. Restrictive covenants on senior securities	9.1	9.7	18.7	35.2	27.3	0.0	3.62
5. Avoiding mispricings of securities to be issued	3.4	10.8	27.3	39.8	18.7	0.0	3.60
6. Corporate tax rate	4.0	9.7	29.5	42.6	13.1	1.1	3.52
7. Voting control	17.6	10.8	21.0	31.2	19.3	0.0	3.24
8. Depreciation and other non-debt tax shields	8.5	17.6	40.9	24.4	7.4	1.1	3.05
9. Correcting mispricings of out-standing securities	14.8	27.8	36.4	14.2	5.1	1.7	2.66
10. Personal tax rates of debt and equity holders	31.2	34.1	25.6	8.0	1.1	0.0	2.14
11. Bankruptcy costs	69.3	13.1	6.8	4.0	4.5	2.3	1.58

[a]These estimates are based on 176 responses.

[b]Means are calculated by assigning scores of 1 through 5 for rankings from "unimportant" to "important," respectively, and by multiplying each score by the fraction of responses within each rank. A score of 0 is assigned when a source is not ranked.

revision in market expectations of the firm's operating performance.[8]

Moreover, a series of questions that asked managers to indicate to what extent they felt their securities were correctly priced also produced results suggestive of a signaling scenario. Although almost half of the managers (47.2%) indicated their securities were correctly priced more than 80% of the time, another 40.3% indicated fair pricing between 50 and 80% of the time, and 11.9% said their securities were correctly priced less than 50% of the time. Thus, many managers disagree with the notion of efficient markets at least part of the time.

Despite theses perceptions, however, managers may not deliberately attempt to signal their firms' true value.

___

[8]This finding also points to the "residual equity method" in evaluating asset choices. See Solomon [23] and Taggart [24] for a discussion of this approach.

The low mean rank in Exhibit 2 on correcting mispricings of outstanding securities (2.66) is inconsistent with an overt signal. Therefore, the relation between the perceptions of market efficiency and managers' rankings of the factors in Exhibit 2 were cross-classified to determine whether financing choices are affected by managers perceptions of fair market prices.

Market efficiency responses were grouped by whether managers believe their securities are correctly priced more than 80% of the time or 80% or less. Exhibit 2 responses were also categorized into 'low' (ranks 1 and 2), 'medium' (rank 3), and 'high' (ranks 4 and 5) ranges. Then, two Pearson chi-square statistics were computed, based first on the high, medium, and low ranges and then on the high and the low.

The p-values for these statistics represent the probability of incorrectly inferring an association between managers' perceptions of market efficiency and the importance assigned to the factors in Exhibit 2. Ideally, such probabilities should be low. However, only two of the factors had p-values of 0.100 or lower.[9] Specifically, perceptions of market efficiency appear to influence the importance assigned to risk (p-values = 0.065 and 0.021) and to the restrictive covenants on senior securities (p-values = 0.194 and 0.071). Almost all of the managers (95%) who said the market is inefficient also said that asset risk is highly important. In comparison, 82% of the managers who believe the market is efficient categorize risk as highly important. The corresponding fractions for the restrictive covenants are 0.83 and 0.70.

Although the above fractions are statistically higher when managers believe the market is inefficient, they are not low even when managers perceive their securities to be correctly priced. Thus, perceptions of market efficiency appear to have little impact on financing decisions, and deliberate signals of firm value through the debt-equity choice seem unlikely.[10]

Tax-Cum-Bankruptcy Cost and Other Static Trade-off Models Of the three capital structure categories discussed above, the static tradeoff models seem least well supported by the data in Exhibit 2. From these models, restrictive covenants on senior securities, the corporate tax rate, voting control, and depreciation and other non-debt tax shields are the most important inputs. Nevertheless, the respective mean ranks of 3.62, 3.52, 3.24, and 3.05 indicate only moderate concern for these factors. (Boquist and Moore [1] also find little support for the hypothesis that non-debt tax shields help determine the debt-equity choice at the individual firm level.) The mean ranks for the personal tax rates of debt and equity holders (2.14) and for bankruptcy costs (1.58) are even less supportive of the static tradeoff theories.

Although the low ranking of bankruptcy costs is not surprising given the size and success of the firms in our sample, the extensive treatment of tax arguments in the finance literature coupled with the recent major changes in the tax law suggest that taxes should be more important to managers in making financing decisions. Nevertheless, responses to a separate series of questions

relating to the Tax Reform Act of 1986 indicate that the relative rankings above are accurate.

The first question of that series asked what effect the Tax Reform Act would have on after-tax cash flows. Half of the managers indicated their cash flows would increase, 26.7% indicated a decrease, and 22.7% indicated the Act would have no effect. Asked next how their capital structure was likely to change as a result of the Tax Reform Act, 82.4% of the managers indicated no revision in their capital structure would be made. Of the managers indicating no change, 83.4% said other factors are more important than tax laws in determining their financing mix. Additionally, 4.8% said that no change would be made because tax laws could change again soon; 0.7% indicated that changes had already been made in anticipation of the new tax law; 3.4% indicated that the precise implications of the tax law were not clear; and 7.6% listed a combination of the above reasons or did not respond to the question. Hence, tax factors do not appear to be the fundamental determinants of the debt-equity choice even for the large, successful firms in our sample.

Financial Planning Principles Managers' relative disinclination toward capital structure theory, in general, is further reflected in their rankings of seven financial planning principles summarized in Exhibit 3. Five of the seven principles there have mean ranks of 3.90 or higher. In contrast, only 3 of the 11 inputs in Exhibit 2 had mean ranks that high. Financial planning principles, therefore, dominate specific capital structure models in governing financing decisions for the firms in the sample. This finding is underscored by the observation from Exhibit 3 that maximizing security prices also has a lower mean rank (3.99) than three of the other financial planning principles. Given these findings and the absence of a strong relation between managers' perceptions of market efficiency and the importance attached to information factors in Exhibit 2, the evidence suggests that the projected cash flow, risk of the assets to be financed, and avoiding dilution of common shareholders' claims are more closely associated with financial planning principles than with information-related capital structure theories.

C. Factors Governing Preferences for Specific Financing Sources

Spearman rank correlations between the preferences listed in Exhibit 1 and the relative rankings listed in Exhibits 2 and 3 were calculated to determine which of the planning principles and/or capital structure inputs

---

[9]The probability of observing at least two significant factors at the 0.100 level by random chance alone is 0.910. Therefore, the association between managers' perception of market efficiency and capital structure inputs is dubious.

[10]A chi-square statistic was also computed to determine whether managers' perceptions of market efficiency influence their preference for a target capital structure or a financing hierarchy. The p-value for that test (0.453) indicates that perceived mispricings are not critical determinants of that choice.

Exhibit 3. Relative Importance of Various Financial Planning Principles in Governing Financing Decisions of Major U.S. Industrial Firms

Planning Principle by Order of Importance	Percentage of Responses Within Each Rank[a]						Mean[b]
	Unimportant	2	3	4	Important	Not Ranked	
1. Maintaining financial flexibility	0.6	0.0	4.5	33.0	61.4	0.6	4.55
2. Ensuring long-term survivability	4.0	1.7	6.8	10.8	76.7	0.0	4.55
3. Maintaining a predictable source of funds	1.7	2.8	20.5	39.2	35.8	0.0	4.05
4. Maximizing security prices	3.4	4.5	19.3	33.5	37.5	1.7	3.99
5. Maintaining financial independence	3.4	4.5	22.2	27.3	40.9	1.7	3.99
6. Maintaining a high debt rating	2.3	9.1	32.4	43.2	13.1	0.0	3.56
7. Maintaining comparability with other firms in the industry	15.9	36.9	33.0	10.8	2.8	0.6	2.47

[a]These estimates are based on 176 responses.

[b]Means are calculated by assigning scores of 1 through 5 for rankings from "unimportant" to "important," respectively, and by multiplying each score by the fraction of responses within each rank. A score of 0 is assigned when a source is not ranked.

guide the selection of each funding source. Significant correlations are reported in Exhibit 4.[11] The funding source, the factor that is significant, and the direction of the relation are listed in the first through third columns, respectively.

For internal equity and convertible preferred stock, no significant correlations exist. The lack of variation in the preferences reported in Exhibit 1 for these sources may explain this finding.[12] In contrast, the negative relation between managerial preferences for external equity and avoiding dilution of common shareholders' claims suggests that dilution deters new equity issues. Straight debt is used to maximize security prices; none of the theoretical factors, however, has a significant correlation. Preferences for convertible debt relate negatively to the importance attached to expected cash flows from new assets and positively to maintaining the long-term survivability of the firm. These relations

suggest that managers concerned about 'hanging' the convertible because of cash flow shortages in early stages of an asset's life nonetheless issue the debt if the investment is crucial to the firm's long-run survivability. Finally, the negative correlation between the preference for straight preferred stock and the importance assigned to maintaining comparability with other firms is consistent with the explanation (given in footnote 7) that preferred stock is used mainly for specialized needs.

Although the above explanations are plausible, they are also almost certainly oversimplified. By definition, the judgment required to make sound financing decisions implies that managers balance the need to avoid dilution against (for example) the need to grow and to maintain financial flexibility. Hence, multiple factors bear on the financing choice, and several financing alternatives may be considered simultaneously. Perhaps such complexities explain why managers are guided more by planning principles than by the implied precision of our theoretical models.[13]

[11]The significance level is 0.05. Obviously, more correlations are significant at the 0.10 level; however, interpreting those correlations is more difficult because higher significance levels induce more "noise."

[12]The same argument explains why maintaining financial flexibility in Exhibit 3 is uncorrelated with any of the financing sources in Exhibit 1. Over 94% of the respondents ranked maintaining financial flexibility as being very important (i.e., as a 4 or a 5). The lack of variability in the responses concerning internal equity and financial flexibility suggests something akin to an identity: internal equity is the most preferred source because it provides the greatest flexibility.

[13]It is possible that planning principles frequently cause managers to finance their firms in ways predicted by capital structure models even though the principles—not the models—provide the motivation. For example, Kim and Sorensen [10] present evidence that supports Myers [15] and many of the tax-cum-bankruptcy cost models. However, the irresponsiveness of most managers in this sample to changes induced by the Tax Reform Act illustrates why knowing the motivation for financing decisions is important.

Exhibit 4. Significant Correlations Between Managerial Preferences for Funding Sources and the Perceived Importance of Capital Structure Model Inputs and/or Financial Planning Principles[a]

Funding Source	Capital Structure Input or Planning Principle	Direction of Relationship
Internal Equity	None	NA
External Common Equity	Avoiding Dilution	Negative
Straight Debt	Maximizing Security Prices	Positive
Convertible Debt	Cash Flow Survivability	Negative Positive
Straight Preferred	Comparability	Negative
Convertible Preferred	None	NA

[a]The correlations are calculated with the nonparametric Spearman rank statistic, and the significance level is 0.05.

D. Financing Decisions and Other Sources and Uses of Funds

The importance of capital structure decisions (in general) relative to other decisions managers make can be assessed by examining responses relating to firms' sources and uses of funds. When presented with an attractive new growth opportunity that could not be undertaken without departing from the target capital structure or financing hierarchy, cutting the dividend, or selling off other assets, 82.4% of the managers indicated they would deviate from their target capital structure or financing hierarchy. In contrast, 1.7% said they would cut the dividend, and 3.4% said they would forgo the investment opportunity. The remainder said they would sell off other assets or pursue some combination of all the alternatives. Thus, the financing decision is the most flexible of all the sources and uses of funds constraints. That is, it is least binding. To the extent this is true and to the extent motivations for capital structure changes are complex and imprecise, interpreting common stock price responses to unanticipated capital structure changes will continue to pose difficult challenges to finance researchers.

IV. Conclusion

Corporate managers in this sample are more likely to follow a financing hierarchy than to maintain a target debt-equity ratio. Further, models based on corporate and/or personal taxes and bankruptcy and other leverage-related costs are not as useful in determining the financing mix as are models that suggest that new financing reveals aspects of the firm's marginal asset performance. However, the importance managers attach to specific capital structure theories is not related to managerial perceptions of market efficiency. Thus, most managers do not overtly signal firm value through capital structure adjustments. In general, financial planning principles are more important in governing the financing decisions of the firm than are specific capital structure theories. Moreover, the capital structure decision, per se, is less binding than either the investment or the dividend decision of the firm.

References

1. J.A. Boquist and W.T. Moore, "Interindustry Leverage Differences and the DeAngelo-Masulis Tax Shield Hypothesis," *Financial Management* (Spring 1984), pp. 5–9.
2. H. DeAngelo and R.W. Masulis, "Optimal Capital Structure Under Corporate and Personal Taxation," *Journal of Financial Economics* (June 1980), pp. 3–29.
3. A. Dewing, *Financial Policies of Corporations*, 5th ed., New York, Ronald Press, 1953.
4. G. Donaldson, *Corporate Debt Capacity: A Study of Corporate Debt Policy and the Determination of Corporate Debt Capacity*, Boston, Division of Research, Harvard School of Business, 1961.
5. E. Fama, "Agency Problems and the Theory of the Firm," *Journal of Political Economy* (April 1980), pp. 288–307.
6. R.A. Haugen and L.W. Senbet, "The Insignificance of Bankruptcy Costs to the Theory of Optimal Capital Structure," *Journal of Finance* (May 1978), pp. 383–393.
7. M.C. Jensen, "Agency Costs of Free Cash Flow, Corporate Finance, and Takeovers," *American Economic Review* (May 1986), pp. 323–329.
8. M.C. Jensen and W.H. Meckling, "Theory of the Firm: Managerial Behavior, Agency Costs and Ownership Structure," *Journal of Financial Economics* (October 1976), pp. 305–360.
9. E.H. Kim, "A Mean Variance Theory of Optimal Capital Structure and Corporate Debt Capacity," *Journal of Finance* (March 1978), pp. 45-64.
10. W.S. Kim and E.H. Sorensen, "Evidence on the Impact of the Agency Costs of Debt on Corporate Debt Policy," *Journal of Financial and Quantitative Analysis* (June 1986), pp. 131–144.
11. A. Kraus and R.H. Litzenberger, "A State Preference Model of Optimal Financial Leverage," *Journal of Finance* (September 1973), pp. 911–922.
12. M.H. Miller, "Debt and Taxes," *Journal of Finance* (May 1977), pp. 261–276.
13. M.H. Miller and K. Rock, "Dividend Policy Under Asymmetric Information," *Journal of Finance* (September 1985), pp. 1031–1051.

14. F. Modigliani and M.H. Miller, "The Cost of Capital, Corporation Finance, and the Theory of Investment," *American Economic Review* (June 1958), pp. 261–297.

15. S.C. Myers, "Determinants of Corporate Borrowing," *Journal of Financial Economics* (November 1977), pp. 147–176.

16. ———, "The Capital Structure Puzzle," *Journal of Finance* (July 1984), pp. 575–592.

17. S.C. Myers and N.S. Majluf, "Corporate Financing and Investment Decisions When Firms Have Information That Investors Do Not Have," *Journal of Financial Economics* (June 1984), pp. 187–221.

18. S.A. Ross, "The Determination of Financial Structure: The Incentive Signalling Approach," *Bell Journal of Economics* (Spring 1977), pp. 23–40.

19. D.F. Scott, Jr. and D.J. Johnson, "Financing Policies and Practices in Large Corporations," *Financial Management* (Summer 1982), pp. 51–59.

20. J.H. Scott, "A Theory of Optimal Capital Structure," *Bell Journal of Economics* (Spring 1976), pp. 33–54.

21. C.W. Smith, "Investment Banking and the Capital Acquisition Process," *Journal of Financial Economics* (January/February 1986), pp. 3–25.

22. C.W. Smith and J.B. Warner, "On Financial Contracting: An Analysis of Bond Covenants," *Journal of Financial Economics* (June 1979), pp.117–161.

23. E. Solomon, *The Theory of Financial Management*, New York, Columbia University Press, 1963.

24. R.A. Taggart, Jr., "Capital Budgeting and the Financing Decision: An Exposition," *Financial Management* (Summer 1977), pp. 59–64.

25. S. Titman, "The Effect of Capital Structure on a Firm's Liquidation Decision," *Journal of Financial Economics* (March 1984), pp. 137–151.

Appendix

The following is a reproduction of the survey sent to chief financial officers.

Instructions Please answer the following questions as they relate to decisions you make in raising new long-term funds.

1. In raising new funds, your firm

   a. Seeks to maintain a target capital structure by using approximately constant proportions of several types of long-term capital simultaneously. (Answer questions 3 through 9.)

   b. Follows a hierarchy in which the most advantageous sources of funds are exhausted before other sources are used. (Answer questions 2 through 9.)

2. Rank the following sources of long-term funds in order of preference for financing new investments (1 = first choice, 6 = last choice).
   Rank

   a. ___ Internal equity (retained earnings)

   b. ___ External common equity

   c. ___ Straight debt

   d. ___ Convertible debt

   e. ___ Straight preferred stock

   f. ___ Convertible preferred stock

3. Please indicate the relative importance of the following considerations in governing your firm's financing decisions. On a scale of 1 to 5, where 1 = Unimportant and 5 = Important.)

   a. ___ Maximizing prices of publicly traded securities

   b. ___ Maintaining financial flexibility

   c. ___ Ensuring long-term survivability of the firm

   d. ___ Maintaining financial independence

   e. ___ Maintaining comparability with firms in the industry

   f. ___ Maintaining a high debt rating

   g. ___ Maintaining a predictable source of funds

4. Approximately what percent of the time would you estimate that your firm's outstanding securities are priced fairly by the market?

   a. More than 80 percent of the time

   b. Between 50 and 80 percent of the time

   c. Less than 50 percent of the time

5. Given an attractive new growth opportunity that could not be taken without departing from your target capital structure or financing hierarchy, cutting the dividend, or selling off other assets, what action is your firm most likely to take?

   a. Forgo the growth opportunity.

   b. Deviate from the target capital structure or financing hierarchy.

   c. Cut the dividend.

   d. Sell off other assets.

6. Indicate the relative importance of the following factors in governing your firm's financing decisions. (On a scale of 1 to 5, where 1 = Unimportant and 5 = Important.)

a. ___ The corporate tax rate

b. ___ Personal tax rates of your debt and equity holders

c. ___ The level of depreciation and other non-debt tax shields

d. ___ Costs of bankruptcy

e. ___ Voting control

f. ___ Restrictive covenants of senior securities

g. ___ Projected cash flow or earnings from the assets to be financed

h. ___ Riskiness of the assets to be financed

i. ___ Avoiding dilution of common shareholders' claims

j. ___ Avoiding mispricings of securities to be issued

k. ___ Correcting mispricings of outstanding securities

7. Other things held constant, the Tax Reform Act of 1986 will have the effect of

a. Increasing your firm's after-tax cash flows.

b. Decreasing your firm's after-tax cash flows.

c. Leaving your firm's after-tax cash flows unchanged.

8. As a result of the Tax Reform Act of 1986, your firm is likely to

a. Increase the proportion of debt used in the capital structure.

b. Decrease the proportion of debt used in the capital structure.

c. Leave the proportion of debt used in the capital structure unchanged.

9. If your firm does not plan to alter the proportion of debt currently used in its capital structure as a result of the Tax Reform Act of 1986, which of the following explanations most closely corresponds to your reasons?

a. Tax laws could be changed again soon.

b. Changes have already been made in the capital structure in anticipation of the Tax Reform Act of 1986.

c. The precise implications of the Tax Reform Act of 1986 are not clear.

d. Other factors are more important than tax laws in determining your capital structure.

Section IV
Changes of Corporate Form

As we have seen in previous sections, the revolution in debt financing has been accompanied by vast changes in capital structure. During the same period, the market for control of firms has undergone a dramatic change as well. The 1980s witnessed one of the greatest mergers waves in history, with the consolidation of many firms and the control of many corporations passing into the hands of private interests. Some observers find an essential link between the debt revolution and the changes in corporate form. This section considers the recent activity in mergers, acquisitions, and bankruptcies.

One of the most prevalent types of mergers in recent years has been the leveraged buyout or LBO. In essence, a leveraged buyout is the acquisition of a target firm that occurs when the acquisition is financed largely with debt. In most cases, the target firm is taken private, so that shares of the target firm no longer are available to the public.

In her article, "The Causes and Consequences of Leveraged Buyouts," Michelle R. Garfinkel explores the concept of the LBO in greater detail. She also presents statistics showing the extent of LBO activity. Many critics have called into question the benefits of LBOs from a social point of view. Garfinkel weighs these concerns and concludes that they may have some validity. However, she also notes that LBOs are not inherently evil or totally lacking in genuine social benefits as some critics seem to maintain.

In his article, "LBOs and Conflicts of Interest," William P. Osterberg focuses on a particular feature of LBOs—the potential conflict among stockholders, creditors, managers, and employees. Without doubt, LBOs can generate changes in the distribution of wealth. For example, an LBO can enrich the parties that buy the corporation at the expense of the existing management. By the same token, LBOs may have benefits by creating a more efficient organizational form. Osterberg explores these issues and shows who is likely to be hurt and who is likely to benefit by LBOs.

In "Hostile Takeovers and the Market for Corporate Control," Diane L. Fortier pursues the issues of wealth creation and wealth redistribution with a focus on hostile takeovers. A hostile takeover is a merger in which the existing management of the target firm attempts to prevent the merger. Fortier investigates whether hostile takeovers create new wealth, perhaps by creating a more efficient corporate form, or whether hostile takeovers merely redistribute existing wealth. On the whole, she concludes that the evidence is mixed.

Besides mergers, firms change their corporate form by passing out of existence in bankruptcies. Currently, we are witnessing a wave of bankruptcies among financial institutions, and there has been a number of significant bankruptcies or near bankruptcies among firms associated with the merger wave of the 1980s. In "The Corporate Bankruptcy Decision," Michelle J. White begins by pointing out that firms voluntarily declare bankruptcy, at least for the most part. Therefore, firms really can decide to go bankrupt. Very recently, for example, Continental Airlines declared bankruptcy to seek protection from its creditors while it attempts to reorganize. Similarly, the already bankrupt Eastern Airlines has been in the news as it struggles to stay alive and straighten out its finances. As a last airline example, Pan Am declared bankruptcy in early 1991.

White reviews the recent history of bankruptcies in the United States and discusses the different kinds of bankruptcies. For example, firms can declare bankruptcy and simply liquidate, or they may declare bankruptcy to seek protection from creditors as they attempt to reorganize. White concentrates on the economic efficiency (or lack of efficiency) in U.S. bankruptcy law.

Article 11

Michelle R. Garfinkel

Michelle R. Garfinkel is an economist at the Federal Reserve Bank of St. Louis. Thomas A. Pollmann provided research assistance

The Causes and Consequences of Leveraged Buyouts

IN THE MARKET for corporate control during the past decade, leveraged buyouts have become increasingly popular. Many observers, speculating about the causes of this recent trend, have expressed concern about the potential problems arising from such activity.[1] Implicit in many casual discussions is the assumption that leveraged buyouts—hereafter LBOs—are merely some type of cosmetic surgery. That is, an LBO has no impact on the productive capacity of the target firm, while unjustifiably inflating the value of the stock.

Under this assumption, any observed gains to the existing shareholders of the target firm are likely to be matched, if not dominated, by losses to others; since there is no net gain and possibly a loss to society, LBO activity should be restricted. Some analysts also argue that LBOs have contributed to the unprecedented growth of outstanding debt in recent years. If, as many contend, the large growth in debt is associated with increased instability in the financial system, public policy might aim to reverse or at least curb debt growth. In addition, tax reform might be an appropriate way to reduce this

debt growth, if it stems chiefly from tax incentives.

This article examines whether LBOs have had a productive impact on the target firm. If economic theory and evidence suggest that LBOs generally are productive, then arguments for legal restrictions on LBO activity are less persuasive. Alternatively, if there are few, if any, gains from LBOs, the idea that LBOs pose a problem for the economy might be valid.

WHAT ARE LBOs?

Despite the ever-expanding literature on LBOs, there does not appear to be a single, clear definition of what an LBO really is. Loosely speaking, an LBO is simply the purchase of a firm by an outside individual, another firm or the incumbent management with the purchase being financed by large amounts of debt; the resulting firm is said to be "highly leveraged." The target firm can be a free-standing entity or a division of a public corporation.[2] Although the target of the LBO can be a private firm, recent discussions about LBO activity have focused primarily

---

[1]For example, see Lowenstein (1986), "When Industry Borrows Itself" (1988), Friedman (1989) and Kaufman (1989).

[2]When the target of an LBO is a division of a public company, the transaction is typically called a "management buyout." Stancill (1988), p. 18, who points out that LBO activity targeting smaller (private) firms is not a new

phenomenon, provides a very general definition of an LBO: "whenever a buyer lacks the requisite cash and borrows part of the purchase price against the target company's assets (receivables, equipment, inventory, real estate) or cash flow (future cash), that's an LBO."

on instances in which a public firm is taken private.[3] Upon this type of transaction, the target firm's stock shares are no longer traded publicly in equity markets.

The greatest ambiguity about what constitutes an LBO concerns the degree to which the purchase is financed with debt.[4] Typically, debt finance provides about 80 percent to 90 percent of the funds for the purchase. Equity finance, in which the resulting shares are held by the purchasers of the target firm and, often, an outside investment group, provides the remaining funds.[5]

Debt Finance in an LBO

Two types of debt are usually employed in an LBO transaction: senior debt and subordinated debt. Senior debt typically accounts for the greatest proportion, usually 50 percent to 60 percent, of financing for the LBO. Sometimes called secured debt, senior debt specifies a lien on a particular piece of property. In the case that the firm's earnings are insufficient to service the firm's debt obligations fully, the holders of senior debt can have the pledged property sold to recover the unpaid interest and principal. Funds through senior debt are often provided by commercial banks, insurance companies, leasing companies and limited partnerships specializing in LBOs and venture capital investments.[6]

Subordinated debt, or "mezzanine" debt, is considered to be more speculative than senior debt because it is issued without a lien against specified property. Although the holders of subordinated debt are protected in the case of default, only assets not pledged explicitly and any cash remaining after paying other creditors are available to satisfy these unsecured claims. Accounting for about 30 percent of the financing for the transaction, subordinated debt is usually provided by pension funds, insurance companies and limited partnerships.[7]

In many LBOs, after the purchase, the new owners sell some of the firm's assets and use the proceeds to retire some of the debt. Cash flows from continued operations are used to service the remaining debt obligations.

Key Features of Recent LBOs

The typical LBO in recent years has two interesting characteristics that distinguish it from other takeover and merger activities. First, the equity of the target firm usually is held by fewer individuals following the financial reorganization. This increased concentration of ownership is especially typical of a "going-private" transaction in which the stock is no longer publicly traded.[8]

Second, although alternative sources of funds are available to obtain corporate ownership, going-private transactions usually are financed heavily with debt, leaving the target firm in a highly leveraged position. In essence, the transaction involves a substitution of debt for equity. For example, in a sample of 58 LBOs between 1980 to 1984, the average debt-to-equity ratio rose from 0.457 to 5.524, a percentage change exceeding 1100 percent.[9]

The higher degree of leveraging means that a larger proportion of claims against the target firm's assets and operations are fixed obligations. Because holders of these claims can push the firm into bankruptcy if these obligations are not met fully, the greater leveraging, holding all else constant, erodes the target firm's insulation from unexpected declines in earnings and, hence, increases the firm's risk of bankruptcy.

RECENT TRENDS IN LBO ACTIVITY

The following discussion defines an LBO as a highly leveraged, going-private transaction. This

[3]See Lehn and Poulsen (1988, 1989) and "Corporate America Snuggles Up to the Buy-Out Wolves" (1988), for example. DeAngelo, DeAngelo and Rice (1984), p. 370, use a narrower definition by making a distinction between pure going-private transactions, where "incumbent management seeks complete equity ownership of the surviving corporation," and leveraged buyouts, where "management proposes to share equity ownership in the subsequent private firm with third-party investors."

[4]The Federal Reserve Board recently established a set of guidelines for banks involved in a broader class of leveraged financing, called "highly leveraged financing." This class of leveraging includes all borrowers having debt-to-

total-asset ratios exceeding 75 percent. See "Board Issues Guidelines for LBO, Other Highly Leveraged Loans ..." (1989). Although LBOs are included in this class, they have not been specifically defined by the Federal Reserve System.

[5]Thomson (1989) and Lehn and Poulsen (1988, 1989).

[6]Ibid.

[7]Ibid.

[8]Many of these firms, however, subsequently go public.

[9]Lehn and Poulsen (1988), table 2, p. 48.

Table 1

**LBO Activity, 1979-88: Going Private Transactions
(dollar amounts in millions)**

Year	Number of transactions	Median purchase price	Total dollar value paid
1979	16	$ 7.9	$ 636.0
1980	13	25.3	967.4
1981	17	41.1	2,338.5
1982	31	29.6	2,836.7
1983	36	77.8	7,145.4
1984	57	66.9	10,805.9
1985	76	72.6	24,139.8
1986	76	84.5	20,232.4
1987	47	123.3	22,057.1
1988	125	79.8	60,920.6

SOURCE: Merrill Lynch Business Brokerage and Valuation, Inc. *Mergerstat Review* (1988), p. 92.

NOTE: These numbers do not include management buyouts. See Merrill Lynch Business Brokerage and Valuation, Inc. (1988), p. 82.

Table 2

Premium Paid Over Market Price in LBOs

Year	Average	Median
1979	106.4%	65.6%
1980	49.2	36.2
1981	31.3	26.7
1982	41.4	38.6
1983	36.7	31.3
1984	36.3	33.7
1985	30.9	25.7
1986	31.9	26.1
1987	34.8	30.9
1988	33.8	26.3

SOURCE: Merrill Lynch Business Brokerage and Valuation, Inc., *Mergerstat Review* (1988), p. 92.

NOTE: Premiums over the market price were calculated on the basis of the market value of the firm's closing stock price five days before the initial announcement. These data are for going-private transactions only.

narrow focus permits the discussion to address recent concerns about LBO activity that appear to revolve around those transactions in which public firms are taken private primarily through debt financing.

As shown in table 1, the number of going-private transactions in 1988 was nearly eight times that in 1979.[10] Just in the past year, the incidence of these transactions has more than doubled. Furthermore, the table indicates that the average as well as the median purchase price rose dramatically over the same period. In 1979, the average purchase price was $39.8 million, whereas in 1988 it was $487.4 million. The average purchase price rose at an annual rate of 32.1 percent, nearly three times the 11.1 percent annual rate of increase in the value of

firms included in the New York Stock Exchange. Even accounting for inflation, the increase in the average purchase price was substantial—from $50.6 million to $400.5 million in 1982 prices, a real annual growth rate of 25.8 percent.

While the average purchase price generally rose during the 1980s, the "premium" or the price paid for these firms above their initial market value (the value of their stock shares before the initial announcement) as a percentage of the market value has been relatively stable. As table 2 shows, average and median premiums paid over the prior market price of the target firms from 1979 to 1988 have been quite large. Even excluding the extremely large 1979 values, the average and median premiums averaged about 36.3 percent and 30.6 percent, respectively.[11] These large premiums indicate

[10]Merrill Lynch Business Brokerage and Valuation, Inc. (1988) reports, "Like the majority of unit management buyouts, most, if not all, of the 'going private' transactions also are leveraged buyouts, i.e., transactions in which the buyers put up only a small part of the purchase price and borrow the rest." (p. 91) Management buyouts have also increased less markedly, from 59 in 1979 to 89 in 1988. See Merrill Lynch Business Brokerage and Valuation, Inc. (1988), p. 82.

[11]Lehn and Poulsen (1988), table 5, p. 52, report the premiums, as determined in the market, for the target firms of LBOs included in the COMPUSTAT data tape be-

tween 1980 and 1984. The "market-valued" premium was measured as the percentage increase in the stock price from 20 days before the LBO announcement until the day of the announcement for LBOs between 1980 and 1984. They find that market-valued premium as a percentage of the market price before the announcement averaged 39.5 percent, ranging from 1.7 percent to 120 percent. During the same period, the "cash-offer" premium (the cash offer above the market price 20 days before the announcement) as a fraction of the market price ranged from 2 percent to 120 percent, averaging 41 percent. The sample standard deviation of both these premiums was 23.2 percent.

that the target firm's stockholders have captured significant capital gains upon the LBO transaction.[12]

ARE LBOs PRODUCTIVE?—SOME FINANCE THEORY AND EVIDENCE

The growing incidence of LBO activity in the market for corporate control has sparked many to question the social value of this activity. Many expressed concerns are predicated implicitly on the notion that the changes in the firm's financial structure associated with the LBO transaction have no positive real effects on that firm's output. If the transaction were merely a device to realize some short-term gain, at the expense of long-term growth and a reduction in social wealth, then these concerns would be justified.

Finance theory, however, suggests that LBOs *can* be productive. The gains derive from two key features of LBOs in recent years—namely, going private and highly leveraged financing. These related features permit a reorganization of the firm to alter its incentive structure and produce an increase in its earnings potential.

The Advantages of Going Private

The theory of corporate finance shows how the distinction between ownership and control, or equivalently the differences between the incentives and constraints of the firm's stockholders and those of the firm's managers, can have important implications for the performance of the firm. Specifically, this distinction can create a situation in which the firm does not achieve its maximum earnings potential—

that is, the firm is not being run efficiently from the stockholder's perspective.[13] By going private, the distinction is removed and earnings can increase.[14]

If the manager's actions were monitored easily and costlessly, going-private transactions would have no implications for the performance of the firm. A contract for compensating the manager could be designed by the owners to encourage the manager to act entirely on their behalf. The ideal contract would specify the appropriate actions to be taken by the manager to maximize the firm's value under all possible contingencies; the contract would penalize the manager if he failed to act in accordance with its specifications, thereby ensuring that the manager always acted in the interests of the owners.

The efficacy of such contracts, however, hinges on the ability and costs of monitoring. Typically, the firm's owners do not observe the actions of the managers directly, nor are they fully aware of the economic environment (specific to the firm) in which a manager's decisions are made. For example, owners do not have complete information about the firm's opportunities for investment and growth or about the daily events that influence a manager's decisions. Holding all else constant, as the number of the holders of the firm's stock increases,—that is, as the firm's ownership becomes more dispersed—the potential gains realized by one owner monitoring the manager's actions decline, because the potential net gains that the individual can capture become smaller relative to the costs he incurs. In this case, monitoring activity declines and contracts designed to align the man-

---

[12]Also, see DeAngelo, DeAngelo and Rice (1984), Torabzadeh and Bertin (1987) and Lehn and Poulsen (1988, 1989), who find that announcements of LBOs have significant positive effects on the target firm's stock price. For example, Lehn and Poulsen (1989, p. 776) calculate the average daily return from holding the stock of the target firm of the LBO for various holding periods, abstracting from movements in the firm's stock price due to economy-wide factors. They find that the "cumulative average daily abnormal return" (CAR) from 20 days before to 20 days after the LBO announcement averaged 20.54 percent across the firms included in the sample during the period 1980-87. This means that an individual buying a stock of an LBO target 20 days before the announcement and then selling it 20 days after the announcement could have made a 20.5 percent return on average above a normal (the market) return over the same period. Even holding the stock from one day before the announcement until the end of the announcement day yielded, on average, a CAR of 16.3 percent, a return too high to be attributed solely to

chance. Similarly, for the period 1973-80, DeAngelo, DeAngelo and Rice (1984), pp. 394-95, estimate a significant CAR of 16.99 percent for the same holding period.

[13]For example, see Manne (1965) and Jensen and Meckling (1976).

[14]Another gain from going private, which is more obvious, involves circumventing the explicit costs that are otherwise incurred with outside ownership, such as registration and listing fees and other stockholder service costs. Relative to the market value of the public firm, these explicit costs can be significant. For example, in the early 1980s, estimates of the costs of public ownership incurred *annually* ranged from $30,000 to $200,000. The value of the stream of this annual cost (for an indefinite time) discounted at a rate of 10 percent, ranges from $300,000 to $2,000,000, whereas the median value of a sample of 72 firms attempting to go private between 1973 and 1980 was $2,838,000. See DeAngelo, DeAngelo and Rice (1984) and references cited therein.

ager's incentives with those of the owners cannot be enforced completely.

To see why the distinction between ownership and managerial control can be important when monitoring incentives are weaker, consider the following extreme example in which a firm has such a large number of owners that no individual finds it worthwhile to monitor the manager at all. As is typical in any publicly owned firm, the owners have voting rights, but do not participate directly in the daily operations and decision-making of the firm. Suppose that the firm's manager, who exercises full control over these operations, has the opportunity to undertake a new project whereby the present value of cash flows (that is, revenues net of operating costs) can increase by $100. If the manager had a fixed salary and no ownership claims in the firm, he would be completely indifferent between exploiting this opportunity and not doing so, as long as the expansion required no additional time by the manager. If the expansion actually required any additional time, however, he might well choose to forgo the opportunity; after all, what's in it for him?

In this example, the distinction between ownership and control is meaningful because the manager does not fully bear the wealth consequences of his actions. In the absence of effective monitoring by the owners, the decisions of the manager, acting on his own behalf, are not likely to maximize the owners' wealth; instead, they will maximize the manager's utility.

As the distinction between ownership and control becomes less clear, the conflict of interests between owners and managers becomes less severe. In the example above, if the manager owned a fraction of the firms' stock, say 5 percent, he would be less reluctant to initiate the new project; the additional cash flow created by the new project would increase the total value of his stock and wealth by $5. Nevertheless, the manager would not act entirely on behalf of all the owners unless the marginal gain from doing so, $5 in this example, exceeded the marginal value of his time used in other ways, including leisure.

The problems that potentially arise from the distinction between ownership and control, called "agency problems," explain why we observe managerial contracts that are more complicated than those that simply specify a fixed income. The problem of "incomplete monitoring" explains why the observed managerial contracts are less complicated than those that could perfectly remove the conflict of interests between owners and managers. A contract that partially links the manager's income to the firm's characteristics observed easily by stockholders—for example, sales, profits or the firm's stock performance—could help alleviate the conflict.[15] A change in the organizational structure of the firm, such as that engendered by an LBO, however, is another and potentially more effective method to circumvent the firm's organizational inefficiencies attributable to the meaningful separation of control and ownership.

In a going-private transaction, the interests of owners and the manager generally are closely, if not fully, reconciled. Once the manager becomes the owner, there is no conflict; the wealth consequences of the manager's actions are entirely internalized by the firm's reorganization. Even when a third party (another company or an individual) finances the purchase, monitoring possibilities improve, simply because the transaction decreases the number of owners—or, equivalently, concentrates the ownership of the firm—thereby raising the level of monitoring and the possibility that enforceable contracts can be designed to resolve the conflict of interests more effectively. By improving the organizational efficiency of the firm through a change of ownership, the LBO can increase the firm's earnings.[16]

---

[15]Note that a manager who dislikes risk would not willingly enter into a wage contract specifying that his compensation be a function only of the market value of the firm's stock. Doing so would involve taking on a large amount of risk—i.e., possible, large fluctuations in income that are not entirely under his control. Provided that there is competition in the market for managers, owners of the firm must bear some of the risks and offer a compensation schedule such that risks are shared by owners and managers. Bennett (1989), however, reports that executives increasingly are taking on some of the risks, in the sense that the link between their salaries and the market value of the firm, through long-term incentive schemes (such as stock options and restricted stock), has become substantial over the past decade. In the absence of complete monitoring, the problems that typically arise from the distinction between ownership and control are being partly mitigated by tying executive compensation to the performance of the firm.

[16]An inefficient organization of a firm provides a motivation for others to take over that firm. Note that such a takeover need not involve taking that firm private. Rather, the takeover is necessary to reorganize the firm to effect a higher concentration of ownership.

The Advantages of Highly Leveraged Financing

That most going-private transactions are financed with a large proportion of debt suggests that leveraging itself must augment the potential gains from the buyout. That is, the high degree of leveraging in the buyout need not indicate that the buyers do not have the requisite cash for the transaction.

One widely mentioned source of gain from extensive leveraging is based on the incentive structure of the tax system. Because interest payments on debt are tax deductible, debt financing is relatively more attractive (*ceteris paribus*) than other methods of finance. The double taxation of dividends, first as corporate income and then as shareholder income, further increases the incentive to issue or sell debt to finance the purchase of the firm.

The gain from leveraged financing, however, need not be restricted to reducing the tax liability of the target firm. Another motive for the use of debt finance stems from the misalignment of the manager's incentives with those of the owners in cases where the firm faces low growth prospects and a large "free cash flow."[17] When the firm's cash flow exceeds what is necessary to finance its own projects that are expected to yield positive (discounted) net revenues, the firm is said to have a positive free cash flow. That is, the firm has reached its optimal size; additional projects to expand its operations would not maximize its profits.

There are cases, however, in which the manager of a firm that has reached its optimal size might choose not to maximize the shareholders' wealth by paying out the free cash flow in the form of dividends. For example, if the manager's compensation were linked to the firm's growth in sales, he would have a greater incentive to invest the free cash in any project that increases the firm's sales, even if the project's net return would be insufficient to maintain the firm's value. The incentive to use the free cash inefficiently (from the stockholders' and society's perspective) to increase the firm's size is greater if the manager values his power as measured by the amount of resources under his control.[18] In this case, the market value of the stock and the wealth of existing shareholders will not be maximized.

The problem of free cash flow, a particular type of agency problem, can be mitigated in a buyout that is financed with debt. Issuing debt and using the entire proceeds to purchase equity in an LBO enables the stockholders to capture the present value of the future free cash flow that otherwise would be used inefficiently. The firm's increased leveraged position after the transaction, in effect, imposes a binding commitment on the manager to not waste future cash flow; specifically, the manager cannot repudiate the firm's debt obligation to pay out the future free cash flow as interest payments because the bondholders could then push the firm into bankruptcy. By circumventing or reducing the agency problem associated with free cash flow, the use of debt essentially improves the productive efficiency of the firm.

Evidence

The empirical observation that the purchase price in an LBO is, on average, considerably higher than the market price before the LBO announcement suggests that these transactions have increased the value of the target firm and, hence, the wealth of the shareholders.[19] The observed gain to shareholders is consistent with the notion that market participants at least expect the changes brought about by the LBO activity to be productive.[20]

The basic idea here is that by increasing the efficiency with which the firm's resources are used, the LBO transaction is expected to in-

---

[17]Jensen (1986, 1988). Also see "Management Brief: The Way the Money Goes" (1989) for a brief discussion of this hypothesis as well as others to explain the increasing degree of leveraging by corporations in recent years and Laderman (1989a) for a discussion of the concept of free cash flow and its relation to cash flow and operating cash flow.

[18]Of course, free cash flow could also explain the growing acquisition activity that has generated losses to stockholders. See Jensen (1986, 1988) for details.

[19]See the evidence cited in footnotes 11 and 12.

[20]The issue of whether merger and acquisition activity in general is productive has also received attention by researchers in finance as well as the news media. See Jarrell, Brickley and Netter (1988) and Jensen and Ruback (1983) for recent reviews of the empirical studies on the effects of merger and takeover activity. These studies generally indicate that stockholders gain, on average, from this activity in the market for corporate control. Also, see Ott and Santoni (1985) who present a useful theoretical discussion of the productiveness of mergers and acquisitions and place this activity into an historical perspective.

crease economic earnings, which would eventually be paid out as dividends. Because the price of a firm's stock is equal, in theory, to the expected present discounted value of future dividends, the transaction also raises the price of the stock. In equilibrium, the gains to stockholders or the premium paid over the market price before the transaction should be identical to the expected increase in the present discounted value of economic earnings to the target firm.[21]

In an attempt to identify the sources of the increase in value from LBOs, one recent study found that the increase in the market price of the target firm's stock is largely explained by its cash flow as a fraction of the market value of its equity before the transaction.[22] This evidence suggests that, with greater cash flow and the greater agency costs potentially associated with that flow, there is more room to improve the firm's productive efficiency and, accordingly, to increase the firm's value. Indeed, although differences in the firm's tax liabilities are associated with significant differences in the observed magnitudes of the premiums, measures of the

firm's tax liability do not add statistically significant information for predicting the market-valued premium above the information provided by the cash flow measure.[23] Hence, the expected gains from the LBO transactions appear to be over-and-above the tax advantages of debt finance.

SKEPTICISM ABOUT THE SOCIAL VALUE OF LBOs

Despite the gains typically realized by a target firm's shareholders, some observers have expressed doubt about the benefits of LBOs. These doubts stem from two types of potential "bad" effects of LBOs: wealth redistributions and increased instability of the economy.

LBOs and Wealth Redistributions

One version of the redistribution criticism is the claim that LBOs generate gains for the stockholders at the expense of those holding the target firm's original bonds; the redistribution presumably results from a reduction in the

---

[21]For example, in the simple case where expected future dividends, d_t for $t > 0$, grow at a constant rate, g, the price of the firm's stock can be written as $\dfrac{d_1}{r - g}$. r is the constant discount rate appropriately adjusted for risk, and d_1 is next period's dividend payment. Hence, by increasing expected dividends (d_t or g)—or, equivalently, expected economic earnings—the transaction can increase the market value of the firm's stock.

Assuming that market participants correctly value the firm's stock, the observed increases in the stock price cast some doubt on the general criticism of activity in the market for corporate control, that managers are exploiting opportunities for short-term gains at the expense of long-term performance. Rather, this activity effectively removes myopic incentives so as to increase long-term economic earnings. Of course, the claim that observed unusual increases in the stock price supports the hypothesis that mergers and acquisitions are productive presumes that capital markets are efficient. In particular, firms are not systematically undervalued (given public information) and daily changes in the price of the firm's stock reflect *new* information that is made available to the public and is relevant for determining the firm's value. Otherwise, the observed increase in the stock price could merely reflect a re-evaluation of the firm's productiveness, without any fundamental change expected to arise from this activity in the market for corporate control.

[22]Lehn and Poulsen (1988), table 6, p. 54. The measure of cash flow used in their empirical analysis, however, does not control for the firm's growth prospects and so only crudely captures the firm's "free cash flow." But in a subsequent analysis, Lehn and Poulsen (1989), using undistributed cash flow (that is, the firm's after-tax cash flow net of interest and dividend payments) and attempting to control for the firm's growth prospects, get similar results for LBOs between 1984 and 1987 (table V, p. 782). Also,

Lehn and Poulsen (1989), table III, p. 778, find that firms going private have a significantly higher flow of undistributed cash flow as a fraction of their equity value and possibly lower growth prospects than a control group of firms.

Recently, Mitchell and Lehn (1988), who attempt to identify the source of gains to shareholders in takeover activity, present some preliminary evidence to support the hypothesis that the growth in productive takeover activity is partly an attempt to prevent the target firm from using free cash flow in an unprofitable way or to reverse the earlier unprofitable takeover activity due to the free cash flow problems.

[23]Lehn and Poulsen (1988, 1989). Lehn and Poulsen (1988), table 9, p. 60, divide their sample into two equal subsamples according to the magnitude of the firm's tax liability as a fraction of the market value of the firm's outstanding equity before the transaction. They find that the mean market-valued premium for those firms with the higher tax liability measure was 47.7 percent, whereas that for firms with the lower measure of tax liability was 32.1 percent. The difference in the premiums for the two subsamples cannot be due to chance alone. (See footnote 11 for their definition of the market-valued premium.) However, the firm's tax liability does not explain variation in the premium not already explained by variation in the firm's undistributed cash flow. See Lehn and Poulsen (1989), table V, p. 782. Also, they do not find a significant difference between the mean tax liability for firms that went private and that for a control group of firms (table III, p. 778).

---

market value of the firm's outstanding debt.[24] The value of debt allegedly falls because the target firm's increased leveraged position, typically in the form of low-quality, high-yielding (junk) bonds, increases the probability that its future revenues will be insufficient to cover its higher interest payments. That is, the value of the firm's bonds outstanding before the announcement of the LBO drops because market participants believe that the probability of default has increased as a result of the LBO transaction.[25]

Even if LBOs were to redistribute wealth in this way, however, whether or not public policy should aim to discourage LBO activity is not obvious.[26] Economics has nothing meaningful to say about the "fairness" of wealth redistributions that leave social wealth unchanged. The key economic issue is whether LBOs reduce the market value of the firm's outstanding debt by more or less than the increase in the value of its outstanding stock. If the net change in the value of stockholders' and bondholders' claims on the firm is negative, then LBOs reduce social wealth. In this case, LBOs would be socially inefficient and public policy to limit such activity could be justified.

The evidence discussed above, however, casts some doubt on the validity of the claim that LBOs merely redistribute wealth among those having claims in the firm with no net gain to society. Specifically, the alleged positive effect of the increase in leveraging on the firm's default probability should not emerge. If such an effect were to emerge, it would first be reflected in the price of the stock. Because the new owners of the firm will be the residual claimants of the firm's earnings, they take on the greatest amount of risk in the transaction. The bidders must expect that, while future debt-servicing increases, the LBO will improve the firm's productivity so

as to augment the future cash flow available for servicing that increased debt obligation; otherwise, they would not be willing to pay such a premium to purchase the firm.

Confirming this line of reasoning, empirical studies indicate that LBO announcements have an insignificant effect on the market value of the firm's outstanding debt. One study found that, for a sample of 13 target firms between 1980 and 1984, the average percentage change in the bond price from 10 days before to 10 days after the announcement was -1.42 percent, much smaller than the average 7.21 percent decline in the Wall Street Journal's 20-bond index over the same period.[27] Another study of 20 LBOs between 1984 to 1988 found that the likelihood of the bond price falling was virtually equal to the likelihood of the price increasing upon the LBO announcement.[28] However, a recent study found that, for 33 successful buyouts between 1974 and 1985, the default risk of the target firms' bonds (as measured by Moody's) typically increased.[29]

Another version of the redistribution hypothesis is based on the widely cited reason for the recent growth of LBOs—that is, the tax system produces a bias for debt finance. By reducing the firm's tax liability, the LBO increases the firm's after-tax earnings and, consequently, the market value of the firm's stock. According to some observers, the observed increase in stock value takes place at the expense of taxpayers. Because these transactions permit the target firms to reduce their tax liability, tax gains to the target firms realized by the shareholders are said to be offset indirectly by increasing the tax liabilities of all taxpayers.[30]

Regardless of the issues related to the fairness of the tax system, the critical economic issue for public policy toward LBOs is whether the

---

[24]For example, see "A Big Event for American Bonds" (1988) and, "When Industry Borrows Itself" (1988).

[25]The value of preferred stock is also said to fall. Specified payments or dividends, distributed to holders of these stock shares unless earnings are insufficient to cover interest payments on outstanding debt, are fixed like interest payments on debt.

[26]The forms of protection, offered in financial markets, against such losses weakens the role for public intervention. See, for example, "The Debt Deduction" (1988) and Lehn and Poulsen (1988).

[27]Lehn and Poulsen (1988), table 8, p. 57. Also, see Marais, Schipper and Smith (1989) who similarly find that bond values did not significantly decline following 290 proposed management buyouts between 1974 and 1985. Further-

more, preferred stock values do not appear to be significantly affected by the announcement.

[28]Fortier (1989). Out of a sample of 20 LBOs, the bond prices of only eight target firms fell. The average change in price as a percentage of the bond's face value, abstracting from general market interest rate movements was only -0.50 percent, too small to be attributed to the LBO announcement. However, she finds that after January 1987, when the elimination of preferential tax treatment of capital gains made debt finance even more attractive, bondholders, on average, experienced significant losses (5.1 percent).

[29]Marais, Schipper and Smith (1989), tables 8 and 9, pp. 184-85.

[30]For example, see Lowenstein (1986).

Table 3
Growth of GNP and Debt

	1960-69	1970-79	1980-88
Nominal GNP	6.89%	10.24%	7.57%
Total credit market debt owed by domestic non-financial sectors	6.80	10.34	10.85
U.S. government	1.95	8.67	13.76
State and local governments	7.56	7.27	8.69
Households	8.54	11.31	9.96
Corporate	8.47	9.09	10.41
Farm corporate	8.95	12.56	−0.31
Nonfarm, noncorporate	13.51	16.07	13.13

SOURCE: Federal Reserve Board, ''Flow of Funds.''

NOTE: All data are annual percentage changes.

net effect on social wealth is negative. But, for example, even if LBOs had no effect on the firm's performance, the *net* effect of LBO activity on tax revenues is unlikely to be negative. While the tax liability of the target firm falls with increased leveraging, that of the shareholders realizing capital gains and new bondholders increases. Moreover, the evidence that the tax benefits do not fully explain the observed gains to shareholders suggests that the gains to shareholders do not simply come at the expense of taxpayers.[31] Thus, the argument that the gains to shareholders are offset by losses to taxpayers ignores the future increased tax base resulting from the LBO's predicted effect on the firm's productivity. If LBOs enhance the firm's performance, then income subject to taxation

would increase later; increased future tax revenues would offset partially, if not fully, the loss in tax revenues now due to the use of debt finance in the LBO transaction.

Macroeconomic Instability

Some individuals have argued that the recent activity in the market for corporate control has contributed to an excessive growth of debt by nonfinancial borrowers in this decade.[32] As table 3 shows, the growth of nominal GNP exceeded that of total debt of nonfinancial borrowers slightly during the 1960s and was marginally smaller in the 1970s. In the 1980s, however, the growth of total outstanding debt for nonfinancial borrowers exceeded that of nominal GNP by more than 3 percentage points. Table 3 indicates that all borrowers contributed to this recent trend except for the farm, and nonfarm, noncorporate sectors. But the primary contributors appear to be the U.S. government and the corporate sector.[33]

Some observers have suggested that the growth rates of corporate and public debt, which appear high relative to GNP growth in the 1980s, especially by post-World War II standards, reflect a greater instability in financial markets and, hence, the economy. According to this view, for any given slowdown in economic activity, the higher degree of leveraging by firms implies a greater likelihood that these firms will be forced to default on their debt obligations; if the affected creditors who suffer from deficient cash flows, in turn, are unable to service their own debt, then the severity of a slowdown in economic activity will be aggravated as the incidence of default is transmitted throughout the financial system.[34]

Despite the fact that the recent growth in corporate debt and LBO activity appear to be striking, whether or not these new trends indicate a threat to the stability of the financial system or

---

[31]See evidence cited in footnote 23.

[32]See Friedman (1989) and Kaufman (1989), for example. Gilbert and Ott (1985) found that the increase in corporate merger activity financed with debt (including LBOs) accounted for a substantial amount of the unusually large growth of business loans in the first half of 1984.

[33]During the 1980s, corporate debt growth has exceeded nominal GNP growth in all but two years and by as much as 9.96 percentage points. See also Bernanke and Campbell (1988), who provide a detailed analysis of the recent trends in corporate debt. They look at disaggregated data in an attempt to determine the financial stability or solven-

cy of those firms most likely to default on their debt obligations.

[34]See, for example, ''Taking the Strain of America's Leverage'' (1988) and Ferguson (1989), Kaufman (1986, 1989), Friedman (1986, 1989) and Greenspan (1989, especially p. 269). Friedman (1989) also argues that ''because of the increased likelihood of debtors' distress in the event of an economic downturn, the Federal Reserve system is likely to be less willing either to seek or to permit a business recession in the United States.'' According to Friedman, a consequence of the higher degree of leveraging is the prospect for greater inflation.

the economy is not obvious. If LBOs or, more generally, merger and acquisition activity had no other benefit than providing a channel through which tax advantages of debt finance could be realized, then the growth of debt that only recently has significantly exceeded the growth of nominal output might seem alarming.

The existing empirical evidence briefly discussed above, however, suggests that LBOs provide anticipated gains over and above the tax gains to the target firm. Since these anticipated benefits include enhancing the earnings potential of the firm, simply comparing debt growth with nominal GNP growth does not provide a complete picture from which to identify the effects of debt growth on the stability of financial markets. Specifically, the increased debt as a fraction of nominal output could reflect an increase in expected future cash flows relative to the prior post-World War II trends. In this case, the increased debt would be associated with a rise in the market value of firms' assets. Indeed, aggregate debt-to-asset ratios, which more accurately indicate financial stability, hardly changed on net from 1969 to 1986. For example, one measure of this ratio using "flow of funds" data, rose from 34 percent in 1969 to 42 percent in 1986, peaking in 1974 at 51 percent.[35]

Aggregate debt-to-asset ratios, however, can be misleading, because they mask the financial condition of those firms with especially high debt-to-asset ratios. In fact, such firms have exhibited only a slightly higher increase in debt-to-asset ratios than would be suggested by the aggregate data. Specifically, a recent study found

that while, for a full sample of firms, the debt-to-asset ratio fell from 31 percent in 1969 to 27 percent in 1986, for those firms in the 99th percentile (that is, having a higher debt-to-asset ratio than 99 percent of the sample), debt-to-asset ratios rose from about 74 percent to 82 percent.[36]

SOME UNANSWERED QUESTIONS AND POLICY IMPLICATIONS

The existing evidence cannot rule out the validity of all critical concerns about LBOs. In particular, most research on LBOs has examined the impact of the transaction on pre-buyout stockholders and bondholders of the firm. As such, these studies provide evidence on financial market participants' expectations about the impact of LBOs on the target firms performance. Although these studies generally indicate that these transactions on average are *expected* to generate gains beyond tax liability reductions, we will have to wait to see if these gains are actually realized. Several recent studies on post-buyout performance of LBO firms provide evidence suggesting that those transactions, on average, have actually improved the firm's performance; however, evidence is preliminary and particularly subject to many methodological problems due to data limitations.[37] Nevertheless, without evidence that LBOs are harmful or are likely to be harmful to the economy, policy actions to restrict LBO activity seem to be premature; indeed, such restrictions could themselves be harmful, especially if LBO activity actually enhances the productiveness of the target firms.

---

[35]Bernanke and Campbell (1988), table 3, p. 98.

[36]Ibid., table 5, p. 104. As predicted by the "free cash flow" theory, the study found a dramatic increase in real and nominal interest expenses as a percentage of cash flows over this same period (see tables 6 and 7, pp. 106-07). Because expectations about increased future cash flows (as reflected in the increased market value of the firms' outstanding assets that has left debt-to-asset ratios virtually unchanged on net from 1969 to 1986) might not be fulfilled, however, concerns about recent trends in debt growth are not entirely unwarranted. Another recent study found that the default rate on junk bonds, commonly used to finance transactions in the market for corporate control, could be as high as 34 percent, much higher than the average 2.5 percent reported by an earlier study. See Laderman (1989b) for a brief discussion of these two studies and Mitchell (1989) and Fidler and Cohen (1989) for discussions of a more recent study by Moody's Investors Services, Inc. Also see Passell (1989) who summarizes two other studies' findings that the greater risk of default has been compensated by higher realized returns on average.

[37]For example, see Deveny (1989), who discusses a recent study indicating that companies involved in the market for corporate control have not, on average, exhibited a decrease in expenditures on research and development, as predicted by some critics. Also, see Yago (1989), who reports one study's finding that target firms of management buyouts are less likely to close plants than are other firms. Francis (1989) discusses evidence from another study indicating that, upon a change in ownership of a firm, the ratio of the administrative employees to plant employees fell 11 percent on average. Indeed, one study found that for LBO firms between 1984 and 1986, average annual growth of the firm's productivity (measured by sales per employee) increased from an average of 3.6 percent before the transaction to 17.4 percent after the transaction. See Yago (1989). Also, Palmeri (1989) recently found that the stocks of 70 LBO target firms that subsequently went public performed significantly better than the market since going public. But see Long and Ravenscraft (1989) for a brief summary of a few other existing studies providing mixed evidence on post-LBO performance and a critical assessment of the validity of these studies.

Although the recent behavior of various debt-to-asset ratios does not indicate a drastic deterioration of corporate solvency, the higher debt-to-income ratios do suggest some increased risk of financial stress. That is, the recent behavior of these latter ratios indicate a higher degree of pressure on cash flows exerted by interest expenses (a reduction in liquidity), which could exacerbate the severity of any given slowdown in economic activity. To the extent the tax advantages of debt finance are not necessary to realize the gains from LBO activity, as well as from other highly leveraged transactions in the market for corporate control, a change in public policy might be warranted.

A widely discussed policy recommendation intended to slow the growth of all corporate debt involves eliminating the tax advantages of debt finance, in particular, by eliminating the tax deductibility of interest payments on debt.[38] Another policy recommendation would involve removing the double-taxation of dividends by relieving the tax burden on dividends at the corporate level or stockholder level. Whether the latter approach to curb debt growth is politically feasible, given the wide concern about the unprecedented growth in public debt along with explicit commitments made by the administration to reduce the budget deficit, remains unclear. In any case, if, as suggested by the empirical evidence, LBO activity has benefits in addition to the tax advantages, these tax reforms should be considered on their own merits, not chiefly as a way to reduce LBO activity.

REFERENCES

"A Big Event for American Bonds," *The Economist* (October 29, 1988), p. 81.

Bennett, Amanda. "A Great Leap Forward for Executive Pay," *Wall Street Journal*, April 24, 1989.

Bernanke, Ben S., and John Y. Campbell. "Is There a Corporate Debt Crisis?" *Brookings Papers on Economic Activity* (1:1988), pp. 83-125.

"Board Issues Guidelines for LBO, Other Highly Leveraged Loans ..." *The Fed Letter*, Federal Reserve Bank of Kansas City (April 1989), p. 1.

"Corporate America Snuggles Up to the Buy-Out Wolves," *The Economist* (October 29, 1988), pp. 69-72.

DeAngelo, Harry, Linda DeAngelo, and Edward M. Rice. "Going Private: Minority Freezeouts and Stockholder Wealth," *Journal of Law and Economics* (October 1984), pp. 367-401.

"The Debt Deduction," *New York Journal of Commerce*, November 29, 1988.

Deveny, Kathleen. "Progress Isn't Drowning in Debt—Yet," *Business Week: Innovation in America* (Special 1989 Bonus Issue), p. 110.

Dowd, Ann Reilly. "Washington's War Against LBO Debt," *Fortune* (February 13, 1989), pp. 91-92.

Ferguson, Douglas E. "Solving the Leverage Problem," *New York Journal of Commerce*, January 9, 1989.

Fidler, Stephen and Norma Cohen. "Widening the Junk Default Debate," *Financial Times*, July 20, 1989.

Fortier, Diana L. "Buyouts and Bondholders," *Chicago Fed Letter* (January 1989).

Francis, David R. "Takeovers Cut Central-Office Costs," *The NBER Digest*, June 1989.

Friedman, Benjamin M. "Increasing Indebtedness and Financial Stability in the United States" in Federal Reserve Bank of Kansas City, Debt, *Financial Stability, and Public Policy* (August 1986), pp. 27-53.

———. "Tread Carefully on Takeovers," *New York Journal of Commerce*, April 27, 1989.

Gilbert, R. Alton, and Mack Ott. "Why the Big Rise in Business Loans at Banks Last Year?" this *Review* (March 1985), pp. 5-13.

Greenspan, Alan. "Statement Before the Committee on Ways and Means, United States House of Representatives," *Federal Reserve Bulletin* (April 1989), pp. 267-72.

Jarrell, Gregg A., James A. Brickley, and Jeffry M. Netter. "The Market for Corporate Control: The Empirical Evidence Since 1980," *Journal of Economic Perspectives* (Winter 1988), pp. 49-68.

Jensen, Michael C. "Takeovers: Their Causes and Consequences," *Journal of Economic Perspectives* (Winter 1988), pp. 21-48.

———. "Agency Costs of Free Cash Flow, Corporate Finance, and Takeovers," *American Economic Review* (May 1986), pp. 323-29.

Jensen, Michael C., and William H. Meckling. "Theory of the Firm: Managerial Behavior, Agency Costs and Ownership Structure," *Journal of Financial Economics* (October 1976), pp. 305-60.

Jensen, Michael C., and Richard S. Ruback. "The Market for Corporate Control: The Scientific Evidence," *Journal of Financial Economics* (April 1983), pp. 5-50.

Kaufman, Henry. "Halting the Leverage Binge," *Institutional Investor* (April 1989), p. 23.

———. "Debt: The Threat to Economic and Financial Stability," in Federal Reserve Bank of Kansas City, Debt, *Financial Stability, and Public Policy* (August 1986), pp. 15-26.

Laderman, Jeffrey M. "Earnings, Schmernings—Look at the Cash," *Business Week* (July 24, 1989a) pp. 56-57.

———. "Does Junk Have Lasting Value? Probably," *Business Week* (May 1, 1989b), pp. 118-19.

Lehn, Kenneth, and Annette Poulsen. "Free Cash Flow and Stockholder Gains in Going Private Transactions," *Journal of Finance* (July 1989), pp. 771-87.

---

[38]For example, see "The Debt Deduction" (1988) and Friedman (1986, 1989) and Dowd (1989). Also see U.S. Congress, Joint Committee on Taxation (1989) for a more detailed and exhaustive list of policy proposals.

_____ . "Leveraged Buyouts: Wealth Created or Wealth Redistributed?" in Murray L. Weidenbaum and Kenneth W. Chilton, eds., *Public Policy Toward Corporate Takeovers* (Transaction Inc., 1988), pp. 46-62.

Long, William F., and David J. Ravenscraft. "The Record of LBO Performance," mimeo (May 17, 1989).

Lowenstein, Louis. "No More Cozy Management Buyouts," *Harvard Business Review* (January/February 1986), pp. 147-56.

"Management Brief: The Way the Money Goes," *The Economist* (July 15, 1989), pp. 70-71.

Manne, Henry G. "Mergers and the Market for Corporate Control," *Journal of Political Economy* (April 1965), pp. 110-20.

Marais, Laurentius, Katherine Schipper and Abbie Smith. "Wealth Effects of Going Private For Senior Securities," *Journal of Financial Economics* (June 1989), pp. 155-91.

Merrill Lynch Business Brokerage and Valuation, Inc., *Mergerstat Review* (1988).

Mitchell, Constance. "Junk-Issuer Rate of Default is Put at Average 3.3%," *Wall Street Journal,* July 20, 1989.

Mitchell, Mark L., and Kenneth Lehn. "Do Bad Bidders Become Good Targets?" mimeo (August 1988).

Ott, Mack, and G.J. Santoni. "Mergers and Takeovers—The Value of Predators' Information," this *Review* (December 1985), pp. 16-28.

Palmeri, Christopher. "Born-Again Stocks," *Forbes* (March 20, 1989), pp. 210-11.

Passell, Peter. "Economic Scene: The $12 Billion Misunderstanding," *New York Times,* July 17, 1989.

Stancill, James McNeill. "LBOs for Smaller Companies," *Harvard Business Review* (January/February 1988), pp. 18-26.

"Taking the Strain of America's Leverage," *The Economist* (November 5, 1988), pp. 87-88.

Thomson, James B. "Bank Lending to LBOs: Risks and Supervisory Response," *Economic Commentary,* Federal Reserve Bank of Cleveland (February 15, 1989).

Torabzadeh, Khalil M., and William J. Bertin. "Leveraged Buyouts and Shareholder Returns," *Journal of Financial Research* (Winter 1987), pp. 313-19.

U.S. Congress. Joint Committee on Taxation. *Federal Income Tax Aspects of Corporate Financial Structures.* (GPO, 1989).

"When Industry Borrows Itself," *The Economist* (October 29, 1988), pp. 17-18.

Yago, Glenn. "LBOs, UFOs and Corporate Perestroika," *Wall Street Journal* (July 19, 1989).

Article 12

LBOs and Conflicts of Interest

by William P. Osterberg

Leveraged-buyouts (LBOs) seem to be firmly entrenched in our financial system and have been growing in volume: in 1988, over 300 LBOs were announced, amounting to over $98 billion; in 1980 LBOs amounted to less than $1 billion. [1] LBOs also appear to be having a significant impact on stock-market movements; the 1988 stock-market rebound after the crash of 1987, for example, coincided with the spurt of LBOs.

There are deep disagreements among economists about the overall costs and benefits of LBOs. Some claim that the stock-price increases associated with LBOs correctly foretell future increases in a firm's productivity and profitability. If this claim is true, then society as a whole may benefit from LBOs. Critics, however, note that rising stock prices directly benefit only shareholders and do not necessarily make society as a whole better off. They claim that stock prices rise only because stockholders use LBOs to redistribute wealth from managers, bondholders, employees, and taxpayers. If this is true, then some people are hurt by LBOs.

Current proposals to change the tax code or to impose regulatory restrictions on LBOs are based on the presumption that the productivity gains from LBOs are overstated or that LBOs primarily benefit one party at the expense of another. Another concern is that LBOs have led to a dangerous increase in the overall level of debt in the economy as a whole.

In this *Economic Commentary*, we discuss how LBOs may benefit some in a corporation at the expense of others. We view the corporation as a set of contracts that tie together the interests of stockholders, managers, bondholders, and employees, and that reduce the conflicts that naturally arise among these groups.

We discuss how the use of LBOs involves replacing existing contracts and possibly redistributing corporate wealth. We also discuss the economic events that have encouraged the use of LBOs and indicate the possible response of our financial system. First, a brief description of the structure and relationships that exist in the modern corporation will help establish a context in which to discuss the effects of LBOs.

■ Conflicts of Interest in the Modern Corporation

The modern corporation is a nexus of contracts between the conflicting interests of stockholders and stakeholders (creditors, managers, and employees). Economists usually view stockholders as running the corporation (indirectly) in order to increase the market value of their stock (equity). Some actions taken by managers on behalf of stockholders increase the market value of equity by improving efficiency, that is, by producing more output with a given amount of input. Other actions redistribute wealth from stakeholders. [2]

The modern corporation has survived largely due to its efficiencies, some of which are associated with the use of

Leveraged-buyouts (LBOs) have had a major impact on our financial system, and have particularly affected traditional corporate relationships between stockholders, bondholders, and employees. It is unclear if LBOs improve economic performance. The growth of LBOs, however, has sparked an evolutionary response that is restructuring the corporation as an institution.

common stock.[3] Since common stock is widely held and easily traded, investors can diversify their investment and thus reduce their risk.

The separation of the ownership of common stock from other roles in the corporation is also beneficial. Managers and employees, for example, make investments in the firm in the form of learned skills. However, such investments cannot be traded as easily as common stock.

Consequently, managers and employees may be less willing to increase their personal exposure to the firm's risk by also buying its stock. If they do purchase their company's stock, they may require a higher rate of return than the average investor. Thus, it may be wise to separate common stock ownership from the roles performed by managers and employees. However, as we discuss below, there are also disadvantages to this separation.

In spite of the various efficiencies of the modern corporation, conflicts arise in *principal-agent* relationships, in which *principals* (for example, stockholders) engage *agents* (managers) to take action on the principals' behalf. A major corporate principal-agent conflict involves the separation of ownership and control. Managers may not have the same goals as stockholders, and may avoid making changes that could jeopardize the investments they have made in their jobs.

The conflict between stockholders and stakeholders centers on the limited liability of stockholders. Stockholders receive the profits, which are the income from earnings, minus payments required to labor, creditors, and taxes. If the corporation's earnings do not cover required payments and the business fails, the stockholders have limited liability and do not have to pay the difference between income and required payments. Stakeholders can only hope to recoup their losses through bankruptcy proceedings

Stockholders therefore may benefit from strategies that increase the variability (risk) of corporate earnings. On the other hand, stakeholders wish to avoid risk because they suffer if earnings are insufficient and do not benefit from the "high" earnings that may result from successful risky business strategies.

As indicated above, employees and managers invest in firm-specific skills, that is, they accumulate human capital in the form of education and training. While such personal investments may be necessary in order to improve productivity, conflicts arise once such investments have been made. It is difficult for employees and managers, for example, to protect themselves by diversifying the risk associated with these firm-specific investments—if a firm goes out of business, they lose their investment. In addition, there may be no guarantee that full compensation will ultimately be received for their learned skills and accumulated experience.

If unresolved, the conflicts between stockholders and stakeholders are costly. Stockholders would expect managers to take advantage of on-the-job perquisites and would lower compensation accordingly. Managers, in turn, would have no incentive to invest in accumulating the skills that would improve their efficiency at a particular job. Bondholders and employees would anticipate the self-serving actions of stockholders and most likely would not provide enough debt or human capital for the firm's efficient operation.

Contracts can reduce the cost of these stockholder-stakeholder conflicts. Bondholders, in particular, use contracts to try to restrict the actions of stockholders. Stockholders agree to such restrictions if the benefits to them, in terms of lower borrowing costs, exceed the costs of the restrictions.

The best set of contracts between stockholders and bondholders will increase both the values of debt and equity. Similarly, all parties gain if contracts induce investment in human capital by

managers and employees. These investments lead to increases in productivity wages, salaries, and market values.

Bond indentures, which are formal agreements between issuers of bonds and bondholders, are the best example of contracts that seem to be written so as to reduce agency costs (the loss in firm value due to conflicts within the corporation). Bond indentures commonly include limitations on issuing debt since additional debt increases the probability of bankrupcty and creates conflicts among bondholders. Issuance of senior debt (debt that has to be paid first in bankruptcy proceedings) is severely limited by convenants negotiated by the initial senior debtholders. Issuance of junior debt is also limited since it may be paid first, either because it matures first, or because the courts may deviate from strict adherence to priority.[4]

Stockholders wish to control managers' incentives to consume, via perquisites, part of the return that could be paid as dividends or that could be reinvested. To do this, managerial compensation is tied to firm performance. However, if compensation is tied to firm solvency, managers will avoid risk, retain too much of the earnings, or not issue enough debt.

Managers in turn must be compensated for investing in firm-specific human capital. Typically, managers have been compensated for growth in sales or revenue rather than for maximizing the firm's stock-market value. Under some circumstances, these objectives may be in conflict. However, managers generally realize that their future salaries will reflect their ability to increase stock-market values and act accordingly.

However, it is impossible to anticipate all the events that may encourage the stockholders or managers simply to redistribute wealth to themselves. In addition, in some cases, it may be too costly to negotiate contracts. In either case, there may be "implicit contracts" that involve the stakeholders' trust that their interests will not be knowingly violated. Appointment of trustworthy managers may be necessary in order to maintain contracts under these circumstances. [5]

LBOs affect the traditional corporate relationships between stockholders, bondholders, and employees described above. In order to change these relationships, however, it may be necessary for control of the corporation to change hands.

■ The Market for Corporate Control

Whoever has a controlling interest in the equity of the corporation chooses the managers and managerial compensation. Bondholders do not become owners since the tax benefits of corporate debt are contingent on the debtholders not being.owners. [6] Employees can be, but typically are not, owners. Increasingly, however, managers have been gaining controlling interest of their firms and have been preempting outside takeovers through MBOs (management buyouts).

In the market for corporate control, outside acquisitions reflect buyers' belief that they will earn an above-market rate of return from owning the firm. The new, higher share value may reflect the fact that the new owners are not necessarily bound by the old set of corporate contracts. It may even be possible to increase share value by replacing the old set of contracts.

In particular, it may be necessary to replace the incumbent management to institute the desired changes. Incumbent management simply may be unaware of potential value-improving strategies, or may not have the proper incentives to increase the firm's stock-market value, especially if such actions would decrease managerial wealth. This could occur if managers were compensated for short-term performance rather than for increasing firm value. Or, incumbent management may not institute such changes if their future salaries will reflect poorly on their trustworthiness in honoring such contracts.

Recent changes in market conditions may have made it generally more

profitable to engage in merger and acquisitions (M&As), of which LBOs are a variation. This increased profitability could either reflect new opportunities to improve efficiency or new chances to redistribute wealth from stakeholders. Other factors may also be involved. The growth of the junk-bond market, for example, has created a new pool of funds and lowered the costs of debt finance.

The increase in funding controlled by institutional investors and the money subsequently available for takeover efforts may have stimulated the concerted analysis of takeovers. Changes in the tax code also may have lowered the cost of debt finance. Increasing international competition may have increased pressures to take advantage of such new, lower-cost financing arrangements. Deregulation in industries such as financial services and oil and gas may also have renewed competitive pressure.

And, finally, some claim that the break-up LBOs of the 1980s reflect an admission that the conglomerate mergers of the 1960s were mistakes. Investors can diversify their market risks without needing to purchase equity in a diversified corporation.

■ Effects of LBOs on Stockholders and Bondholders

Most studies of the impacts of M&As focus on the reactions of financial markets. There is a great deal of evidence on the impacts of the broader category of M&As. One study indicates, for example, that shareholders of target companies clearly benefit from tender offers. However, stockholders of the bidding company at best receive small gains. Others have found that values of bonds do not appear to be adversely affected by M&A activity in general. [7]

Since most firms affected by LBOs go private, there is less evidence of the impacts of LBOs on either stockholders or bondholders. Generally, however, stock prices react positively to financial restructurings that increase leverage, such as issues of new debt or repurchases of equity. Recent studies of management buyouts (MBOs), which also

tend to be highly leveraged, seem to confirm the finding that while bondholders don't gain, they don't lose either. [8]

These results may seem surprising given the well-publicized adverse reactions of bondholders to LBO announcements and the fact that a firm's reorganization may increase the risk of bankruptcy. After all, it is not uncommon for a firm's debt to be downgraded after an LBO. However, bondholders realize in advance that the firm will be run for the benefit of the stockholders. If the bondholders anticipated such actions by stockholders the rates of returns on the bonds should reflect this risk and thus compensate the bondholders.

■ Effects of LBOs on Employees

So far, there is little quantitative evidence about the impact of LBOs on employees. LBOs may eventually push labor towards industries in which labor is more productive. There is some indirect and mixed evidence on the short-run impact of LBOs. One study of M&A activity among small firms in Michigan found no significant decline in employment. Another study, however, found that employment rose by less than industrywide averages for firms going through MBOs. [9]

Any changes in wages or employment associated with an LBO may involve rewriting union contracts or reestablishing the trust necessary to enter implicit contracts. In some cases, such as Carl Icahn's takeover of TWA, union contracts were rewritten with lower wage rates. It is not clear if the lower wages were more competitive and thus led to improved efficiency in airline operations, or if the wage decline represented a transfer of wealth from the employees to the stockholders.

The uses of Employee Stock Ownership Plans (ESOPs) and pension fund assets in LBOs also affect employees. ESOPs are trusts set up to provide employees with direct ownership in their firm. There are substantial tax benefits for a company that establishes an ESOP. ESOPs can be used by companies in takeover defenses since the more stock held in an ESOP, the harder it is for an acquirer to obtain sufficient stock to effect a takeover. On the other hand, employees can use ESOPs to have a greater role in a company's operations or to acquire companies themselves.

Pension funds are large enough to become important sources of financing for LBOs. In addition, companies with surplus pension funds are attractive takeover targets since surplus pension funds revert to the company upon termination of the plan. Or the company may use the pension fund to defend against takeovers. Surplus pension funds are contributions made to the fund in excess of the benefits that the company would be required to pay if the plan were terminated. Recent increases in stock prices (that bloated the value of the funds' equity holdings) and lower rates of wage increases (holding down pension liabilities) may have encouraged these developments.

■ Do LBOs Reduce the Costs of Conflicts Within the Firm?

As discussed above, LBOs operate by replacing contracts governing the corporation. There are costs associated with writing new contracts since trust must be reestablished. Another view, called the *free-cash-flow theory*, emphasizes a way that the post-LBO corporate form may lower the costs of conflicts within the corporation.

The free-cash-flow theory of takeovers emphasizes the costs of having managers' incentives not reflect those of the stockholders. Free cash flow is cash flow in excess of that necessary to fund profitable investments. If managers are rewarded for increased sales or increased revenues rather than for increased stock values, they are likely to accumulate free cash flow. Free cash flow can be regarded as a measure of managers' failure to maximize market value.

LBOs may reduce the costs of free cash flow in at least three ways. First, by incurring higher interest payments, free cash flow is reduced. Second, by giving managers an equity stake, the

agency conflict between owners and managers is mitigated. Third, the eventual need to issue stock will subject the firm to more scrutiny than when it could rely more heavily on internally generated funds.

There is broad evidence in favor of the free-cash-flow theory. [10] LBOs have occurred in industries where changing market conditions are likely to have increased free cash flow. Typically, "streamlining" changes occur such as: rewriting of managerial compensation schemes, rewriting labor contracts, and reducing the size of the company by selling off operations.

Nonetheless, it is unclear if restructuring improves economic performance. Accounting data does not support the efficiency view. A 1987 study of 5,000 mergers between 1950 and 1975 concluded that mergers have led to declines in profitability. More recent studies tend to confirm these results. However, accounting data may not accurately measure performance. [11]

■ The Evolving Response to LBOs

As LBOs become an increasingly accepted part of the financial system, managers, bondholders, and employees will rewrite the explicit and implicit contracts that define the corporation. Or, the prices at which stakeholder services are provided will reflect any increased risk that is not protected through contracts.

Bondholders are responding to the threat posed by LBOs both through contracts and pricing. "Poison puts," which allow bondholders to sell the bonds back to the company at face value if the LBO lowers the bond rating, are now written into some bond covenants. Bondholders are also organizing in an effort to bargain for better terms when new debt is issued.

The response of bondholders to LBOs is obscured by a more fundamental development in the pricing of debt. The distinction between debt and equity has been lessened, largely through the increased use of junk bonds, whose

returns have risk valued by the market in ways similar to that of equity. Other types of debt with equity characteristics, such as convertible debt, are also more common. To some extent then, bond prices may come to reflect the risk associated with LBOs. In fact, there is some evidence that LBOs were encouraged by a decreased emphasis on writing bond covenants in the early 1980s.

Changes in managerial compensation are an important response to LBOs. Managers are now given equity stakes in the form of direct stock ownership or options in order to make the interests between managers and stockholders more compatible.

Labor unions may try to respond to the LBO threat through the terms of new labor contracts, in particular by including antitakeover provisions. Union efforts also have focused on legislative attempts to restrict takeovers. In addition, ESOPs give unions the potential to own the companies themselves as a way of insuring against the risk of LBOs.

Legislative restrictions on takeovers are also part of the overall response to LBOs. Congress could consider changes to aspects of the tax code that currently favor debt over equity or that encourage "abuse" of ESOPs or pension funds. However, even without these responses the profitability of future LBOs will decline. It is likely that market prices of corporate debt and equity will come to reflect the potential increases in value from restructuring. As further evidence of the long-term impact of LBOs, incumbent managers now increasingly perform the analysis that takeover specialists would perform and, if warranted, institute the changes that would follow an LBO. Through this process, LBOs may become institutionalized.

■ Conclusion

There is no conclusive evidence on whether LBOs improve economic efficiency or merely redistribute wealth to shareholders from stakeholders. LBOs were encouraged by events that made the existing set of contracts inconsistent with maximizing the stock market value of firms. The resulting new contracts may make the corporation more efficient. However, if LBOs were unanticipated when the old contracts were written, some parties may be made worse off. Clearly, the traditional corporation is changing: the set of explicit and implicit contracts that define the corporation are being rewritten. It is not yet clear whether the restructured corporation will be more efficient than the one it replaced.

Of course, it is possible that LBOs both improve efficiency and redistribute wealth. In that case, policymakers evaluating proposed changes in the tax code or regulations face a difficult tradeoff between improvements in efficiency that benefit society as a whole and redistributions of wealth that may harm individuals or groups.

■ Footnotes

1. An LBO is a type of takeover. Takeovers involve obtaining a controlling portion of equity. In LBOs, the takeover is financed with a relatively high amount of debt that is generally secured by the assets of the target company. The high levels of debt either force the new company to restrict expenditures or to develop new sources of funds, possibly by selling assets. More than half of the LBOs announced in 1988 went private (after the LBO, the stock was no longer publicly traded). Not all LBOs are hostile; approximately one-quarter were organized by management without the help of an equity sponsor.

2. Stakeholder wealth can be thought of as having two components. One is the value of financial assets such as stocks and bonds. The other represents the value of the investments they have made in accumulating employment skills. The latter component is closely related to expected future earnings.

3. Efficiency in the modern corporation refers to its ability to reduce the costs of the conflicts within the corporation and to organize productive resources in the least costly manner. See Michael C. Jensen and Clifford W. Smith Jr., "Stockholder, Manager, and Creditor Interests: Applications of Agency Theory," in *Recent Advances in Corporate Finance*, eds. Edward I. Altman

and Marti G. Subrahmanyam, Richard D. Irwin, 1985, pp. 93-131.

4. Research has shown that bond yields and prices reflect the protection that bond covenants give bondholders.

5. See Andrei Schleifer and Lawrence H. Summers, "Breach of Trust in Hostile Takeovers," in *Corporate Takeovers: Causes and Consequences*, ed. Alan Auerbach, National Bureau of Economic Research, University of Chicago Press, pp. 33-67. An alternative view to the position that managers and employees negotiate implicit contracts maintained with trust is the view that such relationships may arise because of managerial discretion or even "weakness." Managers may value having a good relationship with employees.

6. The distinction between debt and equity for tax purposes is determined on a case by case basis. However, "…independence between the holdings of the stock of the corporation and the holdings of the interest in question …" is one of the features the courts have come to view as characteristic of debt. See Joint Committee on Taxation, *Federal Income Tax Aspects of Corporate Financial Structures*, U.S. Government Printing Office, Washington, D.C., 1989, p. 36.

7. See Jensen, Michael C., and Richard S. Ruback, 1983, "The Market for Corporate Control: The Scientific Evidence," *Journal of Financial Economics*, 11, 5-50, and Denis, Debra K., and John J. McConnell, 1986, "Corporate Mergers and Security Returns," *Journal of Financial Economics*, 16, pp. 143-187.

8. See K. Lehn and A. Poulsen, "Leveraged Buyouts: Wealth Created or Wealth Redistributed?" in *Public Policy Towards Corporate Mergers*, ed. by M. Weidenbaum and K. Chilton, (Transition Books, New Brunswick, N.J.) and L. Marais, K. Schipper and A. Smith, 1989, "Wealth Effects of Leveraged Buyouts for Senior Securities," *Journal of Financial Economics*, forthcoming.

9. See Charles Brown and James L. Medoff, 1988, "The Impact of Firm Acquisitions on Labor," in *Corporate Takeovers: Causes and Consequences*, ed. Alan Auerbach, National Bureau of Economic Research, University of Chicago Press, pp. 9-31, and Steven Kaplan, "A Summary of Sources of Value in Management Buyouts," paper presented at 1988 Institutional Research Conference, Drexel Burnham Lambert, April 1988.

10. See Michael C. Jensen, 1988, "The Free Cash Flow Theory of Takeovers: A Financial Perspective on Mergers and Acquisitions and the Economy," in *The Merger Boom*, eds., Lynn E. Brown and Eric S. Rosengren,

Federal Reserve Bank of Boston, pp. 102-143.

11. See David J. Ravenscrafts and F.M. Scherer, *Mergers, Sell-Offs, and Economic Efficiency*, Brookings Institution, Washington, D.C., 1987. Accounting measures of profitability are influenced by the chosen methods of depreciation and inventory valuation as well as by other accounting decisions.

William P. Osterberg is an economist at the Federal Reserve Bank of Cleveland. The author would like to thank Mark Sniderman and James Thomson for helpful comments.

The views stated herein are those of the author and not necessarily those of the Federal Reserve Bank of Cleveland or of the Board of Governors of the Federal Reserve System.

Article 13

Hostile takeovers and the market for corporate control

Do hostile takeovers create new wealth? Or, do they simply move wealth from Column A to Column B, enriching some at the expense of others? The evidence is mixed

Diana L. Fortier

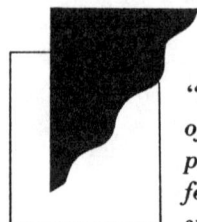

"In recent years, the tender offer takeover has been praised and damned with a ferocity suggesting that the survival of capitalism is at stake. The truth, as in most disputes with substantial metaphysical content, is more prosaic." F. M. Scherer, *Journal of Economic Perspectives*, Winter 1988, pg. 69.

The market for corporate control—firms competing for the rights to manage their corporate resources—has become an increasingly important element of the corporate landscape. Mergers and acquisitions have increased every year since 1982, reaching an all time high of 3,336 net announced transactions in 1986. (See Table I.)

Although contested tender offers— hostile takeovers—only account for a small fraction of all merger and acquisition activity, they involve large publicly traded companies with substantial market values across many industries. The $12.8 billion aggregate dollar value of 15 successful hostile takeovers in 1987 accounted for 7.7 percent of the total dollar value of the 972 mergers and acquisitions for which such data were disclosed. Moreover, the number of unfriendly takeovers was higher in each of the past three years than in any of the previous eleven years.[1]

Hostile takeover activity has a substantial impact on corporate behavior. Indeed, organizations involved incur substantial costs and devote much time to developing defensive or offensive strategies. Such battles may also impose large costs on shareholders, creditors, management, employees, customers, and communities. These private and social costs of takeovers have recently spurred significant legislative interest in hostile takeovers and defensive tactics.[2]

This paper discusses the corporate control market by focusing on hostile takeovers as a mechanism for corporate control. It discusses the causes of hostile takeovers and the methods of defensive action by hostile takeover targets. It then analyzes their effects not only on the bidder and target shareholders but also on other stakeholders (e.g., management and employees). A final section reviews the evidence on the sources of takeover gains. Are such gains redistributions of wealth to one group at the expense of another or are they derived from improved efficiency? Finally, what does this evidence imply about the effect of hostile takeovers on social welfare?

Hostile takeovers: Why do they occur?

Hostile takeovers, those opposed by the target's board of directors, became an "accepted" part of the corporate control market in 1974 with Morgan Stanley and Company's representation of International Nickel Company of Canada in its hostile takeover of ESB, Inc. In a hostile takeover, a bid is made directly to the shareholders of the target rather than to the target's management. The acquirer obtains the needed

TABLE 1

Merger and acquisition statistics[1]

Year	Total mergers & acquisitions	Total tender offers		Contested tender offers							
				Total contested		Successful offers[2]		Target remained independent		Acquired by white knight	
		#	% of col. 2	#	% of col. 3	#	% of col. 4	#	% of col. 4	#	% of col. 4
1978	2,106	90	4.3%	27	30%	13	48%	8	30%	6	22%
1979	2,128	106	5.0%	26	25%	8	31%	9	35%	9	34%
1980	1,889	53	2.8%	12	23%	3	25%	3	25%	6	50%
1981	2,395	75	3.1%	28	37%	13	46%	6	21%	9	33%
1982	2,346	68	2.9%	29	43%	17	59%	10	34%	2	7%
1983	2,533	37	1.4%	11	30%	7	64%	1	9%	3	27%
1984	2,543	79	3.1%	18	23%	10	56%	6	33%	2	11%
1985	3,001	84	2.8%	32	38%	14	44%	9	28%	9	28%
1986	3,336	150	4.5%	40	27%	15	38%	10	25%	15	37%
1987	2,032	116	5.7%	31	27%	18	58%	6	19%	7	23%
Ten year total	24,309	858	3.5%	254	30%	118	46%	68	27%	68	27%

[1]Data refer to net announcements (completed or pending transactions) or publicly announced formal transfers of ownership of at least ten percent of a company's assets or equity where the purchase price is greater than or equal to $500,000 and one of the parties is a U.S. company. Tender offer data refer to tender offers for publicly traded companies. Successful offers refer to both fully and partially successful deals.

[2]Offers still pending as of year-end are also included in these totals.

SOURCE: W.T. Grimm, *Mergerstat Review,* selected years.

votes, gains control, and replaces existing management. But what factors need be present in the target and the bidder firms for hostile takeovers to occur?

Conflicts of interest between the target firm's management and shareholders lie at the root of the hostile takeover phenomenon. These conflicts result from the separation of ownership (shareholders) from control (management). Conflicts arise from management's desire to use the firm's resources to achieve outcomes that do not coincide with shareholders' interest, which is maximizing the net present value of the firm's future profits.

Economists term the lost profits arising from the separation of ownership and control, agency costs. Internal controls are generally sufficient to hold down these agency costs. But when agency costs become too high and internal controls, particularly the board of directors, have failed to protect the interests of shareholders from inefficient performance and non value-maximizing behavior of management, the firm is likely to become the target of a hostile takeover bid.[3]

Several factors can influence the level of agency costs. Often factors such as deregulation and increased competition create a need for valuation and restructuring of corporate assets in an effort to continue to maximize shareholder value. But sometimes current management fails to undertake the necessary steps to do so. New management without prior ties to employees or the community may be more objective and better able to adapt the firm's productive assets to its changing environment. Hostile takeovers are one way of effecting the necessary changes.[4]

Diana L. Fortier is an economist at the Federal Reserve Bank of Chicago. The author thanks Herbert Baer and Bruce Petersen for their helpful comments.

Firms that are undervalued by the market, that is, there is a mismatch between realizable asset value and stock price, for whatever reason, are prime takeover targets. It is often argued that firms with managements that concentrate on long-term investments (e.g., research and development) at the expense of short-term earnings are susceptible takeover targets. The premise to this explanation of hostile takeovers is that markets are short-sighted and poor current profits lead to stock undervaluations which create favorable takeover conditions. Agency costs arise here as the market puts more emphasis on current cash flows and management places greater weight on future cash flows. However, evidence does not support this "myopic market" hypothesis.[5]

Significant amounts of free cash flow also contribute to agency costs. Free cash flow is that cash flow in excess of the amount required to fund all projects that have a positive net present value when discounted at the relevant cost of capital. With high levels of free cash flow, managers may seek to secure their own position by making inefficient low-return investments rather than paying out the free cash flow to shareholders in the form of dividends.[6] Yet, it may be difficult to distinguish this behavior from prudent investing that turns out to be less profitable than expected.

Agency costs may also explain why some companies choose to initiate hostile takeovers. Companies with significant free cash flow and unused borrowing power may engage in unwarranted acquisition activity—paying significant premiums for targets to fulfill objectives other than value maximization. Acquisitions aimed at diversification, geographic expansion, or increased firm size may be pursued in order to further management's goals of self-entrenchment or "empire-building" rather than enrich shareholders. Thus, unwarranted acquisition activity not only explains why firms may become targets, but is also one explanation of bidder behavior in takeovers. This may also explain instances of negative returns to shareholders of acquiring firms—management benefits at the expense of shareholders.

Firms initiating hostile takeovers may also be victims of hubris. This "winner's curse" hypothesis asserts that takeovers may be motivated by the bidder's overestimation of the value of the target firm, when there may not be any true gains to be had.[7]

Defensive tactics—the target's response

Whatever the cause of the hostile takeover attempt, a target or potential target must respond. Data in Table 1 indicate that only 25 percent of all targets are successful in remaining independent. Another 25 percent are saved from the hands of the hostile bidder but are acquired under friendly terms by a "white knight." The remaining 50 percent ultimately fall prey to the hostile acquirer.

Despite the fact that few targets are successful at fending off hostile suitors, there are several defensive measures available to boards, managements, and shareholders to assist them in their efforts to maintain an independent organization or current management.

The best defense

It is often said that the best defense is a strong offense. In the case of hostile takeovers a firm's best defense is the restoration of a closer relationship between asset values and share price. Thus, increased returns to shareholders or increased price/earnings ratios may be the most effective and direct "defensive" measure for an organization. Indeed, taking actions to increase the firm's value (e.g., selling underperforming units) before someone else takes over and does so may also achieve the results of increased stock prices and possible shareholder gains.

An evaluation of the firm's business strategies, ownership composition, and capital structure is a prerequisite to achieving these goals. Internal restructurings have a dual benefit of improving shareholder value through a more efficient allocation of resources and reducing the need to rely on other more costly takeover defenses.

Employee stock ownership plans (ESOPs) and leveraged recapitalizations or leveraged cash-outs (LCOs), are among the commonly used methods of restructuring a firm's capital and equity position and subsequently building its takeover defenses.[8] Both of these methods have a positive impact on shareholder wealth through an improved alignment of shareholder and management interests and shareholder tax benefits.

ESOPs change the equity structure toward a greater proportional ownership by employees. Also, ESOPs may improve takeover defenses because the trustees of the voting stock of the ESOP are often controlled by management. LCOs, which require shareholder approval, increase firm leverage and management's proportional ownership. Efficiency and performance should improve under incumbent management as commitments to debt repayment reduce management's discretionary use of free cash flow. Hence, the agency costs of management/shareholder conflicts decline because default on debt service would have substantial negative financial impacts on management. In addition to increasing capital market scrutiny of the firm, the increased leverage also decreases the opportunity for a bidder to borrow against the assets of the firm to finance its acquisition.

Although size alone was once thought to be an effective takeover deterrent, it has become increasingly evident that it is no longer a reliable defense. Small firms may obtain acquisition resources for larger firms by issuing claims on the value of the target firm's assets, as with any other corporate investment. The ability to do this has been facilitated by the increase in financial market liquidity, particularly with increased acceptance of, and usage of, junk bonds.[9]

Antitakeover amendments

Despite an excellent offense, protection from hostile takeovers may still be difficult without some other line of defense. There are numerous defensive mechanisms or "shark repellents" available through corporate bylaws and charter amendments. Not all of these provisions require shareholder approval. (See Box.)

Yet, as defensive tactics develop, so too do methods to render them ineffective. As a result, antitakeover amendments do not generally halt takeovers, rather they make them more difficult, more costly, more time consuming, and may also be harmful to shareholders. Basically, these defensive tactics impose conditions that must be met before control can be changed, whether by tender offer, merger, or replacement of the board. For example, shareholder rights plans dilute the equity holdings of the bidder and fair price amendments increase the cost of acquisition.

A study of hostile takeover attempts in 1985 indicates that the most often used defensive measures of targets in those cases were acquisition by a white knight, recapitalization such as a stock buy-back, and litigation.[10] As noted earlier, leverage-increasing transactions such as recapitalizations can diminish the attractiveness of the target by decreasing the ability of the acquirer to borrow against the assets of the target to finance the acquisition. LCOs also enhance takeover defenses by reducing the agency costs created when high levels of free cash flow are available. Litigation serves as a defense by increasing the costs and uncertainty of takeover and thus deterring bidders.

The ability of a firm to defend itself is also affected by its state of incorporation. The powers of firms, shareholders, and managers are controlled by state statutes that define and regulate corporations. (See Table 2.) The constitutionality of state restrictions on takeovers was supported by an April 1987 Supreme Court ruling.[11]

Also affecting the battle lines between bidders and targets are administrative and regulatory requirements. Tender offer disclosure, delay rules, and regulatory approval periods slow the acquisition process. This usually gives targets additional time to build defenses and often leads to increases in multiple and preemptive bidding and auction contests, all of which tend to decrease bidder returns by increasing target premiums.[12]

The impact of antitakeover amendments

Several researchers have studied the impact of antitakeover amendments on targets' shareholders. Those amendments adopted by management without shareholder approval are in most cases found to be detrimental to shareholders. Although amendments requiring shareholder approval should be less likely to harm shareholders, about half of them have also been found to result in significant negative abnormal returns to target shareholders. (See Box.)

Among the most common defensive devices that require shareholder approval are fair price amendments, which have been found to have no significant effects on shareholders, and classified boards and supermajority clauses, both of which have been found to have significant negative impacts on shareholder wealth. The poison pill, which does not require shareholder approval, has proven to be an effective and popular, yet controversial, defensive measure. However, its adoption has been shown to have significant adverse effects on shareholders.[13]

Why do shareholders approve amendments that may decrease shareholder wealth? Proponents of antitakeover amendments argue that such amendments are in the shareholders' interest by giving boards the power to ensure that the shareholder receives a fair price reflecting their maximum possible share of expected acquisition gains. Management, by acting as a negotiating agent for diffuse shareholder interests, is better able to hold out for the best price by reducing individual incentives to tender at too low a price. Of course, the composition of ownership will also affect the dispersion of shareholder interests. The greater the proportion of insider (management) stockholders, the more likely antitakeover amendments will be in the shareholders' interest.

According to this shareholder interest hypothesis, antitakeover amendments are a negotiating tool rather than a takeover deterrent. This argument seems to rest on the assumption that antitakeover amendments are ineffective at ultimately deterring takeovers. It suggests that the adoption of anti-takeover amendments should have a positive impact on stock prices not because of the antitakeover amendment per se, but from the anticipation of ultimate takeover and positive returns. However, many of these antitakeover provisions have been found to decrease shareholder value, and research provides weak support for the shareholder interest hypothesis.[14]

Opponents of antitakeover amendments argue that management may abuse their veto power and act in their own interests at the expense of shareholders. They view such amendments as detrimental because they can entrench current management, reduce shareholder wealth by deterring tender offers and potentially valuable take-over bids, or reduce their share of the take-over premiums due to the acquirer's in-creased transactions costs as a result of the amendments. In general, they argue that such amendments have a negative impact on the efficient allocation of real capital in the economy. A fall in equity values resulting from adoption of antitakeover amendments would support the managerial entrench-ment hypothesis.[15]

One way of dealing with, though not eliminating, this shareholder/management conflict of interest is for the board to estab-lish management compensation contracts with ownership stakes (e.g., stock options) to promote value-maximizing behavior by management.[16] Yet, boards often are not ef-fective in controlling management behavior because the managers are able to create a board of directors loyal to management or with financial interests in maintaining existing management. Moreover, directors may lack sufficient information to determine the degree of value-maximizing behavior of management.

Ownership composition

A firm's ownership composition also influences its defensive position. The per-centage of institutional holdings and insider holdings affect the ability to get shareholder approval of antitakeover provisions. The lower the percentage of institutional hold-ings and the higher the percentage of insider holdings, the more likely antitakeover meas-ures, particularly those with negative wealth effects, will obtain shareholder approval.[17]

Although inside holders have financial interests to protect, they also have careers to be concerned about. Thus, inside holders may trade-off wealth accumulation for greater corporate control. Data suggest that the greater the percentage of insider hold-ings of the hostile target the better the tar-get's chances of remaining independent. In-stitutional holders also have large economic interests to protect; however, data do not suggest that relatively large shares of institu-tional holdings are indicative of greater takeover vulnerability.[18]

Also of importance is the percentage of low-stake uninformed shareholders. The costs of assessing antitakeover amendments are high for uninformed shareholders and incentives are relatively low for low-stake holders. Thus, such shareholders tend to vote with management under the assumption that voting more often with management than against them is more likely, in the long run, to yield greater shareholder wealth.

Effects of hostile takeovers and policy implications

The previous actions have presented the major elements of the hostile takeover battle and, as with any battle, there will be a win-ner and a loser. However, the effects of the battle go beyond the direct combatants. The remaining sections will discuss the impact of hostile takeovers on various stakeholders: shareholders, management, labor, and soci-ety in general. Although conclusive evi-dence on the net economic welfare impacts of hostile takeovers is elusive, arguments for and against them are not.

The winners: Target shareholders

Evidence from short-period merger event studies (covering the few weeks around a takeover announcement) clearly indicate that stockholders of target firms benefit by receiving positive abnormal returns—gains above those that would have occurred had the stock followed overall market movements. A recent study conser-vatively estimates the gain to target share-holders from takeovers of publicly traded

Takeover and defense tactics*

There are numerous tactics for taking over corporations. Even more numerous are the modes of defense against takeovers. Following is a list of the major actions available to the offensive and defensive players of this increasingly popular enterprise, corporate takeover. The defensive tactics are grouped according to their impact on shareholder wealth, as indicated by research to date.

TAKEOVERS

■ *Leveraged buyout:* heavily debt-financed buyout of shareholder equity often by incumbent management.

■ *Merger:* bidder negotiates with target management on the terms of the offer which is then submitted to a vote of the target's shareholders.

■ *Proxy contest:* by a vote of the shareholders a dissident group tries to gain a controlling position on the board.

■ *Tender offer:* bidder makes offer to shareholders for some or all of the target's stock.

   Friendly: offer supported by the target company's management.

   Unfriendly (hostile): offer opposed by target management.

DEFENSIVE TACTICS
(Shareholder approval required)

No impact or no evidence of impact on target shareholder wealth

■ *Dual-class recapitalizations:* restructure equity into two classes with different voting rights with the goal of providing management or family owners with voting power disproportionately greater than provided by their equity holdings under a one-share, one-vote rule; typical dual class firm is already controlled by insiders and the recapitalization may also provide needed capital without dilution of control and without harm to the stock value.

■ *Fair-price provision:* a supermajority provision which applies only to nonuniform two-tier hostile takeover bids; insures that all shareholders selling within a certain time period receive the same price; the usual determination of fairness is the highest price paid by the bidder for any of the shares it has acquired in the target during a certain time period; has a low deterrence value and is not detrimental to stock values.

■ *Rights of shareholders:* restricts rights of shareholders to vote on issues between annual meetings or at special shareholder meetings (e.g., only supermajority vote of the shareholders or the president of the board may call a special meeting).

Positive impact

■ *Leveraged recapitalization or leveraged cash-out:* a change in capital structure and equity ownership, retaining a publicly traded company; financial leverage is increased significantly as the company replaces the majority of its equity with debt so that a raider can not borrow against the assets of the firm to finance an acquisition; management (insiders) in essence receives a stock-split and proportional increase in ownership as all but inside shareholders receive a large one-time payout in cash or debt securities and continued equity interest in the restructured company.

Negative impact on target shareholder wealth

■ *Change state of incorporation:* stringency of state antitakeover laws vary; may harm shareholders because it reduces takeover chances; may benefit states as they increase the likelihood of keeping jobs with strict state laws.

■ *Reduction in cumulative voting rights:* increases management's ability to resist a tender offer but appears to reduce shareholder wealth. (Cumulative voting rights allow a group of minority shareholders to elect directors even if the majority opposes because each shareholder is entitled to cast a number of votes equal to the number of shares owned multiplied by the number of directors to be elected—thus one could accumulate votes for a particular director or group of directors.)

■ *Staggered directors or classified board:* directors are broken into classes (usually three groups) with only one class being elected each year; works best with limit on number of board members; makes it difficult for a substantial shareholder to change all of the board at once without approval or cooperation of the existing board, but also makes any change of directors more difficult; also lowers the effectiveness of cumulative voting; has impact of significant negative abnormal returns.

■ *Supermajority clause:* increases the number of votes of outstanding common stock needed to approve changes in control to two-thirds or nine-tenths from a majority of one-half (director must also be removed for cause); found to have significant negative stock-price effects around their introduction and on average they appear to reduce shareholder wealth; important to have an escape clause (provision allowing for simple majority vote) so that friendly offers are not also foreclosed; almost always combined with a lock-in provision.

■ *Lock-in provision:* prevents circumvention of antitakeover provisions; most common provision requires a supermajority vote to change antitakeover amendments or limits the number of directors; has impact of a significant negative abnormal return.

(Shareholder approval not required)

Negative impact on target shareholder wealth

■ *Litigation by target management:* a win by target may harm shareholders in that chances of acquisition may be lost or lowered—this may be reflected by a fall in share price, whereas the acquisition is likely to have increased share prices (examples: charges of securities fraud, antitrust violations, or violations of state or federal tender offer rules); delays control fight, yet also gives management time to find a friendlier deal.

■ *Shareholder rights plans or poison pills:* do not require majority voting approval by shareholders; are triggered by an event such as a tender offer, or by the accumulation of a certain percentage of target's stock by a single stockholder; trigger allows target shareholders with rights to purchase additional shares or to sell shares to the target at very attractive prices; can be cheaply and quickly altered by target management yet makes hostile takeovers very expensive by diluting the equity holdings of the bidder, revoking his voting rights or forcing him to assume unwanted financial obligations; different types include: flip-over, flip-in, back-end, and voting plans; generally harmful to stock values; judicial approval of certain types of plans (e.g., flip-in and back-end) is still not clear.

■ *Target block stock repurchases or greenmail:* target repurchases, at a premium, the hostile bidders block of target's stock; often results in substantial fall in stock returns for the target or reduced shareholder value from foregone takeover potential as opposed to normally positive stock price effects of a repurchase of stock by a nontargeted firm; yet evidence indicates that a net positive stock price may result from the initial hostile bidder purchase (positive impact) to the target repurchase (negative effect); benefits returns for bidder firm shareholders; practice is controversial and has been challenged in federal courts, congressional testimony, and SEC hearings.

---

*For empirical evidence of the effects of defensive tactics and the market for corporate control see footnote 14 of the text.

companies between 1981 and 1986 to be 47.8 percent, or an estimated dollar value of $134.4 billion. Additionally, the average premium on all mergers and acquisitions in 1987 was 38.3 percent whereas the average for hostile takeovers that year was 42.7 percent.[19]

Bidder shareholders may gain or lose

For the acquiring firm, the results from the same studies are not so unequivocal. They indicate that on average there is no significant short-period effect, positive or negative, on shareholder returns, and, if anything, there is at best a slight positive impact on the acquirer's share value.[20] Evidence from longer-period event studies (one to three years) suggests that increases in target stock prices during takeovers overestimate the post-merger increase in firm value. Despite this overvaluation, recent research concludes that the average successful tender offer results in a statistically significant positive revaluation of the combined firm. Such increases have been fairly consistent over time. However, bidder gains have been diminishing over the last two decades while target returns have increased.[21] Thus, it appears that on average takeovers and mergers enhance shareholder value.

While it is concluded that mergers and acquisitions enhance shareholder value, this conclusion does not imply that such value is derived entirely, or at all, from increased efficiency (e.g., resource reallocation, removal of inefficient management, or economies of scale or scope).

Sources of gain: Improved efficiency or wealth redistribution

Although easily measured, shareholder gains do not provide an accurate measure of welfare gains. If takeover gains are a result of wealth transfers, then the increase in share prices overstates the efficiency gains of takeover. Shareholder gains must be weighed against the losses of other stakeholders such as management and employees.

As opponents of hostile takeovers argue, takeover gains result primarily from wealth redistributions: one stakeholder's gain—the target shareholder—is at the expense of another's economic loss—such as the target employee or bondholder. In the extreme, such takeovers are merely costly and disruptive restructurings of corporations that provide no social benefits. Preventing such takeovers would, it is argued, improve economic welfare.

Proponents argue that takeovers provide net gains to society by reducing the agency costs related to management/shareholder conflicts, which, in turn, improves resource allocation and efficiency and encourages value-maximizing behavior. Thus, attempts to prevent a free corporate control market would have negative effects.

Overall, research is not conclusive on the sources of takeover gain and indicates that gains from redistribution as well as increased efficiency may be occurring. The sources of gain vary from deal to deal, from industry to industry, and from year to year. Studies have addressed the wealth transfers to target shareholders from target bondholders, government, and target labor.

One version of the redistribution theory asserts that the gain of one class of security holders comes at the expense of another. For example, bondholder values may decline as common shareholder values increase. This example may be more relevant to highly leveraged transactions in which corporate bond prices may fall and yields rise as increased leverage contributes to uncertainty about the acquirer's ability to service its debt. Despite some recent examples of such behavior related to leveraged buy-outs, studies of both mergers and leveraged buy-outs have failed to find consistent support for this theory.[22] Moreover, when such redistributions have occurred, the increase in shareholder value often more than offsets the fall in bond values. Thus, takeovers appear to result in net gains to investors as a group. In general, target shareholders' gains do not occur at the expense of either bidder shareholders or other classes of target or bidder investors.

The increase in shareholder value resulting from hostile takeovers could also be a redistribution from the government to shareholders. Hostile takeovers may generate tax savings without any underlying efficiency gains. Thus, government becomes another stakeholder in the takeover battle. But the evidence indicates that tax benefits have been only a minor force behind takeovers.[23]

Another form of redistribution espoused recently is that shareholder gains come at the expense of labor through long-term labor contract concessions which reduce employment or wages. Evidence from small firm acquisitions (not hostile takeovers) does not support assertions that acquisitions have an overall negative effect on labor in terms of lower employment and wages.[24] However, hostile takeovers usually involve large organizations and create a fear that both explicit and implicit commitments by target management to labor will be broken following the takeover. A notable example is Carl Icahn's hostile purchase of TWA which resulted in improved management and shareholder premiums worth $300 to $400 million, but also resulted in wealth transfers to Icahn from three labor unions which one researcher valued at $600 million or one and a half times the takeover premium.[25] In this case, it would appear that shareholders gained principally at the expense of labor. The unanswered question is whether such labor concessions are simply wealth transfers or actually enhance efficiency.

Labor-related inefficiencies may result from the inability of management to respond appropriately to factors, such as technological developments, which decrease the demand for labor, or result from failure to deal successfully with a labor force that wields market power. In either case, these inefficiencies create conditions ripe for hostile takeovers, which in turn become the mechanism by which efficiency is enhanced. This does not mean that labor will always be a casualty in a hostile takeover battle. Takeover activity, and hence the fear of takeover, may be favorable to labor in that efficiency gains at potential target companies can lead to job preservation and greater long-run growth and employment.

Economic efficiency theories argue that net gains may occur from increases in economic efficiency achieved through major restructurings and better management of corporate assets. Takeovers can reduce agency costs and result in more efficient capital investments by subjecting the firm to the scrutiny of the capital markets and by reducing resources under management control. Benefits accrue when target shareholder wealth that had been appropriated to target management, employees, suppliers, or customers under non value-maximizing behavior is reallocated to target shareholders and the acquirer upon acquisition.

Business line financial data has been used to test the efficiency enhancement theory of takeovers by analyzing the *ex post* financial performance of acquiring firms. Two implications of the theory that takeovers increase efficiency due to improved management have been tested. First, the target's pre-takeover profits should be less than its industry peers', and second, *ceteris paribus*, post-takeover profitability should be relatively higher than pre-takeover profitability.

Examining these hypotheses, Scherer found that targets were slight underperformers relative to their industry norm, but that "operating performance neither improved nor deteriorated significantly following takeover," and "there is no indication that on average the acquirers raised their targets' operating profitability net of merger-related accounting adjustments."[26]

Generally, studies using accounting data to analyze post-takeover performance do not clearly support the economic efficiency theory of takeover gains. Unless this inconclusiveness can be attributed to measurement problems associated with the use of accounting data or the lack of coordination in the use of market and accounting data in analyzing shareholder gains and the sources of those gains, one must question whether there are any true wealth gains derived from the supposed improved management and efficiency subsequent to takeover.

While operational efficiencies may be elusive, it appears that financial market inefficiencies do create opportunities for takeover gains. If takeovers lead to the revaluation of undervalued firms, the cost of raising additional capital will be lower and more investment will take place. Several studies have tested the market undervaluation hypothesis. Evidence on it is mixed.

Empirical evidence using stock price data do not generally support the theory that target firms are victims of undervaluation. Stock prices of targets successful at fending off hostile bidders decline to approximately pre-bid levels. That is, the tender offer process does not reveal to the market significant new information about the intrinsic value of the target such that substantial price adjustments (increases) occur due to prior undervaluations of the target by the market. It is not merely the information generated from putting a firm into play, but the actual acquisition and expected gains that result in positive stock returns.[27]

However, an analysis of market valuation of large, multidivisional targets using business line financial data as well as market data provide somewhat different results. If the sum of the liquidation or replacement value of the firm's parts is greater than the market value of the firm as a whole then it is undervalued by the market. It is argued that this provides incentive for takeover by creating opportunities to improve performance and add value by divesting the target of certain units whose assets are more productively managed elsewhere. This has been the strategy in the recent takeovers of many conglomerates formed by previous diversification acquisitions.

Recent research suggests "that there is some undervaluation in the market as a whole, which can probably be attributed to underpricing of both multi-industry companies and small companies." Further, this undervaluation is proportional to the number of firm divisions and is more prevalent in certain industries and organizations with low institutional holdings.[28]

Conclusion

Although contested tender offers are a small fraction of all merger and acquisition activity, the target and bidder costs of fighting a hostile battle and the slight chances of targets remaining independent, as well as the attendant social costs of the fight, magnify the importance of understanding and dealing with the corporate control market.

A successful and profitable takeover depends on the extent to which the target firm is undervalued, the inefficiency of target management, the cost of overcoming the target's takeover defenses, the ability of the acquirer to transfer wealth from other stakeholders, and the ability of the bidder to divert some gains from the target shareholders.

Target shareholders are definite winners in the hostile takeover battle. Bidder shareholders, on average, have equal probabilities of gaining or losing and, at best, obtain modest gains.

However, the source and quantification of the gains to target shareholders remain elusive. Research does not provide clear support for the hypothesis that there are real efficiency gains from takeovers. Support for the several versions of the wealth redistribution theory is mixed. Wealth transfers are most likely to have negative effects on target management.

What is clear, however, is that net shareholder gains are not an accurate measure of welfare gains resulting from takeovers. Only with additional research can the social and economic welfare implications and policy directives regarding hostile takeovers be more precisely drawn.

Footnotes

[1] Data on net merger and acquisition announcements are from *Mergerstat Review* 1978-1987. (Chicago: W. T. Grimm & Co.) Of the 2,032 net merger and acquisition announcements in 1987, there were only 972 in which the dollar value of the deal was disclosed.

[2] For instance, S. 1323 and S. 1324, 100th Cong. 1st sess. (1987) (amending Section 14 of the Securities Exchange Act of 1934, 15 U.S.C.).

"Securities Regulation, Hostile Corporate Takeovers: Synopses of Thirty-Two Attempts," United

States General Accounting Office, March 1988, GAO/GGD-88-48FS, a study of 32 hostile takeover attempts in 1985 provides data indicating that, although financial-advisory-related service fees totaled approximately $60 million, this is only a minor fraction of the total value of the deals. Nonetheless, that data also indicate that in successful hostile takeovers, the target spent approximately twice as much as the bidder on such services.

[3] For a sample of papers dealing with the value maximization hypothesis, see Eugene F. Fama and Michael C.

Jensen, "Organizational Forms and Investment Decisions," *Journal of Financial Economics*, Vol. 14, No. 1, (March 1985), pp. 101-119; Eugene F. Fama, E. and Martin H. Miller, *The Theory of Finance*, (Hinsdale, Ill.: Dryden Press, 1972), Chapter 2; and Paul Asquith, Robert F. Bruner, and David W. Mullins, Jr., "The Gains to Bidding Firms from Merger." *Journal of Financial Economics*, Vol. 11, No. 1-4, (April 1983), pp. 121-139. Andrei Shleifer and Robert W. Vishny, "Value Maximization and the Acquisition Process," *Journal of Economic Perspectives*, Vol. 2, No. 1, (Winter 1988), pp. 7-20, examine the failure of internal control mechanisms as one explanation of hostile takeovers.

[4] Randall Morck, Andrei Shleifer, and Robert W. Vishny, "Characteristics of Targets of Hostile and Friendly Takeovers," in Auerbach, *Corporate Takeovers*, pp. 101-136 study the characteristics of hostile takeover targets and suggest that hostile takeovers occur in declining industries and those in a state of change, where management is slow to adjust to the changing environment for whatever reasons--e.g., to maintain their control or to protect employees from pay reductions or job eliminations.

[5] Michael C. Jensen, "Takeovers: Their Causes and Consequences," *Journal of Economic Perspectives*, Vol. 2, No. 1, (Winter 1988), pp. 55.; Randall J. Woolridge, "Competitive Decline and Corporate Restructuring: Is a Myopic Stock Market to Blame?," *Journal of Applied Corporate Finance*, Vol.1, No. 1, (Spring 1988), pp. 26-36 finds that a myopic market is not to blame as "common stock prices react positively to announcements of corporate strategic investment decisions and the market appears to place considerable emphasis on prospective long-term developments in valuing securities." See also Bronwyn H. Hall, "The Effect of Takeover Activity on Corporate Research and Development," Alan J. Auerbach, ed., *Corporate Takeovers: Causes and Consequences*, (Chicago: University of Chicago Press, 1988), pp. 69-100; John J. McConnell and Chris J. Muscarella, "Capital Expenditure Decisions and Market Value of the Firm," *Journal of Financial Economics*, Vol. 14, 1985, pp. 523-553; and Jeremy C. Stein, "Takeover Threats and Managerial Myopia," *Journal of Political Economy*, Vol. 96, No. 1, (Feb. 1988), pp. 61-80.

[6] See Michael C. Jensen, "Agency Costs of Free Cash Flow, Corporate Finance, and Takeovers," *American Economic Review*, Vol. 76, No. 2, (May 1986, Papers and Proceedings, 1985), pp. 323-329.

[7] Richard Roll, "The Hubris Hypothesis of Corporate Takeovers." *Journal of Business*, Vol. 59, No. 2, (April 1986), pp. 197-216.

[8] For a series of articles discussing methods of and effects of corporate restructuring including Employee Stock Option Plans and Leveraged Cash-outs, see *Journal of Applied Corporate Finance*, Vol. 1, No. 1, (Spring 1988). For evidence of stock price reactions to capital structure changes generally indicating a direct correlation between changes in leverage and stock prices, see

[8] Michael C. Jensen and C. W. Smith Jr., "Stockholder, Manager and Creditor Interests: Applications of Agency Theory," in E. Altman and M. Subrahmanyam, eds., *Recent Advances in Corporate Finance*, (Homewood: Richard Irwin, 1985), pp. 93-131.

[9] Although 30-40 percent of the junk bonds issued since 1985 have been used in acquisition-related financing, these junk-bond-financed transactions only accounted for approximately 8 percent of total merger financings in 1986, up from 4.3 percent in 1985. *(Mergers and Acquisitions, 1987).*

[10] GAO, Securities Regulation.

[11] Supreme Court of the United States, *CTS Corp. v. Dynamics Corporation of America*, 107 S Ct 1637(1987). Appeal from the United States Court of Appeals for the Seventh Circuit, No. 86-71. Argued March 2, 1987 and decided April 21, 1987. This decision reverses prior court trends and raises the possibility that state legislation may have a substantive impact on corporate control contests. The case upheld one form of takeover statute, the Indiana control share acquisition provision. For an invalidation of a state control share statute on constitutional grounds, see *RTE Corporation* v. *Mark IV Industries*, Civ. Action No. 88-C-378 (E.D. Wis.) May 6, 1988. Also see Lynn E. Browne and Eric S. Rosengren, "Should States Restrict Takeovers?" *New England Economic Review*, Federal Reserve Bank of Boston, (July/August 1987), pp. 13-21, for a discussion of state antitakeover laws.

[12] Sanford J. Grossman and Oliver D. Hart, "Takeover Bids, the Free-Rider Problem, and the Theory of the Corporation." *Bell Journal of Economics*, Vol. 11, No. 1, (Spring 1980), pp. 42-64 discuss the ability of bidders to gain from takeover, and Andrei Shleifer and Robert W. Vishny, "Greenmail, White Knights, and Shareholders' Interest," *Rand Journal of Economics*, Vol. 17, No. 3, (Autumn 1986), pp. 293-309 discuss the accumulation of shares prior to full disclosure.

The Williams Act, a 1968 amendment to the Securities and Exchange Act of 1933, Public Law No. 90-439, 82 Stat. 454 (July 29, 1968) as amended in 1970 Public Law No. 91-567, 84 Stat. 1497 (December 22, 1970) governs tender offers with disclosure, offer period and other procedural requirements, as well as antifraud provisions. It was intended to protect shareholders by allowing sufficient time and information to properly analyze a tender offer.

[13] For empirical evidence of the effects of defensive tactics and the market for corporate control see Greg A. Jarrell, James A. Brickley, and Jeffery M. Netter, "The Market for Corporate Control: The Empirical Evidence Since 1980," *Journal of Economic Perspectives*. Vol. 2, No. 1, (Winter 1988), pp.49-68; Gregg A. Jarrell and Annette B. Poulsen, "Shark Repellents and Stock Prices, The Effects of Antitakeover Amendments Since 1980." *Journal of Financial Economics*, Vol. 19, No. 1, (Sept. 1987), pp. 127-168; John Pound, "The Effects of Antitakeover Amendments on Takeover Activity: Some Direct Evidence," *The Journal of Law and Economics*,

(Oct. 1987), pp. 353-367; and Michael Ryngaert, "The Effect of Poison Pill Securities on Shareholder Wealth," *Journal of Financial Economics*, Vol. 20, No. 1-2, (January/March 1988), pp. 127-168.

[14]Scott C. Linn and John J. McConnell, "An Empirical Investigation of the Impact of 'Antitakeover' Amendments on Common Stock Prices," *Journal of Financial Economics*, Vol. 11, No. 4, (April 1983), pp. 361-399.

[15]Harry DeAngelo and Edward M. Rice, "Antitakeover Charter Amendments and Stockholder Wealth," *Journal of Financial Economics*, Vol. 11, No. 1-4, (April 1983), pp. 329-359 find weak support for the managerial entrenchment hypothesis.

[16]Kevin J. Murphy, "Corporate Performance and Managerial Remuneration: An Empirical Analysis," *Journal of Accounting and Economics*, Vol. 7, No. 1-3, (April 1985), pp. 11-42 found a positive relationship between stock performance and managers' pay; and James A. Brickley, Sanjai Bhagat, and Ronald C. Lease, "The Impact of Long-Range Managerial Compensation Plans on Shareholder Wealth," *Journal of Accounting and Economics*, Vol. 7, No. 1-3, (April 1985), pp. 115-130; and Hassan Tehranian and James F. Waegelein, "Market Reaction to Short Term Executive Compensation Plan Adoption," *Journal of Accounting and Economics*, Vol. 7, No. 1-3, (April 1985), pp. 131-144 find introductions of incentive-based compensation programs cause stock price increases. The problem of management performance not achieving cost minimization and profit maximization at the expense of shareholders (absentee owners) was first identified by Adolf A.Berle, Jr. and Gardiner C. Means, *The Modern Corporation and Private Property*, 1932, (New York, New York: Macmillan, 1932).

[17]Jarrell and Poulsen, "Shark Repellents and Stock Prices." Today, institutional investors account for approximately 66 percent to 75 percent of equity ownership and trading compared to about 5 percent in the early 1960s.

[18]GAO, Securities Regulation. 1985 data indicate that insider holdings averaged 21.8 percent for nine targets of unsuccessful takeover attempts and averaged 4.8 percent and 9.5 percent, respectively, for nine successful takeovers and seven targets acquired by white-knights. T. Boone Pickens, Jr., "Professions of a Short-Termer," *Harvard Business Review*, Vol. 64, No. 3, (May/June 1986), pp. 77 states that takeover targets from 1981-1984 averaged 22 percent institutional ownership compared to a market average of 35 percent.

[19]Bernard S. Black and Joseph A. Grundfest, "Shareholder Gains From Takeovers and Restructurings Between 1981 and 1986: $162 Billion is a Lot of Money," *Journal of Applied Corporate Finance*, Vol. 1, No. 1, (Spring 1988), pp. 5-15; Michael C. Jensen and Richard S. Ruback, "The Market for Corporate Control," *Journal of Financial Economics*, Vol. 11, No. 1-4, (April 1983), pp. 5-50; Roll, "The Hubris Hypothesis of Corporate Takeovers"; Jarrell, Brickley, and Netter,

"The Market for Corporate Control: The Empirical Evidence Since 1980," *Journal of Economic Perspectives*, (Winter 1988), pp. 49-58; Michael Bradley, Anand Desai, and E. Han Kim, "Synergistic Gains from Corporate Acquisitions and Their Diversion between the Target and Acquiring Firms," Working Paper, School of Business Administration, University of Michigan, 1987; and Asquith, Bruner, and Mullins, Jr., "The Gains to Bidding Firms from Merger."

[20]Jensen and Ruback, "The Market for Corporate Control" provides an extensive review of corporate control market studies and finds shareholders of acquirers do not lose; and Roll, "The Hubris Hypothesis of Corporate Takeovers" finds statistically insignificant results showing that acquirers, on average, do lose on bid announcements. Jarrell, Brickley, and Netter, "The Market for Corporate Control: The Empirical Evidence Since 1980" updates and confirms the earlier Jensen and Ruback (1983) study.

[21]In contrast to the earlier studies using aggregate data, Michael Bradley, Anand Desai, and E. Han Kim, "Synergistic Gains from Corporate Acquisitions and Their Diversion between the Target and Acquiring Firms" study the gains and losses of matched pairs of bidders and targets from 1962-1984 and find a statistically significant synergistic gain of 7.5 percent created from tender offer combinations.

For empirical evidence on post-merger (long-run) negative returns and discussion of the issue, see F.M. Scherer, "Corporate Takeovers: The Efficiency Arguments," *Journal of Economic Perspectives*, Vol. 2, No. 1, (Winter 1988), p. 71; Jensen and Ruback, "The Market for Corporate Control," pg. 20; and Ellen Magenhein and Dennis C. Mueller, "On Measuring the Effect of Mergers on Acquiring Firm Shareholders" in John C. Coffee, Jr. et.al, eds. *Knights, Raiders and Targets*, (New York: Oxford University Press), 1988.

[22]Debra K. Dennis and J. McConnell, "Corporate Mergers and Security Returns," *Journal of Financial Economics*, Vol. 16, No. 2, (June 1986), pp. 143-187; Kenneth Lehn and Annette B. Poulsen, "Sources of Value in Leveraged Buyouts," in *Public Policy Towards Corporate Takeovers*, (New Brunswick, NJ: Transaction Publishers), 1987; Paul Asquith and E. Han Kim, "The Impact of Merger Bids on the Participating Firms' Security Holders," *Journal of Finance*, Vol. 37, No. 5, (December 1982), pp. 1209-1228; and "Buyouts Devastating to Bondholders," *New York Times*, October 26, 1988.

[23]Alan J. Auerbach and David Reishus, "Taxes and the Merger Decision," in J. Coffee and Louis Lowenstein. eds., *Takeovers and Contests for Corporate Control*, (Oxford: Oxford University Press. 1987); D. Breen, "The Potential for Tax Gains as a Merger Motive," Federal Trade Commission, Bureau of Economics. July 1987; and Lehn and Poulsen, "Sources of Value in Leveraged Buyouts."

[24]Andrei Shleifer and Lawrence Summers, "Hostile Takeovers as Breaches of Trust," in Auerbach, *Corpo-*

rate Takeovers, pp. 33-68; and Charles Brown and James L. Medoff, "The Impact of Firm Acquisitions on Labor," in Auerbach, *Corporate Takeovers*, pp. 9-32. In Bernard S. Black and Joseph A. Grundfest, "Shareholder Gains From Takeovers and Restructurings Between 1981 and 1986: $162 Billion is a lot of Money," on pg. 7 the authors noted that "Yago and Stevenson also find 'no evidence that unsolicited deals had systematically different effects than friendly transactions'."

[25]Andrei Shleifer and Lawrence Summers, "Hostile Takeovers as Breaches of Trust," pg. 50.

[26]Scherer, "Corporate Takeovers: The Efficiency Arguments," pp. 75-76; and David J. Ravenscraft and F. M. Scherer, "Life After Takeover," *The Journal of Industrial Economics*, Vol. 36, No. 2, (December 1987), pp. 147-156.

[27]Michael Bradley, Anand Desai, and E. Han Kim, "The Rationale Behind Interfirm Tender Offers: Information

or Synergy?," *Journal of Financial Economics*, Vol. 11, 1983, pp. 183-206. Frank H. Easterbrook and Gregg A. Jarrell, "Do Targets Gain from Defeating Tender Offers?," *New York University Law Review*, 1984, Vol. 54, pp. 277-299 show that stock returns of targets of defeated hostile bidders fall to approximately pre-bid levels. Sanjai Bhagat, James Brickley, and Uri Lowenstein, "The Pricing Effects of Inter-Firm Cash Tender Offers," *Journal of Finance*, Vol. 42, 1987, pg. 965-986 find that increased valuations of target firms are too large to be explained solely by adjustments for prior undervaluations.

[28]See Dean LeBaron and Lawrence S. Speidell, "Why are the Parts Worth More than the Sum? 'Chop Shop,' A Corporate Valuation Model." *The Merger Boom*, Federal Reserve Bank of Boston, pp. 78-101; and Michael E. Porter, "From Competitive Advantage to Corporate Strategy," *Harvard Business Review*, Vol. 65, No. 3, (May/June 1987), pp.43-59.

References

Asquith, Paul, "Merger Bids, Uncertainty, and Stockholder Returns," *Journal of Financial Economics*, Vol. 11, No. 1-4, (April 1983), pp. 51-83.

Asquith, Paul, Robert F. Bruner, and David W. Mullins, Jr., "The Gains to Bidding Firms from Merger," *Journal of Financial Economics*, Vol. 11, No. 1-4, (April 1983), pp. 121-139.

Auerbach, Alan J., ed., *Corporate Takeovers: Causes and Consequences*, Chicago: University of Chicago Press, 1988.

Black, Bernard S., and Joseph A. Grundfest, "Shareholder Gains From Takeovers and Restructurings Between 1981 and 1986: $162 Billion is a Lot of Money," *Journal of Applied Corporate Finance*, Vol. 1, No. 1, (Spring 1988), pp. 5-15.

Browne, Lynn E., and Eric S. Rosengren, eds., "Are Hostile Takeovers Different," *The Merger Boom: Proceedings of a Conference held at Melvin Village, New Hampshire, October 1987.* Federal Reserve Bank of Boston, Conference Series; No. 31, pp. 199-229.

Browne, Lynn E., and Eric S. Rosengren, "Should States Restrict Takeovers?," *New England Economic Review*, Federal Reserve Bank of Boston, (July/August 1987), pp. 13-21.

Brown, Stephen J., and Jerold B. Warner, "Using Daily Stock Returns: The Case of Event Studies," *Journal of Financial Economics*, Vol. 14, No. 1 (March 1985), pp. 3-31.

DeAngelo, Harry, and Edward M. Rice, "Antitakeover Charter Amendments and Stockholder Wealth," *Journal of Financial Economics*, Vol. 11, No. 1-4, (April 1983), pp. 329-359.

Eckbo, B. Espen, "Horizontal Mergers, Collusion, and Stockholder Wealth," *Journal of Financial Economics*, Vol. 11, No. 1-4, (April 1983), pp. 241-273.

Jarrell, Gregg A. and Annette B. Poulsen, "Shark Repellents and Stock Prices: The Effects of Antitakeover Amendments Since 1980," *Journal of Financial Economics*, Vol. 19, No. 1, (Sept. 1987), pp. 127-168.

Jarrell, Gregg A., James A. Brickley, and Jeffry M. Netter, "The Market for Corporate Control: The Empirical Evidence Since 1980," *Journal of Economic Perspectives*, Vol. 2, No. 1, (Winter 1988), pp. 49-68.

Jensen, Michael C., "Agency Costs of Free Cash Flow, Corporate Finance, and Takeovers," Papers and Proceedings of the Ninety-Eighth Annual Meeting of the American Economic Association, New York, New York, Dec. 28-30, 1985, *The American Economic Review*, Vol. 76, No. 2, (May 1986), pp. 323-329.

Jensen, Michael C., "Takeovers: Their Causes and Consequences," *Journal of Economic Perspectives*, Vol.2, No. 1, (Winter 1988), pp. 21-48.

Jensen, Michael C., and Richard S. Ruback, "The Market for Corporate Control: The Scientific Evidence," *Journal of Financial Economics*, Vol. 11, No. 1-4, (April 1983), pp. 5-50.

Linn, Scott C., and John J. McConnell, "An Empirical Investigation of the Impact of 'Antitakeover' Amendments on Common Stock Prices," *Journal of Financial Economics*, Vol. 11, No. 1-4, (April 1983), pp. 361-399.

Malatesta, Paul H., "The Wealth Effect of Merger Activity and the Objective Functions of Merging Firms," *Journal of Financial Economics*, Vol. 11, No. 1-4, (April 1983), pp. 155-181.

Mandelker, Gershon, "Risk and Return: The Case of Merging Firms," *Journal of Financial Economics*, Vol. 1, No. 4, (December 1974), pp. 303-335.

McConnell, John J., and Chris J. Muscarella, "Corporate Capital Expenditure Decisions and the Market Value of the Firm," *Journal of Financial Economics*, Vol. 14, No. 3, (Sept. 1985), pp. 399-422.

Palepu, Krishna G., "Predicting Takeover Targets: A Methodological and Empirical Analysis," *Journal of Accounting and Economics*, Vol. 8, No.1, (March 1986), pp. 3-35.

Pound, John, "The Effects of Antitakeover Amendments on Takeover Activity: Some Direct Evidence," *The Journal of Law and Economics*, Vol. 30, No. 2, (October 1987), pp. 353-367.

Ravenscraft, David J., and F. M. Scherer, "Life After Takeover," *The Journal of Industrial Economics*, Vol. 36, No. 2, (December 1987), pp. 147-156.

Roll, Richard, "The Hubris Hypothesis of Corporate Takeovers," *Journal of Business*, Vol. 59, No. 2, (April 1986), pp. 197-216.

Scherer, F.M., "Corporate Takeovers: The Efficiency Arguments," *Journal of Economic Perspectives*, Vol. 2, No. 1, (Winter 1988), pp. 69-82.

Shleifer, Andrei, and Robert W. Vishny, "Value Maximization and the Acquisition Process," *Journal of Economic Perspectives*, Vol. 2, No.1, (Winter 1988), pp. 7-20.

Stein, Jeremy C., "Takeover Threats and Managerial Myopia," *Journal of Political Economy*, Vol. 96, No. 1, (Feb. 1988), pp. 61-80.

Woolridge, Randall J., "Competitive Decline and Corporate Restructuring: Is a Myopic Stock Market to Blame?," *Journal of Applied Corporate Finance*, Vol. 1, No. 1, (Spring 1988), pp. 26-36.

Article 14

The Corporate Bankruptcy Decision

Michelle J. White

A central tenet in economics is that competition drives markets toward a state of long-run equilibrium in which those firms remaining in existence produce at minimum average costs. In the transition to long-run equilibrium, inefficient firms, firms using obsolete technologies and those producing products that are in excess supply are eliminated. Consumers benefit because in the long run, goods and services are produced and sold at the lowest possible prices. The legal mechanism through which inefficient firms most often are eliminated is that of bankruptcy. In 1984, around 62,000 business firms filed for bankruptcy. Two-thirds of them filed to liquidate in bankruptcy and the rest filed to reorganize in bankruptcy (Administrative Office of the U.S. Courts, 1985). The total liabilities of firms that filed for bankruptcy in 1985 came to approximately $33 billion (Dun & Bradstreet, 1986).[1]

Economic theory suggests that bankruptcy should serve as a screening process designed to eliminate only those firms that are economically inefficient and whose resources could be better used in some other activity. However, firms typically file for bankruptcy voluntarily. When they do, creditors are not all repaid in full and large redistributional effects occur. Managers of firms do not take creditors' losses fully into account in deciding either how to run the firm or whether and when to file for bankruptcy. This suggests that firms in bankruptcy might not always be economically inefficient and that inefficient firms might not always end up in bankruptcy. Rather, firms may shut down and file for bankruptcy versus continuing to operate because managers respond to the potential for redistribution from creditors to equity, rather

[1]This figure includes liabilities of firms (such as Chrysler) that did not formally file for bankruptcy, but whose creditors incurred losses.

■ Michelle J. White is Professor of Economics, University of Michigan, Ann Arbor, Michigan.

than because shutdown or continued operation is more economically efficient. This paper argues that none of the commonly considered bankruptcy priority rules give firms an incentive to choose bankruptcy or to remain out of bankruptcy only when that alternative is more economically efficient. Failing firms may liquidate even in circumstances when their resources are most valuable if they continued operating and they may continue to operate even when their resources could be better employed in some new use. When reorganization is added to liquidation as an additional bankruptcy alternative, the analysis suggests that too many failing firms are likely to continue operating in the same line of business in which they were previously making losses. Thus the U.S. bankruptcy system, rather than helping the economy move toward long-run efficiency, in fact appears to delay the movement of resources to higher value uses.

The paper is divided into separate sections on bankruptcy liquidation and reorganization. In examining each of those topics, it will consider the features of an economically efficient bankruptcy procedure and how such a procedure might differ from actual U.S. bankruptcy law. In a concluding section, I consider the costs of bankruptcy and some proposed reforms. I argue that some deadweight losses are the unavoidable consequence of having a bankruptcy procedure and cannot be eliminated by reforming it. These deadweight losses are the price of having limited liability for corporate equity holders.

Liquidation

A bankruptcy filing initiates a collective legal procedure by which all claims against the firm are settled.[2] Without such a procedure, individual creditors would engage in a costly and unproductive race to be first to sue the firm for repayment of their own claims. As in a bank run, those creditors who sued first would receive payment in full until the firm's assets were exhausted, after which other creditors would receive nothing. Resources would be consumed both by creditors' duplicative monitoring expenses and by the costs of the lawsuits themselves. Even with bankruptcy, there is still an incentive for creditors to race to sue the firm first, but the incentive is muted since any appreciable volume of suits will cause the firm to enter bankruptcy.

Liquidation is the basic bankruptcy procedure. Even for firms that decide to reorganize rather than liquidate, the liquidation procedure sets the framework for bargaining over a reorganization.

---

[2]A firm that closed down and paid all its debts in full would not use the bankruptcy process, nor would a firm in difficulties that merged with a profitable firm if the latter assumed its debts. However, subsidiaries of profitable parent corporations which are losing money normally do use the bankruptcy process, since the parent is not responsible for the subsidiary's debts if the subsidiary is separately incorporated, unless the parent specifically guaranteed some of the subsidiary's debts. If a firm in financial difficulties is going to merge with a profitable firm, then it is in their joint interests for the former to file for bankruptcy before the merger.

U.S. law of bankruptcy liquidation

When a firm files to liquidate under Chapter 7 of the U.S. Bankruptcy Code, the bankruptcy court appoints a trustee who shuts the firm down, sells its assets and turns the proceeds over to the court for payment to creditors.[3] (Note that creditors do not get actual ownership of the firm, as is often assumed. They get the proceeds of selling the firm's assets.) The bankruptcy priority rule then determines in what order individual creditors are paid and how much each receives.

The priority rule in bankruptcy liquidations is called the "absolute priority rule" (APR). The APR specifies that claims are paid in full in a particular order: first, administrative expenses of the bankruptcy process itself, including court costs, lawyers' fees, the trustee's expenses, and any loans incurred by the firm after the bankruptcy filing (with the court's permission); second, claims taking statutory priority, including tax claims, rent claims, consumer deposits, and unpaid wages and benefits which accrued before the bankruptcy filing;[4] and third, unsecured creditors' claims, including trade creditors, utility company creditors, holders of damage claims against the firm (such as claims by users injured by the firm's defective products or claims against the firm for breach of contract),[5] and claims of long-term bondholders. Unsecured creditors' claims rank equally in priority, unless there are subordination agreements between particular creditors and the firm specifying priority orderings within the class. Such agreements are common in long-term bond contracts, and they usually require that subsequent loans to the firm rank below the claims of the particular bondholders. These agreements are followed in bankruptcy by creating subclasses within the class of unsecured creditors. Finally, equity holders come last.

The APR also provides for secured creditors to be outside the priority ordering. Secured creditors are those who have bargained with the firm for the right to claim a particular asset (or its value) if the firm liquidates in bankruptcy. Their liens are recorded in public records. Thus, secured creditors may receive a payoff in bankruptcy even when all other creditors receive nothing.

If creditors perceive the firm's financial condition to be deteriorating, they have an incentive to try to raise their positions in the priority ordering. Creditors holding claims that are long term and due in the future have little bargaining power with management. But creditors holding short-term claims who are willing to make new loans to the firm have substantial bargaining power. These creditors often improve their positions in the priority ordering by bargaining with the firm to convert some or all of their claims from unsecured to secured status (Schwartz, 1981).

For example, suppose creditors A and B both make unsecured loans to the firm which are used to purchase inventory. As unsecured creditors, they have equal priority in bankruptcy. Creditor B's loan comes due first and in negotiating to renew it, the firm agrees to allow creditor B to take a "floating" lien on the inventory, perhaps in return for creditor B increasing the size of his loan. If the firm later files for

---

[3] No creditors' committees are appointed in liquidations.
[4] There are limits on the maximum size of claims in this category.
[5] Pennzoil's claim against Texaco and claims by victims of asbestos disease against the Johns Manville Company fit into this category.

bankruptcy, creditor B will have the right to claim the inventory, while creditor A will be at the bottom of the priority ordering and will probably receive nothing.[6]

It might be argued that unsecured creditors like A anticipate this and will either demand to be secured themselves or will lend on an unsecured basis, but raise the interest rate they charge to compensate for the added risk. However, some types of loans, such as trade credits extended by suppliers and tax claims, are too small or too short term to make arranging a security interest worthwhile. Other claims are involuntarily unsecured, such as damage claims against the firm. Still others, such as long-term subordinate bonds, may be unsecured, but are only extended to large, publicly traded firms whose probability of financial distress was viewed before the fact as being extremely small. While unsecured lenders may demand higher interest rates to cover extra risk, once their loans are made, the higher interest rate becomes merely a negative income effect to the firm. Afterwards, managers have an incentive to arrange new loans to the firm that rank high in the priority ordering, since the new loans will carry a lower interest rate due to their high priority.

Despite these disadvantages, secured loans have an economic advantage in that they reduce transactions costs. Secured lenders need only to monitor the whereabouts and condition of the actual assets subject to their liens. For example, if a lender takes a lien on a drill press, she need only check when the agreement is made that the press is not already subject to a prior lender's lien and later that the press is not being misused. The lender has no need to monitor the firm's financial condition generally. This advantage for the individual lender is purchased at somewhat higher transactions costs, since the lender must agree on a contract with managers which specifies a particular asset to be subject to the security interest; also, the lien must be registered. If all creditors were secured, then no new lender could take a lien on an asset already subject to a lien (unless the new lien were subordinate to the old). This would make it impossible for later lenders to improve their position in the priority ordering at the expense of earlier creditors in bankruptcy. But I show below that even this would not necessarily prevent managers of firms from making inefficient bankruptcy decisions.

Characteristics of firms that liquidate in bankruptcy

In a sample of 500 firms that filed to liquidate in bankruptcy, a study done for the Department of Justice (Ames *et al.*, 1983) found that the ratio of total liabilities to assets at the time of the bankruptcy filing was 7.3 and the ratio of secured liabilities to

---

[6]There are many other ways in which creditors improve their positions in the priority ordering. One involves the practice of "setoff." Here, at the time of the bankruptcy filing, a bank having an unsecured loan outstanding can claim the firm's account balance with the bank in partial payment of the loan. This allows the bank to be paid before other unsecured and statutory creditors. Another involves the firm buying another as a subsidiary and guaranteeing its loans. This in effect allows the subsidiary's creditors to jump ahead of the parent's in the priority ordering. A third possibility is that an unsecured creditor might force the firm to file for bankruptcy as a condition of the creditor renewing its loan. Then the new loan is considered an administrative expense of the bankruptcy proceeding (regardless of whether the firm later liquidates or reorganizes) and is placed in the highest priority class.

assets was 1.0. With these high ratios of liabilities to assets at the time of the bankruptcy filing, it should not be surprising that unsecured creditors receive little in bankruptcy liquidations. White (1984) found that in a sample of 90 firms that liquidated in bankruptcy, the average payoff rate to creditors having statutory priority was 6 percent and the average payoff rate to unsecured creditors was 4 percent. But the average size of firms in this sample was small—the mean level of total liabilities was $1.6 million. Since large firms that file for bankruptcy are likely to reorganize rather than liquidate, the unobserved payoff characteristics of large firms that liquidate could differ substantially from the observed characteristics of firms that liquidate.[7]

Economic efficiency considerations of the liquidation procedure

Since bankruptcy implies that all creditors cannot be paid in full, what priority rule would be economically efficient? Consider three possibilities. The first is the well-known "me-first" rule of Fama and Miller (1972, pp. 150–152). Under this rule, all creditors of the firm are assumed to be unsecured (and no claims have statutory priority). Creditors are ranked in order of the date on which they made their loans to the firm, with the earliest claims ranked highest. In bankruptcy, the proceeds of liquidating the firm's assets are used to pay off claims in full in order of their ranking. If anything remains, it goes to equity holders, who otherwise receive nothing. The second rule is the "last-lender-first" rule, which is identical to the me-first rule except that creditors are ranked in reverse chronological order. Thus the most recent lender ranks first and the earliest lender ranks last. The third rule is the equal priority rule, in which all creditors have the same ranking in bankruptcy and are paid the same fraction of the face value of their claims.

The APR contains some elements of all three of these rules. The me-first rule is followed among long-term bondholders if the firm has several bond issues outstanding and each is covered by a subordination agreement. The equal priority rule applies to unsecured creditors not covered by subordination agreements. The last-lender-first rule frequently prevails among groups of creditors because creditors who make late loans to the firm bargain for high priority or for secured status. They then may be paid in bankruptcy even though unsecured creditors who made their loans to the firm earlier receive nothing.

To analyze the effects of these priority rules on economic efficiency, one must describe a model of how the decision to declare bankruptcy is made and under what circumstances. I will assume either that managers, representing equity, make decisions so as to maximize the value of equity, or else that decisions are made by a coalition of equity and a lender referred to as the "bank." The coalition assumption is used when the firm is failing; that is, when the firm has insufficient assets to pay obligations which are due in the current period, then it must obtain new financing to avoid

---

[7]Unfortunately, the government does not make data available concerning payoff rates to creditors in bankruptcy cases.

bankruptcy, which is assumed to take the form of a loan from the bank. In this case, the decision concerning whether or not the firm files for bankruptcy is made to maximize the total value of the coalition's holdings. The "bank" is a short-term lender that monitors the firm's behavior closely and has bargaining power since it is willing under some circumstances to make new loans to the firm. For simplicity, it is assumed to have no prior loans outstanding to the firm. Other creditors, referred to here as "debt," do not have such bargaining power and are unwilling to make new loans to the firm.[8]

I assume that the failing firm's bankruptcy decision is made in the first period of a two-period model. Suppose the firm has outstanding debt of amount D_1 due in period 1 and D_2 due in period 2. If it filed for bankruptcy and liquidated in period 1, then its assets (sold piecemeal) would be worth L after subtracting the transactions costs of liquidating. I also assume that if the firm was liquidated in period one, its value would be less than the sum of its debts, so equity holders would receive nothing. Alternatively, the firm might continue operating outside of bankruptcy for another period. But by assumption, it has no cash on hand. So in order to avoid bankruptcy in period 1, it must obtain a new loan of amount B_1 equal to the debt owed in period 1, which is D_1. (Interest and discount rates are assumed to be zero for simplicity.) The new loan would have to come from the bank. Since the coalition chooses whichever alternative maximizes the total value of equity plus the bank's claim, this means that equity holders are willing to give the bank up to the entire value of equity to induce it to make a new loan so that the firm can avoid bankruptcy this period. Equity holders are willing to do this since equity would be wiped out if the firm filed for bankruptcy in period 1.

If the firm gets a loan and continues, its earnings in period 2 after non-debt expenses are paid are assumed to be P_2 with certainty. Then from an economic efficiency viewpoint, it is efficient for the firm to continue operating if its period 2 earnings are greater than the amount that would have been received by liquidating in period 1, L, and to file for bankruptcy if its period 2 earnings are less than would be received by liquidating in period 1.

What decision will be made under each of the three priority rules? Consider the me-first rule. If the coalition chooses bankruptcy in the current period, then it will receive nothing. If the coalition chooses continuation, then it will receive P_2, but it must pay off both the debt owed in period 2 and the loan taken out in period 1. Thus, the coalition will choose continuation if $P_2 - D_2 - B_1 > 0$. But this condition must imply that the firm's earnings in period 2 are greater than the amount that would have been received if the firm had liquidated in period 1. After all, the amount received in liquidation was less than the sum of the debts owed, while the amount received in continuation is enough to pay off both period 2 debt and the bank loan

[8]Coalition models of the bankruptcy decision were first proposed by Bulow and Shoven (1978) and have been analyzed by Ang and Chua (1980) and White (1980; 1983).

taken out to cover period 1 debt. Therefore, continuation will only be chosen when P_2 exceeds L, that is, if it is economically efficient. However, suppose that the known earnings from continuing are not enough to pay off period 2 debt and the bank loan. In this situation, both liquidation and continuation lose money, so the bank refuses to make the loan that allows the business to continue to period 2. But either alternative might be more economically efficient, since a loan might allow the business to lose *less* money than the alternative of going into liquidation immediately. When both alternatives lose money but continuation loses less, debt holders would gain the amount $P_2 - L$ if continuation were chosen. But this gain is ignored by the coalition, which chooses liquidation.

Thus under the me-first rule, the coalition chooses continuation only when that alternative is economically efficient, but it may sometimes choose to liquidate even when continuation is more efficient. Therefore some firms end up in bankruptcy when they should continue to operate from an economic efficiency standpoint. This occurs because whenever the coalition chooses continuation, it must share the efficiency gain with debt holders (the infra-marginal creditors) by paying them in full. Therefore the coalition only chooses continuation when the efficiency gain is great enough to pay debt holders their share and still have something left over.

Now let us play out the scenario using the rule of "last-lender first." The coalition's return under liquidation is the same as above. The coalition's net return under continuation remains equal to $P_2 - D_2 - B_1$, if this amount is positive. Here continuation is economically efficient and is preferred by the coalition since it is profitable. But now suppose P_2, the amount received in period 2, is between B_1 and $D_2 + B_1$. Then the coalition's net return is 0, since the bank is paid first in full, but there isn't enough money left to pay off the debt due in period 2 and still have anything left for equity. In this case, the coalition is indifferent between the two alternatives and has no incentive to make the choice that would pay more to debt holders. But while the coalition is indifferent, economic efficiency would require that it have an incentive to choose the more efficient option.

Finally, since under the equal priority rule the repayment of the bank loan is neither first nor last, the return to the coalition if continuation is chosen will fall between those under the other two rules. Thus the coalition also has an incentive under this rule to choose continuation only when it is efficient, but it sometimes will choose liquidation when continuation is more efficient.

In this simple model, all three bankruptcy priority rules have similar results. All have a "one-sided" efficiency property in that they give the coalition an incentive to choose continuation only when it is efficient, but also give the coalition an incentive sometimes to choose liquidation when continuation is the most efficient outcome. None of the three bankruptcy priority rules *always* gives the bank-equity coalition an incentive to make economically efficient bankruptcy decisions. The reason is that when continuation is more efficient but the coalition chooses liquidation, a cost is imposed on holders of debt since they are not repaid in full. But the coalition ignores this cost in making its decision. Therefore it chooses liquidation too often. The bias toward choosing liquidation is worse under the me-first rule than under the last-lender-first rule, since debt holders rank higher under the me-first rule and therefore would have received more of the gains from the coalition making an efficient choice.[9]

Let us now examine the case when the firm's earnings under continuation are uncertain. Now, if the firm continues, it earns $P_2 \pm G$ in period 2, with probabilities p and $1 - p$. A higher value of G implies greater uncertainty. I assume that if the good outcome occurs in period 2, then the firm will be able to pay all its debts. If the bad outcome occurs, then the firm will not be able to pay all its debts and will file for bankruptcy then. However, I also assume that the firm's earnings will be positive in the second period, so $P_2 - G > 0$.

Suppose the me-first rule is in effect. If continuation is chosen, the coalition gets $P_2 + G - D_2$ in the good outcome, but gets no return in the bad outcome, since all the firm's earnings must go to debt holders, who have higher priority. The coalition's expected return is $p(P_2 + G - D_2) - B_1$. (This also presumes that in the bad outcome, second period earnings will be less than or equal to the amount of debt owed in period 2; that is, $P_2 - G \leq D_2$.) Assuming risk neutrality, continuation will be chosen if this expression is positive. But continuation is only economically efficient if the expected value of the firm's earnings in period 2 is greater than the value of its assets in liquidation, L.

The result introducing uncertainty is that continuation may be chosen even if liquidation is economically more efficient and *vice versa*. Continuation becomes more attractive to the coalition, even in situations when liquidation is more efficient, as the variation in earnings, G, and/or the probability of the good outcome occurring, p, gets larger, since the coalition receives all the profits after debtholders are paid in the good outcome, but loses only the amount of the first period bank loan (debtholders lose the rest) in the bad outcome. Continuation is also more attractive if the firm has relatively more debt due in period 2 rather than period 1, since the new bank loan required to finance continuation is smaller.

Introducing uncertainty into the coalition model thus has the effect of reversing the bias in the liquidation/continuation decision from the coalition choosing liquidation too often to the coalition choosing continuation too often. In the certainty case, the coalition had to repay period 2 debt in full if it chose continuation. But in the uncertainty case, choosing continuation forces period 2 debt holders to participate in a risky activity with uncertain returns. The coalition gets the upside benefit, while debtholders disproportionately bear the downside costs. Thus the well-known tension between debt and equity regarding risk-taking—debt holders prefer safer investments while equity holders prefer riskier investments—also emerges here in the bankruptcy decision. When the firm's earnings are risky, continuation itself is a risky investment. Then the coalition prefers continuation even though liquidation may be more eco-

[9] If interest rates are added into the model and they have risen in the market since the firm's long-term debt was issued, then an offsetting effect is introduced which may give the coalition an incentive to choose continuation under any of the three priority rules. This is because choosing liquidation causes debt holders to receive a windfall gain, since their claim in liquidation is for the face value of the debt, which is greater than its market value even ignoring default risk.

nomically efficient.[10] In both situations, the coalition has an incentive to choose the alternative in which it benefits from redistribution away from creditors. But the redistribution possibilities shift when uncertainty is introduced from favoring liquidation to favoring continuation.[11]

The results are similar but even stronger under the last-lender-first rule. In this case, the coalition's gain from choosing continuation is even larger than under the me-first rule, because repaying the bank loan now has priority over repaying previously owed period 2 debt and therefore the bank receives more when the bad outcome occurs. Assuming that the firm's earnings in the bad outcome are enough to pay off the bank loan in full, the coalition chooses continuation as long as it makes a profit in the good outcome; that is, if $p(P_2 + G - D_2 - B_1) > 0$. Thus the coalition has an extremely strong incentive to choose continuation over liquidation when the firm's earnings are risky, since it considers only the firm's earnings in the good outcome, when efficiency would require that it consider the firm's earnings in both the good and bad outcomes.

It is a common assumption in the finance literature that failing firms file for bankruptcy as soon as their liabilities rise to the point that they equal the value of the firm's assets. But if the last-lender-first rule is followed, firms observed in bankruptcy are likely to have liability-to-asset ratios well in excess of one. The reason is that a bank may be willing to loan money even if liabilities exceed assets, as long as it is assured of being repaid first. Many failing firms end up following the last-lender-first rule because banks that are willing to lend demand the security of knowing that they will be repaid first. The data presented above on the characteristics of firms that filed to liquidate in bankruptcy support the prediction of the last-lender-first rule that firms observed in liquidation have high ratios of total liabilities to assets.

Finally under the equal priority rule, the bank loan is neither first nor last in being repaid, so the coalition's return is between its return in the other two cases. Specifically, the coalition chooses continuation if its return,

$$p(P_2 + G - D_2) + (1 - p)\frac{B_1}{(B_1 + D_2)}(P_2 - G) - B_1,$$

is positive.

The analysis has shown that no single priority rule in bankruptcy gives the bank/equity coalition an incentive to choose continuation or liquidation only when that alternative is economically efficient. When the firm's future earnings are certain, all three priority rules sometimes discourage continuation decisions even when they

---

[10]Stiglitz (1972) was the first to make the point that managers of firms have incentives to engage in risky investment projects when there is a possibility that the firm might go bankrupt.

[11]This conclusion may seem odd to those familiar with the finance literature, which has tended to emphasize the desirable properties of the me-first rule. In most finance models, the value of the firm's assets in bankruptcy is assumed to be the same as their value if the firm continues. This assumption means that the firm's decision whether to continue operating or to file for bankruptcy has no economic efficiency implications. Thus the question that is of interest here is assumed away (Kim et al., 1977; Kim, 1978; Scott, 1977; Warner, 1977).

are economically efficient, with the me-first rule having the worst bias. But as the firm's future earnings become increasingly uncertain, all three rules begin to encourage too many firms to continue operating, even when the most efficient outcome is for them to liquidate. The me-first rule works best at discouraging inefficient continuation decisions, but none of the rules always works. Thus, not only does none of the priority rules lead to economically efficient results in all situations, but none of the three rules seems to dominate the others. Inefficient bankruptcy decisions and inefficient investment incentives appear to be the price society pays for limiting the liability of equity holders. From the standpoint of economic efficiency, no simple bankruptcy priority rule works as well as unlimited liability by the firm's owners.

It should be noted that inefficient outcomes might be reversed under any of the priority rules by debt holders offering a side payment to the coalition to induce it to choose the efficient outcome. But transactions costs are likely to be high in bargaining over bankruptcy, because severe free rider problems come up in attempting to collect money from debt holders to pay the transactions costs of bargaining with the coalition and the costs of the side payment itself. Debt holders' interests thus tend not to be actively represented.

Reorganization

Firms filing for bankruptcy have a choice between liquidating under Chapter 7 of the U.S. bankruptcy code and reorganizing under Chapter 11 of the Code. In a reorganization under Chapter 11, the existing managers of the firm usually remain in control and the firm continues to operate. A reorganization plan must be adopted which settles the claims of all pre-bankruptcy creditors. In many reorganizations there is never a sale of the firm or its assets on the open market. Instead, the reorganization plan substitutes for a sale. The reason for having two separate bankruptcy procedures seems to be that Congress has tended to view the role of reorganization as one of providing breathing space to save the jobs of supposedly viable firms that are in temporary financial distress. In contrast, liquidation is viewed as the process of winding up the operation of firms that are not viable.

The coalition model suggested that not all firms observed in bankruptcy liquidation should shut down. Rather, in both the certainty and uncertainty cases, the coalition in some situations has an incentive to choose liquidation even when the expected value of the firm's future earnings if it continues to operate exceeds the liquidation value of its assets. This finding suggests that the additional option of reorganization could potentially improve efficiency by allowing firms for which the expected value of future earnings exceeds shutdown value to continue operating, even though they would end up in liquidation if that were the only bankruptcy procedure available. However, if two separate procedures exist, managers will tend to choose the alternative that is best for themselves and for equity, regardless of whether the firm's assets are more or less valuable if it shuts down or continues operating. Thus a dilemma of reorganization is that, while it may allow some efficient firms to continue operating which would otherwise liquidate, it also is likely to facilitate the rescue of some economically inefficient firms.

U.S. law of bankruptcy reorganization

Firms that file under Chapter 11 must adopt a reorganization plan.[12] There are two separate procedures for formulating a plan. The first is referred to as the "unanimous consent procedure" or UCP, under which all classes of creditors and equity as a class must consent to the plan. The assumption behind the UCP is that the firm's assets will have higher value if it reorganizes than if it liquidates. This value differential—which under the APR would go entirely to high priority creditors—must be divided up among all classes of creditors and equity via a negotiating process, with all parties sharing the gain. The plan must incorporate what is often an inflated valuation of the firm's assets, which makes them worth more than its liabilities under the plan. This makes the firm "solvent," which is required in order that the old equity be retained. (If instead it were determined that the firm is insolvent, then old equity must be eliminated, which means equity is deemed to disapprove the reorganization plan and the UCP cannot be used.) The UCP requires that all classes of creditors and equity as a class vote to approve the plan. For each class of creditors, the required voting margin in favor is at least two-thirds in amount of claims and one-half in number of claimants. For equity, the required voting margin is at least two-thirds in amount.

Thus reorganization plans under the UCP provide for a different division of the firm's assets than would occur under the APR liquidation rules. Under the UCP, everyone must receive something. Under the APR, equity and low priority creditors may quite possibly receive nothing at all.

Management is in a strong bargaining position in negotiations over the reorganization plan under the UCP. During the first six months after the bankruptcy filing (and lengthy extensions are often granted), only a plan proposed by management can be adopted. Managers also can threaten to transfer the firm's bankruptcy filing from Chapter 11 to Chapter 7 if creditors do not agree to a plan—a threat which is often effective in prodding unsecured creditors to accept the plan, since they anticipate receiving little or nothing if liquidation occurs. Managers also run the firm during the negotiating process, so secured creditors often fear that the value of their lien assets is declining. Finally, even after the period when only they can propose a plan, managers remain in a strong bargaining position. Individual creditors are often unrepresented and severe free rider problems crop up when creditors attempt to form groups to raise funds to take an active part in bargaining.

One justification for having a procedure such as the UCP is that something like it would seem likely to emerge in bargaining over the bankruptcy decision if transactions costs were low and all creditors were to participate. For example, suppose liquidation

---

[12] The new U.S. Bankruptcy Code, adopted in 1978, made major changes in bankruptcy reorganization procedures as well as some minor changes in the liquidation procedure. The law as described here is that prevailing under the Code. For a description of differences between provisions of the Code versus the pre-1978 Bankruptcy Act, see White (1984).

were the only bankruptcy procedure and the coalition had decided to liquidate. Then non-coalition debt holders might offer a side payment in the form of a reduction in the interest rate on their debt in return for the firm continuing to operate. Such an agreement would be similar in substance to the UCP, since creditors would accept a reduced return voluntarily in return for the firm continuing to operate.

The second scheme for adopting a reorganization plan is aptly named "cramdown." It comes into play if a reorganization plan is voted on, but fails to meet the standard for approval by all classes under the UCP, or if the firm is clearly insolvent and old equity must be eliminated. In that case, as long as at least one class of creditors has voted in favor of the plan, the bankruptcy court can confirm the plan anyway, or a modified version of it, as long as each dissenting class is treated "fairly and equitably." The "fair and equitable" standard closely reflects the APR in that it requires that all unsecured creditors either receive full payment of the face value of their claims over the period of the plan (usually 6 years) or else that all lower ranking classes receive nothing. It also requires that secured creditors retain their pre-bankruptcy liens on assets (or the "indubitable equivalent") and that they receive periodic cash payments equal to the value of their claims. Cramdown plans usually involve higher transactions costs than UCP plans, since the bankruptcy judge is likely to require appraisals by outside experts and more court hearings before approving the plan.

If no reorganization plan is adopted using either the UCP or cramdown, then sometimes managers will voluntarily sell the firm as a going concern on the open market. In that case, the proceeds of sale are paid to creditors according to the APR. This "liquidating reorganization" is similar to a Chapter 7 liquidation, except that the firm is sold as a going concern, rather than shut down and its assets sold piecemeal. (However, since most firms probably go through extended bargaining and months of disruption before such a sale occurs, their value when sold is likely to be less than if they were offered for sale immediately after filing for bankruptcy.) Finally, if no progress is being made toward completion of the Chapter 11 reorganization, then normally some creditor petitions the bankruptcy judge to order a shift of the firm's bankruptcy filing to a Chapter 7 liquidation. Thus all of the alternatives to adopting a reorganization plan under the UCP involve paying off creditors more or less according to the APR.

Characteristics of firms that reorganize in bankruptcy

In the DOJ study of 500 firms that filed to reorganize in bankruptcy, the average ratio of total liabilities to assets at the time of the filing was 1.4 and the ratio of secured liabilities to assets was 0.60. These ratios are lower than for the DOJ sample of firms that filed to liquidate, suggesting that failing firms which file to reorganize tend to be in better financial condition. In White's (1984) study of 64 firms that filed to reorganize and completed the reorganization process, only around 40 percent of the firms agreed on a reorganization plan under the UCP. For the rest, bargaining over a plan under the UCP did not succeed. Thirty percent of the sample then converted their filings to liquidations under Chapter 7. The remaining firms went through liquidating reorganizations. No firms in the sample formally used cramdown to adopt a reorganization plan.[13]

In the White sample, the average payoff rate to unsecured creditors under the UCP reorganization plans was 16 percent in cash plus 18 percent (undiscounted) in installments payable over up to 6 years. The payoff rate to unsecured creditors of firms that were sold as going concerns while in bankruptcy was 13 percent in total. This evidence suggests that unsecured creditors do better when firms reorganize than when they liquidate and also do better when firms reorganize using the UCP than when bargaining over a plan under the UCP fails. The data are only suggestive, since important characteristics of firms in the different samples are not held constant.

Economic efficiency considerations of the reorganization procedure

The three-way bankruptcy decision among liquidation, reorganization and continuation outside of bankruptcy can be modeled as an extension of the bank/equity coalition decision. Suppose as a third alternative that the coalition might reorganize in bankruptcy using the UCP. I assume that the firm has both unsecured and secured debt which may be due in either period 1 or 2. Managers propose a reorganization plan under which all unsecured claims will receive a payoff rate in period 2 equal to u percent of face value and all secured claims will receive a payoff rate of s percent of face value. The payoff rate on secured claims is likely to be higher, so that s exceeds u. (What values these payoff rates would be likely to take is discussed below.) The amount not paid to creditors under the plan, equal to $(1 - u)$ percent of unsecured debt plus $(1 - s)$ percent of secured debt, is referred to as debt forgiveness. The firm also incurs a fixed transactions cost of reorganizing, T, which I assume must be paid in period 1. This includes court costs, lawyers' fees and the cost of lost management time. If the firm's earnings fall in reorganization as a result of disruption, this can be thought of as part of the fixed cost of reorganization.

The bank/equity coalition makes the decision between the firm reorganizing versus liquidating in bankruptcy. Assume that equity will receive nothing if liquidation is chosen. For the firm to reorganize, the coalition bank must be willing to extend a new loan to the firm that covers the fixed costs of reorganization, T, which is the only payment that must be made in the first period. I assume that the new loan will be available if giving it last-lender-first priority (as a loan made after the bankruptcy filing, it receives highest priority) makes it certain to be repaid. From the coalition's standpoint, one advantage of reorganizing over continuing outside of bankruptcy is that the new loan from the coalition bank is likely to be smaller and easier to obtain if the firm reorganizes. This is both because of debt forgiveness under the reorganization plan and because payments to creditors under actual reorganization plans are spread out over several years (six years is common), making the amount that must be paid in the first period smaller.

---

[13] These firms were again quite small—the average level of total liabilities was around $2 million. Large firms are probably much more likely either to adopt plans using the UCP or to use cramdown.

It is useful again to distinguish between cases when the firm's future earnings are certain versus uncertain. Suppose the firm's future earnings if it reorganizes are P_2 with certainty. Then, neglecting interest and discount rates, the coalition chooses reorganization if P_2 minus the total amount of secured and unsecured debt *not* forgiven under the plan exceeds the fixed cost of reorganizing, T.

What are the efficiency implications of the reorganization/liquidation choice? The economic efficiency gain from the firm reorganizing is the difference between the value of its future earnings, P_2, and the liquidation value of its assets, L, if this difference is positive. The economic efficiency cost of the firm reorganizing is the fixed cost, T. Thus reorganization is economically worthwhile if the efficiency gain $P_2 - L$ exceeds T. But the coalition chooses reorganization if P_2 minus the amount of debt not forgiven under the plan exceeds T. Therefore the coalition may choose reorganization even when liquidation is more economically efficient or may choose liquidation even when reorganization is more economically efficient, depending on whether the firm's liquidation value is larger or smaller than the amount of non-forgiven debt owed to creditors.

Recall the discussion of the liquidation/continuation decision under certainty in the previous section. There, the coalition had an incentive to choose liquidation too often, since it ignored the gain to creditors from continuation being chosen, which was $P_2 - L$, unless the coalition also profited from continuation being chosen. Here exactly the same effect occurs, but with an additional factor affecting the coalition's choice. This additional factor is that when reorganization rather than continuation is the alternative to liquidating, there is a transfer from non-coalition creditors to equity in the form of debt forgiveness on secured and unsecured debt. This subsidy makes reorganization more attractive. As a result, while the coalition may choose either reorganization or liquidation when the other outcome is more efficient, it is more likely under reorganization that inefficient decisions will favor continuing the firm's operations rather than shutting it down.

Since the amount of debt forgiveness affects the coalition's choice between liquidating and reorganizing, there is a level of debt forgiveness under which the coalition has an incentive to make the economically efficient choice. This occurs when the amount of debt not forgiven under the plan equals the liquidation value of the firm, L. The average payoff rate to all creditors under the reorganization plan then must equal the liquidation value of the firm divided by the total face value of non-coalition debt. Thus a justification for using the APR as a default standard in reorganization when bargaining over a plan under the UCP breaks down is that in the certainty case, paying creditors in total an amount equal to the firm's value in liquidation gives the coalition an incentive to make the economically efficient choice between liquidation and reorganization. (However, this result does not hold when the firm's earnings are uncertain.)

Now suppose the firm's future earnings if it reorganizes are uncertain rather than certain. In this situation, reorganizing becomes much more attractive to the coalition than liquidating. The reason is the same as in the previous section: by reorganizing, the coalition forces creditors to invest their remaining claims in a risky activity—the continued operation of the reorganized firm. Again equity receives the upside benefit and creditors disproportionately bear the downside risk. If the firm's earnings are again assumed to be $P_2 \pm G$ with probabilities p and $1 - p$, then the coalition can be shown to choose reorganization whenever the expected value of its earnings in the good outcome are positive. Thus the coalition bases its choice only on its earnings in the good outcome, when economic efficiency would require that the decision be based on both the good and the bad outcomes. The attractiveness of reorganizing increases as both G and/or p rise, and as the payoff rates s and/or u fall.

How are the payoff rates s and u determined? Without a more complete model of the bargaining process in reorganization, the actual payoff rates in reorganization cannot be predicted. However, the bankruptcy rules discussed above suggest the strength of the bargaining power of different creditors' groups. If bargaining over a reorganization plan failed and the firm liquidated, secured creditors could reclaim their lien assets. Each of these assets has an individual liquidation value. Secured creditors are each likely to demand a payoff rate equal to the liquidation value of their assets divided by the face value of their claims. Since individual secured creditors are usually each a separate creditors' class, they can individually block a UCP reorganization plan by voting against it. Therefore, they are in a fairly strong bargaining position. However, they may settle for a payoff rate less than this to avoid prolonged bargaining over a UCP reorganization plan, if disruption to the firm during the bargaining process would cause their lien assets to decline rapidly in value.[14] Unsecured creditors as a group also have the power to block a reorganization plan under the UCP, but if they do and the firm liquidates or goes through a liquidating reorganization, the data discussed above suggest that their returns will be quite low. Their payoff rate u will be at least equal to what unsecured creditors expect to receive if the firm were liquidated.

Since earnings uncertainty increases the attractiveness of reorganization to the coalition compared to the alternative of liquidation, giving non-coalition creditors a total payoff in reorganization equal to the firm's liquidation value, L, would still leave the coalition with an incentive to choose reorganization too often. Thus using the APR as a default standard in reorganization when voluntary bargaining does not succeed leaves the coalition with an incentive to choose reorganization more often than is economically efficient. To give the coalition economically efficient incentives, the default standard in reorganization would have to give creditors more in total than the firm's liquidation value.

The arguments concerning firms' decisions to reorganize in bankruptcy thus suggest that as long as firms' future earnings are risky, too many firms will reorganize in bankruptcy. They are motivated to file for bankruptcy reorganization both by the

---

[14]See Gordon and Malkiel (1981) for discussion of bargaining strategies of high priority creditors in reorganization which suggests that they are willing to give up 20 to 30 percent of their claims to facilitate quick adoption of a plan.

transfer from non-coalition creditors in the form of debt forgiveness under the plan and by the incentive to gamble with creditors' remaining claims by investing them in the firm's continuing operation.

Subsidies to firms that reorganize

Reorganizing firms benefit from some important subsidies relative both to firms that liquidate and to firms that continue outside of bankruptcy, subsidies the model above did not consider. These subsidies come either from the government or from creditors. They give firms in reorganization advantages relative either to firms that continue operating outside of bankruptcy or relative to firms that liquidate.

First, firms that reorganize retain most of their accrued tax loss carryforwards, which would be lost if they liquidated. These loss carryforwards shelter the firm from having to pay corporate profits taxes for a period, even if their operations start to be profitable. They make reorganization attractive relative to liquidation, but do not affect the choice between reorganization and remaining out of bankruptcy. Second, when reorganizing firms settle liabilities for less than their face value, the amount of debt forgiveness is deducted as a loss by the creditor but is not taxable income to the reorganizing firm. However, since 1980, the loan forgiveness amount becomes taxable (although with a long lag) if the reorganized firm becomes profitable, by reducing either its tax loss carryforward or its depreciation allowances.

Third, firms reorganizing under Chapter 11 have the right to terminate under-funded pension plans, and the U.S. government picks up the uncovered pension costs. Three large firms that have recently filed for bankruptcy—LTV, Wheeling-Pitts-burgh Steel and Allis-Chalmers—terminated their pension funds and together trans-ferred around $3 billion of uncovered pension liabilities to the government. Several years before its bankruptcy filing, Allis-Chalmers made an agreement with its union simultaneously to raise pension levels (which were insured by the government) and to lower pension funding. When it filed for bankruptcy, the assets in its pension plan only equalled 3 percent of its guaranteed benefits. The Pension Benefit Guaranty Corporation has attempted recently to transfer LTV's pension plan back to the company on the grounds that LTV is financially able to cover its pension costs, and the matter is being litigated.

Fourth, the Bankruptcy Code provides that when firms file for bankruptcy, their obligation to pay interest to pre-bankruptcy creditors, both secured and unsecured, ceases. They do not have to begin paying interest again until a reorganization plan is approved. The unpaid interest does not become a claim against the firm. This subsidy clearly gives managers of failing firms an incentive to file for bankruptcy earlier and to delay proposing a reorganization plan.

Fifth, firms in reorganization can reject any of their contracts which are not substantially completed. Thus they can get out of any contracts which are unprofita-ble. They are liable for damages to the other party to the rejected contract, but such damage claims are unsecured claims which are likely to receive only a low payoff rate. Thus, the cost to the firm of shedding unprofitable contracts is small. Firms in reorganization can sometimes also reject their collective bargaining agreements, although since 1984 this step has required the approval of the bankruptcy judge. The ability of the firm to "decontract" selectively makes reorganization attractive both relative to continuing outside of bankruptcy (where firms must perform all their contracts) and relative to liquidating (which cancels all contracts).[15]

These subsidies increase the attractiveness of reorganizing to the coalition relative to the alternatives of liquidating or continuing outside of bankruptcy, by increasing the total amount of debt forgiveness in reorganization. However, the subsidies also cause the firm's earnings to become relatively less risky. Therefore the coalition will find reorganization more attractive, but the effect will be smaller than if the subsidies increased rather than reduced the riskiness of the firm's earnings. Finally, the subsidies have no effect on the economic efficiency of reorganization relative to liquidation or continuation. Thus if too many firms were already choosing reorganization, then to the extent that the subsidies cause failing firms to choose reorganization more often, they worsen the problem.

In practice, the subsidies are also likely to change the nature of the bargain made between creditors and the coalition in reorganization. Under the UCP, all creditors' classes and equity must consent to the plan, so that the subsidies strengthen the bargaining position of creditors generally and probably cause all payoff rates to rise. In this case, the subsidies are in effect divided among creditors' groups and equity, with the firm itself retaining equity's share. Alternately, if a liquidating reorganization occurs and the firm is sold on the open market, then the subsidies will cause the firm's sale price to rise, although probably by less than the full amount of the subsidies (since the new owners will also focus primarily on equity's earnings in the good outcome in deciding how much to bid for the firm). In this case, since the sale proceeds must be distributed according to the APR and will be exhausted before paying off all creditors' claims in full, creditors will get the entire increase in the sale price. The new owners of the reorganized firm will get the benefit of whatever proportion of the subsidies was not capitalized into its sale price. In either case, creditors are likely to demand and receive a substantial proportion of the value of the subsidies.

If we assume that the intent of Congress in providing the subsidies was to improve the viability of firms that reorganize and save their jobs, then to the extent that the subsidies "leak" out of the firm as increased payments to creditors, they fail to accomplish their purpose and are wasted. The subsidies could theoretically accomplish their purpose at lower cost if the reorganization procedure were changed to prevent them from leaking out. But it is difficult to see how this could be done. Eliminating at least some of the subsidies, such as by requiring that all firms fully fund their pension plans, seems desirable from an efficiency standpoint.

These subsidies vary in importance for different industries. But they have the potential to enable unprofitable firms to reduce their costs substantially by filing for bankruptcy under Chapter 11. For example, in the steel industry, there is overcapacity

---

[15]Firms not in bankruptcy also have the right to avoid performing their contracts by paying damages. But for firms not in bankruptcy, the damage payment is considerably higher, making it not worthwhile to default except in very unusual cases.

and a need for contraction overall. But analysts have estimated that LTV, one of the large steel companies, was able to reduce its steelmaking costs from $460 to $380 per ton as a result of filing to reorganize in bankruptcy. LTV's costs were then estimated to be $60 per ton below average steel industry costs.[16] This may affect the entire steel industry. The subsidies both enable LTV and other reorganized steel firms to continue to produce steel and put pressure on their competitors to file for bankruptcy (and receive the subsidies) as well. One viewpoint is that the subsidies may enable inefficient firms to remain in operation and slow the contraction of the industry and the movement of assets out of steel production to more valuable uses. An alternative viewpoint is that the subsidies may put previously uncompetitive steel firms on a more even footing with competitive steel firms in other countries. In either case, the subsidies probably save some jobs that would otherwise have been lost, but at a very high cost.

Bankruptcy Costs and Proposed Bankruptcy Reforms

Bankruptcy costs

The previous discussion suggests that bankruptcy costs play an important role in firms' three-way choice among liquidation, reorganization and continuation outside of bankruptcy. Thus it is of interest to know how high these costs actually are. Research on bankruptcy costs has tended to divide them into two categories. The first is the set of administrative costs for which bankruptcy courts keep records—including lawyers' costs, trustees' fees, and auction and appraisal costs. The second, referred to as indirect costs of bankruptcy, consists of lost sales and profits due to disruption, the value of foregone investment opportunities during the bankruptcy procedure, and the lost value of funds that are tied up during bankruptcy.

White (1984) compared the administrative cost items to the total amount paid to creditors in samples both of firms that liquidated and firms that reorganized. The figures were 21 percent for firms liquidating, 3.4 percent for firms that reorganized using the UCP and 10 percent for firms that went through liquidating reorganizations. In a similar study, but only of firms that liquidated, Ang, Chua and McConnell (1982) found a figure of 7.5 percent. These figures seem relatively low. An alternative approach to measuring administrative costs is suggested by Baird (1986), who gives a typical cost estimate of $100,000 for a firm going through a "straightforward" Chapter 11 proceeding. If half of the 17,000 firms that filed for bankruptcy under Chapter 11 in 1985 spent $100,000 each, this would imply a total expenditure on bankruptcy administrative costs of around $0.85 billion per year—which again seems low.

There have been a few efforts to measure indirect bankruptcy costs in reorganization. White (1983) used a coalition model similar to the one discussed above to show

---

[16]See "LTV is Healthier Under Chapter 11, but Not Cured," by C. F. Mitchell and J. E. Beazley, *The Wall Street Journal*, Friday, July 24, 1987, p. 5, col. 1.

that when firms choose reorganization but liquidation is more efficient, then the transfers to the coalition resulting from the decision to reorganize are an upper bound on the level of indirect bankruptcy costs resulting from the inefficient decision. These deadweight costs are in addition to the direct bankruptcy costs. White estimated that direct bankruptcy costs due to reorganization were $0.85 billion in 1980 dollars and that the direct plus indirect bankruptcy costs of inefficient decisions to reorganize were bounded from above at $9 billion in 1980 dollars. Thus total deadweight bankruptcy costs could be as high as 11 times the level of direct bankruptcy costs alone.

Another way to measure the upper bound on the level of total bankruptcy costs involves use of the risk premium on corporate bonds. The spread between interest rates on high risk and low risk corporate bonds having the same term measures investors' expectations of the probability of being repaid less than the contractual amount, converted to an even level over the term of the bond.[17] The spread between Moody's Aaa and Baa corporate bond rates, which are highest quality and medium quality corporate bonds, averaged 0.017 during the period 1980 and 1985. Since the average level of liabilities of U.S. financial corporations from 1980 to 1985 was $1,045 billion, these figures imply that investors expected to lose around $18 billion per year over the period. Actual losses in fact averaged $18 billion per year.[18]

Finally, another indicator of bankruptcy costs is the length of time that the bankruptcy procedure takes. White (1984) found that firms which reorganize using the UCP take 17 months on average in the bankruptcy process. Ang, Chua and McConnell (1982) found that bankruptcy liquidations are somewhat faster but still time-consuming—the average firm in their sample spent 14 months in bankruptcy. These data suggest that reforms of the bankruptcy process might well be directed toward speeding it up.

Proposed reforms of the bankruptcy procedure

The arguments of the previous section suggest that substantial inefficiencies result from having two separate bankruptcy procedures. In liquidation, equity interests rank last, while equity is maintained intact in reorganization under the UCP. This means that managers, representing equity, always prefer reorganization over liquidation, because by reorganizing they can transfer income from creditors to equity. (Managers may not always succeed in attracting a bank lender who will finance reorganization, but they always prefer reorganization over liquidation.) In addition, managers' personal interests also strongly favor reorganization because existing management is usually retained in reorganization, while in liquidation managers' jobs are eliminated. This preference for reorganization over liquidation causes too few firms to liquidate

---

[17]Actually this amount should exceed creditors' expected losses by the costs investors expect to incur if a default occurs (such as costs for participating in bankruptcy negotiations), plus a premium for idiosyncratic risk.

[18]However, during the period, the actual level of failed liabilities rose more quickly than the level expected by investors. Data on interest rates and actual losses are from the *Economic Report of the President* and data on total corporate liabilities are from the *Federal Reserve Bulletin*.

and generates inefficiency by delaying the movement of assets from less productive to more productive uses.

This suggests that reforming bankruptcy by combining the two procedures would improve economic efficiency. For example, suppose that new bankruptcy procedures required all bankrupt firms to be sold on the open market, but as going concerns rather than as piecemeal assets after shutdown. The proceeds of the sale would be paid to creditors and old equity holders according to the APR. The new owners of the firm would choose whether to shut it down or continue its operations. Since they would have an incentive to choose whichever alternative has greater value, the shutdown/continuation decision would be made efficiently. The new owners would also decide whether to keep the old managers on or replace them, and would have an incentive to make the efficient choice. The amount that the firm would sell for is the maximum of what the new owners would pay for its piecemeal assets versus what would be paid for it as a going concern. This would guarantee the maximum total compensation to pre-bankruptcy creditors and equity holders. Requiring that all bankruptcies take place under a single legal procedure would thus eliminate the deadweight cost that arises when firms continue to operate even when their resources are more valuable in some alternative use or when bad managers remain in control.

A number of writers have suggested reforms along these lines. All of the proposals involve establishing a market valuation of the bankrupt firm by selling some or all of its new equity on the open market. The resulting market valuation would be used as a basis for compensating pre-bankruptcy creditors and equity according to the APR. Some of the proposals involve changing the current reorganization procedure to make it more like the liquidating reorganization described above, while others advocate combining reorganization and liquidation into a single bankruptcy procedure.[19] An advantage of these proposals is that the firm would end up with an all-equity capital structure at the end of the bankruptcy procedure, in contrast to the often high debt burdens established by reorganization plans. The all-equity capital structure would make it much easier for the firm to attract a new working capital lender. Another advantage of these proposals is that the bankruptcy procedure would proceed much more quickly, since there would be no need for creditors and managers to bargain to an agreement concerning how each group is compensated. Assuming that length of time in bankruptcy is positively related to indirect bankruptcy costs, any reform which eliminates the need for bargained agreements is likely to reduce deadweight costs.

Despite these advantages, a unified procedure involving market valuation or sale of all bankrupt firms would not be a panacea for bankruptcy ills. The efficiency of the bankruptcy process itself would probably improve if reforms along these lines were adopted. But improving the bankruptcy procedure itself would be likely to exacerbate

---

[19]See Roe (1983), Bebchuk (1986), Baird (1986), and Jackson (1986). Roe's proposal involves selling 10 percent of the bankrupt firm's new equity on the market to establish a valuation for the firm. Under Bebchuk's proposal, the firm's new equity would be issued to high priority creditors, but subject to an option held by low priority creditors to purchase the equity for a pre-specified price. Low priority creditors would in turn be subject to an option given to old equityholders to buy the new shares at a pre-specified, but higher, price. Baird and Jackson both advocate eliminating bankruptcy reorganization completely.

the problem of inefficient decision-making outside of bankruptcy. The critical problem is that the reform proposals all involve compensating pre-bankruptcy creditors according to the APR. But the model of the coalition's liquidation versus continuation decision developed in the first section suggests that managers have an extremely strong incentive (except in the certainty case) to avoid bankruptcy if the bankruptcy procedure follows the APR and puts equity last. Therefore if the unified bankruptcy procedure used the APR, only firms in the worst possible financial shape would file for bankruptcy. Managers would have an incentive to choose the riskiest investment projects, to waste the firm's assets, to do anything possible and for as long as possible to avoid walking into bankruptcy court. A unified APR-based bankruptcy procedure would probably increase dramatically the deadweight costs of inefficient bankruptcy decisions. Only when the worst outcomes occurred and the firm's assets were exhausted would managers consider filing for bankruptcy.

The current two-pronged bankruptcy procedure has the effect of reducing the deadweight costs of inefficient bankruptcy decisions by allowing firms to reorganize in bankruptcy under rules which are more favorable both to equity interests and to managers themselves. In reorganization under the UCP, equity interests are maintained intact even while creditors' claims are cut back. Managers remain in control during the reorganization process. Thus, managers of firms in financial difficulty have less incentive to take extreme steps to avoid bankruptcy when reorganization is an option. The data presented above suggest that a result is for firms to file for bankruptcy reorganization when their financial condition is better on average than that of firms filing to liquidate in bankruptcy. Thus bankruptcy reorganization, which makes the bankruptcy procedure itself more complicated and costly than if all firms were liquidated, has an offsetting advantage in reducing deadweight costs outside of bankruptcy. A further advantage of having reorganization as a bankruptcy alternative is that once the firm has filed under Chapter 11, there is some supervision of managers' decisions by the bankruptcy court, which probably prevents at least the worst abuses.

Thus there is a tradeoff between improving the bankruptcy procedure itself and improving the efficiency of decision-making outside of bankruptcy. As long as streamlining the bankruptcy procedure involves compensating creditors according to the APR, then managers will have an incentive to gamble with creditors' assets as they try desperately to avoid bankruptcy's draconian treatment of equity under the APR. Ironically, while bankruptcy is supposed to be the procedure by which the economy moves toward long-run efficiency, the bankruptcy liquidation procedure gives managers of failing firms incentives to engage in inefficient behavior trying to avoid it.

Are there any possible solutions to this dilemma? One, not very practical on other grounds, would be to eliminate limited liability completely and make equity holders responsible for the firm's losses. This would take away from managers the ability to make transfers from creditors to equity—the source of their incentive to make economically inefficient decisions. Another possibility might be to unify and streamline the bankruptcy procedure along the lines of the reforms discussed above, but with old equity and management treated more favorably than under the reform procedures just discussed. All bankrupt firms could be sold as going concerns on the open market, but existing management would be kept in place during the sale, and the sale proceeds could be divided among various creditors' classes and equity in a way which provides partial compensation to all groups. A reform along these lines would in effect try to strike a balance between conflicting efficiency objectives. But the basic problems of bankruptcy are not caused by design flaws in the bankruptcy system and tinkering with the design of bankruptcy procedures will not "solve" them. As with any tradeoff, the best that can be done is to strike the right balance.

■ *I am grateful to the Cook Fund of the University of Michigan Law School for research support and to Lucian Bebchuk, Roger H. Gordon, Henry Hansmann, Thomas Jackson, Raymond Nimmer, Ariel Pakes, Mark J. Roe, Carl Shapiro, Joseph Stiglitz, Timothy Taylor and James J. White for many helpful comments. Earlier versions of this paper were presented at the N.B.E.R. Conference on Firm Startup, Entry and Exit and the Law and Economics Seminar at Harvard Law School.*

References

Administrative Office of the U.S. Courts, *Federal Judicial Workload Statistics.* U.S. Government Printing Office, Washington, D.C., 1985.

Ames, Nancy, et al., *An Evaluation of the U.S. Trustee Pilot Program for Bankruptcy Administration: Findings and Recommendations.* Consultants' study for the U.S. Dept. of Justice. Cambridge, MA: Abt Associates, 1983.

Ang, James S., and Jess H. Chua, "Coalitions, the Me-first Rule, and the Liquidation Decision," *Bell Journal of Economics,* Spring 1980, *1*, 355–359.

Ang, James S., Jess H. Chua, and John J. McConnell, "The Administrative Costs of Corporate Bankruptcy: A Note," *Journal of Finance,* March 1982, *37*, 219–226.

Baird, Douglas G., "The Uneasy Case for Corporate Reorganizations," *Journal of Legal Studies,* January 1986, *XV*, 127–147.

Bebchuk, Lucian, "A New Method for Corporate Reorganization," unpublished paper, Harvard Law School, 1986.

Bulow, Jeremy I., and John B. Shoven, "The Bankruptcy Decision," *Bell Journal of Economics,* Autumn 1978, *9*, 437–456.

Dun & Bradstreet, *The Business Failure Record,* 1986.

Fama, Eugene R., and Merton H. Miller, *The Theory of Finance.* New York: Holt, Rinehart and Winston, 1972.

Gordon, Roger H., and Burton Malkiel, "Corporation Finance." In Aaron, Henry, and Joseph Pechman, eds., *How Taxes Affect Economic Behavior.* Washington, D.C. Brookings Institution, 1981.

Jackson, Thomas H., *The Logic and Limits of Bankruptcy Law.* Cambridge, MA. Harvard University Press, 1986.

Kim, E. Han, "A Mean-Variance Theory of Optimal Capital Structure and Corporate Debt Capacity," *Journal of Finance,* March 1978, *XXIII:1*, 45–63.

Kim, E. Han, J. J. McConnell, and P. R. Greenwood, "Capital Structure Rearrangements and Me-First Rules in an Efficient Capital Market," Journal of Finance, June 1977, *XXXII:3*, 789–810.

Roe, Mark, "Bankruptcy and Debt: A New Model for Corporate Reorganization," *Columbia Law Review,* April 1983, *83:3*, 527–602.

Schwartz, Alan, "Security Interests and Bankruptcy Priorities: A Review of Current Theories," *Journal of Legal Studies,* January 1981, *X*, 1–38.

Scott, James H., "Bankruptcy, Secured Debt, and Optimal Capital Structure," *Journal of Finance,* March 1977, *XXXII:1*, 1–19.

Stiglitz, Joseph E., "Some Aspects of the Pure Theory of Corporate Finance: Bankruptcies and

Take-Overs," *Bell Journal of Economics and Management Science*, Autumn 1972, *3*, 458–482.

Warner, Jerold B., "Bankruptcy, Absolute Priority, and the Pricing of Risky Debt Claims," *Journal of Financial Economics*, May 1977, *4:3*, 1–38.

White, Michelle J., "Bankruptcy Liquidation and Reorganization." In Logue, Dennis, ed., *Handbook of Modern Finance*. Boston: Warren, Gorham & Lamont, 1984 chapter 35, pp. 1–49.

White, Michelle J., "Public Policy toward Bankruptcy: Me-First and Other Priority Rules," *Bell Journal of Economics*, Autumn 1980, *11*, 550–564.

White, Michelle J., "Bankruptcy Costs and the New Bankruptcy Code," *Journal of Finance*, May 1983, *XXXVIII:2*, 477–487.

Section V

Corporate Financial Management and the Investor

The dramatic changes that we have been considering throughout this book—the swelling of corporate debt, the tilting of capital structure toward debt, and the revolution in corporate control—have all been important in redefining the relationship between the firm and its investors. As we have already seen, mergers can redistribute wealth among shareholders, managers, and employees. Section V explores the new relationship between the firm and its investors that is emerging from these revolutions in the world of finance. The articles in this section emphasize the financial management dimensions of this new relationship.

Paul M. Healy and Krishna G. Palepu explore, "How Investors Interpret Changes in Corporate Financial Policy." Healy and Palepu begin by noting two general tendencies: issuing new equity tends to decrease stock prices, while increasing dividends tends to raise stock prices. As the authors point out, the explanations for these systematic tendencies is new. In essence, changes in financing and dividend policy act as signals to investors. Therefore, the financial manager should be aware of the signals that he or she sends in making a financing decision. This line of thinking suggests that managers might be able to increase the value of the firm by merely sending the right signals, irrespective of the underlying financial realities. However, Healy and Palepu show why false signaling is a losing game for the manager.

Following the signaling theme, John R. M. Hand and Patricia Hughes consider changes in capital structure in their paper, "The Motives and Consequences of Debt–Equity Swaps and Defeasances: More Evidence That it Does Not Pay to Manipulate Earnings." A debt–equity swap is a financing arrangement in which a firm issues new debt to retire existing equity. In a defeasance, a firm buys government debt with cash flows that match the payments due on the firm's existing debt. The government bonds go into a special fund used to make the payments on the firm's debt, effectively retiring the debt of the firm. Corporate managers can be tempted to undertake debt–equity swaps or defeasances to manage either the income statement or the balance sheet. In essence, the managers seek to signal to the market that the firm is in better circumstances than its underlying economics suggest. As Hand and Hughes show, the market is not fooled by this attempt to manipulate earnings. The result of such efforts is a loss of value from the firm.

Anthony Saunders explores the primary market for stocks in his article "Why Are So Many New Stock Issues Underpriced?" By "new stock" Saunders refers to stock that is newly issued as opposed to existing shares. Considerable evidence suggests that newly issued stock is underpriced because the stock price increase after issuance exceeds the appropriate risk-adjusted return. Saunders reviews the evidence supporting this view and asks a deeper question: What does this underpricing suggest about the regulation of investment banking firms and commercial banks? (Currently, the Glass-Steagall Act limits commercial bank participation in issuing new stock.) Saunders concludes that repeal of Glass-Steagall could result in fairer pricing for newly issued stock.

No issue of financial management affects shareholders more directly than decisions about cash payments to shareholders. In their paper, "Cash Distributions to Shareholders," Laurie Simon Bagwell and John B. Shoven discuss the new mechanisms by which firms convey cash to shareholders. As Bagwell and Shoven discuss, firm managers now use a wider array of instruments to reward shareholders, and some of these methods have important advantages over cash dividends. Corporate managers need to be aware of these alternative and superior means of rewarding shareholders.

Article 15

HOW INVESTORS INTERPRET CHANGES IN CORPORATE FINANCIAL POLICY

by Paul M. Healy, Massachusetts Institute of Technology and Krishna G. Palepu, Harvard University

In May 1987, Apple Computer announced that it would pay $5 million in cash dividends on its common stock (four cents per share) for the first time in its history. On the day of the announcement, the market value of Apple's equity rose by $219 million.

In May 1986, Embart announced that it intended to issue 2.75 million shares to raise $102 million in new equity. Following the announcement, the market value of its existing equity fell by $23 million.

In February 1989, General Motors declared a 2-for-1 stock split for the first time since 1955, and increased its dividends. The announcement led the market value of GM's equity to increase by $1.3 billion.

Academic research has confirmed what practicing businessmen have long suspected—namely, that changes in corporate financial policies affect stock prices in systematic and thus fairly predictable ways. Announcements of equity offerings are generally accompanied by large decreases in the stock prices of the issuing firms. Dividend increases and stock splits typically lead to significant price increases.

What is relatively new is the explanation for why the market responds in this way. Finance scholars now argue that corporate policy changes affect stock prices because such changes convey information to investors about future performance.[1] Corporate managements, they reason, often have better information than investors about their companies' future profitability, investment opportunities, and business risks. And managers can be expected to use this information when making

decisions about the appropriate level of dividends or financial leverage. For this reason, investors may look to such policy changes to reveal management's expectations about future earnings and investment opportunities. Hence, the effect on stock prices.

Wall Street analysts and corporate executives, however, tend to tell a different story. The conventional wisdom on common stock offerings, for example, is that they decrease stock prices by increasing the supply of a given company's shares. The popular account of stock price reactions to dividend increases is that investors value current income in the form of cash dividends more highly than capital gains. And stock splits are often said to increase stock prices by expanding the number of potential investors.

What each of these popular explanations have in common is their reliance on some form of market malfunction (economists call them "inefficiencies"). For example, it is true that if each company's stock were really unique, an increase in that stock's supply would cause the price to fall. But, as finance theorists have long argued, there are many close substitutes in our capital markets for any individual stock; and thus an increase in the supply of a single company's stock should have no important effect on price. Conversely, given this implied horizontal demand curve for securities, the attempt to increase potential investor "demand" through a stock split should be equally ineffective.

On the dividend question, financial economists have long argued that, apart from tax effects, investors should be indifferent between receiving income in the form of dividends and capital gains. In fact, when dividend tax rates exceeded those on capital

*We are grateful for the helpful comments of Paul Asquith, Gordon Donaldson, Bob Kaplan, and Richard Leftwich.

1. For examples of information-based models see Stewart Myers and Nicholas Majluf, "Corporate Financing and Investment Decisions When Firms Have Information That Investors Do Not Have," *Journal of Financial Economics*, Vol. 13 No. 2 (1984), Merton Miller and Kevin Rock, "Dividend Policy Under Asymmetric Information," *Journal of Finance*, (1985), and Michael Brennan and Thomas Copeland, "Stock Splits, Stock Prices, and Transaction Costs", *Journal of Financial Economics*, Vol. 22 No. 1 (1988).

gains (before the Tax Reform Act of 1986), taxable investors should actually have preferred capital gains to dividends.

In three recent studies, we attempted to discover which version of the story is correct. Do financial decisions influence stock prices because they provide new information to investors, or because capital markets do not work well? In one study, we looked at companies that decided to pay dividends for the first time. In a second study, we investigated publicly traded companies' decisions to issue additional common stock after a long period of financing by debt and retained earnings. The third examined the performance of companies that split their stock.[2]

HOW DO INVESTORS VIEW FIRST-TIME DIVIDEND PAYMENTS?

The vast majority of public companies pay cash dividends.[3] Moreover, they appear to try to maintain a stable, predictable dividend policy. As early as 1956, John Linter's classic study of corporate dividend policy showed that managers consider expected future earnings as well as current earnings in setting dividend policy—presumably because they are very reluctant to cut dividends in the future.[4]

To the extent this model of dividend policy-making reflects actual behavior, we would expect managers to increase dividends only when earnings increases are expected to be sustained in the future. And, if management turns out to be right more often than not, then reasonably astute investors will come to recognize that dividend increases represent managers' forecast of higher earnings.[5] Such implicit forecasts, moreover, will carry considerably more weight than straightforward earnings forecasts because, unlike mere statements, dividend increases are backed up by a commitment to pay out cash.

One of our recent studies attempted to determine whether a special subset of dividend increases—namely, dividend initiations—provided

reliable signals of future earnings increases. (We defined dividend initiations as either payments for the first time in a firm's history, or after a hiatus of at least ten years.) We tested this proposition by comparing the earnings growth pattern of 131 NYSE and ASE companies that started (or resumed) dividend payments over the period 1970 to 1979.

As shown in Table 1 and Figure 1, this group of companies report relatively flat earnings until the year before the announcement of the first dividend payment. Then, earnings increase markedly and continue to grow at impressive rates for the next three years.

To give some indication of the size of such changes, the average earnings increases are 43 percent in year 1 (the year before the initiation), 55 percent in year 1, 22 percent in year 2 and 35 percent in year 3.[6] When most companies experience a pattern of large earnings increases like this, the increases typically turn out to be temporary and are reversed in later years.[7] For companies initiating dividends, however, the earnings are sustained through year 4 and thus appear to be relatively permanent.[8]

In short, the actual earnings increases following first-time dividend payments suggest that managers' implicit forecasts of unusual earnings growth are indeed realized. It is not surprising, then, that recent research has also shown that the stock market responds very positively to announcements of dividend initiations. In fact, the average market-adjusted increase in stock price in the two days surrounding the dividend announcement is roughly 4 percent.

Furthermore, it turns out that the larger the *yield* of the initial dividend, the more positive is the immediate stock price reaction to a given company's announcement of a dividend initiation. And, perhaps even more telling, the larger the market's positive reaction to the announcement, the larger are the future earnings increases actually realized by companies initiating the dividend.

This, needless to say, is persuasive evidence that dividend changes provide useful "signals" to investors.

2. Our original research on these issues is presented in the following papers: (1) Paul Healy and Krishna Palepu, "Earnings Information Conveyed by Dividend Initiations and Omissions" *Journal of Financial Economics*, Vol. 21 No. 2 (1988); (2) Paul Healy and Krishna Palepu, "Earnings and Risk Changes Surrounding Primary Stock Offers," *Journal of Accounting Research*, (1990); and (3) Paul Asquith, Paul Healy, and Krishna Palepu, "Earnings and Stock Splits," *The Accounting Review*, (July 1989).

3. In 1987, 76% of NYSE and ASE firms listed on Standard and Poor's Compustat files paid cash dividends.

4. John Linter, "Distribution of Incomes of Corporations Among Dividends, Retained Earnings and Taxes," *American Economic Review*, Vol. 46 (1956). See also Eugene Fama and H. Babiak, "Dividend Policy: An Empirical Analysis," *Journal of the American Statistical Association*, Vol. 63 (1968).

5. Managers could also initiate dividend payments when they forecast that their firms' earnings will be more stable relative to past earnings. In this case, investors will view dividend initiations as a signal of a decrease in the riskiness of the initiating firms.

6. In our original research, we compute earnings performance as earning changes divided by stock prices. Here we convert these values to earnings growth rates by assuming that the average P/E ratio is 10 times.

7. For further evidence on this see L. Brooks and D. Buckmaster, "First-Difference Signals and Accounting Time-Series Properties," *Journal of Business Finance and Accounting* (1980).

8. These findings do not change when we control for industry earnings patterns in years surrounding the dividend initiations.

TABLE 1	Year Relative to Dividend Initiation	Number of Firms	Mean Earnings Growth Rate	Median Earnings Growth Rate
EARNINGS GROWTH RATES IN YEARS SURROUNDING FIRST-TIME DIVIDEND PAYMENTS BY 131 FIRMS IN THE PERIOD 1970 TO 1979*	−4	130	14.9%	17.4%
	−3	129	−7.1	7.6
	−2	128	12.9	10.5
	−1	131	42.7**	28.0
	1	130	55.0**	40.2
	2	130	22.0**	35.9
	3	130	35.0**	28.2
	4	128	3.5	19.5

* In our original research we compute earnings performance as earnings changes standardized by stock prices. Here we convert these values to earnings growth rates by assuming that the average price earnings ratio for the sample firms is ten.
** Significantly different from zero at the 10% level or lower.

FIGURE 1
MEDIAN EARNINGS
GROWTH RATES IN YEARS
SURROUNDING FIRST TIME
DIDIDEND PAYMENTS*

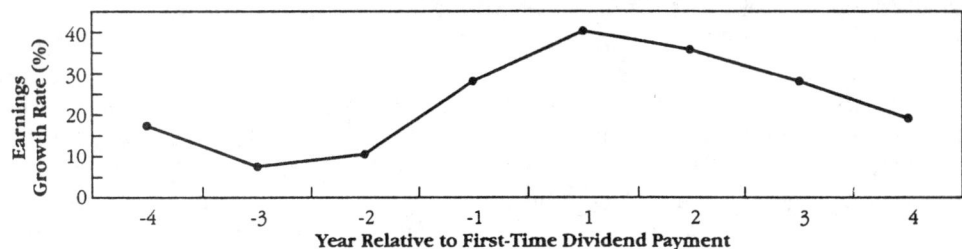

*In our original research we compare earnings performance as earnings changes standardized by stock prices. Here we convert these values to earnings growth ratios by assuming that the average price-earnings ratio for the sample firms is ten.

HOW DO INVESTORS VIEW STOCK OFFERINGS?

Finance theory suggests that corporate management should (if they do not already) determine the mix of debt and equity in their companies' capital structures by balancing the tax benefits of debt financing with the associated costs of financial distress.[9] Companies with high and stable profits are likely to borrow more because they can use interest tax shields without fear of financial distress. Companies with low or volatile profits are likely to borrow less because of the increased threat of financial difficulty.

Studies of actual corporate capital structures tell a somewhat different story about the management decision-making process. These provide strong evidence that, rather than adhering to a stable target ratio that reflects the trade-off between tax benefits and financial distress, managements instead typically fund new investments using retained earnings and, if necessary, external debt financing. Only rarely do they resort to external equity financing; and when they do, it is usually only when they believe that the firm's current debt ratio is too high (or that its debt capacity has been used up) given their expectations about the level or riskiness of future earnings.[10]

Given this reasoning, we might expect managers to make equity offerings when they expect the company's business risk to be higher than previously anticipated, or the level of future earnings to be lower. And, to the extent that managers have better information than investors about the company's future earnings and risk, investors will interpret announcements of equity offerings as "signals" of management's expectations.

Using a sample of 93 seasoned stock offerings over the period 1966 to 1981, we attempted to test whether equity issues convey information about companies' business risk, future earnings, and target

---

9. See Gordon Donaldson, *Corporate Debt Capacity*, Division of Research, Harvard Business School: Boston (1961), and Harry DeAngelo and Ron Masulis, "Optimal Capital Structure under Corporate and Personal Taxation," *Journal of Financial Economics*, (1980).

10. Publicly listed corporations raise additional capital through equity offerings very infrequently. For a discussion of corporate financing practices see Gordon Donaldson, *Managing Corporate Wealth*, Praeger: New York (1984), and Richard Brealey and Stewart Myers, *Principles of Corporate Finance*, McGraw-Hill: New York (1988).

debt-equity ratios. If a company made multiple offerings less than five years apart, we used only the first offering. The sample therefore comprised firms for which equity offers were relatively rare events. All 93 firms were listed on the NYSE or ASE.

We estimated both the mean and median changes in business risk and leverage for the two years before and the two years after the equity offer. We used two measures of a firm's business risk: (1) asset beta and (2) an index of the firm's earnings volatility.[11]

As shown in Table 2, the average asset betas of the companies issuing equity are stable before the offer, but increase markedly after the offer. On average, asset betas increase by 23 percent (from 0.66 to 0.80) in the year after the equity offer. (This increase is, in a statistical sense, quite reliable.) The asset betas remain at the higher level in year 2, indicating that the beta increase in year 1 is not a temporary phenomenon.

We also found that earnings volatility, an alternative measure of business risk, increases sharply after the equity offer. The earnings volatility index is virtually unchanged in years before the offer, but later more than doubles (from 0.9 to 2.5). These patterns in beta and earnings volatility indicate that the offering firms experience a substantial increase in their business risk after the equity offer announcement.

To examine whether equity offerings signal future earnings declines, we analyzed the post-offer earnings performance as well as revisions in *Value Line* analysts' forecasts. We found no evidence, however, that the offering companies have lower earnings after the equity offer relative to either their pre-offer levels or the earnings of other firms in their industries. Further, analysts do not reduce their earnings forecasts after the announcements of equity issues.

It therefore appears that the managers of the offering firms anticipate future increases in business risk and respond by issuing additional equity to reduce financial leverage. The stated uses of equity-offer proceeds reported in the *Wall Street Journal* and in offer prospectuses indicate that a majority of firms intended to use these proceeds to retire debt and thus reduce leverage

ratios. And subsequent changes in corporate debt ratios suggest that results match intentions. After the equity offering, the average debt-equity ratio decreases by 20% (from 0.95 to 0.76), and remains at the lower level.

The net effect of the increase in business risk combined with the decrease in financial leverage is to increase equity betas. On average, equity betas increase by 8 percent in the offer year (from 1.23 to 1.33). (This increase, moreover, is statistically reliable; and there is no significant change in equity betas in other years.)

The economic significance of this average increase in equity betas of the offering firms can be quantified using a simple valuation model. Start by making the following assumptions: cash flows are constant in perpetuity, the discount rate is determined by the Capital Asset Pricing Model, the market's risk premium is 8%, and the risk-free rate is 10%. Given these assumptions, an expected increase in the equity beta from 1.23 to 1.33 will lead to a stock price decline of 4 percent.[12]

And, in fact, we find that the actual stock price reaction to the announcement of equity offers in our sample is consistent with this prediction. The average, risk-adjusted return is − 3.1 percent in the two days surrounding the offer announcement.[13]

Apparently, then, managers of companies issuing new equity forecast an increase in their companies' business risk, and therefore an increase in the probability of financial distress. They respond by issuing common stock and use the proceeds to retire existing debt, thereby reducing their firms' financial leverage. Investors recognize that managers have superior information and interpret offer announcements accordingly: they revise the offering firms' equity betas upward. And increases in earnings volatility of the offering firms in the years following the offer confirm that managers' forecasts of increased business risk are on average correct.

HOW DO INVESTORS VIEW STOCK SPLITS?

Surveys of managers' views on stock splits show that a vast majority regard splits as a means to keep

---

11. Asset betas measure the sensitivity of a firm's stock returns to market fluctuations after controlling for financial leverage. The asset beta B_a for a firm is estimated as follows:

$B_a = B_e (1+D/E)$

where, B_e is the equity beta estimated using the market model, and D/E is the ratio of the book value of debt to the market value equity (financial leverage). See Robert Hamada, "The Effect of Firm's Capital Structure on the Systematic Risk of Common Stocks," *Journal of Business*, Vol. 27 (1972) for a discussion of the relation between asset betas, equity betas, and leverage.

The earnings volatility index is constructed using the variance of changes in EPS as a percentage of stock price across the sample firms. The index for each year is the ratio of the variance in that year to the variance in year −3.

We computed asset betas, earnings volatility indices, and debt-equity ratios also for the offering firms' industries. The industry values are not reported in this paper for brevity, but are used in our tests to confirm that the results for the sample firms are not driven solely by industry-related factors.

12. For Further details on this calculation, see Paul Healy and Krishna Palepu, "Earnings and Risk Changes Surrounding Primary Stock Offers," *Journal of Accounting Research*, (1990).

13. In our sample the average ratio of the offer proceeds to the pre-offer equity value of the firm is 12.5%. Thus, the 3% decline in the stock price of the offer firms translates into a loss of about 25% of the proceeds of the proposed offer.

TABLE 2
CHANGES IN BUSINESS RISK
AND LEVERAGE IN YEARS
SURROUNDING SEASONED
EQUITY OFFERS FOR 93
FIRMS IN THE PERIOD
1966 TO 1981[a]

Variables	Year Relative to Equity Offer				
	−3	−2	−1	1	2
Business Risk:					
Asset Beta					
Mean	0.71	0.67	0.66	0.80	0.83
Median	0.64	0.61	0.62	0.78	0.79
Change in Asset Beta					
Mean		−5.6%	−3.0%	22.7%*	3.8%
Median		−3.1%	−1.6%	24.2%*	1.3%
Earnings Volatility Index	1.0	1.0	0.9	2.5	2.3
Leverage:					
Debt-Equity Ratio					
Mean	1.01	1.05	0.95	0.76	0.80
Median	0.68	0.74	0.72	0.56	0.59
Change in D-E Ratio					
Mean		4.0%	−9.5%	−20.0%*	5.3%
Median		7.4%	−6.8%	−20.8%	1.8%

[a] Two measures of business risk are used: asset betas and an earnings volatility index. Asset betas are unlevered equity betas; the earnings volatility index is the variance of the annual change in earnings as a percent of the stock price before the equity offer in each year relative to the value in year −3. Leverage is the book debt-equity ratio.
* Significant different from zero at the 10% level or lower.

their firm's price within an optimal trading range.[14] Companies typically split their stocks after permanent increases in earnings, since the news of favorable earnings is likely to push their stock prices above the target trading range. By contrast, companies with only temporary increases in earnings are unlikely to split their stock, since their stock prices will not appreciate beyond the target range.

Given this reasoning, we suggest that a company's decision to split its stock could well be determined by its managers' forecasts of whether past or current earnings growth is permanent. If managers have better information than investors about the permanence of earnings growth, investors may infer that past earnings increases are permanent from the announcement of a split.

Using a sample of 121 stock distributions of at least 25 percent over the period 1970 to 1980, we tested whether stock-splitting firms have permanent increases in their earnings. (Since stock splits are often accompanied by explicit or implicit increases in cash dividends and since dividend increases sig-

nal earnings increases, we restricted the sample to firms that did not pay cash dividends at the split date.)[15] None of these firms had made a stock distribution in the prior five years. The sample therefore comprised relatively large and infrequent stock distributions. All the sample firms were listed on the NYSE or ASE.

As shown in Figure 2 and Table 3, companies that split their stocks have large earnings increases for several years before the stock split,[16] as well in the year of the split. In effect, earnings increase by 12 percent two years before the split (year −2), 26 percent in year −1, and 20 percent in year 1.[17] The implied confidence of management about future earnings thus appears to be substantiated; and the earnings of the splitting firms do not decline over the next five years.

While the splitting firms' share prices increase before the split, we find that stock prices do not fully reflect the unusually large earnings increases in these years. Perhaps, without the split, investors would expect such increases to be temporary and reverse

14. H.K. Baker and P.L. Gallagher, "Management's View of Stock Splits," *Financial Management* (1980) report that 94% of the managers surveyed viewed stock splits as a means to keep their firm's price within an optimal trading range. Current finance theories do not address why firms have a preferred trading range. Optimal trading ranges may arise to reduce costs of trading, and to attract a broad and heterogeneous base of stockholders. For further discussion see Josef Lakonishok and Baruch Lev, "Stock Splits and Stock Dividends: Why, Who, and When," *Journal of Finance* (1987).

15. Many firms that split their stock do not decrease their dividend per share proportionally. For these firms the split announcement is accompanied by an increase in the total dividends paid. We have excluded these firms from our sample to isolate earnings changes around stock splits, since we have documented that firms that increase their dividend have large earnings increases.

16. See footnote 6.

17. Pre-split earnings increases are due to both industry- and firm-specific factors. When we controlled for industry earnings patterns in years surrounding the stock splits, we found that the sample firms were in industries that performed well but out-performed their industries in the year before the split.

FIGURE 2
MEDIAN PERCENT
CHANGES IN EPS
SURROUNDING
STOCK SPLITS

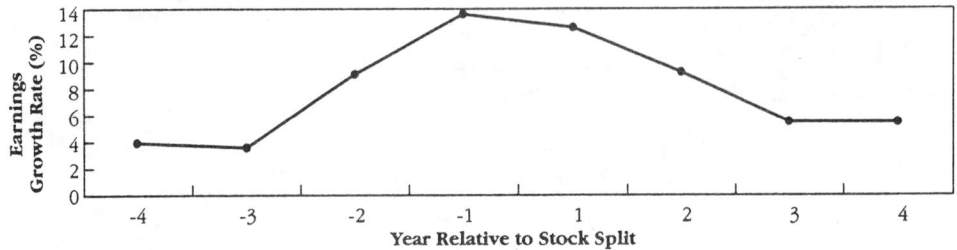

*In our original research we compare earnings performance as earnings changes standardized by stock prices. Here we convert these values to earnings growth ratios by assuming that the average price-earnings ratio for the sample firms is ten.

TABLE 3
EARNINGS GROWTH RATES
IN YEARS SURROUNDING
STOCK SPLITS BY
NON-DIVIDEND PAYING
FIRMS IN THE PERIOD
1970 TO 1980*

Year Relative to Stock Split	Number of Firms	Mean earnings Growth Rate	Median earnings Growth Rate
−4	44	10.5%**	4.1%
−3	61	6.6	3.7
−2	84	12.4**	9.2
−1	100	2.55**	13.7
1	118	20.3**	12.8
2	117	9.1	9.3
3	110	− 6.5	5.6
4	101	21.0	5.5

* In our original research we compute earnings performance as earnings changes standardized by stock prices. Here we convert these values to earnings growth rates by assuming that the average price earnings are for the sample time of ten.
** Significantly different from zero at the 10% level or lower.

themselves in later years—because large earnings increases, as mentioned earlier, are typically followed by declines. A stock split thus may help investors recognize that pre-split earnings increases are permanent.

How does the market respond to announcements of splits? The average market-adjusted stock price increase in the two days surrounding the split announcement is 3.7 percent. Further, the stock price reaction to the split announcement is proportional to earnings increases in *prior* years. That is, firms with higher earnings growth in the two years before the split experience higher stock price reactions to the split announcement.

In short, investors appear to view stock splits as signals that previous earnings increases will be sustained.

■ PAUL HEALY

is Associate Professor of Management at MIT's Sloan School of Management. He is an associate editor of the *Journal of Accounting and Economics* and *The Accounting Review*. His research centers on the effect of accounting methods on managerial behavior and on corporate finance generally

CLOSING REMARKS

There are no obvious reasons why corporate policy changes such as stock splits, dividends, and equity offerings should affect stock prices in any consistent or systematic way.

The evidence from our recent research suggests that managers make capital structure, dividend policy, and stock split decisions when they foresee changes in their companies' business risk or earnings levels. Subsequent changes in the actual values of these business fundamentals tend to bear out the implied management forecasts. Sophisticated investors appear to pay attention to such forecasts, and to incorporate them accurately into their own forecasts of future corporate performance.

■ KRISHNA PALEPU

is Associate Professor of Business at the Harvard Business School. He is an associate editor of the *Journal of Financial Economics, Journal of Accounting and Economics* and *The Accounting Review*. His research focuses on corporate takeovers and other corporate finance issues.

Article 16

THE MOTIVES AND CONSEQUENCES OF DEBT-EQUITY SWAPS AND DEFEASANCES: MORE EVIDENCE THAT IT DOES NOT PAY TO MANIPULATE EARNINGS

*by John R. M. Hand,
University of Chicago, and
Patricia J. Hughes,
University of Southern California*

■

On February 9, 1982, Hammermill Paper registered with the Securities and Exchange Commission to swap as many as 400,000 common shares for $13.4 million of the company's 8.07% promissory notes due February 1, 1997. The resulting swap increased Hammermill's 1st quarter earnings by $3.7 million, accounting for more than a third of its earnings for that period. Between February 9 and 10, the market value of Hammermill's equity fell by 4.5%.

On January 28, 1985, United Airlines announced that its preceding 4th quarter earnings included a $3 million extraordinary gain from the defeasance of $38 million of outstanding notes, and that earnings for all of 1984 included a defeasance gain of $21.5 million, representing 7.6% of UAL's 1984 net income. Between January 28 and 29, the market value of UAL's equity declined by 4.6%.

■

uring the period of high interest rates in the early 1980s, many companies availed themselves of two new techniques for retiring discounted debt: debt-equity swaps and insubstance defeasances. These transactions were touted by investment bankers as a means of increasing reported earnings without increasing taxes. They were also held up as a way of achieving reductions of balance sheet leverage. Using debt-equity swaps, for example, companies could retire an amount of (book value) debt significantly greater than the amount of equity issued in exchange.

Skeptics, however, pointed out that such transactions had no economic substance. The increase in earnings did not represent any increase in corporate operating cash flow; and the value to stockholders of reductions in the market price of the debt below par should already have been reflected in corporate stock prices. In a reasonably sophisticated market, they reasoned, transactions designed primarily to project accounting illusions should confer no benefits on stockholders. And, to the extent swaps and defeasances actually impose costs on stockholders or provide "signals" of bad news ahead, they may well end up reducing corporate stock prices.

In this article, we present the findings of our own recent research on swaps and defeasances. This research was designed to answer the following two questions: What were the principal corporate motives for these transactions? And what were the consequences for stockholders?

SOME BACKGROUND

What is a Debt-Equity Swap? In a debt-equity swap, an investment banker purchases a company's bonds in the open market, exchanges those bonds for a new issue of the company's common stock, and then sells the stock to investors. A swap thus combines a new equity issue with a retirement of debt. Because the difference between the book and market values of retired bonds is included in reported earnings, debt-equity swaps increase earnings during periods of high interest rates.

As mentioned above, however, there is no corresponding increase in corporate cash flow. And in fact the reduction in interest tax shields that accompanies debt-equity swaps may actually reduce after-tax operating cash flow. In addition to higher corporate taxes, an additional cost of debt-equity swaps are investment banker fees that average close to 4% of the market value of the newly issued stock.

What Is a Defeasance? In an insubstance defeasance, a company buys U.S. government securities with cash payouts identical in amount and timing to those promised by some of its own outstanding bonds. The government securities are then placed with a trustee who services the company's bonds using the cash flows from the government securities. While the defeased bonds remain outstanding and continue to trade, they are removed from the firm's balance sheet, and the difference between the book value of the defeased bonds and the cost of the government securities is included in earnings.

As in the case of debt-equity swaps, the accounting income from a defeasance does not correspond to an increase in cash flow. Unlike a swap, the interest tax shield from a defeased debt issue remains intact; but because the company also incurs additional taxes on the interest earned on the portfolio of Treasury bonds, the net effect is also likely to be an increase in the total amount of corporate taxes.

Why Did They Come About When They Did? The rise of debt-equity swaps and insubstance defeasances in the 1980s can be seen as the fairly direct consequence of changes in the tax code.

Prior to the 1980s, companies simply bought back their discounted debt in the open market. Such direct repurchases first became popular in the early 1970s, presumably because the rise in interest rates allowed companies to realize large accounting gains by buying back their debt well below par. The practice became so common that, in 1975, the Financial Accounting Standards Board issued FAS #4, which prescribed that gains and losses from early debt retirement be classified as "extraordinary." Until 1981, moreover, the gains arising from the repurchase of discounted debt were essentially tax-free.

The practice of directly repurchasing discounted debt came to an end with the the Bankruptcy Tax Act of 1980, which eliminated this favorable tax treatment. Then, in 1981, with interest rates again on a sharp rise, Salomon Brothers created the debt-equity swap in order to facilitate tax-free retirements of discounted debt. Between August 1981 and June 1984, approximately 290 swaps were performed by 170 different companies.

This movement in turn came to an abrupt halt when a provision in the Deficit Reduction Act of 1984 made the gains from swaps taxable. As a consequence, insubstance defeasances, aided by a ruling from the FASB (#76) that permitted the defeased debt to be removed from the balance sheet, then became the preferred vehicle for retiring debt. The popularity of defeasances, however, was ended by the decline in interest rates that began at the end of 1984. (See Figure 1, which clearly demonstrates that the frequency of these transactions depends critically on the level of interest rates.)

SOME NEW EVIDENCE

Two recently published studies have examined both the corporate motives for and the stockholder consequences of swaps and defeasances. In the first, one of the present writers looked at a sample of 245 debt-equity swaps completed during the three-year period August 1981 to June 1984.[1] In the second, we (along with a third researcher, Steve Sefcik) analyzed data on 80 defeasances executed during the period April 1981-February 1987.[2]

---

1. John Hand, "Did Firms Undertake Debt-Equity Swaps for an Accounting Paper Profit or True Financial Gain?," *The Accounting Review*, Vol. 64 No. 4 (1989).

2. John Hand, Patricia J. Hughes, and Stephan E. Sefcik, "Insubstance Defeasances: Security Price Reactions and Motivations," *Journal of Accounting and Economics*, Vol. 13 No. 1 (1990).

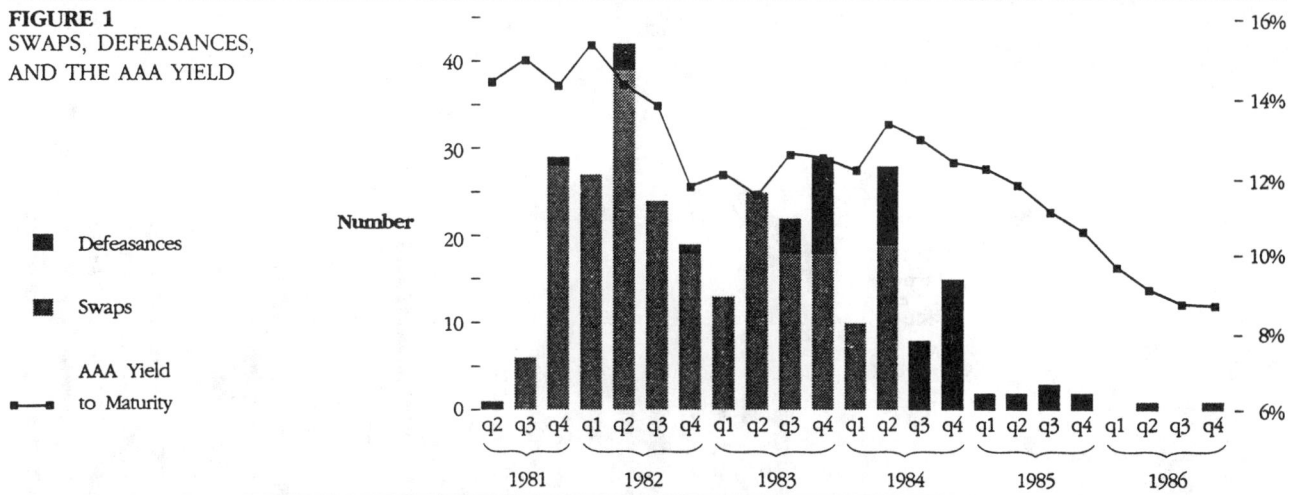

FIGURE 1
SWAPS, DEFEASANCES, AND THE AAA YIELD

■ Defeasances

■ Swaps

■—■ AAA Yield to Maturity

TABLE 1	Item	Minimum	Median	Maximum
SWAPS AND DEFEASANCES	**SWAPS**			
Sample Statistics	Face Value of Debt Swapped	1.1	21.1	197.5
($ in millions)	Market Value of Equity Issued	0.9	15.1	164.4
	Reported Swap Gain	-2.2	4.8	87.3
	Coupon on Bonds Swapped	3.75%	8.1%	14.25%
	Numbers of Years to Maturity for Bonds Swapped	0.25	15.1	28.2
	DEFEASANCES			
	Book Value of Debt Defeased	1.8	21.4	550.0
	Cost of Riskless Securities	2.2	19.6	550.0
	Reported Defeasance Gain	-12.4	0.7	132.0
	Coupon on Bonds Defeased	3.0%	7.9%	14.4%
	Number of Years to Maturity for Bonds Defeased	0.04	6.2	90.0

Corporate Motives

In the case of both swaps and defeasances, the coupons on the retired debt were in most cases significantly lower than market rates (see Table 1). As suggested earlier, the larger this difference, the greater the opportunity for cosmetic improvements of income statements and balance sheets.

'Managing' the Income Statement. The research produced strong evidence that managers used debt-equity swaps to smooth quarterly earnings. In the average swap, quarterly EPS in the quarter the swap was transacted was lower than reported EPS in any of the twelve quarters preceding and twelve quarters following the swap. And, as shown in Figure 2, swaps appear to have been very effective in disguising a temporary downturn in operating earnings.

In the case of defeasances, we chose to focus on trends in annual EPS for only those defeasing companies that reported defeasance gains greater than the median. Our assumption in so doing was that such firms were most likely to be smoothing earnings. The results of this analysis, as shown graphically in Figure 3, provide strong support for our contention that income "management" was a primary motive for defeasances. Further confirming our suspicions, the research also showed that both swaps and defeasances were concentrated near the ends of the quarters in which they were executed.

'Managing' the Balance Sheet. Unlike a debt-equity swap, in which the investment bankers use the proceeds of an equity offering to repurchase the debt, a defeasance requires cash to purchase the portfolio of government securities. How were such defeasances financed? And were they designed to make a permanent change in corporate capital structures?

To answer these questions, we examined the financial statements of 64 defeasing companies and

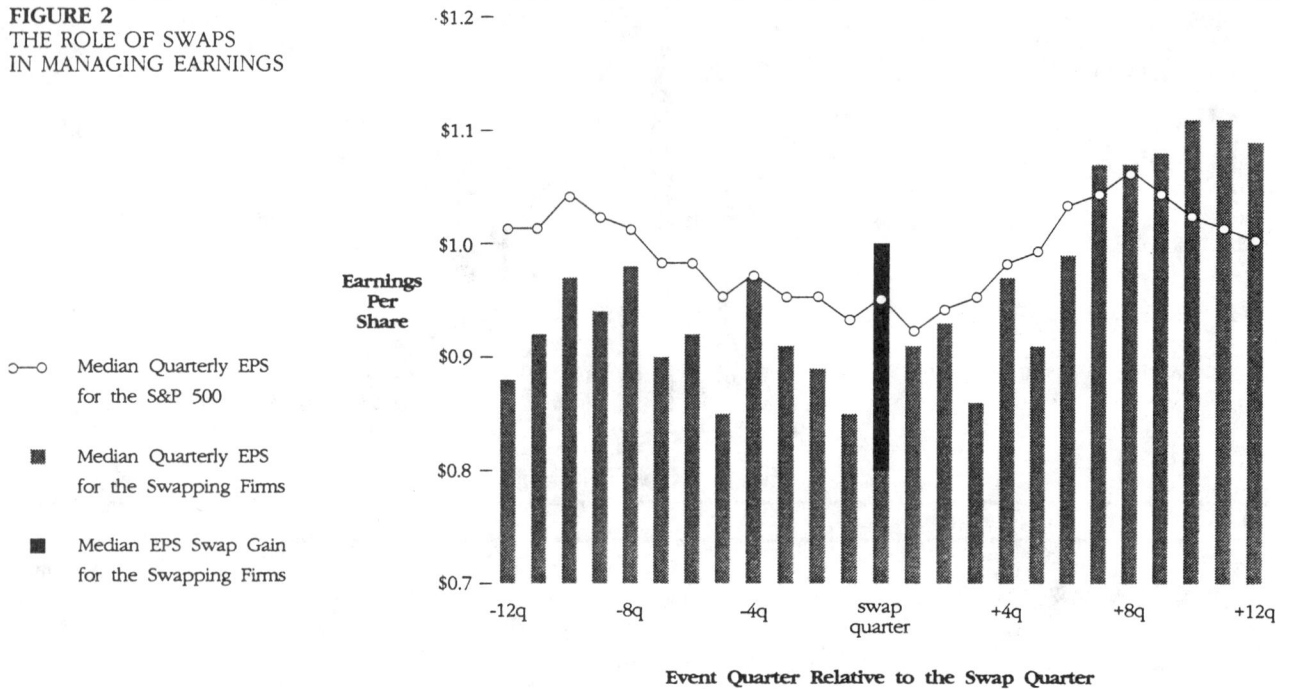

Earnings
Per
Share

○—○ Median Quarterly EPS
for the S&P 500

▨ Median Quarterly EPS
for the Swapping Firms

▰ Median EPS Swap Gain
for the Swapping Firms

$1.2
$1.1
$1.0
$0.9
$0.8
$0.7

-12q   -8q   -4q   swap quarter   +4q   +8q   +12q

Event Quarter Relative to the Swap Quarter

FIGURE 3
DEFEASANCES AND
EARNINGS MANAGEMENT

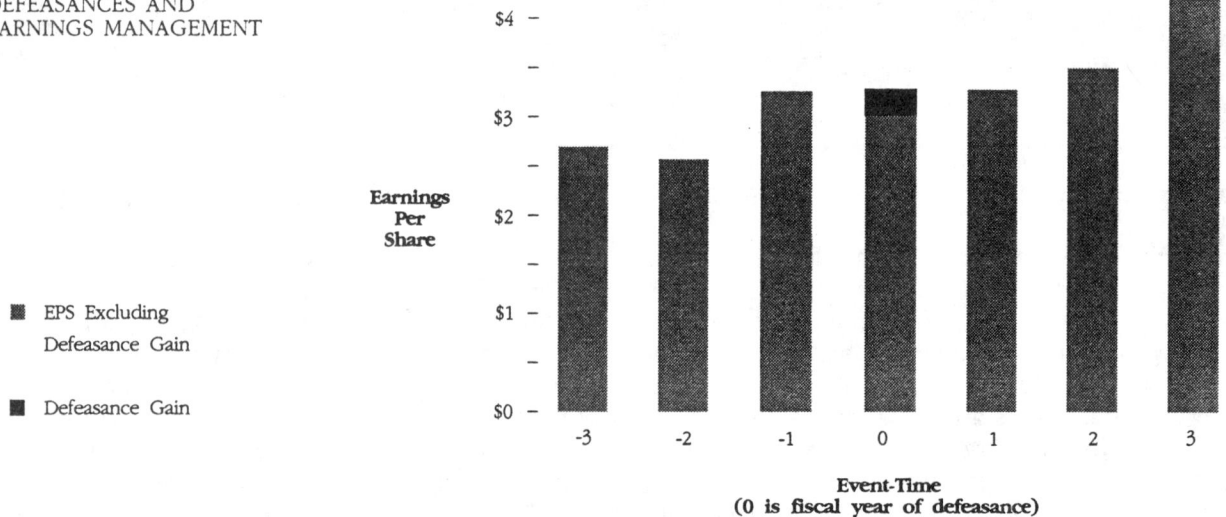

Earnings
Per
Share

$4
$3
$2
$1
$0

▨ EPS Excluding
Defeasance Gain

▰ Defeasance Gain

-3   -2   -1   0   1   2   3

Event-Time
(0 is fiscal year of defeasance)

Note: 64 of the 80 defeasances in our sample had both annual EPS data and information on the amount of the defeasance gain. This figure represents the median of those 32 cases in which the defeasance gain was the largest.

a control group of other companies matched by industry, size, and fiscal year-end. Our results, as summarized in Table 2, show that defeasances were financed, on average, by some combination of excess cash and new stock issues. Also not surprising, they were undertaken by companies with higher debt-equity ratios, possibly either to improve the look of the balance sheet or to avoid running up against restrictions in bond covenants.

What was surprising, however, was that one year after the defeasance, the leverage ratios of defeasing companies actually *increased* significantly

TABLE 2 DEFEASANCE FINANCING ($ in millions)		Year Before Defeasance	Year of Defeasance	Year After Defeasance
	Cash and Marketable Securities			
	Defeasing Firms	610.4	593.4	643.3
	Matched Firms	324.0	325.3	347.1
	Long-term Debt Issued			
	Defeasing Firms	141.4	107.8	164.2
	Matched Firms	156.4	280.9	656.4
	Common and Preferred Stock Issued			
	Defeasing Firms	30.5	47.3	22.1
	Matched Firms	32.0	14.7	31.2
	Debt/Equity Ratio			
	Defeasing Firms	0.74	0.78	1.14
	Matched Firms	0.64	0.59	0.46

relative to the control group. The fact that many companies followed defeasances with new debt issues suggests that there was no underlying intent to reduce the amount of leverage in the target capital structure. And this reinforces our suspicion that the primary corporate motive for defeasances was simply to boost reported earnings.

The Consequences (Or Did the Stock Market Buy It?)

To determine whether investors capitalized such earnings into stock prices, the research examined the stock market reactions to the initial public release of information about the transactions. In the case of the 245 debt-equity swaps, the price movements were measured over the two trading days surrounding the registration of the transactions with the SEC. In the case of defeasances, we looked at two-day price reactions to announcements of 35 defeasances that appeared in the *Wall Street Journal.*

The Market Response

	Swaps	Defeasances
Mean abnormal return	-1.3%	-0.86%
(t-statistic)	(-7.9)	(-2.4)
% of negative returns	69%	66%

The average stock price reaction to debt-equity swaps was -1.3%. In the case of defeasances, the price movement was -0.86%. In the case of swaps, moreover, the larger the accounting gain from the swap, the more negative the market's response.

Stock market investors, then, do not appear to have been misled by such artificial increases in

earnings. In fact, the evidence suggests that investors may have understood the underlying corporate motive for such transactions all too clearly. Anticipating a decline in operating cash flow, they correctly marked down the value of the shares before the lower earnings actually materialized.[3]

Wealth Transfer to Bondholders? Another tenable explanation for the negative market reaction to defeasances concerns its effect on the prices of outstanding bonds. Because the defeasance portfolio is irrevocably dedicated to servicing the defeased bonds, some speculated that a wealth transfer from stockholders to bondholders would result from the reduction in bond default risk. And, in fact, for our 35 public announcements of defeasances, we found the average price response of 24 bond issues to be a positive 1 percent (with a **t** statistic of 3.1). If the total operating value of the firm (debt plus equity) remains unchanged, such increases in bond values represent reductions in the value of the equity.

CONCLUDING COMMENTS

The evidence from our recent research suggests that managers undertake costly debt-equity swaps and defeasances in "bad times" in order to disguise downturns in reported earnings. Stock market investors, far from being fooled by such accounting illusions, respond negatively to these transactions. While reductions in corporate leverage and the associated tax shields partly explain the negative reaction, it also seems likely that investors correctly interpret such attempts to manipulate earnings as a sign of poor operating results ahead.

---

3. The somewhat more negative investor response to debt-equity swaps than to defeasances may have much to do with the fact that swaps involve the issue of new equity. It is now well-documented that announcements of corporate equity offerings reduce stock prices—by 2 or 3 percent, on average.

Article 17

Why Are So Many
New Stock Issues Underpriced?

Anthony Saunders*

Each year hundreds of small firms approach the capital market to issue equity for the first time. These firms are usually growing so fast, or have so many profitable investment projects available to them, that traditional sources of funds (bank loans, retained earnings, and the owners' own equity) are often insufficient to finance their expansion.

Because of this need for finance at a crucial stage in their growth, it is important for these firms that the prices of their shares reflect the

*Anthony Saunders is a Professor of Finance at New York University's Stern School of Business. He wrote this article while he was a Research Adviser to the Federal Reserve Bank of Philadelphia.

true value of company assets or growth opportunities. In particular, if their shares are sold too cheaply, these firms will have raised less capital than was warranted by the intrinsic values of their assets. In other words, their shares will have been "underpriced."

Considerable evidence shows that new or initial public equity offerings (IPOs) are underpriced on *average*. That is, the prices of firms' shares offered to the public for the first time are, on average, set below the prices investors appear willing to pay when the stocks start trading in the secondary market. That is, in the parlance of investment bankers, small firms appear to leave behind considerable "money on the table" at the time of a new issue.

Why small firms raise fewer funds in the new-issue process than the market indicates they should is a crucial public policy issue. Clearly, some degree of market imperfection or lack of competition could cause such an outcome. For example, if, by restricting commercial banks' participation in the market, the Glass-Steagall Act of 1933 has allowed investment bankers to enjoy a type of monopoly (market) power over new equity-issuing firms, then this would suffice to explain underpricing. Alternatively, underpricing may be the premium the issuing firm must pay for having little information about itself to offer potential investors. In that case, underpricing would have little to do with the regulatory structure of the investment banking industry.

Let's examine the reasons for IPO underpricing and evaluate the degree to which underpricing is due to Glass-Steagall restrictions. What is the evidence on the degree of underpricing of U.S. IPOs? What are the various explanations for underpricing? And what are the implications of these explanations, and of the associated empirical evidence, for commercial and investment bank regulation?

EVIDENCE ON UNDERPRICING

In "firm commitment" underwriting ("firm" in that the investment banker guarantees the price), an investment banker (and his syndicate) will undertake to buy the whole new issue of a firm at one price (the *bid* price, or BP) and seek to resell the issue to outside investors at another price (the *offer* price, or OP). In doing so, the investment banker offers a valuable risk-management service to the issuing firm by guaranteeing to purchase 100 percent of the new issue at the bid price (BP). The return for the investment banker in bearing underwriting risk—that is, the risk that investors will demand less than 100 percent of the issue when it is reoffered for sale to the market—is the spread between the public offer price and the bid price (OP - BP) plus fees and commissions. (Here,

and throughout this article, the term "investor" refers to those who buy shares through the investment banker at the offer price.) Thus, the investment banker's spread plus fees and commissions may be viewed as the *direct* cost of going public.

However, there is also potentially an *indirect* cost of going public, measured by the degree to which the issue is underpriced. For example, if the BP is $5 per share and the OP is $5.25 per share, then the underwriter's spread is 25 cents per share. However, suppose that on the first day of trading in the secondary market the share price (P) closes at $7 per share. This indicates that the share has been underpriced in the new-issue process and that, potentially, the firm might have raised as much as $7 per share had it been priced "correctly." This implies that the issuing firm has borne an additional *indirect* new-issue cost of $1.75 per share ($7.00 - $5.25), because the investment banker has set the offer price below the price the market was willing to pay on the first day of trading.

Thus, more formally, the "raw" percentage degree of underpricing (UP) of an IPO can be defined as:

$$(1) \qquad UP = [(P - OP) / OP] \times 100$$

where:

OP = offer price of the IPO
P = price observed at the end of either the first trading day, week, or month

If UP is positive, the issue has been underpriced; if UP is zero, the issue is accurately priced; and if UP is negative, it has been overpriced. The expression for UP is also the expression for a percentage rate of return. Thus, equation (1) can be viewed as the one-day (or one-week or one-month) *initial* return on buying an IPO (that is, UP = R, the initial return on the stock).

Returns calculated by equation (1) are deemed raw returns. However, researchers also compute excess (market-adjusted) returns, as well. The reasons for this are easy to see. Given a lag between the setting of the offer price and the beginning of trading on an exchange (anywhere from one day to two weeks or more), the price observed in the market on the first day of trading may be high (low) relative to the offer price simply because the stock market as a whole has risen (fallen) over this period. Thus, in analyzing underpricing, researchers need to control for the performance of the stock market in general. More specifically:

$$(2) \qquad R_m = [(I_1 - I_0) / I_0] \times 100$$

where:

R_m = return on the market portfolio

I_1 = level of the general market share index at the time of listing (first day, first week, or first month)

I_0 = level of the market share index at the time offer is announced

If R_m is positive, the market has been going up in the time between the setting of the offer price and the listing of the stock on the stock exchange. If R_m is negative, the market has been falling. Excess market or risk-adjusted initial returns (EX) can therefore be defined as:[1]

$$(3) \qquad EX = R - R_m$$

According to equation (3), underpricing occurs only when R is greater than R_m.

The findings of 22 studies that examine the degree of underpricing are summarized in the table on p. 10. Although the time periods, sample sizes, and ways of calculating initial returns (especially raw versus market-adjusted) differ widely across these studies, each finds underpricing on average. For example, studies that use a one-week period to calculate the difference between the offer price and the market price of an IPO find underpricing ranging from 5.9 percent to as much as 48.4 percent.[2]

Thus, an important empirical fact is that U.S. IPOs are underpriced on average, resulting in small firms raising less capital than is justified by the markets' ex post valuation of their shares.

WHY ARE NEW ISSUES UNDERPRICED?

Several reasons have been proposed in the institutional, finance, and economics literature as to why underpricing occurs. Although this article will not discuss all the proposed reasons, it concentrates on four views that have received much publicity. The first view attributes underpricing to "monopoly power" enjoyed by investment bankers. The second regards Securities and Exchange Commission regulations as the primary cause. And the third and fourth see underpricing as a problem of imperfect information among contracting parties—especially between investors and issuers.

---

[1] For a detailed discussion of excess returns, see Robert Schweitzer, "How Do Stock Returns React to Special Events?" this *Business Review* (July/August 1989) pp. 17-29. For IPOs, researchers adjust the initial return on the stock by deducting the return on the market. This is equivalent to assuming that a new IPO's returns move exactly with the market's. That is, they have a unit degree of systematic risk (or their β is 1). The reason for this assumption is that since IPOs have no past history of returns, one cannot estimate directly the IPO's β at the time of issue. The only researcher

who has tried to address this problem was Ibbotson (1975), who developed an ingenious method of constructing synthetic β's for IPOs.

[2] It should be noted that these are one week's returns and are thus very large. These underpricing "costs" swamp the direct costs of a new issue, which are, on average, in the range of 2 to 5 percent of the issue's dollar size.

The Monopoly Power of Underwriters. One possible explanation for pervasive underpricing is the monopoly power the investment banker enjoys over the issuer.[3] Given that commercial banks are barred from entering into corporate equity underwriting (a result of the Glass-Steagall Act, which effectively separated commercial banking from investment banking), investment bankers may have a degree of monopoly power that they use to earn "rents" by underpricing new issues. Of course, competition among investment banks would limit the extent of this monopoly power.

But how real is this monopoly power? Compared to U.S. commercial banks, U.S. noncommercial banking firms and foreign banks have always faced fewer restrictions on entry into investment banking. Moreover, thrifts also can enter investment banking. In recent years, for example, nonbank firms such as General Electric and Prudential have entered the investment banking industry via acquisitions, as has Franklin Savings Bank, a thrift. This potential competition presumably places a limit on the degree of monopoly power enjoyed by investment bankers.

In addition, foreign banks were not subject to Glass-Steagall regulations until passage of the International Banking Act of 1978. Even then, those already possessing investment banking powers had them grandfathered. The emphasis on investment banks is due to their traditional dominance of the underwriting market and to their potential economies of scope (cost savings from offering a combination of services) in extending to their underwriting customers a broader range of financial services.

If investment bankers have monopoly power

over the new issuer, they might use it to increase both the spread between the offer price and bid price (the underwriters' spread) as well as the degree to which the offer price is set below the markets' true valuation (P). A monopolist investment banker might have the incentive to underprice, since by doing so he can increase the probability of being able to sell the whole issue to outside investors (thereby minimizing his underwriting risk) while earning a high investment banking spread (OP - BP) on the issue.[4]

Clearly, if this was the prime reason for underpricing, it would tend to make a case for allowing commercial banks into the underwriting business. This argument would be based on the expectation that pro-competitive effects would reduce the average degree of underpricing.[5] But this argument would, of

---

[3]For a discussion of the reasons for and effects of investment bankers' potential monopoly power, see Ibbotson (1975) and Pugel and White (1984).

---

[4]Implicitly, this argument presumes that investment bankers are risk-averse. This is reasonable, given the private nature of many companies, their limited capital bases, and the potential for a large loss if they take a "big hit" (loss) on an underwriting. For example, many U.S. investment bankers suffered significant losses in underwriting an issue of British Petroleum shares at the time of the October 1987 stock market crash.

[5]A different monopoly-based argument, advanced in Baron (1982), is that investment bankers possess monopoly power through their private access to *information* about the likely size of the demand for a new issue. Since issuers are viewed as being relatively uninformed about the nature of this demand, they can easily be exploited by the investment banker. Indeed, since the issuer has no way of knowing ex ante the size of investor demand, the underwriter has an incentive to save resources on distribution and search ("shirking") by simply underpricing enough to ensure that the whole issue is sold. In this context, the presence of potential competitors, such as commercial banks, and the importance of maintaining a reputation might be viewed as potential controls on the investment bankers' temptation to shirk. This presumes, however, that commercial banks, if they entered into underwriting, have the same abilities to "place" (sell to investors) a new issue as investment bankers do. In reality, it might take commercial bankers a number of years to build up the same placement powers.

course, be tempered by the need to maintain safety and soundness of the banking system, which could be lessened if the spread (P - OP) is small enough to risk inability to sell the entire issue.[6]

Due-Diligence Insurance. A second reason given for why underwriters underprice IPOs is the fear of potential legal problems stemming from overpriced issues. Underwriters, along with company directors, are required to exercise "due diligence" in ensuring the accuracy of the information contained in the prospectus they offer to investors.[7] Since passage of the Securities Acts of 1933 and 1934, both underwriters and directors may be held legally responsible under SEC regulations for the accuracy of this information.

Investors who end up holding heavily overpriced issues may well have an incentive to sue the underwriter and/or the company directors for publishing misleading or incomplete information in the prospectus. The investors could contend they were misled into believing this was a "good" issue rather than a "bad" one. To avoid any negative legal effects, as well as adverse publicity and damage to reputation, a risk-averse underwriter may try to keep investors happy by persistently underpricing IPOs. Hence, some researchers believe that the legal penalties for due-diligence failures are what have created incentives for investment bankers to underprice.

The Problem of the "Winner's Curse." The academic literature has paid a great deal of attention to a theory first advanced by Rock (1986) and extended by Beatty and Ritter (1986) and McStay (1987), among others. This theory considers underpricing as a competitive outcome in an IPO market in which some investors are viewed as informed while a larger group is viewed as uninformed. As a result, underpricing is directly related to the degree of information imperfection—or, more specifically, information asymmetry—in the capital market and to the costs of collecting information. Both this theory and the one that follows view underpricing as a way of resolving the problem of costly information collection.

In Rock's model, there are two types of IPOs: good issues and bad issues. Informed investors, defined as those who expend resources collecting information on IPOs, will bid only for those issues that are good. (This search effort is assumed to allow the informed investor to assess exactly the true value of the IPO.) Those investors who are uninformed, however, will not engage in expensive search, but rather will bid randomly across all issues, good and bad. It is further assumed that informed investors are never sufficiently large as a group to be able to purchase a whole issue.

First, consider a good issue. In this case, both informed and uninformed investors will bid for the issue (the uninformed in a random manner). Because both groups bid for the issue, it is likely to be oversubscribed, so that any single *individual* bidder (informed or uninformed) will get fewer shares than he bid for. Thus, for good issues, uninformed investors get only partial allotments.

Next, consider bad issues. In this case, informed investors will not bid at all. The only bidders will be the uninformed. Moreover, owing to the absence of competing informed bidders, any individual bidder will more likely achieve his full allotment (or a higher probability of an allotment). That is, the uninformed bidder suffers from the problem of the "winner's curse": he achieves a large allotment for bad IPOs and a small allotment for good IPOs.

Rock's argument is that, because of the winner's curse, IPOs have to be underpriced on average so as to produce an expected return for

---

[6] Since P is not known with certainty, a small spread (P - OP) risks occasional negative spreads, in which case the underwriting firm suffers a loss.

[7] See, for example, Tinic (1988).

the uninformed investor that is high enough to attract investment in IPOs regardless of whether the issue is good or bad.[8] That is, underpricing is a phenomenon perfectly consistent with competitive market conditions in a world of imperfect information flows. Thus, monopoly power is rejected as an argument explaining underpricing.

Underpricing as a Dynamic Strategy. In the most recent literature, underpricing is seen as a dynamic strategy employed by issuing firms to overcome the asymmetry of information between issuing firms and outside investors.[9] Implicitly, underpricing is viewed as a cost to be borne by the issuing firm's insiders to persuade investors to collect (or aggregate) information about the firm and in that way establish its true value in the secondary market. Moreover, the better the firm (a "good" issue), the more it will be underpriced relative to the bad issue.

Specifically, a good firm will underprice its issue to attract outside investors.[10] Investors (such as analysts) collect information about the firm and, in the secondary market, establish its true value above its offer price. The owners of the firm benefit from this strategy because once the true (higher) market value is established, the owners have an incentive to "cash in" by coming out with new (further) secondary offerings at the higher market price. Thus, the cost or losses of underpricing the IPO are offset by the benefits from cashing in on the secondary offering.[11]

By comparison, a bad firm—one that knows it is a bad firm—will have the opposite incentives. In particular, the firm may seek to price the IPO as high as possible, since it knows that once investors collect information and discover that it is a "bad" firm, its stock's price will fall on the secondary market.[12]

As in the Rock model, these types of dynamic-strategy models view underpricing as a phenomenon that is consistent with competition in a world of imperfect information among issuing firms and investors. The difference is that, here, IPO underpricing is viewed as a cost to be borne by good firms, which is offset by the revenue benefits from making a secondary ("seasoned") offering later on at a higher price.

IMPLICATIONS FOR BANK REGULATION

What do these models imply for bank regulation and, in particular, the Glass-Steagall Act? If underpricing is indeed due to information imperfections in the capital market—especially between firms and investors—it is difficult to see how commercial banks' entry into underwriting will have much effect, unless these banks somehow collect more information and alleviate the degree of information imperfection in the market. Since the modern theory of banking views banks as major collectors and users of information, increased production of information about small firms may indeed be a benefit from repealing Glass-Steagall.

However, a better test of whether Glass-

---

[8] Technically, the *conditional* expected return for the uninformed investor, across both good and bad issues, must be at least as great as the risk-free rate.

[9] See, for example, Chemmanur (1989) and Welch (1988).

[10] In these models, the investment banker plays a largely passive function, operating as an agent on behalf of the principal (the firm). The failure of the investment banker to take a more active role may be seen as a weakness of these information-based models.

---

[11] Welch (1988) offers preliminary evidence that these issues that are more underpriced tend to follow up more quickly with a secondary (seasoned) offering.

[12] This is not to imply that the bad firms necessarily overprice. However, the theory has the *aggregate* implication that the greater the proportion of good to bad issues in the market, the greater the degree of underpricing on *average*.

Steagall has undesirable costs is whether it confers monopoly power on existing investment banks that is reflected in the degree of underpricing. That is, what, if any, is the empirical evidence linking underpricing to the monopoly power of investment banks?

One implication of the monopoly-power hypothesis[13] is that an underwriter, because of his expertise and more precise knowledge of the issuing firm's true value, can save effort (shirk) by ensuring maximum sales through underpricing while still earning a high underwriting spread (OP - BP). However, even in a world of asymmetric information, presumably firms would learn that they are being exploited and, if competition exists, would switch to other underwriters. In contrast, monopoly power would imply that issuing firms would fare as well with one investment bank as with another and that underwriters could ignore all problems or considerations related to maintaining a reputation.

Beatty and Ritter (1986) have sought to test this reputation–monopoly power effect. That is, do investment bankers who heavily underprice in one period lose business from issuing firms in the next? Beatty and Ritter's results tended to confirm that the more an investment banker underpriced in one period, the greater his loss of business in the next—a result suggesting that monopoly power is temporary at best.

A second implication of the monopoly-power hypothesis is that the investment banker—to avoid risk—will have a greater incentive to underprice relatively risky issues so as to ensure maximum sales. For example, it can be argued that the more uncertain are firms' uses of the proceeds of the issue (for example, to pay off existing debt, to develop new projects, and so on), the riskier the issue. Or, alternatively, the more variable the after-market returns on an issue—measured by the standard deviation of returns over a period subsequent to listing on the stock exchange—the riskier the issue. Thus, we would expect underpricing to increase as the number of potential uses of proceeds, and the volatility of its (expected) price in the after-market, grows.

Beatty and Ritter (1986) found a positive relationship between number of uses of proceeds and underpricing; Ritter (1984) and Miller and Reilly (1987) found a positive relationship between the standard deviation of after-market returns and the degree of underpricing. Both these results are consistent with the monopoly-power hypothesis; however, it *must* be noted that both findings are also consistent with the competitive-market, information-imperfection "winner's curse" theory of Rock (1986).[14]

A third potential implication of the monopoly-power model is that the degree of underpricing should have been less prior to passage of Glass-Steagall—that is, the pre-1933 *average* degree of underpricing should have been less than the post-1933 average degree. In a recent study, Tinic (1988) tested the degree of underpricing in the period 1923-30 and compared it with the period 1966-71. He found that underpricing was higher in the 1966-71 period. While Tinic interpreted these results as consistent with the due-diligence-insurance hypothesis—that is, the passage of the Securities Act of 1934, which forced investment banks to underprice to avoid potential lawsuits—they are also consistent with the monopoly-power hypothesis. That is, in a period preceding Glass-Steagall (when commercial banks had greater power to

---

[13] See Baron (1982), who developed a theory of investment banker monopoly power based on the inability of issuers to accurately monitor the investment bankers' effort in placing new shares with investors.

[14] That is, the greater the risk or uncertainty about the issue, the greater the cost of becoming informed and thus the greater the degree of underpricing required in equilibrium.

underwrite corporate securities),[15] the degree of underpricing was less than in a period following the Glass-Steagall separation of powers.

A fourth implication of the monopoly-power hypothesis is that IPOs of investment banks (for example, Morgan Stanley going public) should *not* be underpriced, since the investment bank brings its "own firm" public. Looking at 37 IPOs of investment banks that went public in the 1970-84 period and participated in the distribution of their own issues, Muscarella and Vetsuypens (1987) find an average degree of underpricing of *8 percent* on the first day of trading. At first sight this tends to contradict the monopoly-power hypothesis as the sole reason for underpricing; however, it could be argued that 8 percent underpricing is less

---

[15]This was particularly true in 1927-33, when commercial banks had the same powers as investment banks. Since technology and the structure of the financial services industry are continuously changing, a more valid test might have been to compare underpricing in the period *immediately following* passage of the Glass-Steagall Act.

than the median or mean underpricing found in the majority of studies listed in the table below and that monopoly power may offer a partial explanation for underpricing.

Nevertheless, the results favoring monopoly power as the major determinant of new-issues underpricing appear somewhat weak. Indeed, the evidence is largely consistent with the existence of competitive markets in which investors have incomplete or imperfect infor-

Initial Returns, According to Various Studies

Study	Sample Period	Sample Size	Initial Returns 1 Week	Initial Returns 1 Mo.
Reilly/Hatfield (1969)	1963-65	53	9.9%	8.7%
McDonald/Fisher (1972)	1969-70	142	28.5%	34.6%
Logue (1973)	1965-69	250	—	41.7%
Reilly (1973)	1966	62	9.9%	—
Neuberger/Hammond (1974)	1965-69	816	17.1%	19.1%
Ibbotson (1975)	1960-71	128	—	11.4%
Ibbotson/Jaffe (1975)	1960-70	2650	16.8%	—
Reilly (1978)	1972-75	486	10.9%	11.6%
Block/Stanley (1980)	1974-78	102	5.9%	3.3%
Neuberger/LaChapelle (1983)	1975-80	118	27.7%	33.6%
Ibbotson (1982)	1971-81	N/A	—	2.9%
Ritter (1984)	1960-82	5162	18.8%	—
	1977-82	1028	26.5%	—
	1980-81	325	48.4%	—
Giddy (1985)	1976-83	604	10.2%	—
John/Saunders (1986)	1976-82	78	—	8.5%
Beatty/Ritter (1986)	1981-82	545	14.1%	—
Chalk/Peavy (1986)	1974-82	440	13.8%	—
Ritter (1987)	1977-82			
Firm commitment		664	14.8%	—
Best efforts		364	47.8%	—
Miller/Reilly (1987)	1982-83	510	9.9%	—
Muscarella/Vetsuypens (1987)	1983-87	1184	—	7.6%

mation about new firms. While new issues did appear to be *less* underpriced before Glass-Steagall (consistent with the monopoly-power hypothesis), evidence suggests that those investment banks that excessively underprice today lose future business from prospective issuing firms and that investment banks' own IPOs are also underpriced on average (although less so than those of other firms). The gains from allowing commercial banks to compete directly with investment banks for corporate equity underwritings may come less from creating more potential competition than from collecting, producing, and disseminating more information about small firms in the new-issue process. This conclusion suggests that allowing banks into investment banking activities may indeed bring about price changes that benefit the public; however, those changes may be smaller and occur for different reasons than once thought.

REFERENCES

Baron, D.P. "A Model of the Demand for Investment Banking and Advising and Distribution Services for New Issues," *Journal of Finance* (1982) pp. 955-77.

Beatty, R., and J. Ritter. "Investment Banking, Reputation, and the Underpricing of Initial Public Offerings," *Journal of Financial Economics* (1986) pp. 213-32.

Block, S., and M. Stanley. "The Financial Characteristics and Price Movement Patterns of Companies Approaching the Unseasoned Securities Market in the Late 1970s," *Financial Management* (1980) pp. 30-36.

Chalk, A.J., and J.W. Peavy. "Understanding the Pricing of Initial Public Offerings," Southern Methodist University Working Paper 86-72 (1986).

Chemmanur, T.J. "The Pricing of Initial Public Offerings: A Dynamic Model With Information Production," mimeo, New York University (1989).

Giddy, I. "Is Equity Underwriting Risky for Commercial Bank Affiliates?" in I. Walter, ed., *Deregulating Wall Street* (New York: John Wiley, 1985).

Ibbotson, R.G. "Price Performance of Common Stock New Issues," *Journal of Financial Economics* 3 (1975) pp. 235-72.

Ibbotson, R.G. "Common Stock New Issues Revisited," Graduate School of Business, University of Chicago, Working Paper 84 (1982), unpublished.

Ibbotson, R.G., and J.J. Jaffe. "'Hot Issue' Markets," *Journal of Finance* 30 (1975) pp. 1027-42.

John, K., and A. Saunders. "The Efficiency of the Market for Initial Public Offerings: U.S. Experience 1976-1983," unpublished (1986).

Logue, D.E. "On the Pricing of Unseasoned New Issues, 1965-1969," *Journal of Financial and Quantitative Analysis* (1973) pp. 91-103.

McDonald, J.G., and A.K. Fisher. "New-Issue Stock Price Behavior," *Journal of Finance* (1972) pp. 97-102.

McStay, K.P. *The Efficiency of New Issue Markets*, Ph.D. thesis, Department of Economics, U.C.L.A. (1987).

Miller, R.E., and F.K. Reilly. "An Examination of Mispricing, Returns, and Uncertainty for Initial Public Offerings," *Financial Management* (1987) pp. 33-38.

Muscarella, C.J., and M.R. Vetsuypens. "A Simple Test of Baron's Model of IPO Underpricing," Southern Methodist University Working Paper 87-14 (1987a).

Muscarella, C.J., and M.R. Vetsuypens. "Initial Public Offerings and Information Asymmetry," Edwin L. Cox School of Business, Southern Methodist University, unpublished (1987b).

Neuberger, B.M., and C.T. Hammond. "A Study of Underwriters' Experience With Unseasoned New Issues," *Journal of Financial and Quantitative Analysis* (1974) pp. 165-77.

Neuberger, B.M., and C.A. LaChapelle. "Unseasoned New Issue Price Performance on Three Tiers: 1975-1980," *Financial Management* (1983) pp. 23-28.

Pugel, T.A., and L.J. White. "An Empirical Analysis of Underwriting Spreads on IPO's," Working Paper 331, Salomon Brothers Center for the Study of Financial Institutions, Graduate School of Business Administration, New York University (September 1984).

Reilly, R.K., and K. Hatfield. "Investor Experience With New Stock Issues," *Financial Analysts Journal* (September/October 1969) pp. 73-80.

Reilly, R.K. "Further Evidence on Short-Run Results for New Issue Investors," *Journal of Financial and Quantitative Analysis* (1973) pp. 83-90.

Reilly, R.K. "New Issues Revisited," *Financial Management* (1978) pp. 28-42.

Ritter, J. "The 'Hot Issue' Market of 1980," *Journal of Business* 57 (1984) pp. 215-40.

Ritter, J. "The Costs of Going Public," University of Michigan Working Paper 487 (1987a).

Ritter, J. "A Theory of Investment Banking Contract Choice," University of Michigan Working Paper 488 (1987b).

Rock, K. "Why New Issues Are Underpriced," *Journal of Financial Economics* 15 (1986) pp. 187-212.

Tinic, S.M. "Anatomy of Initial Public Offers of Common Stock," *Journal of Finance* 43 (1988) pp. 789-822.

Welch, I. "Seasoned Offering, Imitation Costs and the Underpricing of Initial Public Offerings," University of Chicago Working Paper (1988).

Article 18

Cash Distributions to Shareholders

Laurie Simon Bagwell and John B. Shoven

conomists have long been puzzled by why firms pay dividends when alternative methods of rewarding shareholders and financiers exist which involve less taxes. Dividend paying equity appears to be the most heavily taxed capital instrument available. It is subject to two levels of taxation: first, the federal corporation income tax (currently at a 34 percent marginal rate in the United States) and second, the personal income tax if the shares are owned by households. Even with the new lower marginal tax rates of the 1986 Tax Reform Act, most household shareholders have marginal personal tax rates of 28 or 33 percent, meaning that the combined corporate and personal taxes on dividends exceed 50 percent.

There are more lightly taxed alternative methods of finance. Equity which retains and reinvests earnings generates accrued capital gains on which taxes can be deferred until realization. There is even the possibility of completely escaping taxation on accrued gains if they remain unrealized until the asset passes through an estate. This paper will highlight the fact that firms can distribute cash to equity holders in ways more lightly taxed than dividends. The two methods we examine are share repurchase programs and cash-financed mergers and acquisitions. With either of these alternatives, corporations transfer cash to shareholders in return for their shares, thereby reducing outstanding equity claims. In both mechanisms, the immediate tax consequences of the cash distribution are unlike dividend taxation, as will be described below. Finally, of course, there is corporate debt. While this paper emphasizes equity finance, it should at least be noted that interest payments escape the double taxation

■ *Laurie Simon Bagwell is Assistant Professor of Finance, J. L. Kellogg Graduate School of Management, Northwestern University, Evanston, Illinois. John B. Shoven is Professor of Economics, Stanford University, Director of the Center for Economic Policy Research, and Research Fellow, National Bureau of Economic Research, all in Stanford, California.*

of dividends since interest is a deductible cost of doing business under the corporation income tax.

Despite the relative tax disadvantage of dividends, they are a major element in the leading models of share valuation. There are several models which attempt to solve the dividend puzzle. There are those in which dividends convey a sufficiently valuable signal (presumably about the firm's true financial position and prospects) to overcome the tax handicap (Bhattacharya, 1979; Miller and Rock, 1985). There are models in which the payment of dividends restricts the action of management in a manner which helps control problems brought about by the separation of management and ownership (Jensen and Meckling, 1976). There are models whereby dividend payments are used by firms to maintain the desired leverage ratios (Feldstein and Green, 1983). And, there is a recent Bagwell–Judd (1988) paper which explains dividends as a result of shareholder diversity and issues of corporate control. Despite these many theories, it is safe to say that none of the explanations have been accepted as the final word on why dividends are paid.

The taxation at the personal level of share repurchases is potentially quite small. When corporations buy shares, either in a repurchase plan or as part of a merger, the tax paid by those who receive the cash is based on their capital gain. Cash received which represents a return of the initial investment (or "basis") is tax free, and only increases above the basis value are treated as a realized capital gain and subject to taxation. In share acquisitions where only a fraction of the outstanding shares of a particular company is acquired, one would expect the sellers to be amongst the holders with the highest basis values (including ones with capital losses), who are therefore those facing the lowest tax bills.

Both the sellers and the nonsellers can gain from a corporate program of share repurchase. When outstanding shares are repurchased, the price of the remaining shares will be higher than if an equivalent amount of cash had been distributed as a dividend. This higher price on the remaining shares results in accrued capital gains on which taxes can be deferred until the gain is realized by selling the shares. The tax advantage of share repurchases relative to dividends was reduced but not eliminated when the taxation of realized capital gains was increased in the Tax Reform Act of 1986.

So why should cash distributions from firms to shareholders ever take the form of dividends? This paper first provides evidence on the explosive growth in non-dividend cash payments, and then discusses how this evidence should affect theories about corporate finance.

The Importance of Non-Dividend Cash Payments

As just described, shareholders can get cash from corporations through dividend payments, cash-financed acquisitions, or share repurchases. Estimates of the quantitative importance of these alternative methods are not readily available in official government statistics. One major contribution of our research is the compilation of these numbers.

Table 1

Annual cash distributions to shareholders, 1977-1987

| | A) Millions of current dollars | | |
Year	Cash via acquisitions	Dividends	Share repurchases
1977	4,274	29,450	3,361
1978	7,228	32,830	3,520
1979	16,888	38,324	4,507
1980	13,081	42,619	4,961
1981	29,319	46,832	3,973
1982	26,247	50,916	8,080
1983	21,248	54,896	7,709
1984	64,244	60,266	27,444
1985	69,971	67,564	41,303
1986	74,522	77,122	41,521
1987	62,240	83,051	54,336

| | B) Millions of 1986 dollars[a] | | |
Year	Cash via acquisitions	Dividends	Share repurchases
1977	7,233	49,842	5,688
1978	11,402	51,791	5,553
1979	24,472	55,535	6,532
1980	17,386	56,643	6,594
1981	35,526	56,747	4,814
1982	29,896	57,993	9,203
1983	23,293	60,179	8,451
1984	67,942	63,735	29,024
1985	71,864	69,392	42,421
1986	74,522	77,122	41,521
1987	60,231	80,370	52,582

Source: Data compiled by authors aggregating the Compustat Primary, Supplementary and Tertiary Industrial Files

[a]1986 Constant dollar figures adjust current dollar numbers using the GNP deflator from the 1988 Economic Report of the President, Table B-3

Table 1 contains the annual time series information regarding cash mergers and acquisitions, dividends, and share repurchases. The figures are aggregated over the 2,445 firms on the Compustat Primary, Supplementary and Tertiary Industrial files. A summary of Compustat firm inclusion can be found in the Appendix. Though this data set does not cover all firms, it does include the largest and most significant market participants from the major stock exchanges.

Table 1 displays the figures in both current dollars and in constant 1986 dollars. Between 1977 and 1987, real dividends grew smoothly by a total of 61.3 percent. Both cash acquisitions and share repurchases grew explosively, with real cash acquisitions up by a multiple of roughly nine and share repurchases up 824 percent. In real terms, both roughly tripled between 1983 and 1984. The annual figures of Table 1 show that

204   Section V   Corporate Financial Management and the Investor

Table 2

Quarterly cash distributions to shareholders, 1984:1-1988:2

(*millions of current dollars*)

Year: quarter	Cash via acquisitions	Dividends	Share repurchases
1984:1	13,705	13,965	5,414
1984:2	29,434	14,893	6,617
1984:3	10,116	13,059	8,370
1984:4	11,468	15,937	7,973
1985:1	11,514	14,010	10,327
1985:2	10,698	16,253	11,155
1985:3	17,915	14,454	8,533
1985:4	29,985	20,113	12,382
1986:1	15,120	15,051	10,063
1986:2	13,038	20,855	8,854
1986:3	15,354	15,425	9,414
1986:4	33,476	22,784	15,430
1987:1	7,877	15,485	8,739
1987:2	16,745	23,465	11,117
1987:3	10,053	20,156	11,934
1987:4	27,565	23,945	22,546
1988:1	18,274	20,976	14,486
1988:2	14,323	22,096	11,570

Source: Data derived from Compustat

dividends were the primary mechanism for firms to make cash payments in 1977 (accounting for 80 percent of the total cash distributions). But by 1986, dividends had fallen to 40 percent of cash distributions.

Table 2 contains quarterly time series information from 1984 through the first half of 1988 for the three alternative cash distribution methods examined here. (The figures are consistent with the annual ones because they are derived from the same Compustat data source.) The 1987 information is of special interest, since it shows the initial period in which the taxation of realized capital gains was increased by the 1986 Tax Reform Act.

Table 2 indicates that there may have been a modest bunching of share repurchases and cash acquisitions in the fourth quarter of 1986 (perhaps to beat the tax law changes). However, acquisition activity is often bunched in the fourth quarter, so the "under the tax wire" theory is not resoundingly illustrated. The other notable fact is that total share repurchases in 1987 exceeded those for 1986. In fact, the figures for each quarter starting in 1987 are higher than the annual totals for all years before 1984.[1] There were some predictions that the higher capital gains tax rate in the Tax

---

[1]It should be noted that our data for the first half of 1988 are less complete, and the final tabulations will certainly show first half 1988 share repurchases greater than these figures.

Reform Act would slow the practice of share repurchases, but the evidence presented here says otherwise.

Evidence regarding cash distribution mechanisms from other sources supports the conclusions presented here. Shoven (1986) created a time series for share repurchases and cash acquisitions from 1970 to 1985 using the monthly Center for Research in Security Prices data. The same qualitative picture emerged there, namely that dividends had been overtaken by the sum of the two share acquisition mechanisms by the end of the sample. We chose to use the Compustat data for this study because it includes explicit information regarding each of the cash distributions examined here.

The New York Stock Exchange compiles monthly reports of changes in Treasury Stock holdings for member companies. We have examined their data in detail from January 1985 through December 1987. This information argues even more forcefully than does the Compustat data that share repurchase activity accelerated in 1987 relative to the two previous years.

We also examined other sources for mergers and acquisitions. We identified, using *Mergers and Acquisitions*, the 25 largest transactions for each quarter from January 1984 to December 1987. The terms of each deal were extracted from *Mergers and Acquisitions* and the *Wall Street Journal* to determine the amount of cash distributed. The time series of the aggregated results were consistent with the Compustat results reported here.

There seems little doubt that during the last decade dividends have lost their place as the primary mechanism for firms to distribute cash to shareholders, a change that represents a major realignment of corporate financial policy.

Theories to Explain the Trends

The evidence presented here demonstrates that the hypothesis that dividends are the only vehicle by which cash can be distributed to shareholders is no longer viable. While the real dividend series has been rising fairly smoothly over the past decade, there has been a meteoric rise in the share acquisition methods of cash distribution. In the most recent years, the majority of cash payments have been in these nondividend forms. Economists are therefore challenged by these market trends to understand both why firms distribute a certain amount of cash to shareholders, and the changing motivations for choosing a specific form of cash distribution.

The framework for understanding optimal financial policy stems from the seminal papers of Modigliani and Miller (1958; 1961).[2] They set forth conditions under which firm financial policy is irrelevant, in the sense that it has no effect on the firm's market value. A firm's investors need not care about its financial decisions, because private portfolio adjustments, "homemade dividends," can offset any action at the firm level. If the firm chooses to pay dividends, some of the recipients could use

---

[2]An extensive discussion of the Modigliani–Miller theorem and its implications can be found in the 30th anniversary symposium on the Modigliani–Miller propositions in the Fall 1988 issue of this journal. Therefore, its discussion here will be brief.

the money to buy additional shares, thus replicating the percentage ownership they would have held as a nonparticipant owner of a firm repurchasing shares. Conversely, if the firm chooses a share repurchase, each shareholder can sell sufficient shares to match the amount they would have received if dividends had been paid out.

A cash–financed acquisition of the shares of another firm is analogous to a share repurchase. As long as the assets acquired offer a market rate of return, the value of the shares of the acquiring firm will capitalize the new investment. Those who want a dividend-like cash flow can achieve it by selling a fraction of their shares.

Since the underlying assumptions of the Modigliani–Miller propositions are unrealistic, most economists use the model to organize their thinking regarding the effects of relaxing the assumptions. These researchers attempt to explain why the various forms of cash distributions to investors—cash dividends, share repurchases, mergers and takeovers, and capital gains in share values—all exist side by side. And given the trends documented above, theory should address changes in the relative use of these alternative forms through time.

One set of theories examines the implications of allowing taxes to enter the model. The personal tax advantage of using share acquisition programs has been discussed above. Because taxes may differentially impact shareholders, tax clienteles have been considered as an explanation of cross-sectional differences in firms' financial decisions. As first suggested in Miller and Modigliani (1961), perhaps "each corporation would attract itself to a 'clientele' consisting of those preferring its particular payout ratio." Taxpayers with high marginal tax rates may disproportionately be found in firms accruing capital gains, while taxpayers with zero or low marginal tax rates and preference for steady cash flow, including pension funds and taxable corporations, may actually prefer dividends.[3] If one takes seriously the notion of tax clienteles, then the Tax Reform Act of 1986 may have resulted in a shifting of such niches. The difference for an individual investor in the effective tax rate on dividends vis-a-vis capital gains was decreased. Though this might suggest a relative shift from share acquisitions to dividends, no such trend emerges in the data. Taxes alone, therefore, seem unable to fully explain the observed behavior.

It is therefore valuable to examine the implications of relaxing additional assumptions of the Modigliani–Miller paradigm. Bagwell (1989) considers whether, in the presence of costs of making transactions, the form of distribution differentially affects the likelihood of takeovers. She finds that in the presence of an upward sloping supply curve for shares, the cost to the bidding firm of acquiring control of the target will be larger if the potential target distributes a fixed amount of cash through share repurchase rather than through dividends. Since shareholders willing to tender shares to management in the repurchase are those with the lowest reservation values, a repurchase skews the distribution of reservation values that the potential acquirer faces towards a more expensive pool.

One explanation of why the supply curve for the firm's shares slopes upward involves transaction costs. In particular, an upward sloping curve can be derived from

---

[3]For evidence consistent with dividends and clienteles, see Elton and Gruber (1970) and Pettit (1977). For evidence consistent with share acquisition clienteles, see Bagwell and Shoven (1988).

capital gains tax considerations: investors with different basis values impute different reservation values to their holdings. In a study of defensive responses to hostile takeovers, Dann and DeAngelo (1988) find that the bidder was unsuccessful in all eight cases where repurchase was used, whereas in ten of the remaining twenty-five defensive restructurings the hostile bidder successfully acquired a substantial stake and board representation. This evidence shows that takeover threats may dictate the form of the distribution,[4] and the simultaneous increase of repurchase and acquisitions is consistent with this theory that repurchases may deter takeovers.

Bagwell and Judd (1988) examine the effect of share repurchase and dividends on the distribution of ownership. Since a dividend leaves the distribution unchanged, while a repurchase may systematically alter the composition of ownership, a dividend may be chosen by the current dominant interest group as the means of distributing cash. It assures them of maintaining control. Even in the presence of a tax advantage to share repurchase, control over future firm decisions in the presence of shareholder diversity and transaction costs may dictate that dividends are chosen.

An alternative explanation for optimal financial structure is that distributions may be made in the presence of asymmetric information. The potential benefit of a distribution that has been considered most extensively is that there may be information revealed in a payout. In order for the distribution to signal an increase in firm value, the management must be better informed than the marketplace, and there must be a cost to a "bad" firm of mimicking the "good" firm.

The good news revealed by dividends or share repurchase can include unobserved firm value (Bhattacharya, 1979; Ofei and Thakor, 1987), unobserved current cash flow (Miller and Rock, 1985), or unobserved future cash flow (Ross, 1977; John and Williams, 1985; Huberman, 1984; Constantinides and Grundy, 1986). The cost of false signaling can include the cost of raising new capital externally to finance future investments (Huberman, 1984; Ofer and Thakor, 1987), the probability of going bankrupt trying to meet future distribution obligations (Ross, 1977), taxes on distributions (Bhattacharya, 1979; John and Williams, 1985; Bernheim, 1988), or necessitating a cutting back on today's investment (Miller and Rock, 1985). Unexpected changes in dividends have been confirmed to provide information about unexpected increases in the level of earnings in addition to the information found in earnings announcements. Repurchases have also been found to signal favorable information.[5] These signaling models explain cash payout more satisfactorily than they explain the choice between dividends and repurchase.

We believe that there exists yet another explanation of optimal financial structure, based on learning by the managers and markets about the technologies of repurchases and cash acquisitions. There are some aspects of share acquisition which

---

[4]Cash acquisitions can also be motivated by the threat of takeovers. The most obvious illustration is the "Pac Man" defense, when the target responds to a takeover threat by attempting to acquire its pursuer. This defense has been employed between Martin Marietta and Bendix in 1982 and between E-II Holdings and American Brands in 1988.

[5]For evidence of the informativeness of dividends see, for example, Aharony and Swary (1980) and Ofer and Siegel (1987). For evidence consistent with repurchase signaling see Dann (1981) and Vermaelen (1981).

are learned only by experience. For repurchases, there has been learning through time about how large or frequently a repurchase can be done without being deemed ordinary income by the IRS, and taxed accordingly. According to Section 302 of the U.S. Internal Revenue Code, if the redemption is "substantially disproportionate," then the excess of the payment over shareholder basis is taxed as capital gain. Firms have also learned how to use repurchase as part of an anti-takeover strategy, and firms and shareholders have recognized that a repurchase can be a less costly signal of favorable news than a dividend.

Management may be reluctant to choose a signal that the market does not interpret correctly. As familiarity with repurchase has increased, the magnitudes and frequencies have increased. There was very little repurchase used prior to 1973. At the inception of Nixon's price and wage ceilings, the ceiling imposed on dividends was met by an increased use of repurchase. In the Dann sample covering of 1962–1976, 73 of the 143 repurchases occurred in 1973 or 1974. It was not until 1977, however, that a major corporation did a large repurchase (IBM, $1.4 billion). Subsequently, repurchase has become a common event for even the largest firms, and the market has learned about the IRS's reaction to and tax treatment of such repurchases.

If one imagines a simple epidemic model where what is spreading is information about repurchase as a cash distribution technology, then we would expect to find a learning curve with firms increasingly using repurchase. Looking at our data for the last ten years, one first sees repurchase used on a large scale in 1984. Evidence of the past three years suggests that dramatic learning has already been achieved. However, it is too soon to predict whether repurchase will continue at its current level, or whether additional technological learning will occur.

There has also been learning about the technology of acquisitions. The most obvious is the use of junk bond financing, commencing in 1984. These below-invest-ment-grade high-yield bonds allow the raising of capital necessary for acquisitions. The junk bond innovation may have been stimulated by changes in the relative taxation of debt and equity. By 1987 they represented one-fourth of the total market for corporate bonds (Jensen, 1988). A second technology increasingly used during this period is the bridge loan. Many Wall Street commercial banks, insurance companies, and pension funds have risked their own money in short term merchant banking to facilitate takeovers and leveraged buyouts.[6] As the successful use of these new technologies has been demonstrated, their use has increased.

Conclusion

The major realignment in the relative importance of alternative cash distribution methods has serious implication for corporate managers, private investors, financial

---

[6]This behavior took on new magnitude in 1985, when Merrill Lynch put up a $1.2 billion loan in the Comcast takeover of Storer Communications.

economists, and the federal tax authorities. Corporate management now uses a wider array of instruments to reward shareholders, some with distinct advantages over traditional dividends. Private investors as well need to expand their equity valuation models to include these nondividend payments. The availability of alternative cash distribution technologies gives investors the opportunity to acquire equity in firms which use particular distributional forms. This may allow tax driven clienteles to form, thus addressing more precisely the particular tax circumstance of the investors.

The Internal Revenue Service certainly needs to take account of the use of alternative methods of cash distribution. Their differential tax treatment implies that the IRS must consider the form of distributions to correctly estimate tax revenue. To the extent that some are tax efficient methods for firms and investors, they are also revenue-losing technologies from the IRS's perspective. Shoven (1986) estimated that the increased use of nondividend payments reduced federal revenues by roughly $25 billion per year in 1984 and 1985 (relative to taxing the payments as dividends). Since corporate equity is often perceived to be "double"-taxed or "over"-taxed, the tax revenue reduction is not necessarily harmful to economic efficiency or bad policy for the country.

The presence of alternative distributional forms must also be recognized in the creation of tax policy and legislation. However, this task is made difficult by the multiplicity of effects any law change may have. Though many investors predicted the 1986 Tax Reform Act would sharply curtail nondividend methods of cash payment, this has proven to be incorrect. To understand why not, further research is needed on the effect of tax changes on firm and investors' decisions.

Finally, the findings presented here dictate that financial economists must adapt some of their most popular models. In the standard discounted cash flow model[7] of share valuation the equity investor receives return in two forms: dividends and capital gains. Since dividends are the only mechanism in this model for transmitting cash between the firm and its shareholders, capital gains simply reflect a change in the present value of expected future dividends. Therefore, at any moment in time, the share price is equal to the present value of all future dividends, adjusted for risk. In a number of other models that explain why dividends should be paid, dividends are also the only explicit means of transmitting cash to shareholders. These models must be generalized to include cash flows resulting from corporate share acquisitions.

The trapped equity model (for example, see King, 1977; Auerbach, 1979; Poterba and Summers, 1985) in which dividends are the only form of payment to shareholders must also be reconsidered. The trapped equity model implies the corporate retained earnings are immediately capitalized into the share value at less than dollar for dollar, or less than par.[8] Retained earnings are therefore a relatively cheap source of funds, since only their capitalized value must offer competitive market

---

[7]This model is often called the Discounted Cash Flow, or DCF, model. See Brealey and Myers (1988) for a discussion.

[8]In fact, each dollar is valued at $(1 - Tp)/(1 - Tc)$ where Tp and Tc are the personal tax rate and the effective tax rate in accrued capital gains for the marginal shareholder reflecting the eventual and inevitable taxes on dividends that will be paid in those earnings.

returns. Once more tax efficient means of cash transmission are allowed, the resulting cost of capital financed by retained earnings must be adjusted upwards.

To enhance our understanding of corporate financial behavior, it is necessary to recognize that alternative forms of compensating shareholders have become dominant. We hope that the evidence presented here will encourage future research on the implications of this major realignment of corporate financial policy.

Appendix
Compustat Data Availability

Inclusions by File

The Primary Industrial File (814 companies) specifically includes all companies in the S & P 400, some companies in the S & P 40 Utilities Index, the S & P 20 Transportation Index, and the S & P 40 Financial Index, plus companies of greatest interest, primarily companies on the New York Stock Exchange.

The Supplementary Industrial File (812 companies) contains companies which are followed on the major exchanges but which may have a lesser degree of investor interest.

The Tertiary File (819 companies) completes the coverage of industrial companies with common stock listed on the New York and American Stock Exchanges. It also includes approximately 300 nonindustrial companies which have been modified for comparability to the industrials. The nonindustrial companies are from the following industries: Banks, Utilities, Life Insurance, Railroads, Property and Liability, and Real Estate Investment Trusts (REIT). These nonindustrial companies include some of the companies in the S & P 40 Utilities Index, the S & P 20 Transportation Index, and the S & P 40 Financial Index.

Compustat Companies by Exchange

NYSE (400 INDUSTRIALS)	394
NYSE (40 UTILITIES)	40
NYSE (20 TRANSPORTATION)	18
NYSE (40 FINANCIAL)	35
NYSE (NON-S & P 500)	963
ASE (400 INDUSTRIALS)	1
ASE (NON-S & P 500)	801
OTC (400 INDUSTRIALS)	5
OTC (20 TRANSPORTATION)	2
OTC (40 FINANCIAL)	5
OTC (NON-S & P 500)	175
REGIONAL (NON-S & P 500)	6
TOTAL COMPANIES	2,445

■ *This paper was begun while the first author was a John M. Olin graduate fellow as a doctoral candidate at Stanford; financial support from the Olin Foundation and from Stanford's Center for Economic Policy Research is gratefully acknowledged. Research assistance was provided by Tom Gosline and Leah Sonnenschein.*

References

Aharony, Joseph and Itzhak Swary, "Quarterly Dividend and Earnings Announcements and Stockholder's Returns: An Empirical Analysis," *Journal of Finance*, 1980, *35*, 1–12.

Auerbach, Alan J., "Wealth Maximization and the Cost of Capital," *Quarterly Journal of Economics*, August 1979, 433–46.

Bagwell, Laurie Simon, "Share Repurchase and Takeover Deterrence," Northwestern University Department of Finance Working Paper No. 53, latest revision, February 1989.

Bagwell, Laurie Simon and Kenneth L. Judd, "Transaction Costs and Corporate Control," Northwestern University and the Hoover Institution, unpublished manuscript, November 1988.

Bagwell, Laurie Simon and John Shoven, "Share Repurchases and Acquisitions: An Analysis of Which Firms Participate." In *Corporate Takeovers: Causes and Consequences*. University of Chicago Press: Chicago, Illinois, May 1988.

Bernheim, B. Douglas, "Dividends versus Share Repurchases as Signals of Profitability," unpublished manuscript, June 1988.

Bhattacharya, Sudipto, "Imperfect Information, Dividend Policies, and 'The Bird in the Hand Fallacy,'" *Bell Journal of Economics*, Spring 1979, 259–270.

Brealey and Myers, *Principals of Corporate Finance*. McGraw Hill Inc.: New York, 1988.

Constantinides, George and Bruce Grundy, "Optimal Investment with Share Repurchase and Financing as Signals," Stanford Graduate School of Business, working paper #887, May 1986.

Council of Economic Advisors, *1988 Economic Report of the President*. Washington, D.C.: U.S. Government Printing Office, February 1988, 68–74.

Dann, Larry Y., "Common Stock Repurchases: An Analysis of Returns to Bondholders and Stockholders," *Journal of Financial Economics*, June 1981, *9*, 113–38.

Dann, Larry Y. and Harry DeAngelo, "Corporate Financial Policy and Corporate Control: A Study of Defensive Adjustments in Asset and Ownership Structure," *Journal of Financial Economics*, January 1988, *20*, 87–127.

Elton, Edwin J. and Martin J. Gruber, "Marginal Stockholder Tax Rates and the Clientele Effect," *Review of Economics and Statistics*, February 1970, *52*, 68–74.

Feldstein, Martin and Jerry Green, "Why Do Companies Pay Dividends?" *American Economic Review*, March 1983, *73*, 17–30.

Huberman, Gur, "External Financing and Liquidity," *Journal of Finance*, July 1984, *39:3*, 895–908.

Jensen, Michael C., "Takeovers: Their Causes and Consequences," *Journal of Economic Perspectives*, Winter 1988, *2:1*, 21–48.

Jensen, Michael C. and William Meckling, "Theory of the Firm: Managerial Behavior, Agency Costs, and Ownership Structures," *Journal of Financial Economics*, 1976, *3*, 305–360.

John, Kose and Joseph Williams, "Dividends, Dilution and Taxes: A Signalling Equilibrium," *Journal of Finance*, September 1985, *40:4*, 1053–70.

King, Mervyn, *Public Policy and the Corporation*. London: Chapman and Hall, 1977.

Masulis, Ronald W., "Stock Repurchase by Tender Offer: An Analysis of the Causes of Common Stock Price Changes," *Journal of Finance*, May 1980, *35:2*, 305–21.

Miller, Merton H., "The MM Propositions after 30 Years" and comments by Joseph E. Stiglitz, Stephen A. Ross, Sudipto Bhattacharya and Franco Modigliani, *Journal of Economic Perspectives*, Fall 1988, *2:4*, 99–158.

Miller, Merton H. and Kevin Rock, "Dividend Policy Under Asymmetric Information," *Journal of Finance*, September 1985, *40:4*, 1031–51.

Miller, Merton H. and Franco Modigliani, "Dividend Policy, Growth and the Valuation of

Shares," *Journal of Business*, October 1961, *34*, 411–33.

Miller, Merton H. and Franco Modigliani, "Corporation Income Taxes and the Cost of Capital," *American Economic Review*, June 1963, 433–43.

Modigliani, Franco, and Merton H. Miller, "The Cost of Capital, Corporation Finance and the Theory of Investment," June 1958, *American Economic Review*, 261–97.

Ofer, Aharon R. and Anjan V. Thakor, "A Theory of Stock Price Responses to Alternative Corporate Cash Disbursement Methods: Stock Repurchases and Dividends," *Journal of Finance*, June 1987, *42:2*, 365–94.

Ofer, Aharon and Daniel Siegel, "Corporate Financial Policy, Information, and Market Expectation: An Empirical Investigation of Dividends," *Journal of Finance*, 1987, *42:4*, 889–911.

Pettit, R.R., "Taxes, Transaction Costs and Clientele Effects of Dividends," *Journal of Financial Economics*, December 1977, 419–36.

Poterba, James M. and Lawrence H. Summers, "The Economic Effects of Dividend Taxation." In Altman, E. I. and M. G. Subrahmanyam, eds., *Recent Advances in Corporate Finance*. Homewood, Illinois: Richard Irwin, 1985, pp. 227–84.

Ross, Stephen, "The Determinants of Financial Structure: The Incentive-Signalling Approach," *Bell Journal of Economics*, Spring 1977, 23–40.

Shoven, John B., "The Tax Consequences of Share Repurchases and Other Non-Dividend Cash Payments to Equity Owners." In Summers, Lawrence, ed. *Tax policy and the Economy Vol. I.* Cambridge, MA: NBER and MIT Press, 1986, pp. 29–54.

Vermaelen, Theo, "Common Stock Repurchases and Market Signalling: An Empirical Study," *Journal of Financial Economics*, June 1981, 139–83.

Sources

"Recent Developments in Corporate Finance," Leland E. Crabbe, Margaret H. Pickering, and Stephen D. Prowse, *Federal Reserve Bulletin*, August 1990, pp. 595–603.

"Globalization in the Financial Services Industry," Christine Pavel and John N. McElravey, Federal Reserve Bank of Chicago *Economic Perspectives*, May/June 1990, pp. 3–18.

"The Changing American Attitude Toward Debt, and its Consequences," Frank E. Morris, *New England Economic Review*, May/June 1990, pp. 34–39.

"What is an "Acceptable" Rate of Inflation?—A Review of the Issues," Michelle R. Garfinkel, Federal Reserve Bank of St. Louis *Review*, 71:4, July/August 1989, pp. 3–15.

"Is There Too Much Corporate Debt?," Ben Bernanke, Federal Reserve Bank of Philadelphia *Business Review*, September/October 1989, pp. 3–13.

"The Case for Junk Bonds," Eric S. Rosengren, *New England Economic Review*, May/June 1990, pp. 40–49.

"The Truth About Junk Bonds," Sean Becketti, Federal Reserve Bank of Kansas City *Economic Review*, July/August 1990, pp. 45–54.

"The Modigliani-Miller Propositions After Thirty Years," Merton H. Miller, *Journal of Applied Corporate Finance*, 2:1, Spring 1989, pp. 6–18.

"Still Searching for Optimal Capital Structure," Stewart C. Myers, in *Are The Distinctions between Debt and Equity Disappearing?*, edited by Richard W. Kopcke and Eric S. Rosengren, Boston: Federal Reserve Bank of Boston, 1990, Conference Series No. 33, pp. 80–95.

"What Managers Think of Capital Structure: A Survey," J. Michael Pinegar and Lisa Wilbricht, *Financial Management*, 18:4, Winter 1989, pp. 82–91.

"The Causes and Consequences of Leveraged Buyouts," Michelle R. Garfinkel, Federal Reserve Bank of St. Louis *Review*, 71:5, September/October 1989, pp. 23–34.

"LBOs and Conflicts of Interest," William P. Osterberg, Federal Reserve Bank of Cleveland *Economic Commentary*, August 15, 1989, pp. 1–5.

"Hostile Takeovers and the Market for Corporate Control," Diana L. Fortier, Federal Reserve Bank of Chicago *Economic Perspectives*, January/February 1989, pp. 2–16.

"The Corporate Bankruptcy Decision," Michelle J. White, *Journal of Economic Perspectives*, 3:2, Spring 1989, pp. 129–151.

"How Investors Interpret Changes in Corporate Financial Policy," Paul M. Healy and Krishna G. Palepu, *Journal of Applied Corporate Finance*, 2:3, Fall 1989, pp. 59–64.

"The Motives and Consequences of Debt-Equity Swaps and Defeasances: More Evidence that it Does Not Pay to Manipulate Earnings," John R. M. Hand and Patricia J. Hughes, *The Journal of Applied Corporate Finance*, 5:3, Fall 1990, pp. 77–81.

"Why Are So Many New Stock Issues Underpriced?," Anthony Saunders, Federal Reserve Bank of Philadelphia *Business Review*, March/April 1990, pp. 3–12.

"Cash Distributions to Shareholders," Laurie Simon Bagwell and John B. Shoven, *Journal of Economic Perspectives*, 3:3, Summer 1989, pp. 129–140.